The STORY Of

FAITH, HOPE and LOVE

The STORY Of

FAITH, HOPE and LOVE

WILLIAM EDWARD DEWBERRY

authorHOUSE®

AuthorHouse™ LLC
1663 Liberty Drive
Bloomington, IN 47403
www.authorhouse.com
Phone: 1-800-839-8640

Published by AuthorHouse 10/11/2013

ISBN: 978-1-4918-2542-6 (sc)
ISBN: 978-1-4918-2543-3 (e)

Library of Congress Control Number: 2013918199

Contents

William Edward Dewberry-Author

Preface

The Story of Faith, Hope and Love was written to present an understanding of God and His eternal plans and hope for the people He created. It is written in easy to understand language. The book tells the story about God's plan to redeem people and fully explains His relationship with the people He created and the responsibility of all people to personally learn and fulfill their obligation to God.

The ability of people to think and draw conclusions comes from God our creator. Rationalism is the guide for learning about God. We are constantly surrounded by material and spiritual evidence to support the existence of a Supreme Being that is responsible for the creation.

The Story of Faith, Hope and Love gives an account of the story of God's interaction with people from the beginning of life to the end of life on earth. This book interprets the scriptures of the Bible in a way that the readers gain a comprehensive understanding of God's complete plan of redemption including the events of the future at the end of time.

An overall understanding of the Bible is the most important element to promote faith in God and Christ and have spiritual unity on earth. God inspired a man named Moses to write about the creation, the beginning of time and the history of man. The first five books in the Bible are called the Pentateuch. After the Pentateuch there were 51 inspired books added by other inspired men writing over a period of several hundred years completing the Bible of 66 books.

Introduction

God's existence is conspicuous as a result of His creation, and the most important thing in life is faith in the God of creation that leads to hope and love. God knows the complete record of a person's life. He knows our every thought and everything we do. God clearly reveals himself in the creation and in the inspired account of the Bible so that we can know Him.

God is known by His Self revelation in the Bible, and He is represented as a Spirit; not subject to scientific examination or proof. Most people are not scholars or scientists, but they can accept the creation account in the Bible by reading with a common sense view of the beginning of God's story of the people He created and their obligation to their creator. God made people in a way that they can independently think, reason, and find God in nature and in the Bible.

The Bible is the only inspired book and guide available, and the Bible is dedicated to the pursuit of immortality. The Bible was written so that God could communicate with the people He created. The authenticity of the Bible was established many years ago, and people of every generation since its completion believes it is a divinely inspired book. God welcomes people to establish a relationship of faith in Him in order to avoid the consequences of sin. The Bible is the story of faith, hope, and love based on the belief that the only means of a happy and successful life is to have faith in God and fill our heart with a hope of eternal life and love for God and our fellow man.

The Bible tells us about God and welcomes us to have a relationship with Him. *Psalm 145:18 "The Lord is near to all who call on Him in truth."* The knowledge and understanding of God's plan is truth and is based on the inspired scriptures of the Bible. Men who were chosen by God and inspired by the Holy Spirit wrote the Bible so that all men everywhere could know God and obey Him. Forty different authors wrote the books of the Bible over a period of 1500 years, and each author added God's Word to God's story of redemption in the Bible.

The Bible contains the Old Testament and the New Testament. There are 66 separate books. Each book reveals a part of the entire story of the creation and the history of God's plan of redemption. Each book is a supernatural work of God in which He communicated divine truth to men who were inspired by the Holy Spirit. The Bible is the world's all-time, best selling book, and countless millions of copies of it have been printed and distributed; in one year alone 627,000,000 copies (United Bible Societies, 1999).

The Bible has been accurately preserved for thousands of years and has had a definite effect on the life of people of every generation. Discovering the truth contained in the Bible could be one of the most exciting adventures you will ever have. God depends on the intelligence He gave us to discover Him through His word that He graciously supplied for us in the Bible.

The Bible contains 66 individual books written by 40 individual authors over a period of 1,600 years. The Bible was completed nearly 2,000 years ago but has been carefully preserved. The Holy Spirit of God inspired the men who wrote it. The Bible begins with the first days of the creation story and moves from there to the history of God's dealings with man from the beginning to the end of time.

The book of Genesis, the first book of the Bible, is a book of beginnings. Genesis begins with the events of the creation of the earth and the history of the life of the first people. It explains that there is a need for redemption because of the sinful nature of people.

Since the beginning of creation people have been confused and mistaken in their views of whom God is and what He expects of the people He created. The Bible was not written to prove the existence of God but to reveal Him and explain His importance in the life of the people. Today people have the advantage to understand God's creation because of the Bible.

The Bible explains that the true God has a Divine Nature and cannot be worshiped with men's hands. God must be worshiped from people's heart. God made all people to live on the earth, and He expects them to know Him and realize their need for Him and search for Him. God is not far away from any of us, and we can know Him because we are His offspring. We see the evidence of God everywhere we look. Paul said at one time God overlooked the ignorance of people who did not believe in Him, but now the evidence of God is so great that there is no excuse for not believing in God.

The Bible's claim of inspiration has been proved by the fulfillment of the countless prophecies contained in the Bible. The evidence of God's existence is too great to ignore. It is evident that God created the universe specifically for human life, and He created man to fill the earth with offspring and rule over all other creatures.

People can read the scriptures and learn how the creation came into existence and how we can best serve God as we worship, obey, honor and glorify Him. The Christian religion claims that God can be known as a personal God by the revelation of the scriptures in the Bible.

The Bible answers important questions that inquiring minds might wonder about: for example, where did people come from? What is the purpose of their existence? What happens to them when they die? Does their spirit live forever and what happens to the spirit of people when the body dies?

The Bible answers these questions and offers people hope for eternal life. The inspired men who wrote the Bible called the words and writings of the Bible scripture. These men explained the significance and importance of the scriptures in the Bible. *2nd Timothy 3:16-17 "All scripture is given by inspiration of God, and is profitable for doctrine, for reproof, for correction, for instruction in righteousness, that the man of God may be complete, thoroughly equipped for every good work."*

Everyone will give an account to God at the end of time. The Bible tells *the **Story of Faith, Hope and Love*** and redemption from the guilt of sin. Sin simply means a person has missed the mark that God set for their life, and the ultimate punishment is spiritual death—meaning their spirit no longer has fellowship with God and no hope of eternal life. Sin entered into the world first through the disobedience of Adam and Eve in the Garden of Eden. Many years later in the first century A.D. God's Son came to earth to live as a human and to sacrifice His life to redeem sinful people.

Redemption is a personal matter between an individual person and God. In the Bible we discover God's nature and character, His love, His justice, His forgiveness, and His truth. If the Bible is read without prejudice, it will have the intended effect of producing faith in most people. Faith will lead to a desire to obey God and the story of Jesus Christ leads to eternal life.

The story of Jesus' birth, ministry, death, burial and resurrection is documented in the four gospel books: Matthew, Mark, Luke and John. The story about faith, hope and love begins with the universal problem of sin among all people in the Old Testament and includes the story of the birth of God's Son Jesus in the New Testament.

Faith is defined as a conviction based on hearing without seeing. We cannot see God and Christ with our eyes but we firmly believe and are persuaded that God and Christ are real through faith that gives us hope and love. With faith God and Christ are as real as the things we see clearly with our eyes. In Romans 10:17 Paul said faith comes by hearing the word of God. Faith is unquestioning belief of the existence of things that are unseen. *Hebrews 11:1 "now faith is the substance of things hoped for, the evidence of things not seen."*

Romans 8:24-25 "For we were saved in this hope, but hope that is seen is not hope; for why does one still hope for what he sees? But if we hope for what we do not see, we eagerly wait for it with perseverance."

The word love describes the attitude of God towards Christ and towards those who have faith in Christ.

John 3:16-18 "For God so loved the world that He gave His only begotten Son, that whoever believes in Him should not perish but have everlasting life. For God did not send His Son into the world to condemn the world, but that the world through Him might be saved."

God's Son Jesus Christ is the answer to God's promise of hope from the beginning of time. God promised to send His Son to become a sacrifice to redeem sinful people. The promise to send God's Son is revealed in the book of Genesis, then by promise and prophecy throughout the rest of the Bible.

People who are redeemed by faith in God's Son have hope that the death of the body is not a loss but a new beginning of life with Christ in a new body, in a new heaven, and a new earth at the end of time.

God's Son was born to a virgin woman by the seed of God—making Him both God and man. He lived on earth as a human and died as a human, thereby becoming a sacrifice for the guilt of sin even though He had no sin. God's Son Jesus lived approximately 33 years on earth and He ministered to the people demonstrating His love for people and giving them hope.

God sent His Son to be a propitiation or payment for all sin by being sacrificed on the cross. God promised forgiveness to all people who have faith in Christ. Romans 3:21-26 *"But now the righteousness of God apart from the Law is revealed, being witnessed by the Law and the prophets, even the righteousness of God, through faith in Jesus Christ, to all and on all who believe. For there is no difference; for all have sinned and fall short of the glory of God, being justified freely by His grace through the redemption that is in Christ Jesus, whom God set forth as a propitiation by His blood, through faith, to demonstrate His righteousness, because in His forbearance God passed over the sins that were previously committed, to demonstrate at the present time His righteousness, that He might be just and the justifier of the one who has faith in Jesus." God's righteousness extends beyond any law.*

The author of the book of Hebrews defines faith in chapter 11: 1-3 "Now faith is the substance of things hoped for, the evidence of things not seen. For by it the elders obtained a good testimony. By faith we understand that the worlds were framed by the word of God, so that the things which are seen were not made of things which are visible."

The book of Hebrews reveals that God's creation is made from things that were invisible. Today we have a great advantage over the people who were living when the Bible was first written. Today we know that all material things are made of atoms that are too small to be visible unless the atoms are combined in countless masses. Atoms are the building blocks of all material objects. People living in ancient times who accepted God did so by faith. They had much less evidence Of God's creation than people today, yet they developed a faith in God.

People may wonder: why did God, who is self-sufficient, create people?

God created people in His image, so they would know Him, glorify Him and have faith in Him. God's glory is recognized through His creation and His word. God did not create people because He needed them. God created people for His Own glory, and He expects them to glorify, worship, obey and honor Him because of who He is. There are consequences set forth by God for failing to glorify Him and for failing to obey the rules of His law.

Faith is what binds people to God and makes it possible for them to accept every aspect of God and obey Him. God loves the people He created like a father loves his children, and He has continually appealed to people since the creation to glorify Him. The Psalmist expresses God's love for people and their responsibility to Glorify God. Throughout the Bible we find commands to glorify God.

Psalm 34:1-3 I will bless the Lord at all times; His praise shall continually be in my mouth. My soul shall make its boast in the Lord; the humble shall hear of it and be glad. O, magnify the Lord with me, and let us exalt his name together."

The greatest manifestation of God's glory was through His Son Jesus Christ. Jesus was raised from the dead by the glory of God so we could have forgiveness from sin and have eternal life.

Psalms 86:9-13 "All nations whom You have made shall come and worship before You, O Lord, and shall glorify Your name. For You are great, and do wondrous things; You alone are God. Teach me Your way, O Lord; I will walk in Your truth; Unite my heart to fear your name. I will praise You, O Lord my God, with all my heart, And I will glorify Your name forevermore. For great is Your mercy toward me, And You have delivered my soul from the depths of Sheol."

Glorifying God is a key subject in both the Old and New Testaments. *John 17:1-5 "Jesus spoke these words, lifted up His eyes to heaven, and said: "Father, the hour has come. Glorify Your Son, that your Son also may glorify You, as You have given Him authority over all flesh, that He should give eternal life to as many as You have given Him.'*

"And this is eternal life, that they may know You, the only true God, and Jesus Christ whom You have sent. I have glorified you on the earth. I have finished the work, which, You have given Me to do. And now, O Father, glorify Me together with Yourself, with the glory, which I had with you before the world was."

The word glorify used in reference to God means to give praise, honor, fame and obedience to God. The purpose of the angels in heaven and all creatures is to glorify God. *1ˢᵗ Chronicles 16:28 "Give to the Lord the glory due His name; Bring an offering and come before Him, Oh, worship the Lord in the beauty of His holiness." Romans 14:4-6 "For whatever things were written before were written, for our learning that we through the patience and comfort of the Scriptures might have hope. Now may the God of patience and comfort grant you to be like minded toward one another, according to Christ Jesus, that you may with one mind and one mouth glorify the God and Father of our Lord Jesus Christ."*

God's glory can be seen through His creation; by events in history and in nature. Throughout the Bible people are told to glorify God. In John 15:8-10 Jesus told His disciples that God is glorified if you keep His commandments and remain in His love. Everything we do in the name of Christ to glorify God is an expression of our faith, hope and love.

The Beginning of Time

Time is described as all of the days that have been or ever will be, the past, present, and future. In the Bible, the beginning means when time on earth began; the time that God created everything including the earth. God is eternal; He is not restricted by time. Time as we know it began with the creation of the universe and the earth as a temporary home for the people God created.

To paraphrase Genesis chapters 1 through 3: In the beginning of time when God created the heavens and the earth the earth had no form. There was darkness, and the Spirit of God was above the waters that covered the earth. God made light, and He said it was good. God separated the light from the darkness at regular intervals and called them day and night. God called the time of the first light morning. When the light of the day began to become dark, He called that part of the day evening. The time of darkness He called night.

God made a firmament, the arch or vault of the heavens above the earth, and the arch He called the sky. God separated the land from the water and created dry ground. God made a firmament beneath the arch or vault of the heavens. God divided the waters on earth from the waters above the firmament. On the first day God created two great lights in the sky called the sun and the moon and He made the stars. The sun, the moon and the stars were for signs and seasons, days and years based on regular timed intervals. The sun and moon were made to give light on the earth. The sun furnished light during the day and the moon gave lesser light for the night. God also made the stars that shine at night.

God created the plants on the earth for environmental beauty and for food to eat. He created the various types of animal life that exist on the earth on the land in the sea and the sky. The Lord God made man from the dust of the ground and breathed into his nostrils the breath of life. He called the man Adam, and He put him in the garden He had prepared, which was a beautiful place with an environment made especially for the purpose of sustaining life and exhibiting peace, beauty and happiness.

The Lord decided it was not good for man to be alone so He created a woman from the rib of man to be a helpmate for him, and Adam named her Eve. God put a spirit in the body of the people He created. He told the man and woman to multiply by childbirth and fill the earth with people.

On the seventh day God ceased His creation of the heavens and earth and all things therein. The creation revealed the great glory of God, and He was pleased with His creation and said, "It is good."

Of all the things God created, man was His crowning glory. The Spirit God placed in man is immaterial and invisible and has a mind, which can think, understand and reason. God created people in this way so they could worship, praise and glorify Him. The mind is the sentient part of people and is able to perceive, reflect, feel and exhibit love, anger, hope and desire. People are somewhat like the nature of God. He created them in His image. God has supreme authority over people because He is the creator.

God is infinite, eternal, holy, unchanging, impassable, omnipotent, omni present, all knowing self-sufficient, gracious, merciful, loving and sovereign.

The people God created possess the ability to ignore and rebel against the authority of God, but people have no legitimate reason or excuse for ignoring and disobeying the law of their creator. When God put Adam and Eve in the Garden of Eden, He allowed them to eat the fruit and other plants in the garden to sustain physical life. At that time God set forth the first law for the man and woman. His first law is revealed in *Genesis 2:17 "But of the tree of the knowledge of good and evil you shall not eat, for in the day that you eat of it you shall surely die."*

The command do not eat is easy to understand but Adam and Eve deliberately disobeyed God's law. Before they ate the forbidden fruit, God told them if they disobeyed Him they would die. So why did they disobey God? The Devil (Satan), disguised as a serpent, was in the garden. The serpent lied to Eve and said, "You will not die if you eat fruit from the tree." Eve, then Adam, made a personal choice to disobey God.

Satan was successful in his attempt to cause Adam and Eve to sin. Adam and Eve sinned when Satan deceived them with a lie, and they willingly disobeyed God. The evil effect of Satan in the Garden of Eden was only the beginning of Satan's attempt to destroy the fellowship of God and His people. Satan is an evil angel who hates God and attempts to cause God's people to sin.

Sin is a governing principle or power that often acts out in the thoughts and attitudes of the heart, and it is an affront to God. God has always wanted and expected the spirit of people to seek Him, find Him and have faith in Him. Sin is the disobedience of God's commandments that acts out from the thoughts and attitudes of the heart and is expressed by the actions that results from those thoughts. Sin is committed the moment evil things are conceived in the heart.

James 1:13-15 Let no one say when he is tempted, "I am tempted by God;" for God cannot be tempted by evil, nor does He Himself temp anyone. But each one is tempted when he is drawn away by his own desires and enticed. Then, when desire has conceived, it gives birth to sin; and sin, when it is full-grown, brings forth death.

The sixth chapter of Proverbs describes a worthless and wicked person. A Paraphrase of Proverbs 6:12-19: "A worthless and wicked person has a perverse mouth, winks with his eyes and shuffles his feet and points with his fingers. Perversity is in his heart and he continually thinks of evil and sows discord. His calamity comes soon and he will be broken without remedy. Seven things God hates are a proud look, a lying tongue, shedding innocent blood, a heart that devises wicked plans, feet that are swift in running to evil, a false witness that lies, and one that sows discord among brethren."

These seven things are not the only things God hates but they are a good indicator of what God expects from people in their association with Him and with each other.

Adam and Eve had no worries or tribulation in their life until they disobeyed God's law. The sin of Adam and Eve was the first of the doctrine of sin, and it brought bad consequences. Eve disobeyed God and ate fruit from the tree. When Eve ate the forbidden fruit and gave some to Adam and he ate, they both sinned. Adam and Eve heard the voice of God, and they tried to hide from the presence of God, because they felt guilty and feared punishment. Nothing can be hidden from God for He sees all and He knows all. Adam and Eve disobeyed God and God said they would surely die.

God was talking about a spiritual death. Adam and Eve were still alive after they sinned. Spiritual death means a separation of a person's spirit from the fellowship of God and leads to eternal death after the body dies. The death of God's Son is the only sacrifice great enough to remove the guilt of sin. God's laws were given for the benefit of people, and when Adam and Eve ignored God's law, they established a pattern for every generation after them.

People living together in societies usually establish laws for their community, and they assess penalties for those who transgress those laws. Laws are necessary, and it is not unreasonable to believe that God would expect the people He created to obey His law. When Adam and Eve disobeyed God and ate from the tree, they tried to hide from God. God knows and sees everything everywhere all of the time and nothing can be hidden from Him.

Jeremiah 23:23-24 "Am I a God near at hand," says the Lord, And not a God afar off? Can anyone hide himself in secret places, so I shall not see him?" says the Lord; "Do I not fill heaven and earth?" says the Lord. Psalm 44; 20-21 "If we had forgotten the name of our God, or stretched out our hands to a foreign god, would God not search this out? For He knows the secrets of the heart."

A paraphrase of Psalm 147:1-11: The Psalmist declares it is good to sing praises to God. It is pleasant, and praise is beautiful. The Lord builds up Jerusalem; He gathers together the outcasts of Israel. He heals the brokenhearted and binds up their wounds. He counts the number of the stars; He calls them all by name. Great is our Lord, and mighty in power; His understanding is infinite. The Lord lifts up the humble; He casts the wicked down to the ground. Sing to the Lord with thanksgiving; sing praises on the harp to our God, who covers the heavens with clouds, Who prepares rain for the earth, Who makes grass to grow on the mountains. He gives to the beast its food, and to the young ravens that cry.

A paraphrase of Isaiah 59:1-2: Behold the Lord's hand is not shortened, That it cannot save, nor His ear heavy that it cannot hear, but your iniquities have separated you from your God; And your sins have hidden His face from you, so that He will not hear.

The Lord punished the serpent by causing him to be a curse on earth and by making him crawl on his belly. To paraphrase Genesis 3:15: God predicts the defeat of Satan's evil influence to cause people to sin by sending Christ the Messiah to redeem people from the guilt of sin (but it would be a few thousand years before Jesus Christ was born).

From this point on in our story of faith, hope and love, we will look at the lives of many people of faith who were important in God's plan of redemption.

The first sin mentioned after the sin of Adam and Eve was murder. Adam and Eve's son, Cain killed his brother Abel because of jealousy.

Genesis 4:1-5 "Now Adam knew Eve his wife, and she conceived and bore Cain and said, "I have acquired a man from the Lord." Then she bore again, this time his brother Abel. Now Abel was a keeper of sheep, but Cain was a tiller of the ground."

Eve gave birth to a son and they named him Cain. Eve had anther son and they named him Abel. Cain tilled the soil and planted crops for food, and Abel raised sheep to supply meat and wool. Adam and Eve and their sons, Cain and Abel, knew God because He had revealed himself to them, and they served God by offering sacrifices to God. The Bible doesn't mention a commandment from God to offer sacrifices until much later in the history of mankind, but from the story of Cain and Abel we learn that God did accept sacrifices if they were offered with a proper attitude from the heart (faith).

Cain offered some of his produce from the ground and Abel offered meat from the firstborn of his sheep. God was pleased with Abel's offering, but God was not pleased with Cain's offering. The Lord said to Cain, "If you do not do well, sin is at your door." God was pleased with Abel's offering, but He was not pleased with Cain's offering. Cain's offering wasn't offered in faith. When Cain realized that God wasn't pleased with his offering, he became angry.

Why was God pleased with Abel's sacrifice and displeased with Cain's sacrifice? The brothers offered God what they had to offer, but offering sacrifices to God also has to do with one's attitude of faith as well as what is offered. Abel offered his sacrifice from faith in God because he wanted to please God. Cain did not offer out of faith as Abel did, and he became jealous and angry with Abel because God accepted Abel's sacrifice and rejected his sacrifice.

Hebrews 11:4 "By faith Abel offered to God a more excellent sacrifice than Cain, through which he obtained witness that he was righteous, God testifying of his gifts; and through it he being dead still speaks." "If you do well, you will be accepted, but if you do not do right, sin lies at your door."

Cain did not do right, because he did not offer his sacrifice from faith. Cain became jealous of Abel and he murdered him, a sign of Cain's sinful attitude. *Genesis 4:8 "Now Cain talked with Abel his brother; and it came to pass, when they were in the field, that Cain rose up against Abel his brother and killed him."*

The result of Abel's faith and Cain's lack of faith serves as an example that faith in God is necessary to please God. *Hebrews 11:4 "By faith Abel offered to God a more excellent sacrifice than Cain, through which he obtained witness that he was righteous, God testifying of his gifts; and through it he, being dead, still speaks."*

God punished Cain for murdering Abel. His crops didn't produce, so he became a restless person and a wanderer. Cain missed out on the contentment and joy that comes from being true to God with all of your heart. God's plan of salvation by faith in Christ became possible because of the few people who, by faith, obeyed God. The offering of animals by Abel in the beginning was an expression of his faith in God.

Even though God needs nothing from people, He does want people to glorify Him. He accepts the sacrifices from the hearts of people and rewards them because of their faith. To paraphrase Hebrews 13: The writer admonishes people to offer sacrifices of praise to God by the fruit of their lips giving thanks to God and not forgetting to do good and to share, because God is pleased with those sacrifices. Real faith is known by the attitudes and deeds of those who possess faith.

Today our worship of Christ from the heart is our expression of faith in Him. In the very first book of the Bible, we learn what is most important to God and what He wants from His creation. God wants the spirit of mankind to seek Him, find Him and develop a faith in Him with an attitude of faith, hope and love. The sacrifices that are pleasing to God must be offered in a true faith when you worship God.

From the time of Adam and Eve to today people continue to sin. Most people in the beginning ignored God and were involved in many kinds of sin. Some people did offer sacrifices, but their sacrifices did not atone for their sins because the sacrifice was not great enough. The death of God's Son is the only sacrifice that will take away the guilt of sin. Beginning with Abel and later with Noah sacrifices consisted of animals sacrificed on an altar, and they were acceptable to God, but they did not erase the guilt of sin.

Hebrews 13:15-16 "Therefore by him let us continually offer the sacrifice of praise to God that is the fruit of our lips, giving thanks to His name. But do not forget to good and to share, for with such sacrifices God is well pleased."

Later in the redemption story of the bible, God gave a written Law. Paraphrase of Hebrews 10: In the beginning the law that required sacrifices was not sufficient to remove the guilt of sin. It was impossible for the blood of animals to take away the guilt of sin. Animal sacrifices in the Old Testament foreshadowed the sacrifice of Christ and served as a reminder of the future sacrifice of Christ on the cross.

The sacrifice of Christ would take away the guilt of sin for all who had faith in Christ from the time of Adam to the end of time. After the time of Adam, Eve, Cain and Abel, people ignored God and continued to sin. There were only a few individuals who had faith in God.

The few people who remained faithful played a significant part in God's redeeming plan through faith in Christ. God's plan is documented in the Bible all of the time before the birth of Christ. The story in the Bible and in this book ***The Story of Faith, Hope and Love*** explains the history of the people of faith chosen by God who had a part in God's redemption plan.

After the death of Abel, Adam and Eve had another son named Seth and during that time people began to call on the name of the Lord. Calling on the name of the Lord suggests faith in God that leads to obedience of God's commandments. In Romans the first chapter Paul wrote about faith, and he said the righteousness of God is revealed from faith to faith, and those who are righteous live by faith. Chapter 5 of Genesis gives us the generations of Adam through the line of his son Seth.

Genesis 5:25-27 "Methuselah lived one hundred and eighty seven years and begot Lamech. After he begot Lamech, Methusaleh lived seven hundred and eighty-two years and had sons and daughters. So all the days of Methusaleh were nine hundred and sixty-nine years and he died."

From the time of Adam and Eve, God's presence and His Word was made known to the people, but morality steadily declined, and all who were still living were unrighteous except for one man Noah and his family. Everyone else ignored God and lived as they pleased.

God decided to destroy the people on earth because of their sinfulness and begin again with Noah and his descendants. Any time a person disobeys God they become a sinner.

After Noah there was a man named Enoch, of the seventh generation from Adam, he was a man of faith who had fellowship with God and God communicated with Him. Enoch prophesied about Christ several thousand years before the birth of Christ. He also prophesied of the future coming of the end of time when Christ will come with thousands of angels to punish the ungodly sinners.

Enoch was faithful to God all the years he lived meaning He obeyed God, and the Bible says that God took him, indicating that Enoch didn't die a natural death, because God took him from the earth directly to heaven.

Hebrews 11:5-6 "By faith Enoch was taken away so that he did not see death, and was not found because God had taken him; for before he was taken he had this testimony, that he pleased God. But without faith it is impossible to please Him, for he who comes to God must believe that He is, and that He rewards those who diligently seek Him."

In the beginning people had a long life span, but God shortened the physical life span because of the evil ways of mankind. Adam lived nine hundred and thirty years. When Adam was one hundred and thirty years of age his son Seth was born. Seth was faithful like his father Adam. The descendants of Seth were believers in God, but they married the daughters of unbelievers, and their descendants became exceedingly sinful.

Unbelievers corrupted the morals of the righteous people, so God decided He would let that generation of unrighteous people live for only one hundred and twenty years. Man, being a mortal creature subject to the commands of God was subjected to a shorter lifespan because of their wickedness. Eventually mankind became so sinful that every thought of their heart was evil continually.

God gave up His fellowship with sinners meaning they were dead in a spiritual sense. God separated Himself from them, and they were without any way to be forgiven of their sins. Because of their sin God decided to destroy all sinners with a great flood and save the people of faith.

Noah found grace in the eyes of the Lord. Grace means loving kindness and goodwill. Noah's life was spared because he had faith in God and he obeyed God. Faith is a belief without visual evidence. The people could not see God but there was a lot of evidence that He existed. Noah could not see God, but he believed in Him and obeyed Him. The Greek word pistis is the equivalent of faith and means a firm conviction of belief based on hearing alone. This word also means trust.

Genesis 6:1-3 *"Now it came to pass when men began to multiply on the face of the earth, and daughters were born to them, that the sons of God saw the daughters of men, that they were beautiful; and they took wives for themselves of all whom they chose. And the Lord said, "My Spirit will not be with man forever'*

"for he is flesh. His days shall be one hundred and twenty years." Genesis 6:5-8 "Then the Lord saw that the wickedness of man was great in the earth, and that every, intent of the thoughts of his heart was only evil continually. And the Lord was sorry that He had made man on the earth, and He was grieved in his heart. So the Lord said, "I will destroy man whom I have created from the face of the earth, both man and beast, creeping things and birds of the air, for I am sorry that I have made them." But Noah found grace in the eyes of the Lord and he and his household were saved.

God Destroys the Earth With a Great Flood

Genesis 6:9-12 "This is the genealogy of Noah. Noah was a just man, perfect in his generations. Noah walked with God. And Noah begot three sons Shem, Ham and Japheth. The earth also was corrupt before God and the earth was filled with violence. So God looked upon the earth, and indeed it was corrupt; for all flesh had corrupted their way on the earth."

Hebrews 11:7 "By faith Noah being divinely warned of things not yet seen, moved with godly fear, prepared an ark for the saving of his household, by which he condemned the world and became heir of the righteousness which is according to faith."

God told Noah to build an ark, a huge boat, because He was going to destroy all life with a great flood. He told Noah exactly how to build the ark, so Noah obeyed God and built the ark. Noah and his wife and his three sons Shem, Ham and Japheth and all who were in their household entered the ark and lived there during the flood until God told them to leave the ark on dry ground. God caused it to rain for forty days and forty nights and the earth became covered by water. Noah and his family and the animals he put in the ark survived the flood. When the earth dried up God told Noah and his family to leave the ark and to bring all of the animals, birds, cattle and every thing that creeps out of the ark on dry ground.

When Noah left the ark, he built an altar and offered animals on the altar as a sacrifice to God. God was pleased with the sacrifice and God said He would never again curse the ground. God promised while the earth remains, seedtime and harvest, cold and heat, winter and summer, and day and night would not cease.

God promised Noah and his sons that He would never again destroy all life on earth with a flood, and He created the rainbow as a sign that He would keep His word. The rainbow today still reminds us of God's promise.

God blessed Noah and his sons and told them to have children and fill the earth. Noah lived three hundred and fifty years after the flood. He was six hundred years old at the time of the flood, so he lived a total of 950 years. After the flood, there was a new beginning in the relationship between, God and the people

The descendants of Noah increased greatly on the earth and the people began to sin and practice evil like they did before the flood. All the people at that time spoke the same language, and together they thought of all kinds of ways to practice evil and they ignored God. People depended on their own wisdom instead of the word of God.

They began to make their own lifeless gods and to worship them instead of the true God, so God confused their language and scattered them all over the earth. They still practiced evil after they were scattered, but they were no longer united in their evil ways.

The sons of Noah who came out of the ark were Shem, Ham and Japheth and from these three the whole earth was repopulated. The descendants of Shem are given special attention in the Bible, because God's Son would be born through a line of Shem's descendants many years later.

Two years after the flood, Shem was one hundred years old, and he was the father of Arphaxad who is in the birth line of Jesus. Shem lived for five hundred years after the birth of Arphaxad.

He settled in Mesopotamia and was the ancestor of the Semitic peoples, including the Hebrews, Arabs and Syrians. Shem's descendants spoke Semitic languages. Several nations, languages and peoples emerged from the three sons of Noah.

The history of Noah's son Shem and his descendants is mostly obscure from the time of the flood to the time of Abram, a descendant of Shem, and a great man of faith in God. Shem's first son was Arphaxad. Arphaxad's first son was Salah, and Salah's first son was Eber. Eber's son was Peleg, Peleg's son was Reu, Reu's son was Serug, and Serug's son was Nahor. Nahor's son was Terah and Terah's sons were Abram, Nahor, and Haran.

Millions of people have lived on the earth since the time of the flood. Most have been motivated by pride and arrogance forgetting about God and becoming evil and sinful. Many at that time failed to put their faith in God.

However there have always continued to be people of faith. Such were some of the people God used to fulfill His plan to redeem people who would have faith in Him.

This is a Timeline of Dates from Creation until Christ Came

Creation of Adam around 4174 B.C.
Flood was around 2518-2517 B.C.
Birth of Abraham in 2235 B.C.
Birth of Christ in the first century A.D.

God Calls Abram and Makes a Covenant

God changed Abram's name to Abraham. Abraham the man of faith obeyed God even when most of the people during his time ignored God.

Romans 4:3-7 "For what does the scripture say? Abraham believed God, and it was credited to him as righteousness. Now to the one who works, his wage is not credited as a favor, but as what is due. But to the one who does not work, but believes in Him who justifies the ungodly, his faith is credited as righteousness, just as David also speaks of the blessing on the man to whom God credits righteousness apart from works: Blessed are those whose Lawless deeds have been forgiven, And whose sins have been covered."

Abram was born in Ur, a city located along the Euphrates River in ancient Sumer, a part of Babylonia. The region of Sumer is in the lower part of Mesopotamia (now Iraq). Sumer was settled about 3000 or 4000 B.C.

In Genesis 12 God made promises to Abram and told him to leave his country and his fathers house and go to a land God would show him.

Genesis 12: 1 "Now the Lord had said to Abram: Get out of your country, From your family And from your fathers house, to a land I will show you. I will make you a great nation; I will bless you and make your name great; and you shall be a blessing. I will bless those who bless you, and I will curse him who curses you; And in you the families of the earth shall be blessed."

When Abram was living in Mesopotamia, God told him to go to the land of Canaan across the river from Mesopotamia. God had great plans that included Abram and his descendants in His plan of redemption. God's plan included forming a great nation from Abram's descendants who would live in the land of Canaan. God's Son would come from the birth line of Abram's descendants. The Lord God told Abram he would become a father of many nations, and God changed Abram's name to Abraham meaning father of many nations.

Abraham was known as a Hebrew when he crossed over from Mesopotamia into Canaan. Hebrew means 'one who crosses over.' God blessed Abraham and promised him that He would make of him a great nation and that all people on earth would be blessed through him. He was referring to His plan to redeem the people of the earth through his descendants. God communed with Abraham through visions and by angels.

If we fast-forward a few thousand years, the Bible explains how all nations of people can be blessed through the promise God made to Abram and Abraham. *Galatians 3:26-29 "For you are, all sons of God through <u>faith</u> in Christ Jesus. For as many of you as were baptized into Christ have put on Christ. There is neither Jew nor Greek, there is neither slave nor free, there is neither male nor female; for you are all one in Christ Jesus. And if you are Christ's, then you are Abraham's seed, and heirs according to the promise."*

Jesus would be a descendant of Abraham. *Galatians 3:6-9 "Just as Abraham believed God and it was accounted to him for righteousness. Therefore know that only those who are of faith are sons of Abraham. And the Scripture, foreseeing that God would justify the Gentiles by faith, preached the gospel to Abraham beforehand, saying, "In you all the nations shall be blessed." So then those who are of faith are blessed with believing Abraham."*

The process of redemption through Abraham to Christ would take approximately 2000 years and would involve the descendants of Abraham, Isaac, and Jacob. The story of God's redeeming plan follows the events of the life of Abram first then Abraham and Isaac and Isaac's son Jacob.

Paraphrase of Genesis 17:1-8: Abram was ninety-nine years old when the Lord appeared to him and said, "I am almighty God; walk before me and be blameless, and I will make a covenant between you and Me and will multiply your descendants. God told Abraham the covenant would be between them and Abraham's descendants after him in their generations for an everlasting covenant.

"I will be a God to you and your descendants after you. Also I give to you and your descendants after you the land in which you are a stranger, all the land of Canaan, as an everlasting possession; and I will be their God."

The Bible makes, reference to covenants as promises made by God, but promises are gifts that are bestowed, not negotiated. A covenant is a solemn agreement (contract) between two or more parties, and in order for a covenant to remain in force, both parties of the covenant must obey the terms of the covenant. If Abraham or his descendants after him did not keep their part of the covenant, the covenant would be broken and no longer binding on either party. A covenant is a mutual agreement between two parties that means if you will do what I tell you to do, then I will do whatever I obligated myself to do.

The first agreement God made with Abraham depended on Abraham leaving his home and family and going to a place that God would show him. If Abraham fulfilled his part of the agreement, God promised to make him into a great nation and bless him. God promised to bless all people on earth through Abraham. Abraham believed that God would keep his promises, and it was faith in God's word and hope and love that motivated Abraham to continue to do what God commanded him.

Abraham agreed to go to the land of Canaan, and God promised to give the land to Abraham's descendants. Since we have the recorded history in the Bible of God's redeeming plan, we understand that the ultimate blessing of all people is the forgiveness of sin for everyone who would have faith in Jesus a descendant of Abraham. Abraham played a great part in our salvation. Paraphrase—Galatians 3:6-9 says Abraham believed God, which was an act of faith, and God credited him as being righteous. And the Scripture, foreseeing that God would justify the Gentiles by faith, preached the gospel to Abraham beforehand saying, "In you all the nations shall, be blessed." So then those who are of faith are blessed with believing Abraham.

God continually reminded Abraham and his descendants of the agreement between them. God made several other covenants with Abraham before he died. He told Abraham that he would bless him and his descendants would be as numerous as the stars in heaven, and Abraham believed God even though as yet he did not have a son with his wife Sarah because she was barren and Abraham was very old. When God told Abraham that his descendants would be as numerous as the stars. Abraham asked for a sign to help him believe God's promise. God instructed him to bring animals for an offering. Abraham arranged the animals for sacrifice just as God told him to do, and then he fell into a deep sleep. God then spoke with Abraham as he slept and told him that his people would become slaves in a foreign land, and they would be mistreated for four hundred years.

He also promised that He would punish the foreign nation that made slaves of His people and Abraham descendants would leave that land with great wealth. Abraham's son Isaac was the descendant that would inherit the promises God made to his father Abraham. The foreign land where the Israelites would be slaves was the land of Egypt during the time of Isaac's son Jacob. Jacob's name was to be changed to Israel and the Israelites would be a great nation of God's people.

God made a covenant with Abraham and promised that the land from the river of Egypt to the Euphrates River would some day belong to Abraham's descendants. The descendants of Abraham would become slaves in Egypt, then leave Egypt, wander through the wilderness between Egypt and the Jordan River for forty years, afterward cross the Jordan River and occupy the land of Canaan that God promised them.

Abraham's wife Sarah was barren and Abraham wondered how he could become the father of many nations without an heir. Sarah offered her Egyptian handmaid Hagar to Abraham to produce a son for Abraham. Sarah was Jealous of Hagar and she made Hagar leave and Hagar went toward Shur. An angel of the lord appeared to Hagar and told her to return to Abraham and she returned and bore Abraham a son. Abraham's first child by Hagar was named Ishmael.

The angel prophesied about Ishmael saying he would be a wild donkey of a man and his hand would be against everyone and everyone's hand against him. He would act with hostility toward all his brothers. Ishmael had several sons and the Ishmael's descendants may possibly be the Bedouin tribes that gave rise to the Arab nations living in the north and west of the Arabian Peninsula. They now follow Mohammad with Ishmael as their spiritual father. They lived in the area that we call the Middle East (Saudi Arabia, Iraq and Iran).

When Abraham was ninety years old God appeared to him and said He was God Almighty and He commanded Abraham to obey Him and he would make a covenant with him. That was when God changed Abram's name to Abraham because he would be the father of many nations. The covenant between God and Abraham would be an everlasting covenant. God had said He would be Abraham's God and his descendants God forever and He gave them the land of Canaan forever.

The sign of the covenant between God and Abraham was that he and every male of his descendants would be circumcised at the age of eight days. Genesis 17:17-God told Abraham and Sarah that she was going to have a baby and Sarah laughed.

On another day Abraham was sitting in the doorway of his tent in Mamre by the terebinth trees and he saw three strangers and he ran to meet them and bowed himself before them. Abraham addresses one of the men as Lord and sought his favor Genesis 18:13. The consensus of bible scholars is that the men were actually angels sent to deliver the message about Sarah's son and to destroy the evil cities of Sodom and Gomorrah where Abraham's nephew Lot lived. One of the three strangers told Abraham that he would return next year and Sarah would have a son.

Abraham was one hundred years old when God visited Sarah in a miraculous way and she became pregnant and Sarah had a son and they named him Isaac. Hagar and Ishmael had already left Abraham's house. Abraham and the three visitors walked over to a peak that overlooked the cities of the plain and they discussed the fate of Sodom and Gomorrah. The Lord was going to destroy the two cities because of the gross immorality of the people that lived in the cities *Genesis 19:29 "And it came to pass, when God destroyed the cities of the plain, that God remembered Abraham, and sent Lot out of the midst of the overthrow, when He overthrew the cities in which Lot had dwelt."* Abraham looked toward the cities from a distance and he saw the smoke rising from the land like smoke from a furnace.

Abraham left Mamre and settled in Gerar between Kadesh and Shur in the land occupied by the Philistines. While he was living in Gerar he claimed that Sarah was his sister and Abimelech the king had Sarah brought to him but God warned him in a dream that he would die if he laid a hand on Sarah.

Abimelech sent Sarah to Abraham and gifted Abraham with sheep, oxen and servants and he told Abraham he could live anywhere he wanted to. Abraham planted a grove in Beersheba and worshiped God. Sarah became pregnant and bore a son like God had promised and he was named Isaac. Ishmael was thirteen years old at the time of Isaac's birth and Abraham gave Hagar and Ishmael bread and water and sent them away and they wandered in the wilderness of Beersheba. They ran out of water and were in complete despair when an angel of God came to them and told Hagar that Ishmael would become a great nation. A well of water miraculously appeared and their life was saved.

Genesis chapter 22-when Isaac was still young Abraham was commanded by God to offer Isaac as a sacrifice on an altar. Becoming a sacrifice would mean death to Isaac but Abraham was faithful to obey God. Everything was made ready for the sacrifice but God prevented the death of Isaac by sending the angel of the Lord to Abraham.

God was testing the faith of Abraham and Abraham proved to be faithful so God provided a ram for the sacrifice. Because of Abraham's faith God promised to bless him and multiply his descendants as the stars in heaven and the sand on the seashore. Besides the physical descendants of Abraham all Christians are spiritual descendants of the promise God made to Abraham.

Isaac becomes the next in line be engaged in the carrying out the promises God made to Abraham and his descendants because Isaac was the son of the promise God made to Abraham. When Isaac was forty years old Rebekah became his wife but Rebekah was not able to have children. Isaac pleaded with the Lord God for Rebekah to give him children and the Lord answered his prayer and Rebekah became pregnant with twin sons, the babies struggled in her and she didn't understand what was going on so she asked the Lord about it, and the Lord told her that there were two nations in her womb. He said, "Two people shall be separated from your body; one people shall be stronger than the other, and the older shall serve the younger." When Isaac died, the promises and blessings that God gave Abraham and Isaac would be passed on to one of Isaac's sons. God would be the one to choose between the twin sons of Isaac. Isaac lived in the land of Canaan with Rebekah his wife. The oldest son of Isaac would normally be the one in line to inherit the promises God had made to Abraham that passed to Isaac.

Isaac's sons, Jacob and Esau, were born at the same time, but Esau was the first one from the womb, making him the oldest. There was an ancient birthright custom that gave the firstborn son of a family special honor and privileges. When a father died, his oldest son would receive twice as much inheritance as the other male siblings and he would become the head of the family.

The birthright was rightfully Esau's, and normally the promises made by God to Abraham would, continue through the line of Esau's descendants, but Esau was not as wise as Jacob and Esau sold his birthright to Jacob. It was God's will that the promises made to Abraham would continue through Jacob and his descendants.

Approximately one-fourth of the book of Genesis is a biography of Jacob and his descendants, the family through whom the birth line of Christ would come.

Romans 9:6-13 "For they are not all Israel who are of Israel, nor are they all children because they are the seed of Abraham; but in Isaac your seed shall be called, That is, those who are the children of the flesh, these are not the children of God; but the children of the promise are counted as the seed.

For this is the word of the promise; At this time I will come and Sarah shall have a son. And not only this, but when Rebecca also had conceived by one man, even our father Isaac (for the children not yet being born, nor having done any good or evil, that the purpose of God according to election might stand, not of works but of Him who calls), it was said to her, the older shall serve the younger, As it is written, "Jacob I have loved, but Esau I have hated."

Rebekah (Rebecca) remembered what the Lord told her about the older boy serving the younger. Esau would serve Jacob. Rebekah tricked Isaac in order to obey God. God knew before the boys were born that the younger son was the right choice. Isaac became reconciled to the fact that Jacob was to be the blessed one instead of Esau, and Isaac blessed Jacob with these words, *"May God Almighty bless you, and make you fruitful and multiply you, That you may be an assembly of peoples; And give you the blessing of Abraham, to you and your descendants with you, That you may inherit the land in which you are a stranger, which God gave Abraham." (Genesis 28:3-5)*

The promises that God gave Abraham were passed on from Abraham and Isaac to Jacob and his descendants. When Jacob was a young single man, he left his father's house in Beersheba and went toward Haran where his uncle lived. Jacob stopped somewhere along the way and laid down to sleep.

As he slept, he had a very strange dream; a dream from the Lord. In his dream, Jacob saw a ladder reaching from the earth all the way to heaven with the angels of God ascending and descending on the ladder.

The Lord stood at the top of the ladder and said, *"I am the Lord God of Abraham your father and the God of Isaac; the land on which you lie I will give to you and your descendants. Also your descendants shall be as the dust of the earth; you shall spread abroad to the west and the east, to the north and the south; and in you and in your seed all the families of the earth shall be blessed. Behold, I am with you and will keep you wherever you go, and will bring you back to this land; for I will not leave you until I have done what I have spoken to you."* (Genesis 28: 13-15)

Jacob's dream was the first of his personal encounter with the Lord God of Abraham and Isaac, and it made a lasting impression on Jacob. The dream of the ladder established a link between God in heaven and Jacob and his descendants. The dream of the angels ascending and descending was a message that God would be with Jacob, and by the intervention of the angels, God would protect and take care of him and his family.

Jacob received the promises of God, which were made earlier to his father and grandfather, Abraham and Isaac.

Christ the Son of God would come later and become a sacrifice for redemption and He would come through Jacob's line of the nation of Israel. When Jacob woke up from his dream, he declared that God was in that place, and he called the place 'The house of God,' and it became known as the city of Bethel.

Jacob went on his way to his uncle Laban's house to find a wife. He met a girl named Rachel, the daughter of Laban, his mother's brother and a descendant of Abraham's brother. He wanted Rachel for his wife, but Laban would not give Rachel to Jacob unless he first married Leah Rachel's older sister. Jacob married both Leah and Rachel, and together they bore him twelve sons. These twelve sons later became the ancestors of the twelve tribes of Israel. Those who were chosen by God to be ancestors of the birth line of Christ were not perfect people without human weaknesses but they were people who had **faith** in God and **hope** for the future promises of God.

After many years of working for his uncle, Jacob took his wives and children and left Laban's home to go back to his homeland. Jacob wanted to win the favor of his brother Esau from whom he had stolen his birthright. The last time he saw Esau, his brother hated him and wanted to kill him, so Jacob was afraid of Esau. Esau was a hunter and a warrior and Jacob was a person with a gentle nature.

As Jacob drew near to his homeland, Esau got word that he was on his way home. Esau left to meet Jacob with four hundred armed men. Jacob prayed to God for deliverance from Esau thinking that Esau might attack him. As they came to the River Jabbok, Jacob crossed the river to Esau and bowed before him seven times, expressing sorrow for the way he had treated Esau. Esau ran to him, fell on his neck and kissed him, and they wept and were glad to see each other.

Jacob's Name Changed to Israel

Paraphrase—Genesis 32:22-32: Jacob left that night with his two wives two female servants, and his eleven sons. They crossed over the brook of Jabbok and left Jacob alone. That night an angel wrestled with Jacob until the breaking of day.

Now when the angel saw that he could not prevail against him, He touched the socket of Jacob's hip; and the socket of his hip came out of joint. Jacob said, *"Let me go, for the day breaks." But he said 'I will not let you go unless you bless me! So He said to him, what is your name?" He said Jacob. And he said your name, shall no longer be called Jacob, but Israel; for you have struggled with God and with men, and have prevailed."*

Then Jacob said, tell me your name I pray." And He said why is it that you ask My name? And He blessed him there."

Jacob called that place Peniel, which means the face of God. The man who wrestled with Jacob was a manifestation of God, most likely an angel whom God had sent because Jacob had not believed the promise God made to protect him. Jacob held on to the angel and would not let go unless the angel promised to bless him. The angel asked Jacob what his name was, and when Jacob told him, the angel changed Jacob's name to Israel and blessed him.

When Jacob wrestled with the angel he was in effect wrestling with God. Jacob failed to have absolute trust and faith in God's word. For a reminder of Jacob's lack of faith Jacob walked with a limp to remind him of his encounter with God. The name Israel means 'God strives.' God struggled with Jacob in order to make him obey Him.

Jacob lived with his sons in the land of Canaan, the land God promised Abraham, Isaac and Jacob. Abraham's descendants from then on were known as the Israelites. Jacob returned to Bethel, and God appeared to Him again and blessed him. *Genesis 35:10-15 "God said to him, "Your name is Jacob; your name shall not be called Jacob anymore, But Israel shall be your name." So he called his name Israel. And God said to him, "I am God Almighty. Be fruitful and multiply; a nation and a company of nations shall proceed from you, and kings shall come from your body.*

The land, which I gave Abraham and Isaac I give to you; and to your descendants after you I give this land. So Jacob set up a pillar in the place where he talked with him, a pillar of stone; and he poured a drink offering on it, and then he poured oil on it. And Jacob called the name of the place where God spoke with him, Bethel

The word Bethel means 'the house of God.' As we said before, the name Israel means 'God strives,' and God changed Jacob's name to Israel, God struggled with the nation of Israel from then on. The nation of Israel often rebelled against the commandments of the Lord before they finally took possession of Canaan, the land God promised them. The fulfillment of God's promises (covenants) depended on the willingness and faithfulness of the people of Israel to remain faithful to obey God.

The Lord established a covenant with Jacob saying the Israelites would multiply greatly and that his descendants would become kings of nations, and the land of Canaan would belong to them. Later in the story of faith, hope and love God's promises of a great nation and kings of nations was realized. The story of faith hope and love continued through Jacob. Jacob's name was changed to Israel and Jacob's people became the nation of Israel. Jacob had twelve sons whose names were: Reuben, Simeon, Levi, Judah, Dan, Naphtali, Gad, Asher, Issachar, Zebulun, Joseph and Benjamin. These sons would eventually become the twelve tribes of the nation of Israel and possess the promised land of Canaan. This would happen after many years of hardships and struggles with their enemies.

In ancient times the term Patriarch meant 'father or ruler of a family'. Abraham, Isaac and Jacob became patriarchs. God's promises to Abraham passed to Isaac, then Jacob, and eventually to Jacob's son Judah. Judah was chosen by God to inherit the covenant God had made with Abraham. Christ would eventually come through the descendants of Judah.

The destiny and future of Judah, the son of Jacob and Leah, was more important to God's plan of redemption than the other sons, because his descendants would become the progenitor of King David and Solomon, and of Jesus the Son of God.

Jacob and his family become slaves in Egypt and before they were permitted to leave Egypt, Jacob blesses his sons.

Genesis 49: 8-10 "Judah you are he whom your brothers shall praise; your hand shall be on the neck of your enemies; Your fathers children shall bow down before you. Judah is a lion's whelp;'

"From the prey my son you have gone up. He bows down he lies down like a lion; and as a lion, who shall rouse him? The scepter shall not part from Judah, Nor a lawgiver from between his feet, Until Shiloh comes; And to Him shall be the obedience of the people. Binding his donkey to the vine."

The blessing from Jacob to his sons was prophetic and it pictured the future history Of God's people the nation of Israel. Judah would receive the national leadership of Israel.

The emblem of a lion is a symbol of the strength of the leaders of the tribes and Judah would be strong like a lion the king of beasts. Shiloh makes reference to Jesus the last in the line of the kings of Israel.

Jesus the Prince of Peace would be the giver of rest and peace. Jesus said, "Come to me all you who are weary and I will give you rest to your soul." God promised Abraham that all the families of the earth would be blessed through him. And He would judge between the nations, and render decisions for many peoples.

In the fifteenth chapter of Genesis, God said that his people would be strangers in Egypt and then God would judge Egypt, and Abraham's descendants would leave that land with great possessions.

It would be a long time before the Israelites left Egypt and eventually came back to the land of Canaan that was promised to Abraham's descendants. Exodus 12:40-42

The children of Israel lived in Egypt four hundred and thirty years. And at the end of the four hundred and thirty years—on that very same day—it came to pass that all the armies of the Lord left out from the land of Egypt.

It is a night of solemn observance for all the children of Israel throughout their generations. (Paraphrase) Before the children of Israel left Egypt they observed a memorial feast that the Jewish people still observe today.

The Israelites In Egypt

Genesis 37

The Israelites going to Egypt was a fulfillment of prophecy. God had told Abram that his descendants would be strangers in a foreign land and would serve the people there. The Israelites would become slaves of the Egyptians and God would judge the Egyptians and the Israelites would leave Egypt with great possessions. The Israelites would come back to the land of Canaan in the fourth generation.

Ancient Egypt was a great nation that came to power many years ago. The Egyptians were creative and inventive people with discoveries in mathematics and other sciences that enabled them to make great achievements. Egypt, with the help of captive slaves from other lands, built the pyramids. Compared to the Israelite culture, the Egyptians were very far advanced in most areas of civilization except religion.

The Egyptians worshiped many false gods and they did not know the Lord God of the Israelites. The rulers of Egypt were known by the title Pharaoh.

Joseph, next to the youngest son of Jacob, led by God was responsible for the Israelites going to Egypt to fulfill the prophecy of the Lord. Joseph was the favorite son of Israel (Jacob), because he was the son of Rebekah, the wife that Jacob loved most. Joseph was his youngest son until Benjamin was born. When Benjamin was born, Rebekah died in childbirth.

Joseph always obeyed his father and would tell his father when his brothers didn't obey Jacob. This was another reason Jacob favored Joseph and made him a coat of many colors a very fine and expensive gift. Joseph's older brothers hated him because he told on them when they did not obey Jacob and they were jealous of him because he was the favorite son of Jacob.

Joseph had a special gift from the Lord, which enabled him to be favored by his father. The Lord communicated with Joseph of future events through dreams, and he blessed Joseph with the ability to interpret his dreams and the dreams of other people. One day Joseph told his brothers about a dream he had that meant that he, Joseph, would some day reign over his brothers.

One day Joseph's brothers were sent to Shechem to feed their fathers flock. Jacob then sent Joseph to go check on them to see if they were doing what he had told them to do and to report back to him. Joseph couldn't find his brothers at first, because they were not in Shechem where they were supposed to be. A man saw Joseph and told him that his brothers had gone to Dothan. As Joseph came toward Dothan his brothers saw him coming and said, "There comes that dreamer," and they talked about killing Joseph.

Reuben, the oldest brother, refused to let his brothers kill Joseph, so they took the beautiful coat Joseph's father had made for him, and threw Joseph in a deep pit. Then the brothers sat down to eat their lunch. While they were eating, a group of Ishmaelites came by, so Joseph's brothers took him out of the pit and sold him to the Ishmaelites (Midianite traders). The land of Midian where the Ishmaelites lived was not far from Egypt, so the Ishmaelites sold Joseph to Potiphar, an officer of the Pharaoh of Egypt. Joseph's brothers then dipped Joseph's coat in goat's blood, and took it home and showed it to Jacob. When Jacob saw the coat, he thought a wild animal had killed Joseph, and he grieved for him.

While in Egypt, Joseph became Potiphar's house servant and through various events of the Lord blessing him Joseph rose to a prominent position because of his God-given gift to interpret dreams. The Pharaoh of Egypt had a dream one night, and Joseph was able to interpret Pharaohs dream when no one else could. The interpretation was that there were to be seven years of plenty and then seven years of famine in Egypt and in Canaan where Joseph's family lived. Joseph advised Pharaoh to store up as much grain as was possible for the seven years of plenty so Egypt would have plenty of grain when the famine came. So Pharaoh placed Joseph in charge of collecting grain in his storehouses. God is controlling the events in Joseph's life in Egypt in order to bring the Israelites to Egypt to live and Joseph's faith and hope encouraged him to obey the Lord.

When the famine came, there was no grain in Canaan, so Israel sent his sons (Joseph's brothers) to Egypt to buy grain. Since Joseph was the person in charge of the grain in Egypt, the brothers had to deal with him. Joseph's brothers didn't recognize Joseph, so with a little deceit Joseph persuaded his brothers to bring Benjamin his youngest brother with them when they returned again for more grain. When Jacob's family had eaten all of the grain, Jacob sent them back to Egypt with Benjamin to buy more grain. Joseph eventually made himself known to his brothers.

Genesis 45: 4-5,7-8a "And Joseph said to his brothers, "Please come near. Then he said, "I am Joseph your brother, whom you sold into Egypt. But now, do not therefore be grieved or angry with yourselves because you sold me here; for God sent me before you to preserve life. (V7)—And God sent me before you to preserve a posterity for you in the earth, and to save your lives by a great deliverance. So now it was not you who sent me here, but God."

He then told his brothers to bring their father to Egypt.

Genesis 46:1-6 "So Israel took his journey with all he had, and came to Beersheba, and offered sacrifices to the God of his father Isaac. Then God spoke to Israel in the visions of the night, and said Jacob, Jacob! And he said "here I am." So He said "I am God the God of your father; do not fear to go down to Egypt, for I will make of you a great nation there. I will go down with you to Egypt, and I will surely bring you up again; and Joseph will put his hand on your eyes."

Israel left Beersheba; and the sons of Israel carried their father, their little ones, and their wives in the carts that Pharaoh had sent to carry them. So they took their livestock and their goods, which they had acquired in the land of Canaan, and went to live in Egypt.

Genesis 15:13-14 "Know certainly that your descendants will be strangers in a land that is not theirs, and will serve them, and they will afflict them four hundred years. And also the nation whom they serve I will judge and afterward they shall come out with great possessions."

The Descendants of Jacob were destined to go to Egypt in order to fulfill God's prophecy that they would be strangers in a foreign land. From Joseph's experiences we see the hand of God intervening in the lives of people to further His plan to bring Christ and his kingdom into the world through Jacob's descendants. The kingly line of Christ would come through the Israelites. The fulfillment of the promise made to Judah would continue through Judah's line until Jesus was born to become the Savior God promised Abraham, when He said that all people would become blessed through Abraham's descendants.

Joseph was thirty years old when he entered the service of the Pharaoh of Egypt around 1954 B.C., and the great famine in Egypt and Canaan began around 1947 B.C. The descendants of Abraham, Isaac and Jacob would live as foreigners in Egypt for many years before they were brought out of Egypt by the mighty hand of God. Jacob and his family came to Egypt a little after 1945 B.C. and the famine ended around 1940 B.C.

While Jacob and his descendants lived in the land of Egypt they were known as Israelites. the Egyptians were friendly toward the Israelites because of Joseph. The Egyptians allowed the Israelites to live in the land of Goshen in Egypt. Goshen was an area that was well suited for sheep, cattle and other livestock and was suitable for the Israelites. The Israelites were shepherds that tended cattle and sheep and the Israelites grew to become a large nation while in Egypt.

Genesis 47:11-12 "And Joseph situated his father and his brothers, and gave them a possession in the land of Egypt, in the best of the land, in the land of Rameses, as Pharaoh had commanded. Then Joseph provided his father, his brothers and all his father's household with bread according to the number in their families."

Israel (Jacob) was one hundred and thirty years old when he went to Egypt, and while he was there he died at the age of one hundred and forty seven. Before Israel died, he called Joseph to him and made him promise that when he died, they would carry him out of Egypt to Canaan and bury him in the burial place of his ancestors.

Joseph had married an Egyptian, and he had two sons: Ephraim and Manasseh. It was customary for a father to bless his sons before he died, so Joseph brought his two sons to his father for him to bless them. Jacob claimed Ephraim and Manasseh as his own sons. When the Israelites left Egypt and returned to the land of Canaan, the sons of Israel, along with Ephraim and Manasseh became leaders of the twelve tribes of Israel.

And he blessed Joseph and said, God before whom my fathers Abraham, and Isaac walked, The God who has fed me all my lifelong to this day, The angel who has redeemed me from all evil, Bless the lads; Let my name be named upon them, and the name of my fathers Abraham and Isaac; And let them grow into a multitude in the midst of the earth."

The book of Exodus contains the history of the events leading to the expansion of Israel as a great nation while they lived in Egypt and then their exodus from Egypt. The children of Israel remained in Egypt for 430 years. Then they left Egypt, crossed the wilderness and camped at the Jordan River on their way to the Promised Land of Canaan where their history had first began when Abraham was living there.

The Israelites had increased in number and were living in peace in Egypt. Then a new Pharaoh was admitted to the throne. The new Pharaoh recognized the size of the population of the Israelites, and he became afraid that the Israelites might become a threat to his throne and fight against the Egyptians. He began to deal harshly with the Israelites and made slaves of them.

Exodus 1:8-10 "Now there arose a new king over Egypt, who did not know Joseph And he said to his people, "Look, the people of the children of Israel are more and mightier than we; come let us deal shrewdly with them, lest they multiply, and in the event of war, they may also join our enemies and fight against us, and so go up out of the land."

The Egyptian King (Pharaoh) ordered the midwives to kill the Hebrew male babies as soon as they were born.

However the Hebrew midwives refused to obey the Pharaoh. So Pharaoh issued a new order that all of the Hebrew newborn male babies were to be thrown into the river to drown.

There was a man among the Israelites named Amram, and his wife's name was Jochebed. They were both descendants of Levi, one of the twelve sons of Israel. Jochebed gave birth to a son, a beautiful child, and they named him Moses. Jochebed refused to throw him in the river, so she hid him for three months.

When she could no longer hide him, she made a basket and waterproofed it. She put her baby boy in the basket and put the basket in the Nile River. One day Pharaoh's daughter came to the river with her maid to bathe. When she saw the baby in the basket, she knew it was one of the Hebrew children. The baby's sister, Miriam, had been watching, and she asked Pharaoh's daughter if she could get a nurse for the baby. Phadaho's daughter agreed, so she got the baby's own mother, Jochebed, to care for the baby.

Pharaoh's daughter favored the child and kept him for her own son. She asked Jochebed to nurse the baby and take care of him until he was older. When the boy was old enough, Jochebed brought him to Pharaoh's daughter, and she raised him as an Egyptian.

Pharaoh's daughter named the young boy Moses, because she took him out of the water. The word Moses sounds like the Hebrew word meaning to draw out.

The birth of Moses was very significant because God had already chosen Moses to become the great leader that would bring the Israelites out of slavery in Egypt.

Pharaoh's daughter brought Moses up as her own son. And Moses was taught in all the wisdom of the Egyptians, he was mighty in words and deeds When he was grown, he decided to visit his own people. He began to see how the people of Egypt were mistreating the Israelites.

Moses saw an Egyptian mistreating an Israelite and he defended the Israelite. In doing so, he killed the Egyptian and hid him in the sand. When the Pharaoh heard that Moses had killed an Egyptian, he wanted Moses killed, but Moses ran away to the land of Midian.

Moses In The Land of Midian

Hebrews 11:24-27 "By faith Moses, when he became of age, refused to be called the son of Pharaoh's daughter, choosing rather to suffer affliction with the people of God than to enjoy the passing pleasures of sin esteeming the reproach of Christ greater riches than the treasures in Egypt; for he looked for the reward. By faith he forsook Egypt, not fearing the wrath of the king; for he endured as seeing Him who is invisible."

The land of Midian was a land inhabited by the Midianites who were associated with the Ishmaelites through Keturah, a concubine of Abraham and the mother of Midian. Ishmael was the son of Abraham and was Isaac's stepbrother. Midian was east of the northern tip of the Red Sea. Unlike the Egyptians who worshiped many false gods the Midianites worshiped Yahweh, the Lord the same God the Israelites worshiped. Moses learned much about Yahweh (God) the Lord while he was living in the land of Midian. The people of Midian also called God 'El Elyon, the Most High God.' When Moses arrived in Midian he went to a well and he met seven young women there watering their animals.

The women had come to water their father's sheep, but some shepherds were there and would not let them. Moses rescued the women from the shepherds and he watered the sheep for them. The women were daughters of Reuel, the priest of Midian. (Reuel was also called Jethro.) When the women told their father what Moses had done for them, Jethro invited Moses to eat with his family. Moses stayed with the Midianites and eventually married Zipporah, one of Reuel's daughters. Moses and Zipporah had a son whom they named Gershom.

While Moses was in Midian God appeared to Moses, and Moses acquired a great faith in God. Moses had an association with God that lasted the rest of his life. While Moses was in Midian, the Israelites were still slaves in Egypt. The Israelites continued to ask God to free them from their oppression, and God heard their prayers. God had already determined that Moses would lead his people out of Egypt, but first He had to convince Moses of who He was, the God of the Israelites. Moses developed a relationship with God and God chose Moses to follow His instructions to lead the Israelites.

At first Moses was not willing Moses had not yet experienced a personal presence of the Lord God that would cause Him to have faith In God and hope for the freedom of his people. During Moses time in Midian (Paraphrase, Acts 7:30-34) When Moses was forty years old an angel of the Lord appeared to him in flames of fire from a burning bush.

Moses was in the wilderness of Mount Sinai tending sheep when he saw a bush on fire, but it wasn't consumed. Suddenly the Lord spoke to Moses out of the flames of the bush and said, "Moses, Moses!" And Moses said, "Here I am." The Lord told him to remove his sandals, because he was standing on holy ground. The ground was holy because the presence of the Lord was there. The Lord identified Himself as the God of Abraham, Isaac and Jacob.

Exodus 3:7-15 "And the Lord said, "I have surely seen the oppression of My people who are in Egypt, and have head their cry because of their taskmasters, for I know their sorrows. So I have come down to deliver them out of the hand of the Egyptians, and to bring them up from that land to a good and large land flowing with milk and honey, to the place of the Canaanites and the Hittites, and Amorites and the Perizzites and the Hivites and the Jebusites." Now therefore, behold, the cry of the children of Israel has come to Me, and I have also seen the oppression with which the Egyptians oppress them. Come now, therefore, and I will send you to Pharaoh that you may bring My people, the children of Israel, out of Egypt." But Moses said to God, "Who am I that I should go to Pharaoh, and that I should bring the children of Israel out of Egypt?"

Moses was afraid to go back to Egypt but the Lord said to Moses, *"I will certainly be with you. And this shall be a sign to you that I have sent you: When you have brought the people out of Egypt, you shall serve God on this Mountain."*

Moses did not know God's name, and he asked, *"When I come to the children of Israel and say to them, 'The God of your fathers has sent me to you,' and they say to me, 'what is His name?' what shall I say to them?"*

Moses feared the children of Israel would not listen to him unless he knew the name of the Lord God. The people would have to be convinced that the Lord had sent him, so God said to Moses, *"I Am who I Am." And He said, "Thus you shall say to the children of Israel, I Am has sent me to you." Moreover God said to Moses, "Thus you shall say to the children of Israel: The Lord God of your fathers, the God of Abraham, the God of Isaac, and the God of Jacob, has sent me to you. This is My name forever and this is My memorial to all generations."*

God has been known by several names that describe who He is at any particular time. 'I Am' is the same as saying, 'I Am who I will be when I deliver you from Egypt.' The Lord's name at the time the Lord spoke to Moses was Yahweh, the Lord. Yahweh was the name of God in Genesis. When Abraham or Isaac built an altar, they called on the Lord.

Psalm 100:3 "Know that the Lord, He is God; It is He who has made us, and not we ourselves; We are his people and the sheep of His pasture."

God is total Spirit, and He is self-determining. When we call on God from a heart of faith, hope and love, God hears us and He answers us.

God said, *Exodus 3:16-17 "Go and gather the elders of Israel together, and say to them 'The Lord God of your fathers, the God of Abraham, of Isaac, and of Jacob appeared to me, saying, "I have surely visited you and seen what is done to you in Egypt; and I have said I will bring you out of the affliction of Egypt to the land of the Canaanites, and the Hittites, and the Amorites and the Perezzites and the Hivites and the Jebusites to a land flowing with milk and honey."*

Moses did not want to go back to Egypt even after God revealed Himself to him. He was afraid the Israelites would not accept him. The Lord told Moses that He would perform miracles to convince the people that Moses was a spokesman for God. The Lord also told Moses that He would perform mighty miracles to convince the Pharaoh of Egypt to let the Israelites leave. It was inevitable that the Israelites leave Egypt and go to the land of Canaan, because God had promised the land of Canaan to the descendents of Abraham, Isaac and Jacob and his descendants.

Moses asked God, "Suppose they will not believe me or listen to me? Suppose they say, 'The Lord has not appeared to you.'" Moses had a staff in his hand and the Lord told him to throw it on the ground. When Moses threw his staff down, it became a snake. Then the Lord told him to pick up the snake by its tail. When Moses reached down and picked it up, it became his staff again.

The Lord showed Moses a few other miraculous things that Moses would be able to perform, but Moses was still not convinced. He was still afraid to go back to Egypt, and he thought of reasons why he should not go. He said the people wouldn't listen to him, because he was not a good speaker, and he didn't know what to tell the people of Israel. The Lord told Moses that He had the power to help him speak, and He would tell him what to say.

Exodus 4:11-17 "So the Lord said to him, Who has made man's mouth? Or who makes the mute, the deaf, the seeing or the blind? Have not I the Lord?"

Moses still did not want to go and he asked the lord to send someone else. God became angry with him. God told Moses that his brother Aaron was a good speaker, and Aaron would speak for him. Moses was told to speak to Aaron and put the words in him and He the lord would put the words in His mouth and teach him what to say.

God gave Moses a rod to hold in his hand and use to perform miracles to convince the Pharaoh to let the people of Israel leave Egypt. God then told Aaron to go out into the wilderness and meet Moses on the mountain. When they met, Moses told Aaron all that God had said to him, and Aaron agreed to speak for Moses. So Moses, along with his family and his brother Aaron, left the land of Midian and returned to Egypt.

Moses had been in the land of Midian for forty years when the Lord told him to return to Egypt and He was eighty years old and his brother Aaron was eighty-three years old when they returned to Egypt. Moses and Aaron gathered the elders of the children of Israel, and Aaron told them everything that God had told Moses. Then they did miracles before the people, which the Lord had told them to do. The people of Israel were convinced that God had sent Moses, and when they heard that the Lord was concerned about their oppression, they bowed down and worshipped the Lord. The Egyptians greatly oppressed and afflicted the Israelites and when God heard the groaning of the children of Israel enslaved in Egypt, He remembered the covenant He made with the Israelites to give them the land of Canaan. The Lord God told them He would redeem them with an outstretched arm and with great judgments. He said, *"You will be My people and I will be your God. You shall know that I am the Lord your God who brings you out from under the burdens of the Egyptians."*

God promised Moses and all of the people of Israel that He would make the Egyptians let them leave, and the Israelites would be a nation of people belonging to the Lord, and the Lord would help them go to the promised land of Canaan.

The great plagues that God would bring against Egypt would be so severe that The Pharaoh would beg the Israelites to leave. The Lord said to Moses, "Now you will see what I will do to Pharaoh with a strong hand and he will be so glad to let them go, that he will drive them out of his land. God also told Moses.

"I am the Lord. I appeared to Abraham, to Isaac, and to Jacob, as God Almighty (El Shaddai), but by my name Lord (Yahweh) I was known to them. I have also established my covenant with them, to give them the land of Canaan."

God told Moses to go to Pharaoh and demand that he free the Israelites, telling him that the Lord said, "Let My people go. The Pharaoh refused to let the Israelites leave Egypt and God told Moses that Pharaoh's heart was hard meaning he was very stubborn, so God began to send plagues on the Egyptians.

God performed great miracles and signs to convince Pharaoh, but each time Pharaoh's heart was hardened, and he would not let the people of Israel leave and each time Pharaoh's magicians duplicated the same signs with their magic. God sent ten great plagues on the Egyptian people. (The story of the plagues begins in Exodus 7:14 and ends in chapter 11.

The first plague God sent was turning all the fresh water in Egypt into blood. That was followed by nine other plagues: plague of frogs, lice, flies, livestock, disease, a plague of boils, hail, locusts, and darkness. Each time God would remove one plague and then send another one. The Israelites were protected from the plagues. Each time Pharaoh stubbornly hardened his heart because of God's plagues and he refused to let the Israelites leave. Pharaoh became more stubborn and defiant after every plague.

Passover Feast

Before God struck the Egyptians with the death plague of the firstborn, God told Moses to speak to the Israelites and tell them to ask their neighbors for articles of silver and gold. He wanted to Israelites to leave Egypt with great wealth and articles to use later in the construction of the tabernacle, a place where the Israelites could worship God. The Lord caused the Israelites to have favor with the Egyptians and the Egyptian people gave the Israelites what they asked for. These things they would take with them when they left Egypt.

The Feast of Unleavened Bread, also called the Passover Feast, was a feast the Israelites observed before they left Egypt and they have continued to observe every year since that time. The Passover was instituted to remind the Israelites of God's grace and kindness toward them when He delivered them from Egypt. The Jews today observe the Passover Feast or Seder. Before the Lord caused the death plague of the firstborn of Egypt, He gave the Israelites a memorial called the Passover feast that they would observe forever so they would always remember what the Lord did for them in Egypt. Passover literally means to pass over in the sense of sparing the life of the firstborn of Israel on the night that all of the firstborn in Egypt died.

Exodus 12 Observing the Passover the Israelites would remove all leaven from their house and eat unleavened bread for seven days. The only work that was permitted during the seven days was the preparation of the food. The individual families were to pick out lambs according to the size of their family, kill the lamb and use the blood of the lamb to identify their houses by placing blood on the lintel above the door and on the two doorposts.

God said that when he saw the blood on the doorposts and lintel, He would pass over that house and not kill the firstborn of the Israelites. God was testing the faith of the Israelites.

The Lord said to Moses, "I will bring one more plague on Pharaoh and on Egypt. Afterward he will let you go from here. When he lets you go he will surely drive all of you out of Egypt. The death of the firstborn would be the last and worst plague. Each family lost their first-born even the first-born son of Pharaoh. After the ninth plague, Moses and Aaron appeared before the Pharaoh and he said, Get away from me! Take heed to yourself and see my face no more! For in the day you see my face you shall die! So Moses said, you have spoken I will never see your face again.

All of Egypt's firstborn died. The Lord acted with great violence against the Egyptians because of the stubbornness of Pharaoh. The Lord used the only means that would convince Pharaoh to do the right thing and let the Israelites leave Egypt. God demonstrated His great power and Glory for all the Egyptians and the Israelites to see.

Exodus 11: 4-7 (Vs 4-7) Then Moses said, "Thus says the Lord: about midnight I will go out in the midst of Egypt; and all the firstborn in the land of Egypt shall die from the firstborn of Pharaoh who sits on his throne even to the firstborn of the female servant who is behind the hand mill, and all the firstborn of the animals." "There shall be a great cry throughout the land of Egypt, such as was not like it before, nor shall be like it again. But against none of the children of Israel shall a dog move its tongue, against man or beast that you may know that the Lord does make a difference between the Egyptians and Israel."

Exodus 12:29-30 "And it came to pass at midnight that the Lord struck all the firstborn in the land of Egypt' from the firstborn of Pharaoh who sat on his throne to the firstborn of all the captive who was in the dungeon, and all the first born of livestock. So Pharaoh rose in the night, he, all his servants, and all the Egyptians; and there was a great cry in Egypt, for there was not a house where there was not one dead."

At midnight the Lord killed all the firstborn in the land of Egypt, the firstborn of Pharaoh, the firstborn of the prisoner who was in the dungeon, and all the firstborn of livestock. Pharaoh and his servants, and all the Egyptians made a great cry in Egypt, because there was not a house where there was not one dead. Pharaoh sent for Moses and Aaron and told them that all of the Israelites could leave Egypt with their children, animals and all of their possessions and go into the wilderness to serve the Lord.

The Israelites left Egypt with great wealth of the gold, silver and other things they received from the Egyptians, plus all of their livestock. And they went toward the wilderness of the desert of Sinai.

Hebrews 11-23-24 "By Faith Moses, when he was born, was hidden three months by his parents, because they saw he was a beautiful child; and they were not afraid of the King's command. By faith Moses, when he became of age, refused to be called the son of Pharaoh's daughter, choosing rather to suffer affliction with the people of God than to enjoy the passing pleasures of sin, esteeming the reproach of Christ greater riches than the treasures of Egypt; for he looked for the reward. By faith he forsook Egypt, not fearing the wrath of the king; for he endured as seeing Him who is invisible. By faith he kept the Passover and the sprinkling of blood, lest he who destroyed the firstborn should touch them."

Hebrews 11:28-29 "By faith he (Moses) kept the Passover and the sprinkling of blood, lest he who destroyed the firstborn should touch them. By faith they passed through the Red Sea as by dry land, where-as the Egyptians, attempting to do so, drowned."

When the people of Israel left Egypt, the Lord led them through the Red Sea. The Israelites camped in a place called Etham that was at the edge of the wilderness between Egypt and the Jordan River. The Lord went ahead them with the presence of an angel. He led them by a cloud during the day and a pillar of fire at night.

Exodus 13:18-22 "God led the people around by the way of the wilderness of the Red Sea. And the children of Israel went up in orderly ranks out of the land of Egypt. And Moses took the bones of Joseph with him, for he had placed the children of Israel under solemn oath, saying, "God will surely visit you, and you shall carry up my bones from here with you."

There were more than two million Israelites that left Egypt and headed for the wilderness. Pharaoh went back on his word and made his chariot ready and took his troops with him and attempt to catch up to the Hebrews. He took 600 choice chariots, and all the chariots of Egypt with captains over every one of them. And he pursued the children of Israel but the children of Israel continued to run from the Egyptians and the Lord protected them.

Exodus 14:13-18 "And Moses said to the people, Do not be afraid, Stand still and see the salvation of the Lord which He will accomplish for you today, for the Egyptians you see today, you shall see again no more forever. The Lord will fight for you and you shall hold your peace. The Israelites set up their camp at Migdol near the Red Sea. Pharaoh led an army of charioteers after them and the Israelites were trapped between the Egyptians and the waters of the sea."

The Israelites became frightened with Pharaoh's army closing in on them from behind and the Red Sea in front of them, and they began to cry out to God and Moses. The children of Israel stood on the shore of the Red Sea and the angel of God and the pillar of cloud moved behind them so the Egyptian army couldn't see them and come close to them. Moses said, *"Do not be afraid. Stand still, and see the salvation of the Lord, which He will accomplish for you today."*

Moses lifted up his staff over the sea, and a pathway opened up through the waters, and Moses and the people walked across the Red Sea on dry land. The Egyptians came after God's people on the dry path through the sea, but the Lord caused their chariot wheels to become stuck in the mud to slow them down, and the Egyptians became afraid and turned around to go back. Moses stretched out his arms over the sea and the walls of water on each side of the pathway came down on the Egyptians and drowned them. Because of this miracle the people of Israel began to have more faith and trust in the Lord.

Exodus 14:30-31 "So the Lord saved Israel that day out of the hand of the Egyptians, and Israel saw the Egyptians dead on the seashore. Thus Israel saw the great work which the Lord had done in Egypt; so the people feared the Lord, and believed the Lord and his servant Moses."

Moses and the people of Israel celebrated and sang to the Lord. Miriam the sister of Moses and Aaron led them in song. They continued their journey from Succoth and camped in Etham at the edge of the wilderness. And the Lord continued to go before them by day in a pillar of cloud to lead the way, and by night in a pillar of fire to give them light.

While they were in the wilderness of Sinai God told the people of Israel that He was sending an angel to go before them and guard them through the wilderness. The people were warned to listen to the angel and follow his instructions. God told Moses that the name they were to use when speaking of God was Yahweh meaning the Lord.

The children of Israel numbered an estimated two million people. The wilderness was a barren place, a desert sand dunes and rock no vegetation and not enough water. God tried the faith of the Israelites by bringing them out of a land of plenty into a desert wilderness where there was little water and not enough food. The Israelites constantly complained against the Lord and against Moses.

At one time both the Lord and Moses disowned the whole nation. God said to Moses they are your people, but Moses said, Lord they are your people. However, the Lord and Moses continued to help them. God constantly exhorted the people of Israel to have faith in Him. He wanted them to become a great nation of people that would be prepared for the birth of the Messiah their final king.

The Lord sent the Israelites food from heaven, a substance like bread to fall from heaven every morning, which they called manna. The word manna means 'what is it.' because the Israelites had never seen anything like it before. The Lord also sent them quails for meat, and the quails covered the campgrounds every evening.

The Lord established the seventh day of every week as a holy day, and a Sabbath day because God created everything in six days and on the seventh day He ceased. The word Sabbath means to cease or to come to the end of an activity. The Sabbath was a day of much needed rest for the Israelites.

The Lord provided for the daily needs of the people but they were not satisfied and were not grateful.

Hebrews 3:7-11 "Therefore as the Holy Spirit says: "Today if you will hear His voice, Do not harden your hearts as in the rebellion, in the days of trial in the wilderness, where your fathers tested Me, tried Me and saw My works forty years. Therefore I was angry with that generation, and I said, 'They always go astray in their heart, And they have not known My ways.' So I swore in My wrath, They shall not enter My rest."

When the people had walked all of the way to Rephidim, there was no water to drink. The people were angry and argued with Moses, and Moses told them they were temping the Lord. The people did not trust the Lord to provide for them even though He had always done so. Moses was angry with the people and he asked God what he should do with the people. Moses was ready to leave them, but the Lord told him to stay with them. The Lord told Moses to take some of the elders of Israel with him to Horeb and strike a certain rock with his staff and water would come out of the rock. When they came to Horeb, Moses found the rock, and when he struck it, water flowed from the rock. (Exodus 17:7) The place was called Massah and Meribah, because they argued with the Lord and because they tempted the Lord saying, "Is the Lord among us or not?" Moses chose men with ability to lead and made them heads over the people. The problems of the people that were too hard to judge they sent to Moses.

The Israelites continued to walk through the desert, and on the third month after leaving Egypt, they came to the Sinai wilderness near Mt Sinai where they set up camp at the base of MT Sinai (Mt Horeb). Jethro the priest of Midian was Moses father in-law and Jethro came to Moses with Moses sons when they were at Mt Sinai.

The Lord at Mt Sinai

Moses went part of the way up the mountain, and the Lord spoke to him and gave him instructions for the people. The Lord reminded Moses of how He protected the Israelites from the Egyptians by carrying them on Eagles wings—a metaphor concerning God's protection of them like an eagle that protects their young.

Moses went up the mountain and the Lord called to him saying, *"Thus you shall say to the house of Jacob, and tell the children of Israel: You have seen what I did to the Egyptians, and how I bore you on eagles wings and brought you to Myself. Now therefore, if you will indeed obey My voice and keep My covenant, then you shall be a special treasure to Me above all people; for all the earth is Mine. And you shall be to Me a kingdom of priests and a holy nation."*

When Moses came down off the mountain, he called the elders of the people and told them what the Lord had said to him. The people agreed to do everything the Lord commanded, so Moses returned to the Lord to tell Him what the people said. The Lord told Moses that He would come before the people in a thick cloud. (The Lord covered Himself with the cloud because no one can see the Lord's face and live.)

The Lord said He would speak with Moses, but the people could also hear Him so the people would trust Moses.

The people were to be consecrated by making their bodies and their clothes clean before they could come near to the Lord. Moses had three days to prepare the people, and on the third day the Lord would come down on the mountain as the people watched. Moses was told to mark off boundaries all of the way around the mountain so that the people would not be able to touch the mountain. If anyone touched the mountain when the Lord was on the mountain, they would be put to death by being stoned or shot with an arrow. The people were not to go up to the mountain until they heard a loud blast from a ram's horn. Rams horns were used like trumpets to signal the people.

Exodus 19:16-20 "Then it came to pass on the third day, in the morning that there were thunderings, and lightnings and a thick cloud on the mountain; and the sound of the trumpet was very loud, so that all the people who were in the camp trembled. And Moses brought the people out of the camp to meet with God, and they stood at the foot of the mountain. Now Mt Sinai was completely in smoke, because the Lord descended upon it in fire.

The smoke went up like the smoke of a furnace, and the whole mountain quaked. The blast of the trumpet sounded and became louder and louder, Moses spoke and the Lord answered him by voice. Then the Lord came down to the top of Mt Sinai. And the Lord called Moses and Moses went up to the top of the mountain. The Lord told Moses to go back down the mountain and warn the people not to try to break through the cloud and see the Lord. He then told Moses that when he comes back up the mountain to bring Aaron, his brother, with him.

When Moses and Aaron went up the mountain, God gave Moses the Ten Commandments plus a very detailed and lengthy law of rules and regulations, which the people were to observe. Moses received the law and taught the law to the people of Israel. The Law of Moses would remain in effect until the Messiah (Jesus) came and fulfilled the Law in the first century. The law was called the Law of Moses, because through the inspiration of God, Moses received and wrote down the law and taught it to the people. When Jesus was born the Jews were still observing the law. Aaron went up the mountain with Moses to receive the law, and Aaron became the first high priest of the Israelites. As a priest he had certain responsibilities to the Lord and to the people. The covenant the Lord made with the Israelites included divine services administered by the priests and the high priest, including the offering of sacrifices to the Lord.

The title 'priest' means one who offers sacrifices to the Lord God. The priests offered sacrifices to the Lord for themselves and the people.

Hebrews 5:1-3 "For every high priest taken from among men is appointed for men in things pertaining to God, that he may offer both gifts and sacrifices for sins. He can have compassion on those who are ignorant and going astray, since he him self is also subject to weakness. Because of this he is required as for the people, so also for him self, to offer sacrifices for sins. And no man takes this honor to himself, but he who is called by God, just as Aaron was."

"Hebrews 9:6-10 "Now when these things had been thus prepared, the priests always went into the first part of the tabernacle, performing the services.'

"But into the second part the high priest went alone once a year, not without blood, which he offered for himself and for the people's sins' committed in ignorance; the Holy Spirit indicating this, that the way into the Holiest of All was not yet made manifest while the first tabernacle was still standing.' It was symbolic for the present time in which both gifts and sacrifices are offered, which cannot make him

who performed the service perfect in regard to the conscience—concerned only with foods and drinks, various washings, and fleshly ordinances imposed until the time of reformation."

The Israelites were obligated to offer to the Lord a service consisting of fleshly ordinances. This type of worship could not free a person from the guilt of their sin and give them a clear conscience but it would satisfy the Lord at that time if the people were faithful to obey the law.

If the people under the old covenant remained faithful to God according to the ordinances of worship, the sacrifice of Christ would be retroactive in forgiving their sins. The time of reformation refers to the time of the death of Christ that brought to an end the old Law and began the process of salvation by faith in Christ including hope and love.

Speaking of Christ, Paul said in *Ephesians 2:14-16 "For He Himself is our peace, who has made both one, and has broken down the middle wall of separation, having abolished in His flesh the enmity, that is the law of commandments contained in ordinances, so as to create one new man from the two, thus making peace, and that He might reconcile them both to God in one body through the cross."*

The sacrifice of Christ would reconcile all people of faith from the beginning of time to the end of time. The law was very lengthy and Moses was on the mountain for a long time.

The law included every component of the Israelites life including the building of the tabernacle and various articles used for worship while they were in the wilderness.

The people of Israel began to doubt if Moses would ever come down from the mountain, so they encouraged Aaron to take Moses' place. They rebelled against the Lord God when they asked Aaron to make idol gods for them to worship. The Lord told Moses to go down the mountain to tend to the people, calling them a stiff-necked people. He was angry enough to destroy them and start over with Moses and choose another nation of people, but Moses pleaded with the Lord to save the people of Israel. Moses reminded the Lord of His promise to Abraham and how He had told Abraham that he would bless and multiply his descendants. The Lord chose not to destroy the people of Israel because of Moses and the Lord was willing to acknowledge them as His people after Moses pleaded for them.

The promises God made to Abraham did not depend on the Law of Moses. The Law was added because the people were exceedingly sinful. God promised Israel that the time would come when he would make a new covenant with Israel, because redemption of sin could not come through the Law of Moses. The covenant of faith, hope and love.

The Law of Moses regulated the external acts of morality without regards to the heart and sacrifices had to be offered continually. The attitudes of the hearts of the people did not change, and the people continued to sin and sacrifices were offered regularly.

The Lord established the priesthood from the men of the tribe of Levi; therefore it was called the Levitical priesthood. Moses brother Aaron was chosen as the first high priest.

Aaron's sons Nadab, Abihu, Ithamar and Eleazar were priests who assisted Aaron. The main duty of the priests included teaching the Law of Moses as well as offering the animal sacrifices and conducting the ritual religious services according to the Law. The priests served God's people, but later the priesthood became corrupted by the selfish ambition of men.

The Israelites Prepare Articles of Worship

God instructed the Israelites how to make a tabernacle, a portable tent in which to perform their spiritual duties where the priests and the high priest would serve. The Israelites built the portable tabernacle and the articles to use in worship while they were in the wilderness, and they took the tabernacle with them as they moved from place to place on their journey to the Land of Canaan. When the Israelites would camp a in a new place the tabernacle was set up in the middle of the camp. The tribe of Levi was responsible for transporting the tabernacle and its furnishings when the people moved.

Hebrews 9:1-5 "Then indeed even the first covenant had ordinances of divine service and the earthly sanctuary. For the tabernacle was prepared: the first part in which was the lamp-stand, the table, and the showbread, which is called the sanctuary; and behind the second veil, the part of the tabernacle which is called the Holiest of All, which had the Golden censer and the ark of the covenant overlaid on all sides with gold, in which were the golden pot that had the manna Aaron's rod that budded, and the tablets of the covenant; and above it were the cherubim of glory overshadowing the mercy seat."

The people were instructed to make dishes and plates of gold and pitchers to pour out offerings. They were to make a table of acacia wood overlaid with gold, which was called the table of showbread. Twelve loaves of bread, one for each of the twelve tribes of Israel, were to be placed on the table. The bread was called the bread of presence indicating the presence of God. The altar for burning incense, the table for the bread of presence, and a lamp stand to give light were placed in the Holy Place.

God told them to build an ark (chest) made from acacia wood and cover it with pure gold inside and out. The Israelites would be moving from place to place for a long time before they were settled in the promise land, so the chest and the table had rings on each side and poles that could be inserted in the rings allowing men to carry them.

Placed inside the ark were the stone tablets containing the Ten Commandments, Aaron's rod that had budded to show that God had chosen him to be the high priest, and a sample of the manna from heaven that God had sent to feed the people in the wilderness.

This chest was called the Ark of the Covenant and was the only thing placed in the Most Holy Place. On top of the Ark of the Covenant were two cherubim (angels) with their wings outspread covering the mercy seat where God's awesome presence was. The high priest was the only one who was authorized to enter the Most Holy Place.

If anyone else entered the Most Holy Place they would die. The Most Holy place represented heaven as God's dwelling place and God's presence was there. The death of Jesus opened the way for anyone with faith in God and Christ to enter into the holy place, which refers to heaven.

Paraphrase: Hebrews 9:6-10 When every thing was prepared, the priests went into the first part of the tabernacle and performed the services. The high priest went alone once a year with blood, which he offered for himself and for the people's sins that were committed in ignorance. The Holy Spirit indicated this was the way into the Holiest of All but was not yet made manifest while the first tabernacle was still standing. It was symbolic for that time in which both gifts and sacrifices were offered but could not make him who performed the service perfect in regard to the conscience, because the sins were not forgiven.

The service was concerned only with food and drinks, washings, and animal sacrifices This type of worship would continue until the time of Christ who would sacrifice his own blood for the guilt of the sins of the people.

The Law of Moses and the ordinances of the tabernacle and temple worship would end when Jesus died. Since the death of Jesus, His body and blood have become the sacrifice of atonement.

In the courtyard of the tabernacle there was an altar for burnt offerings. The people would bring the animals to be sacrificed, and the priests would offer the animals on the altar for the people. There was also a copper basin called a laver, which was filled with water for the priests and high priest to wash their hands and feet before entering the tabernacle.

The priesthood, the tabernacle and the animal sacrifices were only a foreshadowing of the salvation that would be provided by Christ when he came and was sacrificed on the cross. A blood sacrifice was necessary for the remission of sins, but the blood of animals could never take away the guilt of sin; the sacrifices reminded the people year after year that they were sinners.

The Israelites in the Wilderness

The Israelites often changed their attitude about the Lord from the time of the wilderness wandering until God's Son was sacrificed. Israel would remain faithful to God for a while and then they would rebel against God's commandments. God would threaten them or inflict punishment on them to keep them on the course he planned for them, but later they would become unfaithful again.

When the Israelites had been in the wilderness for about two years, they came to Kadesh-Barnea close to the Negev, God told Moses to send twelve spies into the land of Canaan to explore the land. The land of Canaan was the land God had promised them but they had to forcibly take the land. Two of the spies, Joshua and Caleb, came back with a pleasing report and a sample of some of the fruit grown there, but ten of the spies said the people were powerful and so large that the Israelites looked like grasshoppers in their sight.

When the people heard the report of the ten spies, they were afraid to go forward and they began to complain and grumble against Moses and Aaron. They said, "If only we had stayed in Egypt." The Lord had enough of their complaining, and he said to Moses, "How long will these people treat me with contempt? How long will they refuse to believe in me in spite of all the miraculous signs I have performed among them?" God was very angry with the people of Israel but Moses intervened for them and God did not punish them but God decreed that not one of that generation would see the land He had promised except for the two spies who had given them hope of entering Canaan with their good report.

The Lord made the Israelites wander in the desert until all of that generation was dead. It would be thirty-eight more years before they would get to enter the Promised Land of Canaan. The consequence of Israel's rebellion cost them thirty more years of wandering in the wilderness. God planned to make the Israelite people into a great nation and help them gain the homeland He promised them. The Lord expected the Israelites to obey Him but Israel was not responding to the Lord with faith.

Deuteronomy—Another Statement Of The Law

After all the generation of those who came out of Egypt were dead, except for Moses, Joshua and Caleb, God told Moses to prepare the people to enter Canaan the promised land. Moses taught the people the Law that God had given at Mt Sinai first then warned them to never become idolaters but to remain faithful to the Lord God. He addressed the people with three important speeches and exhortations to encourage them.

Deuteronomy 1:5-8 "On this side of the Jordan in the land of Moab, Moses began to explain this law saying, "The Lord our God spoke to us in Horeb: saying you have dwelt long enough at this mountain. Turn and take your journey and go to the mountains of the Amorites, to all the neighboring places in the plain, in the mountains and in the lowland, in the South and on the seacoast, to the land of the Canaanites and to Lebanon, as far as the great river, the River Euphrates. See I have set the land before you; go in and possess the land which the Lord swore to your fathers—to Abraham, Isaac, and Jacob—to give them and their descendants after them."

The Israelites were to go into lands that were occupied by idolatrous people that had lived in Canaan for many years. They would encounter opposition from the people in Canaan but Moses encouraged the people to be courageous and cross over the Jordan River and take possession of the land. The Israelites would have to fight for the land but God would help them if they remained faithful to Him.

Moses had a great responsibility over many people, so he selected men from the twelve tribes who were wise and respected and gave them jurisdiction over groups of people. The nation of Israel grew to a large size in Egypt, and in the wilderness. A census was taken according to the twelve tribes of Israel and they numbered approximately two million people. Every male twenty years or older that was able to fight in a war would be eligible and expected to fight to drive the Gentile people out of the land of Canaan. Each tribe had their leaders of the army.

The tribe of Levi was the tribe of the priests. They were not a part of the army and therefore would not fight.

Ephraim and Manasseh, the two sons of Joseph, were leaders of tribes, and they would receive an allotment of land. Moses exhorted the people to carefully follow every command of the Law.

Deuteronomy 7:9-11 "Therefore know that the Lord your God, he is God, the faithful God who keeps His covenant and mercy for a thousand generations with those who love Him and keep His commandments; and He repays those who hate Him to their face, to destroy them. He will not be slack with Him who hates Him; He will repay Him to his face. Therefore you shall keep the commandment the statutes and the judgments which, I command you today to observe them."

"Deuteronomy 8:1-2 "Every commandment which I command you today you must be careful to observe, that you may live and multiply, and go in and possess the land of which the Lord swore to your fathers. And you shall remember that the Lord your God led you all the way these forty years in the wilderness to humble you and test you, to know what was in your heart, whether you would keep His commandments or not."

Moses had warned the people to be careful not to worship the idols of the people in the land, which is an abomination to the Lord. Moses reviewed the Passover Feast and the other annual feasts the people were to observe and he said to wait for the Messiah. The word Messiah means the 'Lord's Anointed One.' The New Testament reveals that the Messiah was Jesus Christ, the promised Messiah of the Old Testament, the Messiah that was promised when Jacob blessed his sons in Egypt (Genesis 49: 8-12).

Moses was now one hundred and twenty years old, and there were many things he needed to do to prepare his people before he died. He encouraged the people to obey God's law, and he taught the law of God to the younger generation that had been born during their wandering.

The Lord wanted the people to know that he would go with them as they drove out the people in the land.

Moses told the Israelites that God's commandments were not too hard for the people to comply with, and they must choose life or death. If the Israelites loved God and obeyed His commandments, they would live and be blessed, but if they rebelled against God and His commandments, they would die. The Lord would not kill them, but He would not defend them unless they were faithful to obey Him. Moses told the people that if they obeyed the Lord, the Lord would fight for them like a destroying fire. Moses was one of the most faithful servants of the Lord, and he pleaded with God to let him cross over the Jordan.

God would not allow Moses to go into Canaan, because at one time Moses had taken credit for bringing forth water from a rock instead of giving the glory to God. (Numbers 20:12). In the book of Deuteronomy Moses taught about the importance of the covenant between God and the Israelites before they crossed the Jordan River on their way to the land of Canaan. The tribal leaders were appointed and Moses reminded the people of the events of the wilderness wandering. Deuteronomy 3 Moses is not allowed to cross the Jordan.

Deuteronomy 3:23-29 Paraphrase, Moses pleaded with the Lord to let him cross the Jordan and see the land between the Jordan and the mountains of Lebanon. The Lord was angry with Moses and would not listen to him. God refused to let Moses cross the Jordan and told him to go to the top of Mt Pisgah, and look in every direction so he could see the land. Joshua would be the leader of the Israelites after Moses and he would lead the children of Israel.

The Lord told Moses to encourage Joshua. When Moses was one hundred and twenty years old and no longer able to lead the nation of Israel. God told Moses to choose Joshua, a young man from the tribe of Ephraim as his assistant. Joshua had watched the Tent of Meeting (Tabernacle) when Moses was with God at Mt Sinai. He was also one of the spies who trusted God to lead them into the Promised Land. Moses instructs the people and told them not to add to or take away anything he commanded them.

The Lord had commanded Moses at that time to speak to the people. Moses warned the Israelites not to become idolaters like the people in the land where they would be going. Moses restated the ten commandments of the Law God gave them and stated the greatest commandment.

Deuteronomy 6:3-7 "Therefore hear, O Israel, and be careful to observe it, that it may be well with you, and that you may multiply greatly as the Lord God of your fathers has promised you—a land flowing with milk and honey.' Hear O Israel: The Lord our God, the Lord is one! You shall love the Lord your God with all your heart, with all your soul, and with all your strength. And these words, which I command you today, shall be in your heart. You shall teach them diligently to your children and shall talk of them when you sit in your house, when you walk by the way, when you lie down, and when you rise up."

Moses taught Joshua everything he needed to know about taking command over Israel. Before he died, Moses climbed to the top of Mt Nebo, so he could see the Promised Land. Then he died and was buried in a valley in Moab.

Moses had a personal association with the Lord. He was a very humble man (Num. 12:3), and the greatest of the prophets, because the Lord talked with him face to face (Num. 34:10), and no one has ever had access to the mighty miraculous power of the Lord like Moses. He performed awesome deeds for Israel.

Joshua Leads Israel Across the Jordan (1460 B.C.)

The book of Joshua is about the history of Israel's crusade to conquer the land in Canaan that God had promised them. The Law of Moses united the tribes of the nation of Israel and they divided the land in Canaan and tribal leaders governed each tribe.

Paraphrase: Joshua 1:1-9: After the death of Moses the Lord spoke to Joshua and told him to go over the Jordan River with all the people to the land He was giving them. The Lord told Joshua that He would be with him like He was with Moses all the days of his life. The lord said I wont forsake you or leave you, be strong and courageous and obey all of the Law of Moses and He the Lord would be with him everywhere he went. Joshua had complete faith, hope and love as he served his God.

God told Joshua, "Every place that the sole of your foot will tread upon, I have given you, as I said to Moses." God gave them the land when they took it away from the people who were living there.

Their promised territory would extend from the wilderness to Lebanon and from The Mediterranean Sea (Great Sea) to the Euphrates River. God told them from the land of the Hittites to the Great Sea shall be your territory. God also told them no one would be able to defeat them, because He would be with them and no man would be able to stand before them.

God said He would not forsake or leave them. God said, "Be strong and of good courage, for to this people you shall divide as an inheritance the land, which I swore to their fathers to give them." Before Moses died he instructed them, *"Do not turn from it to the right hand or to the left, that you may prosper wherever you go. This book of the Law shall not depart from your mouth, but you shall meditate in it day and night, that you may observe to do according to all that is written in it. For then you will make your way prosperous, and then you will have good success.'*

"Have I not commanded you? Be strong and of good courage; do not be afraid, nor be dismayed, for the Lord your God is with you wherever you go."

The Promised Land was to be free from idolatry and free from the sins of the heathen people. The people of Israel were told to drive all the foreign people out of the land so that the people of Israel would not be tempted to engage in idolatry. God intended to make Israel a holy nation to serve the Lord.

Joshua led Israel in their military battles to take the land of Canaan by force. The land would be divided among the twelve tribes. Joshua trusted God and the Spirit of God was with him, but the people of Israel often rebelled and failed to obey God's commandments.

The conquest of Canaan was an important part of God's plan to bring His Son into the world. The nation of Israel, the descendants of Abraham, were chosen by the Lord for that purpose, and it was important for them to survive as a nation of people until the right time for Jesus to be born. Under Joshua's leadership the Israelites defeated the kings of several cities and took their land. There was not a single city that was too strong for them to conqueror if the obeyed the Lord.

The two kings of the Amorites were defeated and all of the cities of the plain. Reuben, Gad and Manasseh conquered territories east of the Jordan River. When they had settled their wives and children in the territories they had conquered, the men of those tribes left their wives and children and went with the rest of the Israelites to aid them in conquering the territories west of the Jordan. The first city across the Jordan River was Jericho.

Joshua sent spies across the Jordan River to the city of Jericho, their first planned conquest on the other side of the Jordan River. When the spies entered Jericho, they went to the house of a harlot named Rahab for lodging. While they were there, someone reported to the King that spies from Israel were in Rahab's house. By the providence of God, Rahab was informed that the Lord was going to take the city for the Israelites. The spies promised Rahab that the lives of her and her household would be spared if she would hide them.

Rahab knew that the king would be looking for the two spies, so she took them up to the roof and covered them with flax so the king's men couldn't find them. When the king sent his men to Rahab demanding her to bring the men out, she told them that the men had been there but had left the city.

When the king's men went away, Rahab lowered the spies of Israel on a rope through a window in the wall to the outside of the city. The two spies reported to Joshua all that had happened, and they were confident that the Lord would give them a victory over the city of Jericho.

Joshua led the children of Israel to the Jordan River, but when the people neared the river, they were hesitant about crossing it. For three days the leaders went to all of the people telling them to watch for the Ark of the Covenant that would be carried across the Jordan River by the priests, and the people were to follow the Ark across the river. The people watched the Ark, and as soon as the priests stepped into the water carrying the Ark, the river flowing downstream stopped flowing, and there was a dry path all the way across the river to the other side for the Israelites to cross over. As long as the priests carrying the Ark stood in the water, the water ceased to flow, and all of the Israelites crossed over on dry ground. When they had all crossed over and the priests were on shore, the water began to flow again.

After they crossed the river, they camped at a place called Gilgal. Joshua instructed one man from each tribe to pick up a stone from the riverbed as they crossed the river. They took the twelve stones and built a memorial. Joshua told the people that in the future when their children asked what the stones meant, they were to tell them that God dried up the river and kept it dry until they were all across, just as he had done when they crossed the Red Sea with Moses.

From Gilgal they advanced toward Jericho. As the Israelites were nearing Jericho, Joshua saw an angel in the form of a man.

Joshua asked him who he was, and the angel answered that he was the commander of the army of the Lord. Joshua asked the angel what he wanted him to do, and the angel said to Joshua, "Take off your shoes, because the place where you are standing is holy."

The children of Israel were given specific instructions about how to destroy the city of Jericho. The Lord told them to march around the city once every day for six days. Seven priests were to sound trumpets made from rams' horns while the other priests carried the Ark of the Covenant. On the seventh day they marched around the city seven times with the priests blowing the trumpets then the priests made a long blast on the trumpets, all the people shouted with a loud voice, and the walls fell down. The Israelites rushed in and took the city. The only people in Jericho who were saved were Rahab and her household. The Israelites were involved in many wars in the process of possessing the land of Canaan. Under the leadership of Joshua, with the help of the Lord, Israel gained many victories.

The Lord worked miracles to help the Israelites defeat the nations of the people in the land, however some of the tribes failed to drive out the Canaanites and their false gods from the land like the Lord had said. The Gentile nations lived among the tribes and tempted the Israelites to sin.

Judges 2:1-4 "The angel of the Lord came up from Gilgal to Bochim, and said: I led you up from Egypt and brought you to the land of which I swore to your fathers; and I said, I will never break My covenant with you. And you shall make no covenant with the inhabitants of this land; you shall tear down their altars. But you have not obeyed My voice. Why have you done this? Therefore I also said, I will not drive them out before you; but they shall be thorns in your side, and their god's shall be a snare to you. So it was when the Angel of the Lord spoke these words to all the children of Israel that the people lifted up their voices and wept." When Joshua dismissed the people, the children of Israel each went to their own inheritance to possess the land."

Joshua died at the age of 110, and after his death Israel was without a national leader. The people's faith in God declined and the people began to engage in the worship of foreign god's. Finally most of Israel forgot the Lord, and since there was no one to guide them everyone did what he or she determined was right instead of following the Law of the Lord.

Judges 2:20-23 "Then the anger of the Lord was hot against Israel; and He said, "Because this nation has transgressed My covenant which I commanded their fathers, and has not heeded My voice, I also will no longer drive out before them any of the nations which Joshua left when he died, so that through them I may test Israel, whether they will keep the ways of the Lord, to walk in them as their fathers kept them, or not." Therefore the Lord left those nations, without driving them out immediately; nor did He deliver them into the hand of Joshua."

The priesthood was failing the people, and the tribes of Israel failed to govern themselves responsibly. Without a national leader they continued to drift away from following God. Israel needed someone with faith in the Lord and integrity and wisdom to lead and govern them.

Judges Rule Israel For 450 Years

The conquest of Canaan began with Joshua, but it was not completed before his death. After the death of Joshua, there was a time of disorganization and disunity among the twelve tribes of Israel. Israel's enemies took advantage of the Israelite tribes who had begun practicing idolatry and they were disobedient to the Lord's law of commandments.

Israel broke their covenant with God and consequently God's protection was not with them any longer because the Israelites had not driven their enemies from the land of Canaan when they first occupied the land.

The Lord allowed the enemies of Israel to defeat them as He had said He would do if they forsook Him but the Lord did not leave his people without national leadership for long. He gave them leaders called Judges who judged the people according to the Law and delivered them from their enemies by the power of the Lord.

The Hebrew word for Judges means 'one who administers justice.' Othneil was the first of the Judges, and Samuel was the last. The book of Judges is a historical account of God's faithfulness to His people and Israel's failure to remain faithful to God. It was written to show the consequences of disobedience and the need for a national leader. The Judges, as national leaders of Israel, took the place of Joshua until the time the people asked the Lord to give them a king.

The Lord gave Israel the Judges to deliver them out of the hand of their enemies, but they would not always listen to their Judges. They turned away from the way their fathers walked and failed to obey the commandments of the Lord, they worshiped false gods. When a Judge died, the Israelites behaved more corruptly than their fathers had. Enemies would oppress the nation of Israel, and when the people asked the Lord for help He would appoint a Judge to defeat their enemy. God's Holy Spirit enabled the Judges to make proper decisions, and gave them power to do miraculous things to help Israel.

The Judges did not rule continuously. There were many times when there was not a Judge over the people. God was Israel's Sovereign, but they ignored Him until they were in trouble and asked the Lord for help. Under the leadership of the Judges the Israelites continued their conquest to take and inhabit the land of Canaan.

The Judges became national heroes and governed the people. The people of Israel were now a younger generation, and they ignored the Lord. The Judges were Israel's leaders during battles, and they also ruled during times of peace. They ruled according to the Lord's instructions and the Law of Moses.

Altogether there were fifteen Judges who ruled from the time of Othneil, the first Judge, until Samuel, the last Judge. Othneil became a Judge after the children of Israel were settled in the land of Canaan and they began worshiping false gods called the Baals and the Asherahs. The king of Mesopotamia conquered and ruled over the Israelites, so the children of Israel cried out to the Lord for help. The Spirit of the Lord came upon Othneil and empowered him to defeat the king of Mesopotamia. After that the people of Israel had peace for forty more years.

After the forty years of peace, the children of Israel began to do evil again, and Eglon, the king of Moab, attacked the Israelites. Israel served Eglon for eighteen years, and then Ehud, the second Judge, killed Eglon.

Judges 3:20-23 "So Ehud came to him (now he was sitting upstairs in his cool private chamber.) Then Ehud said "I have a message from God for you." So he arose from his seat. Then Ehud reached with his left hand, took the dagger from his right thigh, and thrust it into his belly. Even the hilt went in after the blade, and the fat closed over the blade, for he did not draw the dagger out of his belly; and the entrails came out. Then Ehud went out through the porch and shut the doors of the upper room behind him and locked them."

Israel had peace for eighty years after Eglon's death. When Ehud died, the children of Israel began doing evil again, and Jabin, the King of Canaan, oppressed Israel for twenty years. Deborah, who was a prophetess as well as a Judge, judged Israel at that time.

On one occasion Deborah sent for Barak, an Israelite from the tribe of Napthali, and told him that the Lord would deliver Jabin and his army of chariots into the hands of Barak and his troops. Barak wouldn't go unless Deborah went with him. Deborah accompanied Barak along with ten thousand troops against nine hundred chariot troops of Sisera, the commander of Jabin's army.

Jabin and his army were destroyed, and after that there was peace for forty years. Then the Midianites began to oppress Israel.

Paraphrase of Judges 6:7-10: The children of Israel complained to the Lord because of the Midianites. The Lord sent a prophet to the children of Israel, and he said, "Thus says the Lord God of Israel: I brought you up from Egypt and brought you out of the house of bondage. Then I delivered you out of the hand of the Egyptians and out of the hand of all who oppressed you. I drove them out before you and gave you their land."

"Also I said to you, 'I Am the Lord your God; do not fear the gods of the Amorites, in whose land you dwell. But you have not obeyed My voice." Each new generation of the Israelites made the same mistake their fathers made and began worshiping the idol gods of the Gentiles.

The angel of the Lord came to a man named Gideon who was from the tribe of Manasseh and said to him, "The Lord is with you, you mighty man of valor!" The Spirit of God was with Gideon, and he became the next judge of Israel. The Lord gave Gideon power through the Holy

Spirit to defeat the Midianites and He convinced Gideon to do what the Lord told him. He was instructed to tear down the altar of Baal and cut down the wooden image that was beside it. He was then told to build an altar to the Lord with the wood from the image he had cut down. Gideon waited until that night, and then he did everything he was told to do. So the Lord gave the Israelites victory over their enemies.

The Israelites had peace for forty years after Gideon. The Judges following Gideon were: Tola who judged for 23 years, Jair for 22 years, Jephthah for 6 years, Ibzan for 7 years, Elon for 10 years, Abdon for 8 years, and Samson for 20 years. The Bible tells us something interesting about Abdon. He judged Israel after Elon, and he had forty sons and thirty grandsons who rode on seventy young donkeys.

The major enemy of Israel during the time of Sampson was the nation of the Philistines. The Philistines came to the coastal plain circa 1200 B.C. and attempted to settle in land belonging to Israel. Sampson waged war against the Philistines and became a Judge by the providence of God. An angel announced Sampson's birth, and the Lord gave Sampson superhuman strength to defeat the Philistines. The story of Sampson is in Judges 13 through chapter 16 and is very interesting.

For several years the Lord had communicated with Israel through the Judges. During the years of the Judges and throughout the rest of the history of Israel, there were also men called prophets who were used by God to communicate to His people. The prophet Samuel was the most important Israelite in the period between the judges and the monarchy.

Samuel was the first in the line of prophets. The prophets were not rulers like the kings; they served as spokesmen to deliver God's commands and messages to the kings and to the people.

The word prophet is an English word designating someone who is directed by the Holy Spirit of God to make God's will known to man. Prophets were also referred to as Holy men of God. Prophets spoke the word of God to the people whether it was good or bad. The prophets were ordinary men who faced many hazards, including wrath from the rulers of the nations they prophesied against, however the prophets remained faithful to the Lord.

The prophets were sometimes stoned to death, sawed in two, or put to death by the sword. The prophets were often depressed, discouraged and fearful, yet their faith, hope and love for the Lord was steadfast. They depended on the Lord for strength, and the Lord was there to lend comfort and encouragement to them and to rescue them from those who wished to harm them. The prophets helped weave God's plan of redemption into the scriptures all the way through the Bible. They were given a major role in the history of Israel after Israel became a monarchy. The Bible contains seventeen books of prophecy.

When we read what the prophets have written, it will be obvious that they were God's messengers who prophesied about events that would take place. The prophets revealed the Lord's message for the present and future events. Some of the events took place soon after they spoke of them, but other events would take place many years later. The prophets had a major role in God's story of Faith, Hope and Love during the entire time of God's plan of redemption. Most of the prophets lived a solitary life. They went about in sheepskins and goatskins, destitute, persecuted and mistreated. They sometimes wandered in deserts and mountains and lived in caves and holes in the ground. All of God's prophets were commended for their faith, yet none of them lived to receive what had been promised.

The prophets didn't usually preach to large audiences; they often went alone to preach to individuals. The Bible contains seventeen books of prophecy written by the prophets. Prophecy always had its origin from the will of God. Paul told Timothy that all scripture is God breathed

(2ⁿᵈ Tim 3:16). Peter stated that none of scripture was written according to the prophet's own interpretation. People respected the prophets, because they knew the prophet spoke for the Lord and received miraculous power from Him. God continued to use prophets to proclaim His word in the first century when Christ was born and during the early years of the church.

The foretelling of future events was not a necessary function of a prophet, but most of the prophets did predict future events as the Lord revealed them.

Samuel was a prominent prophet before and after Israel became a monarchy. The prophets who followed him worked directly with the king's of Israel advising them, helping them, and warning them when they acted contrary to the Lord's will. The work of some prophets was similar to that of a teacher. The prophets preached, taught and instructed the people and their leaders.

There are five major books of prophecy including Isaiah, Jeremiah, Lamentations, Ezekiel and Daniel. They are called Major Prophets because of the size of the contents of the book not the importance of the prophet or of his message. The Bible contains 17 books of prophecy all together if we count the book of Lamentations as prophecy. Lamentations is credited to Jeremiah. God continued to use prophets to proclaim His word in the first century when Christ was born and during the early years of the church. The foretelling of future events was not a necessary function of a prophet but most of the prophets did predict future events as the Lord revealed them. The work of some prophets was similar to that of a teacher.

A man named Samuel was a priest, a prophet and Judge even though he was not mentioned in the book of Judges. The book of 1ˢᵗ Samuel mentions a priest named Eli who judged Israel for forty years after Samson. Eli was living in Shiloh situated north of Bethel. The tent of meeting also called the tabernacle and house of God was set up in Shiloh north of Bethel and it was the principle sanctuary for the Israelites during the time of the Judges.

The Lord chose Samuel to be a judge even before he was born. There was a Jewish woman named Hannah who had no children. She prayed to God and asked Him to give her a male child. She told God that if He would answer her prayer, she would give her child to the Lord for all the days of his life. God answered her prayer, and she had a son and named him Samuel. The name Samuel means 'name of God.'

When Samuel was weaned from his mother's breast, she took him to live in the Tabernacle with Eli, the priest. Hannah said to Eli, "For this child I prayed, and the Lord has granted me my petition which I asked of Him. Therefore I also have lent him to the Lord; as long as he lives he shall be lent to the Lord." (1ˢᵗ Samuel 1:27)

Samuel ministered before the Lord even as a child wearing a linen ephod. Moreover his mother used to make him a little robe and bring it to him year after year when she came up with her husband to offer the yearly sacrifice. (1ˢᵗ Samuel 2:18-19)

Eli was very old and almost blind. One night after they had gone to bed, Samuel heard someone calling his name. He ran to Eli and asked him if he called him, but Eli told him he hadn't and told him to go back to bed.

This happened three times. "Now Samuel did not yet know the Lord, nor was the word of the Lord yet revealed to him."

And the Lord called Samuel again the third time. So he arose and went to Eli, and said, "Here I am, for you did call me." Then Eli perceived that the Lord had called the boy. Therefore Eli said to Samuel, "Go, lie down; and it shall be, if He calls you, that you must say, 'Speak, Lord, for Your servant hears.'" So Samuel went and lay down in his place. (2ⁿᵈ Samuel 3:7-9)

When the Lord called to Samuel the next time, Samuel did as Eli said, and the Lord talked to him about Eli's wicked sons and what He was going to do to them. As Samuel grew, the Lord favored him and revealed himself to Samuel by the Holy Spirit. Samuel was a man of faith in God and with much hope he loved God with all of his heart. Samuel spent his entire life serving the Lord and the people of Israel. The Lord blessed Samuel as he grew, and all the people from one end of Israel to the other recognized him as a prophet.

While Samuel was judge and prophet to the Israelites the Philistines captured the Ark of the Covenant, took it to Ashdod and set it up in the house of their false god, Dagon. The next morning, the idol Dagon had fallen on his face in front of the Ark.

The Philistines set Dagon back up, but the following morning they found that Dagon had fallen again. This time his hands and his head were broken off and lay on the threshold of Dagon's temple. The Philistines never went into the temple again, because they were afraid. The Lord then caused the people of Ashdod to come down with tumors. The people became afraid of what the Israelite God would do to them next, so they moved the Ark to Gath.

The Lord destroyed Gath, and the people there broke out with tumors. The ark was sent to the city of Ekron and the people there were stricken with tumors. The Philistines became afraid to keep the Ark of the Covenant any longer, so they returned the Ark to the Israelites and it was placed in Kirjath Jearim in the house of Abinadab.

Nation of Israel Becomes a Monarchy

After several years of being ruled by the Lord through the Judges, the people of Israel complained and asked God to give them a King like the other nations. All of the elders of Israel came to Samuel at Ramah saying, "You are old, and your sons do not walk in your ways. Now make us a king to judge us like all the nations." The people of Israel under the leadership of a King would still be obligated to worship the Lord as Sovereign and obey God's commands.

The Lord would continue to direct them spiritually through the words of the prophets when Israel needed guidance, help or punishment. The blessings, advice, warnings and rebukes came upon the kings by the will and word of the Lord as the prophets spoke for the Lord. One of the duties of the prophets was to anoint God's selection of a person to be the king over Israel.

The Lord told Samuel to let the people have a king, but to warn them what a king could do when power is given to only one man. The king would take whatever he wanted from the people, and the people would become like slaves in their own land. With the help of Samuel and the prophets, the transition from the leadership of Judges to the monarchy took place in the latter years of Samuel's life. After Samuel, the Lord depended on the prophets to deliver His messages to the people and to the kings they selected.

Samuel anointed Saul as the first king of Israel. At first Saul was a good king and a good military leader, but God was not pleased with him, because Saul didn't obey God in everything He told him to do. The heart of Saul was not completely converted to doing the Lord's will and Saul used his own judgment to rule and failed to do what the Lord commanded him. For that reason the Lord rejected Saul and took the kingdom of Israel away from him. The Lord told Samuel He rejected Saul as king and instructed him to anoint one of the sons of Jesse as king over Israel in the place of Saul. Jesse lived in Bethlehem and he was the father of David a descendant of Abraham in the birth line of Jesus. David was one of the greatest and most beloved kings of

Israel. The prophet Samuel foretold that Christ would be born from the birth line of king David in 2nd Samuel 7:12-14, Luke 1:32, and Isaiah 11:1.

2nd Samuel 7:12-14 "When your days are complete and you lie down with your fathers, I will raise up your descendants after you, who will come forth from you, and I will establish his kingdom forever. He shall build a house for My name, and I will establish the throne of his kingdom forever."

Samuel filled his horn with oil and went to Jesse's house in Bethlehem and anointed David, a descendant of Judah, to replace Saul as King over Israel. The story of David is recorded in 1stSamuel 16 and 1stKings 2.

David had a heart for God, and he was endowed with many talents. He was a musician, a poet and a singer. David became a great military leader and was engaged in several battles with the Philistines.

The Lord said that David was a man after His own heart because of David's honest, faithful and loving attitude towards God.

Samuel died during the reign of David, and the prophet Nathan followed Samuel as the major prophet in Israel. The time of the Judges no longer existed. Nothing is known about Nathan's background except that he was from the tribe of Judah. Nathan appears without explanation in the 7th chapter of 2nd Samuel where he has a conversation with King David. Nathan spoke the word of the Lord to David, and he spoke convicting words from the Lord when David sinned.

God loved David, because he was contrite and very humble in his attitude towards the Lord even though he had many faults. To paraphrase Psalm 31: David said, "I put my trust in You Lord. Let me never be ashamed. Deliver me by Your righteousness. Hear me and deliver me speedily. Be my rock of refuge and a fortress to save me. You are my rock and my fortress. For Your name's sake, lead me and guide me for You are my strength. Into your hand I commit my spirit; you have redeemed me, O Lord God of truth."

David was only thirty years old when he began to reign over Israel. During his reign, the nation of Israel experienced a golden age. David reigned for forty years; he reigned in Hebron for seven years and six months and later in Jerusalem for thirty-three years. Early in the life of David, he conquered the city of Jerusalem, which became the capital city of the Israelites.

The Ark of God was placed on a new cart and brought to Jerusalem, and Jerusalem became known both as the city of God and the city of David. In many ways David was a good person who loved God with all of his heart but David was not a perfect or sinless man. David committed some grievous sins, but he confessed his sins and repented and God forgave David. David had faith, hope and love.

God accepted David's humble repentance and promised that his descendants would be heirs to the same promise the Lord had made to Abraham by establishing a royal line from which the Messiah would come. After David, the royal line continued to follow the line of David until Jesus was born in the first century A.D. David was favored by God, because he did everything the Lord asked him to do. David was the greatest and best loved king in the history of the nation of Israel, and the Jews today still favor him as the greatest.

Acts 13:16-23 "Then Paul stood up, and motioning with his hand said, "Men of Israel, and you who fear God, listen: The God of this people Israel chose our fathers, and exalted the people when they dwelt as strangers in the land of Egypt, and with an uplifted arm He brought them out of it. Now for a time of about forty years He put up with your ways in the wilderness.

And when He had destroyed seven nations in the land of Canaan, He distributed their land to them by allotment. After that He gave them judges for about four hundred and fifty years, until Samuel the prophet. And afterward they asked for a king; so God gave them Saul the son of Kish a man of the tribe of Benjamin, for forty years. And when He had removed him. He raised up for them David as king to whom also He gave testimony and said, "I have found David, the son of Jesse, a man after My own heart, who will do all my will." From this man's seed, according to the promise, God raised up for Israel a Savior—Jesus."

The kingdom of Israel under the leadership of David remained faithful to the Lord, and the Lord blessed Israel, and David's Kingdom was enlarged. David had several sons, including Solomon his son by Bathsheba, and David selected Solomon to become his successor to the throne.

Before David died, he called Solomon to his bedside and explained what his responsibilities would be when he ruled the kingdom after David's death. David told Solomon to walk in the ways God showed him and to keep all of the commandments of the Law of Moses. He told Solomon that as long as he and his descendants were faithful to God with all of their heart and soul, God would be with them. So when David died, Solomon became the king of Israel.

After Solomon was anointed king, the Lord appeared to him in a dream and told him he could ask for anything he wanted, and his wish would be granted. Solomon asked for wisdom, and the Lord was pleased and gave him great wisdom as well as riches and honor.

Solomon became known as the wisest man in the world, and under his rule the kingdom of Israel became very wealthy. With all of Solomon's wisdom he accomplished many great things. Solomon was successful in everything he did but in spite of all of his accomplishments Solomon disobeyed many of the commandments of the Lord and his heart turned away from strict obedience to God. God commanded Solomon twice not to worship false gods, but he refused to obey what the Lord commanded. Solomon desired to carry out is father's wishes and build a temple to the Lord as a place of worship.

1st Kings 5:1-6 "Now Hiram king of Tyre sent his servants to Solomon, because he heard that they had anointed him king in place of his father, for Hiram had always loved David. Then Solomon sent to Hiram saying: You know how my father David could not build a house for the name of the Lord his God because of the wars which were fought against him on every side, until the Lord put his foes under the soles of his feet.

But now the Lord my God has given me rest on every side there is neither adversary nor evil occurrence. And behold I propose to build a house for the name of the Lord my God, as the Lord spoke to my father David, saying, Your son, whom I will set on your throne in your place, he shall build the house for my name."

The tabernacle served the Israelite nation for many years as the house of God, but it was a temporary structure that could be moved from place to place. Four hundred and eighty years after the children of Israel left the land of Egypt and were settled in Canaan, and after Solomon had reigned for four years, he began building the temple in Jerusalem. When the temple was complete, Solomon had a dedication ceremony. The temple became the place for the presence of the Lord. The temple was still the focal point of the Jewish religion when Jesus was born in the first century.

Solomon wrote the books of Proverbs, Ecclesiastes and Songs of Solomon. The book of Ecclesiastes is rich in wisdom. It describes some of the pitfalls of life and the misery that can occur in life. Solomon saw the tears of the oppressed and observed that death comes to everyone. He also discovered that the wise, the foolish, the rich, and the poor will all ultimately come face to face with death. Solomon said that everything God has set in order is forever, and men cannot change it. He observed that there is nothing new in God's relationship with mankind and that there is nothing new under the sun. That which is now, has been before, and what is to be, has already been.

Solomon summed up all of the activities in life and came to the conclusion that success in life is achieved only if we stand in awe of God and keep His commandments. He observed that this life is meaningless unless it leads to a greater life of faith in God. He concluded that the whole duty of man is to fear God and keep his commandments.

Ecclesiastes 12:9-14 "And moreover because the Preacher was wise, he still taught the people knowledge; yes, he pondered and sought out and set in order many proverbs. The Preacher sought to find acceptable words; and what was written, was upright-words of truth. The words of the wise are like goads, and the words of scholars are like well-driven nails, given by one Shepherd.

In spite of Solomon's wisdom, he failed to take his own advice to fear God and keep His commandments. The Lord became angry with Solomon because of his disobedience and told Solomon that He would take the kingdom away from his descendants.

He promised to leave the kingdom in Solomon's hand as long as he lived. After Solomon's death, the kingdom of Israel was taken away from Solomon's son, Rehoboam.

1ˢᵗ Kings 11:9-13 "The Lord became angry with Solomon, because his heart had turned from the Lord God of Israel who had appeared to him twice, and had commanded him concerning this thing, that he should not go after other god's; but he did not keep what the Lord had commanded. Therefore the Lord said to Solomon,'

"Because you have done this, and have not kept My covenant and My statutes, which I have commanded you, I will surely tear the kingdom away from you and give it to your servant."

"Nevertheless I will not do it in your days, for the sake of your father David; I will tear it out of the hand of your son. However I will not tear away the whole kingdom; I will give one tribe to your son for the sake of My servant David, and for the sake of Jerusalem which I have chosen."

Kingdom of Israel is Divided (931 B.C.)

The Lord's prophetic words were fulfilled a few years after Solomon's son Rehoboam took his father's place on the throne. When Rehoboam became king he put a burdensome tax on the people, and they rebelled against him. At that time, the Lord split the kingdom of Rehoboam. He took away ten of the tribes of Israel from Rehoboam and placed a king named Jeroboam over them. They were known as the ten northern tribes. The two southern tribes became the Kingdom of Judah, and Rehoboam remained king of them. The ten tribes of Israel chose the city of Samaria as their capital, and the tribes of Judah and Benjamin, the Southern Kingdom, continued worshiping the Lord in the temple in Jerusalem.

God continued to fulfill his plan of redemption through the descendants of the Israelites after the kingdom was divided even though they sinned against Him. At times most of Israel turned away from following the Lord, but there was always a remnant of the Israelites in Judah who remained faithful. The Lord blessed the remnant and continued to work with them to complete his story of faith, hope and love through Jesus Christ.

Under Jeroboam's rule, the ten northern tribes of Israel soon turned to idolatry. God became very angry with them, and He raised up prophets to warn them that God's judgment would come against them if they didn't repent of their idolatry. They made two golden calves and set them up as gods—one at each end of the kingdom—so the people of the northern kingdom could worship the golden calves instead of going to Jerusalem to worship in the temple.

There was constant conflict between the Northern Kingdom and the Southern Kingdom. The Lord ended the first war between Rehoboam and Jereboam but there were wars between them the rest of the time they reigned. Later Jeroboam led the ten northern tribes wholly into idolatry, and the prophet Ahijah, brought bad news from the Lord to Jereboam and his household, denouncing Jereboam.

1ˢᵗ Kings 14:7-10 "Go tell Jeroboam, 'thus says the Lord God of Israel: "Because I exalted you from among the people, and made you ruler over My people Israel, and tore the kingdom away from the house of David, and gave it to you; and yet you have not been as My servant David, who kept My commandments and who followed me with all his heart, to do only what was right in My eyes; but you have done more evil than all who were before you, for you have gone and made for yourself other gods and molded images to provoke Me to anger, and have cast Me behind your back—therefore behold I will bring disaster on the house of Jeroboam, and will cut off from Jeroboam every male in Israel, bond an free; I will take away the remnant of the house of Jereboam, as one takes away refuse until it is all gone."

There were 20 kings who reigned over Israel before they went into captivity to the Assyrians in 722 B.C. The books of Kings and Chronicles give the history of the kings of both the Northern Kingdom of Israel and the Southern Kingdom of Judah. The prophets also wrote about the sinful deeds and troublesome times of the two kingdoms. The Northern Kingdom was never restored to the fellowship of God.

Ahab and Jezebel Rule Northern Kingdom

Ahab reigned from 874B.C. to 853B.C., and was on the throne during the time of the prophets Elijah and Elisha. Ahab was the son of Omri, and he reigned over the Israelites in Samaria for twenty-two years. Ahab fortified the cities of Israel and used his own capital. During his reign Israel had frequent wars with Syria. A random arrow killed Ahab during a battle with Syria and he was buried in Samaria.

Ahab did more evil to provoke the Lord than all of the kings of Israel before him. He built a temple for Baal in Samaria, the capital city, and built a wooden image of the false god Baal and worshiped it. Jezebel, Ahab's wife, was not an Israelite. She was the daughter of Ethbaal, the king of Sidon. Jezebel worshipped the false god Baal, and she insisted that Baal have equal rights with the Lord God of Israel.

Jezebel's insistence brought her into direct conflict with the prophet Elijah. Jezebel was so wicked that her name has always been associated with evil women.

Elijah, the prophet, warned King Ahab of Israel that as surely as the Lord God of Israel lived, and as he stood before God, there would not be any dew or rain for a few years, and it did not rain again until Elijah prayed to God for the rain to return. Ahab and Jezebel were very angry with Elijah and wanted to kill him. The Lord told Elijah to travel eastward and hide from Ahab and Jezebel in the Kerith Ravine, east of the Jordan. There was a brook in the ravine where Elijah hid, so he would have water to drink, and God sent ravens with food for him each day. Elijah was solely dependent on the providence of the Lord during that time.

After many days, the Lord told Elijah to go back to King Ahab, and then he would cause it to rain. When Ahab saw Elijah, he said, "Is that you, O trouble maker of Israel?"

Elijah said he wasn't the one who had made trouble for Israel but Ahab himself had, because he had forsaken the Lord and worshipped Baal. Then Elijah told Ahab to gather all the prophets of Baal and meet him on Mount Carmel. When all the prophets of Baal were assembled on Mount Carmel, Elijah had a contest with them to see whose god was the real God. Each side built an altar to their God and placed a bull on their altar.

Then the prophets of Baal prayed long and hard for Baal to send fire down on their sacrifice, but no fire came. Elijah had water poured over his sacrifice and prayed for God to send fire down on his sacrifice. God sent fire down, which burned up the sacrifice of Elijah. When the people saw it they said, "The Lord, He is God!" After that, Elijah went off by himself and prayed to God to send rain. The sky turned dark, and it began to rain. Elijah had 450 prophets of Baal put to death in the Kishon valley.

When Ahab told Jezebel what Elijah had done, Jezebel threatened to have Elijah killed. Jezebel, as the queen of Israel, had the power to have Elijah hunted down and killed. Elijah decided to hide in the wilderness, so he arose and ran for his life to Beersheba, which belongs to Judah. Elijah ran toward the wilderness, and sat down under a tree and prayed that he might die. He said, *It is enough! Now Lord, take my life, for I am no better than my fathers!* Fearing for his life, Elijah became so depressed that he wanted to die alone there in the wilderness.

An angel touched him and told him to get up and eat. Elijah saw a cake baked on coals, and a jar of water. He ate and drank and lay down again. And the angel of the Lord came back the second time, and touched him and said, "Get up and eat, because the journey is too long for you."

Elijah had asked the Lord to take his life, but the Lord had other plans for him, and He treated Elijah with kindness. An angel came to Elijah in the desert and fed him. Then the angel told Elijah to go to Mt Horeb, the mountain of God. When Elijah reached Mt Horeb, he spent the night in a cave.

The next morning the Lord asked Elijah what he was doing there, and Elijah replied, "I have been very zealous for the Lord God Almighty. The Israelites have rejected your covenant, broken down your altars, and put your prophets to death with the sword. I am the only one left, and now they are trying to kill me too." The Lord knew that Elijah was very distraught. He had served the Lord faithfully in all kinds of circumstances, and now the Lord was about to reward him for his faithfulness. The Lord told Elijah two important things to do: to go and anoint Hazael king over Israel, and then to find Elisha and appoint Elisha to succeed him as prophet. Elijah dutifully left the mountain, went to Hazael and anointed Hazael to be the next king of Israel, then found the prophet Elisha and made him his attendant.

God was getting ready to take Elijah to heaven, and Elisha would take his place as the prophet of Israel, but before that took place, Elisha would witness a very unusual thing. Elijah would be taken up to heaven in a fiery chariot. The Lord was going to reward Elijah by taking him to heaven before he died. When the Lord was ready to take Elijah to heaven, he sent him to Bethel. Elijah and Elisha were coming back from Gilgal, and Elijah told Elisha to stay where he was and he would go on to Bethel alone. Elisha said, *"As the Lord lives, and as your soul lives, I will not leave you!"* (2nd Kings 2:2) They both went to Bethel. There was a company of prophets there, and the prophets knew the Lord was going to take Elijah. They told Elisha about it, but Elisha told them he already knew but asked them not to speak about it. It must have weighed heavily on Elisha knowing that Elijah would soon be gone, and he would be taking his place.

Elijah told Elisha to stay at Bethel while he went to Jericho. Elisha again refused to stay and he went with Elijah. When they reached Jericho some prophets told Elisha that the Lord was going to take his master that day. Elisha said *"Yes I know, but do not speak of it."* Then Elijah told Elisha he was going to the Jordan River, and again he told Elisha to stay there, but Elisha again said, *"As surely as the Lord lives and as you live, I will not leave you."*

When they got to the Jordan River, Elijah rolled up his cloak and struck the water with it. The water parted and Elijah and Elisha walked across the river on dry ground. Elijah asked Elisha what he could do for him before the Lord took him, and Elisha asked for a double portion of Elijah's spirit.

Elijah possessed a great inner spirit that was evidenced by his great ministry. The Holy Spirit of the Lord was in him in a large measure. Elisha wanted to carry on Elijah's ministry with an even greater power than Elijah's. Elijah told Elisha he had asked for something that was hard to do, but it would be granted if Elisha were there when God took him. Elijah was still testing Elisha to see if he would be faithful in replacing him. Elijah and Elisha continued to walk away from the river.

"Then it happened as they continued on and talked, suddenly a chariot of fire appeared with horses of fire, and separated the two of them; and Elijah went up by a whirlwind into heaven. And Elisha saw it, and he cried out, "My father, my father, the chariot of Israel and its horsemen!" So he saw him no more. And he took hold of his own clothes and tore them into two pieces." (2nd Kings 2:11-12)

After Elijah ascended to heaven, Elisha picked up Elijah's cloak and walked back to the river, struck the waters with Elijah's cloak and called out to the Lord saying, "Where now is the Lord, the God of Elijah?"

The waters parted again and Elisha walked across the bed of the river. Elisha wanted to see if the Lord had given him the power he was promised.

A company of prophets witnessed what took place and the company of prophets said, *"The spirit of Elijah is resting on Elisha."* The Lord honored Elisha's request for a double measure of Elijah's spirit. Elijah was often described as a man of God. He was a Tishbite from the town of Tishbeh in Gilead, and his name means 'Yaweh *is God*.' He wore a garment of hair and a leather belt around his waist. His outer garment was probably made from sheepskin or goatskin and was loose fitting like a cloak.

Ahaziah succeeded Ahab as the king of Israel but he died after two years, and Joram succeeded him. It was during the reign of Joram that Elijah went to heaven, and Elisha succeeded Elijah. The deeds of Elijah and Elisha are recorded from 1st Kings 17 through 2nd Kings 13. After Ahab, Israel was ruled by 12 kings in succession until 722 B.C. The last king on the throne of Israel is Hoshea, and the children of Israel continued to sin against the Lord. In the final difficult days of the Kingdom of Israel (from 760 to 722 B.C.), the prophet Hosea ministered to Israel. This was during the days of the six kings who followed Jereboam the Second: Zechariah, Shallum, Menahem, Pekahiah, Pekah and Hoshea (2nd Kings 15,16, and 17).

Northern Kingdom of Israel Goes Into Exile

Shalmaneser, the king of Assyria, invaded the land of Israel and laid siege to Samaria for three years. During the reign of King Hoshea of Israel, the Assyrians completed the destruction of the northern kingdom, and in 722 B.C, Israel was exiled to Assyria. Shalmeneser settled them in Halah, in Gozan on the Habor River, and in the towns of the Medes. (2nd Kings 17.)

The prophet Amos threatened Israel with a judgment from the Lord several years before the exile, and the prophet Hosea identified the enemy as Assyria. The purpose of Hosea's ministry was to point out Israel's sins and their unfaithfulness. Hosea put much of the blame for Israel's sin on their lifestyle, borrowed from their pagan neighbors in Canaan. The pagans worshiped the false god Baal, and the Israelites were influenced by their worship of Baal. Hosea wrote about the judgment of God and His salvation. God's judgment was altogether punitive. Out of love, God punished His people to bring them to repent. The Lord reminded the Israelites that it was He who brought them out of Egypt, and that they should not acknowledge any God but Him (Hosea 13:4). According to Hosea 13:16, the people of Samaria would have to bear the burdens caused by their own guilt.

The Lord warned what the other nations would do to them without His protection: the sword would slaughter them, their little ones would be dashed to the ground, and their pregnant women would be ripped open. The prophet gave the Lord's warning in plenty of time for Israel to repent but she would not. The Lord would turn His wrath away if they repented. He sent the prophets to plead with the people to return to Him but the message of the prophets fell on deaf ears.

The prophet Hosea prophesied about the Northern Kingdom of Israel in the eighth century B.C. Hosea issued the Lord's threats against Israel and rebuked them when they failed to heed His warnings. Hosea prophesied that the Lord would destroy Israel but would save Judah. Judah would be saved because the Messiah would come from the descendants of Judah. Israel did not repent, and as Joel and Amos predicted, Israel was exiled to Assyria in 722B.C.

In the first chapter of Hosea, the Lord compares Israel to a prostitute; she was married to the Lord, but she became unfaithful and served idols. The Lord is a jealous God and will not tolerate spiritual adultery. God's people symbolize his wife. The Lord commanded his prophet Hosea to marry Gomer; an adulterous wife with children of unfaithfulness, to illustrate that Israel was guilty of spiritual adultery by leaving the Lord for other god's.

Beginning with chapter 1:10, there is a promise of restoration. Judah and Israel would be united under one leader, and they would be called sons of God. This is a prophecy of the coming of the kingdom of Christ. Paul quoted Hosea in Romans 9:25-26 saying that Hosea's prophecy predicted the restoration of Israel and Judah, which would include the Gentiles.

The restoration began when John the Baptist and Jesus began their ministries in the first century A.D. The gospel of Christ was preached to the Jews from every nation on the first Pentecost after Christ's death, burial, resurrection and ascension (Acts 2). The apostle Paul preached the gospel to the Gentiles later (Acts 10), and from then on the gospel was preached to people all over the world.

In Romans 9:22-25, Paul states that God chose to show his wrath in order to make His power known. Throughout the history of the Old Testament, the people of Israel and Judah sinned then would repent. Israel's sins were many, but God's compassion and love was enduring. The Gentiles sinned from the beginning, but God graciously sent his Son to die for all people.

In chapter 3 of Hosea, Hosea reconciles with his wife. Hosea's love for Gomer, his unfaithful wife, illustrates God's love for the unfaithful Israelites and His willingness to reconcile with his people if they will return to him.

The time from their exile till the coming of Christ in the first century Israel sowed the wind and reaped the whirlwind. (Hosea 8:7) The nation of Israel sowed the wind of disregard for God's law and became idolatrous, and as a result, they reaped a whirlwind of judgment. Israel sowed idolatry, and they reaped the mighty power of God that swallowed them up by the Gentile nations.

In chapters 9 and 10 Hosea wrote about Israel's punishment for rejecting the Lord; they would become wanderers among the nations. The people of the nation of Israel went into exile in 722 B.C. and afterwards did become wanderers throughout the world.

In chapter 11, Hosea wrote about God's love for Israel. God loved his people, the descendants of Abraham, but he punished them for their multitude of sins and stubborn refusal to repent. God's purpose in punishing his people was an effort to make them return their loyalty to Him. God's love for his people didn't change even when they sinned or failed to repent. The more God called on them to return to him, the further they drifted into sin and idolatry.

In chapters 12-13, Hosea continued to expose the sins of Israel and Judah and exhorted the two nations to return to the Lord and maintain love and justice. Justice points to the sin of selfishness, greed, and pride. The merchants use dishonest scales; they love to defraud. Ephraim boasted about becoming wealthy, and he thought his wealth would cover his sin. Some people today believe they are rich because they are righteous. That is a false belief. The Lord loves those whose hearts are right regardless of their economic position. The kingdom of Israel continued in their sinful ways, and in the ninth year of King Hoshea, the king of Assyria besieged the city of Samaria. Israel was carried away from their own land to Assyria.

Southern Kingdom of Judah (626-586 B.C)

Judah remained loyal to the Lord when the northern tribes split off and became idolatrous. The promise of the kingdom of Christ through Judah goes all the way back to the prophecy of Jacob.

One of the good kings who reigned over Israel was King Hezekiah. The prophet Isaiah prophesied during Hezekiah's reign. Hezekiah was twenty-five years old when he began to reign in Jerusalem, and Hezekiah did what was right in the sight of the Lord. He removed the altars and images of the false gods from Judah. Hezekiah was on the throne in Judah when the king of Assyria carried the northern kingdom of Israel into captivity.

When King Hezekiah had reigned in Judah for fourteen years, Sennacherib, King of Assyria, attacked Judah and captured the fortified cities. Hezekiah agreed to pay tribute money to Sennacherib and paid him with all of the silver and gold that was in the temple, but Sennacherib sent a large army against Jerusalem anyway. The Assyrian king sent a message to Hezekiah insulting Hezekiah, his army, and the Lord God. The Lord said that He would save a remnant from Judah, and they would again take root downward and bear fruit upward.

The Lord made reference to a remnant from the tribe of Judah that would remain faithful to Him when He made the statement that they would take root downward. Bearing fruit upward meant that they would provide a people through whom Jesus Christ would come. The Lord swore that the king of Assyria would not enter Jerusalem at that time, because He would defend the city.

2ⁿᵈ Kings 19:35-36: "And it came to pass on a certain night that the angel of the Lord went out and killed in the camp of the Assyrians one hundred and eighty five thousand; and when the people arose early in the morning, there were the corpses—all dead. So Sennacherib, King of Assyria departed and went away, returned home and remained at Nineveh."

When Sennacherib returned home, he went into the temple of his god to worship, and while he was there, his sons killed him with a sword.

Later King Hezekiah of Judah became very sick, and the prophet Isaiah told him that the Lord said he was going to die. Hezekiah, out of misery and grief, wept and prayed earnestly to the Lord, reminding the Lord that he had served Him with truth and loyalty.

The Lord told Isaiah to go to Hezekiah and tell him that the Lord had heard his prayers and had seen his tears, and He would heal him. So Hezekiah's life was extended.

2 Kings 20:20-21 "The rest of the acts of Hezekiah—all his might, and how he made a pool and a tunnel and brought water into the city—are they not written in the book of the Chronicles of the kings of Judah? So Hezekiah rested with his fathers."

Hezekiah had given orders to dig a tunnel through the mountain that Jerusalem sits on. The tunnel was used to bring water from the Gihon springs down into the city. The tunnel still exists today as it winds its way 1900 feet under the city of Jerusalem.

Then Manasseh, Hezekiah's son, took his place. Manasseh was only twelve years old when he became king. Manasseh had the reputation of being one of the worst kings in the history of Judah. He was involved in the practices of the Canaanite religion of worshiping false god's. However, Manasseh eventually repented and turned back to the Lord.

Amon came to the throne of Judah after Manasseh. When Amon was twenty-two years old he led the Israelites back into idolatry, and within two years of Amon's reign his servants murdered him.

Josiah followed Amon on the throne. Josiah was eight years old when he came to the throne. When Josiah was older, he began a religious reform destroying the idols and executing the Canaanite priests.

2nd Kings 23:21-25 "Then the king commanded all the people saying, 'Keep the Passover to the Lord your God, as it is written in the book of the covenant.' Such a Passover surely has never been held since the days of the judges who judged Israel, nor in all the days of the kings of Israel and the kings of Judah. But in the eighteenth year of King Josiah, this Passover was held before the Lord in Jerusalem. Moreover Josiah put away those who consulted mediums and spiritists the household gods and idols, all the abominations that were seen in the land of Judah and in Jerusalem, that he might perform the words of the law which were written in the book that Hilkiah the priest found in the house of the Lord.

Now before him there was no king like him, who turned to the Lord with all his heart, with all his soul, and with all his might, according to the Law of Moses; nor after him did any arise like him."

Joahaz followed Josiah on the throne of Judah and was king for three months, and then he was taken to Egypt for the rest of his life. Jehoiakim succeeded Joahaz and reigned from 609 to 598 B.C.

Nebuchadnezzar the king of Babylon when his father died around 605 B.C. demanded that Jehoiakim of Judah swear allegiance to him and pay tribute. At that time Nebuchadnezzar also took some of the young princes of Israel to Babylon as exiles, including Daniel.

In 597 B.C., Jehoiakim rebelled and allied Judah with Egypt, and Nebuchadnezzar's army captured Jerusalem. They put Jehoiakim in prison and placed his son, Jehoiachin, on the throne of Judah. Nebuchadnezzar moved his army against Egypt, and Jehoiachin rebelled against Nebuchadnezzar against the advice of Jeremiah the prophet. Nebuchadnezzar returned to Jerusalem and exiled Jehoiachin, his family, servants, and princes, including Ezekiel to Babylon. Nebuchadnezzar controlled Judah, and he placed Jehoiachin's uncle Zedekiah on the throne of Judah.

2nd Kings 24:8-12 "Jehoiachin was eighteen years old when he became king, and he reigned in Jerusalem three months. His mother's name was Nehushta, the daughter of Elnathan of Jerusalem. And he did evil in the sight of the Lord, according to all that his father had done.'

The servants of Nebuchadnezzar came up against Jerusalem, and the city was besieged. Nebuchadnezzar came against the city, as his servants were besieging it. Then Jehoiachin king of Judah, his mother, his servants, his princes, and his officers went out to the king of Babylon; and He became a prisoner.

Zedekiah was the last king of Judah, and he reigned for eleven years. Zedekiah sent two young men to ask for the help of Jeremiah the prophet, because Nebuchadnezzar made war against Jerusalem. Zedekiah wanted Jeremiah to plead with the Lord for help, but Zedekiah did not receive the message he wanted from the Lord the Lord decided to send them into exile in Babylon.

God's punishment would be severe, but it would have a lasting effect on his people. Jeremiah's answer to Zedekiah is recorded in chapter 21 of Jeremiah. The Lord would not help Judah, and in fact, would fight against Judah. The Lord's anger and wrath against Judah was great because of their idolatrous ways.

Jeremiah 21:8-10 "Now you shall say to this people, "Thus saith the Lord: Behold, I set before you the way of life and the way of death. He who remains in this city shall die by the sword, by famine, and by pestilence; but he who goes, out and defects to the Chaldeans who besiege you, he shall live, and his life shall be as a prize to him. For I have set my face against this city for adversity and not for good," says the Lord. "It shall be given into the hand of the king of Babylon, and he shall burn it with fire."

The Babylonians quickly captured the nation of Judah except for the walled city of Jerusalem. They laid a siege against Jerusalem that lasted for several months, and then in the summer of 586 B.C. the Babylonians broke through the walls. Zedekiah was forced to watch the execution of his sons, and then they put out his eyes. He was then put in chains and taken to Babylon where he died in prison.

The Lord had two major complaints against Israel and Judah. The first was idolatry, and His second complaint was greed, selfishness and pride, which caused them to oppress their own countrymen. The Lord stated that they were wicked men full of evil deeds who were liars, and they were waiting to trap anyone they could. Jeremiah wrote about the prophets lying and the leaders and priests ruling by their own authority instead of the law of the Lord, and the people loved it that way. The Lord promised that he would not completely destroy his people. They would be exiled, then after the exile, some would return to Jerusalem. The wicked people from Judah, such as King Zedekiah, were dealt with by the sword, plague and famine when the Babylonian's destroyed the city of Jerusalem in 586 B.C.

The exile of the people of Judah was to last for 70 years, and then they would be allowed to return to Jerusalem. When the people did return to Jerusalem, they were allowed to take the things that had been taken from the temple.

In chapter 23, Jeremiah wrote about a day when the Lord would raise up a righteous king. The righteous king refers to Jesus Christ the Messiah who would rule wisely and do what is just and right. Jeremiah refers to Jesus as a branch. (Jeremiah 23:5-8, 33:15, Isaiah 4:2,11:1) The branch comes up from the stump of a tree; David was that stump. Christ was the descendant of David (Mt 1:1) who would restore the throne of David. In Matthew 2:1-2 the Magi saw his star in the east and recognized the sign as the birth of the King of the Jews.

Before the exiles returned to Jerusalem, the combined nations of the Medes and Persians conquered the Babylonian empire, fulfilling the word of the Lord. In Jeremiah 30, Jeremiah prophesied of a time when the Lord would restore Israel and Judah to the land. This was a promise of restoration to the fellowship of the Lord and, most likely, a prophecy with dual meaning. The first was a prophecy of the return of the exiles to Jerusalem after 70 years, and instead of serving Babylon, they would serve the Lord. The second was a prophecy of Messianic fulfillment; Christ the King would sit on David's throne when He came to establish His spiritual kingdom.

The Lord had promised to discipline his people with justice, but he would not completely destroy them. The Lord would leave a remnant of the Jews through whom Jesus the Messiah would come. Christ was born in the first century A.D. and His parents Mary and Joseph were both descendants of David. The people during the time of the Old Testament lived by faith in God but they did not receive the things that were promised while they were living—they saw them by faith in the distant future. They longed for a better country—a heavenly city that God had prepared for them.

In Jeremiah 23:5-6, Jeremiah wrote about a righteous branch of David, referring to the birth of Christ. In Jeremiah 33:15, Jeremiah set the time of the beginning of the restoration when he wrote: *"In those days, at that time, I will make a righteous branch sprout from David's line."* This is the time in history when Christ would be born in the first century A.D. The remnant would provide an ancestor of David through whom Christ would come. The Israelite people from Judah would spend seventy years in Babylon, and in the latter years of their time there, the Persians would conquer Babylon, and Cyrus, the king of Persia, would allow some of the exiles to return to Jerusalem and build another temple.

The Persians and Medes treated the Jews well during their captivity. The exiled Jews experienced a time of cleansing and restoration of their hearts to the Lord. The Lord said he would forgive the remnant he spared. The remnant refers to the Jews who remained faithful in their hearts to the Lord. Jeremiah ended writing about the fall of Jerusalem while Zedekiah was king over Judah. Jehoachin, a former king of Judah who was exiled to Babylon and imprisoned, was freed from prison and was given a seat of honor at the king's table and received an allowance for the rest of his life.

The birth line of Jesus began with Adam and passed through Abraham and the Patriarchs to King David, and at the time of the exile of Judah to Babylon, the lineage of Jesus went as far as Josiah, the seventeenth king of Judah. The lineage of Christ continued among the exiles of Judah who would remain in Babylon for seventy years and then would return to Jerusalem.

As we continue to read about God's redeeming plan, we will go into more detail about prophecies of Daniel. In the book of Daniel we jumped ahead of the history of the Jews that were destined to return to Jerusalem in the books of Ezra and Nehemiah.

Book of Ezra—Return Of The Exiles To Judea

The Medes and Persians defeated Babylon during the time of the exile, and the Jews were under the rule of the Medes and Persians. During the reign of King Cyrus of Persia, Cyrus let the people of Judah return to Jerusalem. Cyrus became a part of God's divine plan for the Jews.

The Lord influenced Cyrus in such a way that he was moved to fulfill Jeremiah's prophecy of the return of the Jews.

The Lord commanded Cyrus to build Him a house in Jerusalem, so the family heads of the tribes of Judah and Benjamin, the priests and Levites, and all the people who were anxious to help would return to Jerusalem to build another temple of the Lord.

Cyrus gave the silver and gold articles taken from Solomon's temple to Sheshbazzar, the prince of Judah, to take back to Jerusalem with him. The Jews began their return in 537-538 B.C. As they returned, the people settled in their homes and rebuilt the altar for burnt sacrifices and sacrificed to the Lord. Worship to the Lord was restored in Jerusalem.

Ezra 2:64-67 "The whole assembly together was forty two thousand three hundred and sixty, besides their male and female servants, of whom there were seven thousand three hundred and thirty seven; and they had two hundred men and women singers.'

"Their horses were seven hundred and thirty six, their mules two hundred and forty five, their camels four hundred and thirty five, and their donkeys six thousand seven hundred and twenty."

The Jewish exiles who returned to Jerusalem were people who had lived well in Babylon and Persia and had amassed great wealth as indicated by the animals they brought with them. The people who returned were of high intellect and talented people who were able to rebuild their civilization and practice their religion freely. The people banded together in unity determined to restore the city of Jerusalem and the temple of the Lord.

Among those who returned to Jerusalem was a Levitical priest named Zerubbabel. He and some of the other Jews were determined to re-establish the sacrifices of worship to the Lord in a new temple. The Jews were very liberal in their offerings for the work. First they built an altar for sacrifices on the site of the first temple and later laid out the foundations for a new temple.

When the people from Samaria who were Israelites from the former northern kingdom heard about the building of the temple, they offered to help, but Zerubbabel and the leading families of the Jews refused their help. They didn't want to have any association with the people of Samaria. The Samaritans were a mixture of the northern tribes of Israel and the Gentiles. There were bad feelings between the people of the southern kingdom and the northern kingdom of Israel. The Samaritans forcefully opposed the re-building of the temple, so the work ceased until the second year of the reign of Darius over Persia in 520 B.C.

Then the prophet Haggai delivered the word of the Lord to Zerubbabel. The message from the Lord encouraged the people to work hard to complete the rebuilding of the temple.

Haggai 2:1-9 "In the seventh month on the twenty-first of the month, the word of the Lord came by Haggai the prophet, saying: Speak now to Zerubbabel the son of Shealtiel, governor of Judah, and to Joshua the son of Jehozadak, the high priest, and to the remnant of the people, saying: "Who is left among you who saw this temple in its former glory?

And how do you see it now? In comparison with it, is this not in your eyes as nothing?" Yet now be strong, Zerubbabel,' says the Lord; and be strong, Joshua, son of Jehozadak, the high priest; and be strong, all you people of the land,' says the Lord, 'and work; for I am with you,' says the Lord of hosts. According to the word that I covenanted with you when you came out of Egypt, so My Spirit remains among you; do not fear!'

For thus says the Lord of hosts: 'Once more (it is a little while) I will shake heaven and earth, the sea and dry land; and I will shake all nations, and they shall come to the Desire of All Nations, and I will fill this temple with glory,' says the Lord of hosts. 'The silver is Mine, and the gold is Mine,' says the Lord of hosts. 'The glory of this latter temple shall be greater than the former,' says the Lord of hosts. 'And in this place I will give peace,' says the Lord of hosts."

Haggai's messages stirred up the people to complete the rebuilding of the temple. He encouraged the people by assuring them that they would be successful, because the Lord was with them. Haggai preached during a period of four months in 520 B.C. The temple was completed in 516 B.C. when Darius the Mede was reigning over Persia.

Ezra, the priest, was sent to Jerusalem in 458 B.C. He was well educated in the scriptures and taught the Law of Moses to the people who returned from Persia.

The priests, singers and temple servants also returned to Jerusalem, and temple worship was restored in the seventh year of King Artaxerxes, king of Persia.

Zechariah was a priest and a prophet who prophesied to the people who were returning to Jerusalem at the end of the exile.

Zechariah encourages the people to return their hearts to the Lord, and he made them realize that they had deserved to be exiled, because they had turned away from the Lord God of Israel.

Zechariah rekindled their belief in a Messiah (Christ) who would come and bring eternal peace to God's people.

Nehemiah

Ezra led a group of the Jews back to Jerusalem around 458 B.C. to rebuild the temple and restore the worship of the Lord in the hope that the kingdom would be restored like it was in the time of David. Nehemiah led a group back to Jerusalem to rebuild the walls of the city of Jerusalem. The book of Nehemiah records the restoration of these walls. The great walls of a city were the city's best protection against their enemies.

In the twentieth year of King Artaxerxes, there was a Jew named Nehemiah who was the cupbearer for the king. He had the responsibility of tasting the king's wine, a position of great trust. Nehemiah served King Artaxerxes during the period of 465-424 B.C. It was during this time that Nehemiah learned of the desolate state Jerusalem was in. He asked King Artaxerxes for permission to go to Jerusalem to help rebuild the city and its walls, and the king agreed he could go. God's plan to preserve a remnant of the Jews for the birth of Christ was renewed in the Jews that returned from the exile.

Nehemiah 2:1-6 "And it came to pass in the month of Nisan, in the twentieth year of King Artaxerxes, when wine was before him, that I took the wine and gave it to the king. Now I had never been sad in his presence before."

Therefore the king said to me, "Why is your face sad, since you are not sick? This is nothing but sorrow of heart." So I became dreadfully afraid and said to the king, "May the king live forever! Why should my face not be sad, when the city the place of my father's tombs lie's waste, and its gates are burned with fire? Then the king said to me, "What do you request? So I prayed to the God of heaven.

And I said to the king, "If it pleases the king, and if your servant has found favor in your sight, I ask that you send me to Judah, to the city of my fathers tombs, that I may rebuild it."

Then the king said to me (the queen also sitting beside him), "How long will your journey be?" "And when will you return?" So it pleased the king and I set him a time.

The king gave Nehemiah permission to go back to Jerusalem. He also gave him lumber to rebuild the gates. When Nehemiah arrived in Jerusalem, he surveyed the damage to the walls. Then he went to the people and told them how God had blessed him in the king allowing him to go back to Jerusalem, and he told them what he had observed in surveying the walls. Then the people said, "Let us rise up and build." Then they set their hands to this good work. (Nehemiah 2:18)

Sanballat, an official in Samaria who had married into an Israelite family, wanted control of Judea and he was against the rebuilding of the walls of Jerusalem. When Sanballat heard that the Jews were rebuilding the walls, he tried to hinder the work.

Nehemiah 4:1-3 "But it so happened, when Sanballat heard that we were rebuilding the wall, that he was furious and very indignant, and mocked the Jews. And he spoke before his brethren and the army of Samaria, and said, "What are these feeble Jews doing? Will they fortify themselves?" will they offer sacrifices? Will they complete it in a day? Will they revive the stones from the heaps of rubbish—stones that are burned? Now Tobias the Ammonite was beside him, and he said, "Whatever they build, even if a fox goes up on it he will breakdown their stone wall."

Nehemiah made no reply to Sanballat, but he prayed to the Lord, "Hear, O our God, for we are despised turn their reproach on their own heads, and give them as plunder to a land of captivity! Do not cover their iniquity and do not let their sin be blotted out from before you; for they have provoked You to anger before the builders." So we built the wall, and the entire wall was joined together up to half its height, for the people had a mind to work." (Nehemiah 4:4-6)

The Jews continued to work on the wall in spite of opposition from their enemies, and the wall was completed in 52 days. The people of the nations around Jerusalem were disheartened, because they realized that the Lord had helped Judah re-build the walls.

Book of Daniel

The book of Daniel is a source of the history of the exiles from Judah for the seventy years they were in captivity until their return to Jerusalem. The theme of the book of Daniel is the sovereignty of God and His triumph over the kingdoms of men.

The people of Judah became known as Jews while they were in Babylon. They were allowed to raise families as long as they didn't rebel against the Babylonian rulers. The Jews could not worship the way they did in the temple in Jerusalem, but they worshiped the Lord in their hearts.

Daniel and Ezekiel were among the young princes of Judah who were taken to Babylon in 605 B.C. before the exile of Judah. Both young men became prophets during the exile. Daniel prophesied about God's plan of redemption. The Babylonians held Daniel in high esteem, because the Lord had given him special gifts of prophesying and interpreting dreams.

The Lord spoke through Daniel about future events in history and events concerning the future spiritual kingdom of Christ.

The Lord had purposed that the Jews would return to Jerusalem, rebuild the walls of the city, build another temple, and serve Him in Jerusalem as they waited for the birth of the Messiah and His kingdom. The prophecies of Daniel and Jeremiah reinforced the faith and hope for God's people to return to Jerusalem.

A man by the name of Nebuchadnessar was king over Babylon. One night the king had a dream, and he was so troubled by his dream that he couldn't sleep. The king's astrologers, wise men, and magicians in the kingdom could not explain the king's dreams. Daniel was chief over the magicians, astrologers, Chaldeans and soothsayers, because God had blessed him with knowledge, understanding and the ability to interpret dreams, solve riddles and explain enigmas, so the king sent for Daniel and asked him if he could interpret his dreams. Daniel told the king that he couldn't interpret them, but his God could.

That very night, the meaning of the king's dream was revealed to Daniel, and Daniel was able to interpret the king's dreams. Daniel praised God for revealing deep and mysterious things to him. He understood that God would control world events by deposing and establishing the kings he wanted on the throne and that God would give wisdom to the wise.

Daniel told the king what he had dreamed, and then he explained the interpretation of the dream. In Nebuchadnezzar's dream he saw a huge statue of a man that frightened him. The head of the statue was made of gold, the chest and arms were silver, its belly and thighs were bronze, the legs were iron and the feet were a mixture of clay and iron. Daniel told the king that the head of gold represented the king of Babylon. He told Nebuchadnezzar that God is Sovereign over heaven and earth and that it was He who made the kings who rule over the earth.

Daniel, still interpreting the king's dream, said that the kingdom of Babylon would be replaced by another kingdom. The chest and arms of silver in the dream represented that kingdom. Then a third kingdom, represented by a bronze belly and thighs, would replace the second kingdom. A fourth kingdom, represented by iron and miry clay, would replace the third kingdom, and it would crush all previous kingdoms and be strong like iron. The kingdoms represented in the dream were kingdoms that would arise in this order after Babylon: the Medo-Persian Empire, the Greek Empire and the Roman Empire. The Roman Empire would be the last and most significant kingdom, because during the time of that empire Jesus the Son of God would be born in Bethlehem.

From world history, we know that the king's dream proved that God decided who would be king over the Babylonian, Persian, Greek and Roman Empires that existed in succession. The most important part of the interpretation of the dream was that during the time of the Roman Empire, Christ's kingdom, the church, would be established according to God's timing. Also, in the days of the last kingdom in the dream, the Roman Empire, the God of heaven would set up a kingdom on earth, which shall never be destroyed. The kingdom of Christ's church will remain forever. The dream is certain, and its interpretation is sure.

Belshazzar King of Babylon

After the death of Nebuchadnezzar, a man named Belshazzar became king over Babylon. *Daniel 5:1-2 "Belshazzar the king made a great feast for a thousand of his lords, and drank wine in the presence of the thousand. While he tasted the wine, Belshazzar gave the command to bring the gold and silver vessels which, his father Nebuchadnezzar had taken from the temple which had been in Jerusalem, that the king and his lords, his wives, and his concubines might drink from them."*

King Belshazzar insulted God when he and his guests drank wine from the gold and silver vessels that were taken from God's temple in Jerusalem. As a result, God responded to Belshazzar's insult. As the king and his guests were drinking from the gold and silver vessels in the great room where the feast was held, the fingers of a man's hand appeared on the wall and wrote a message to the king. *"Then the king's countenance changed, and his thoughts troubled him, so that the joints of his hips were loosened and his knees knocked against each other."* (Daniel 5:6)

The king was afraid of God's power and he called for his wise men to explain the writing on the wall, but no one could explain what was meant by the message. The queen told the king, "There is a man in your kingdom in whom is the Spirit of the Holy God." She told him that during the time that his father Nebuchadnezzar was king, Daniel had interpreted his dreams. So Daniel was brought before the king to explain the meaning of the writing on the wall.

"This is the inscription that was written: Mene, Mene, Tekel, Upharsin. This is the interpretation of each word. Mene: God has numbered your kingdom, and finished it; Tekel: You have been weighed in the balance and found wanting; Peres (singular for Up-Harsin): your kingdom has been divided, and given to the Medes and Persians."

Then Belshazzar gave the command, the clothed Daniel with purple and put a chain of gold around his neck, and made a proclamation that he should be the third ruler in the kingdom. That very night Belshazzar was slain. And Darius, the Mede, received the kingdom. (Daniel 5:25-30)

The Medes And The Persians Rule Babylon

According to history, the Medo-Persian Empire followed the Babylonian Empire. An alliance between the Medes and the Persians enabled them to conquer Babylon in 558 B.C. The Persians were more influential and powerful than the Medes, but King Darius the Mede, was the great conqueror that took the city of Babylon.

Later in the history of the Medes and Persians, Cyrus the Great took the throne of Media and Persia including the former Babylonian Empire. Cyrus was wise and generous, and he permitted the Jews to return to Jerusalem. The prophet Isaiah wrote about Cyrus the Great in the book of Isaiah. The Lord made Cyrus an instrument in His hands to accomplish His will on earth, especially in regards to God's people in exile.

The Lord called Cyrus His anointed and disclosed that He, the Lord, called Cyrus by name even though Cyrus did not know the Lord. The Lord said to Cyrus by the pen of Isaiah in *Isaiah 45:5-7 "I am the Lord and there is no other; there is no God besides Me. I will gird you though you have not known Me, that they may know from the rising of the sun to its setting that there is none besides Me. I am the Lord; there is no other; I form the light and create darkness, I make peace and create calamity; I the Lord do all these things.*

Isaiah 45:12-13 "I have made the earth, and created man on it. I—My hands—stretched out the heavens, And all their host I have commanded. I have raised him up in righteousness, and I will direct all of his ways; He shall build My city and let My exiles go free. Not for price nor reward," Says the Lord of hosts."

The fall of Jerusalem took place in 586 B.C. Cyrus issued the decree to free the Jews as Isaiah prophesied in 516 B.C., 70 years after their exile. Darius accepted the God of Daniel and even accepted His sovereignty over the rulers of the earth. Cyrus the Persian reigned with Darius over the former Babylonian Kingdom, and Cyrus also recognized the Lord. Cyrus was an instrument in God's hand's to be a part of God's redeeming plan by helping the Jewish people return to Jerusalem and re-establish their religion.

Vision of Four Beasts (Daniel 7)

When Daniel was in captivity in Babylon, God revealed to Daniel the future history of great kingdoms that would exist before the kingdom of Christ. The fourth kingdom, the Roman Empire, would control the people of the earth at the time of the birth of Jesus.

To Paraphrase Daniel 7:1-14: In Daniel's dream he saw visions of four great beasts and he wrote down what he saw. The beasts represented kingdoms of men. After the four beasts, Daniel saw one like the Son of Man (Jesus) coming with the clouds of heaven! To Him was given dominion and glory and a kingdom where all peoples, nations, and languages should serve Him.

His dominion would be an everlasting dominion, which shall not pass away, and His kingdom will be one, which shall not be destroyed. Daniel asked for an explanation of what he saw, and he was told the interpretation of the things he saw. The great beasts represented four kingdoms.

He said: "The fourth beast shall be a fourth kingdom on earth, Which shall be different from all other kingdoms, And shall devour the whole earth, Trample it and break it in pieces. The ten horns are ten kings who shall arise from this kingdom. And another shall arise after them; He shall be different from the first ones, And shall subdue three kings. He shall speak pompous words against the Most High, Shall persecute the saints of the Most High, And shall intend to change times and law."

Then the saints shall be given into his hand For a time times and half a time. But the court shall be seated, and they shall take away his dominion, and the greatness of the kingdoms under the whole heaven shall be given to the people, the saints of the Most High. His kingdom is an everlasting kingdom, and all dominions shall serve and obey Him."

Daniel saw a vision of God that is described as the Ancient of Days, the Sovereign of all creation, and the One who judges all the people of the earth.

The four successive empires represented as beasts are: (1) the Babylonian Empire (lion) that exiled the kingdom of Judah, (2) the Persian Empire (bear) that allowed the people of Judah to return to Jerusalem and helped them in their efforts to restore their nation and their religion, (3) the Greek Empire (leopard) under the rule of Alexander the Great that conquered the world and spread Greek culture and the Greek language all over the world making communication among the peoples of the world possible, (4) the Roman Empire (the terrifying beast) that allowed the Jews to live in the Roman Empire as long as they paid taxes to Rome.

The influence of all of these Empires helped to make favorable conditions on earth for the birth of the Jewish Messiah (Jesus) to be born at the right time during the Roman Empire and establish the Kingdom of God, a spiritual kingdom that will exist forever. The reference to the four beasts are given to show how other nations would affect the lives of God's people throughout history and at the time Jesus was born.

Three beasts (the Babylonian, Persian and Greek Empires) had already been stripped of their power when Daniel saw the slaying of the fourth beast, the Roman Empire. The Roman Empire cruelly persecuted God's people. Daniel saw one like the son of man (Christ) and God gave Him authority, glory and Sovereign power over all peoples of the earth. Christ's kingdom was established in the first century A.D. and will exist on earth until Christ returns at an unknown time. Christ's kingdom (church) was established in the first century A.D.

Christ is now in heaven at the right hand of God ruling over His creation and His kingdom the church, but He will return some day to glorify His people. At that time all of the kingdoms of this world will be destroyed, and God's people will inherit a new heaven and a new earth in a heaven God has prepared for them. *Revelation 21 "Now I saw a new heaven and a new earth, for the first heaven and the first earth has passed away."* The church on the earth, which is the kingdom of God, will at the end of time be given a new home somewhere in God's heavens. The existing earth will be destroyed by fire at that time.

The vision Daniel saw was prophetic, a prediction that the worldly empires would fall. The mighty empires are like pawns in the hands of God who can do as He wills with them. God's glorious kingdom will prevail over all kingdoms when Christ the King of Kings comes back to gather up His church and take it to the new heaven and earth, therefore the Kingdom of God shall never be destroyed. Today the church on earth represents the Kingdom of God.

The battle for the hearts and souls of mankind is a spiritual battle that continues and will continue until Christ returns.

The account of God's redeeming plan in the Old Testament ends with the books of the two prophets Zechariah and Malachi. Zechariah wrote about the coming of Christ, His humanity, His rejection and His betrayal. He predicts Christ's crucifixion, His priesthood, and His kingship.

Zechariah had a vision of a man on a red horse. Behind this man were red, brown and white horses. The horses were sent by the Lord on a mission throughout the earth to search out the condition of the people.

The man on the red horse may have been the angel of the Lord, and the other horses may have represented angelic messengers who reported to the angel of the Lord. The messengers represented by the horses reported that the whole earth was at peace.

The angel asked the Lord how long he would withhold mercy from Jerusalem and Judah. The insinuation is that if the Lord was merciful and would soon return his people to Jerusalem. The people of Judah had been in exile for sixty-six years, but they would begin returning in four more years. The Lord said He would return to Jerusalem with mercy, and his house would be rebuilt. The people did return and rebuild the temple at the end of the seventy years of exile because of the influence the Lord had on King Cyrus of Persia.

In chapter 2 of the book of Zechariah, Zechariah sees a man with a measuring line to measure Jerusalem. Jerusalem was going to be rebuilt by the returning exiles, and its size would surpass that of the old city. The city of Jerusalem was to be rebuilt by human hands.

In chapter 3:1-7 the angel showed Zechariah a scene in heaven, a court scene in which Joshua, the high priest, was standing before the Lord for judgment. Satan was there to accuse Joshua. The Lord rebuked Satan and told him that Jerusalem was a chosen city. Joshua, representing Israel, is described as a burning stick that was taken out of the fire. The burning stick removed from the fire refers to the Jews who were exiled to Babylon but would return to Jerusalem.

The angel said he would put rich garments on Israel, a symbol of a return to righteousness. Jesus would be born, and at the end of His ministry He would be crucified to restore righteousness by providing forgiveness for sin. The angel stood by while Joshua was clothed in clean garments. The angel of the Lord told Joshua that God would give him a place in heaven if he would walk in His ways and keep His requirements.

Joshua and his fellow priests were men who symbolized things to come. In the book of Revelation, those dressed in white symbolize those who will be in heaven (Rev 3:4, 18, 6:11, 7:9,13, 4:4, 19:14). This indicates that this prophecy probably had a dual fulfillment. The first would represent the return of the exiles to Jerusalem to rebuild the temple and restore worship and obedience to the law. The future fulfillment would be the coming of Christ who would come to redeem sinners for the new heaven and new earth.

In Zechariah 3:8 the Lord Almighty promised to bring forth '*My Servant the Branch.*' This was God's promise to send His Son to the earth. The word 'Branch' is a Messianic title for Christ (Isaiah 4:2, 11:1).

Jeremiah 23:5, 33:15). In the 9th verse the Lord said, *"Behold the stone that I have laid before Joshua: upon the stone are seven eyes. Behold I will engrave its inscription,"* says the Lord of hosts. *"And I will remove the iniquity of that land in one day."* The day He was speaking of was the day that Christ would die on the cross.

The Lord indicated that in that day there would be peace, security and contentment. When Jesus was born, the world was under the rule of the Roman Empire, and the Jews were free to practice their religion. They were secure in their land as long as they did not rebel against Rome. Zechariah was writing about the Christian age when the branch (Christ) would come and offer forgiveness for sin. God could then be at peace with His people.

In chapter 4 of Zechariah, Zechariah saw a golden lamp stand and two olive trees. In the book of Revelation, golden lamp stands are associated with heaven, and lamps associated with the Holy Spirit (Rev 1:12, 4:4-5).

Zechariah asked the angel who was talking to him what the golden lamp stand and two olive trees were, and the angel said they were the word of God by the Holy Spirit to Zerubbabel. Zerubbabel was the grandson of King Jehoiachin, and he and Joshua were leaders in the rebuilding of the temple by the exiles from Babylon.

The word of God is given to man by the power of the Holy Spirit of God. The two olive branches were the two who were anointed to serve the Lord of all the earth. Zerubbabel, who was from David's lineage, and Joshua, the priest, were the two anointed by the Holy Spirit to serve the Lord in the rebuilding of the temple. Christ was the ultimate fulfillment of this symbolism; He was from the royal line of David, He was to be both king and high priest, and He was anointed by the Holy Spirit to preach the word of God.

In chapter 5 Zechariah saw a flying scroll and a woman in a basket. The flying scroll symbolizes the law or word of God. The scroll represents a judgment against those who did not obey the word of God. The land of Judah would be purged of sinners. The reason for the exile was to purge the land of sin and restore fellowship with God.

In chapter 6:9-15, the crowning of Joshua, the high priest, is a symbolic oracle relating to Christ, the high Priest and King. The man whose name is 'the Branch' is Jesus (Isaiah 4:2, Ezekiel 17:22, Jeremiah 33:15-16)). The Branch would build the temple of the Lord. There were four Jewish temples, three of which were: Solomon's temple, Zerrubbabel's temple built by the exiles, and Herod's temple that was destroyed in 70 A.D. The fourth temple is the church, a spiritual temple built by Christ in the first century.

The definition of the temple is a place on earth where the presence of God resides. Jesus said, "Destroy this temple, and I will raise it again in three days." Jesus was speaking of his body. The Father lives in Jesus and Jesus lives in our hearts, and we are members of the kingdom of God.

Chapters 9 through 14 contain more oracles about the coming of the Messiah and the Messiah's Kingdom. The judgment of Israel's enemies was seen in the light of the coming of Christ, the Prince of Peace. The first oracle is about judgment on Israel's enemies. The kingdoms in particular are listed in chapter 9, verses 1-8, and the judgment occurred after the exiles had returned. Some historians consider the conquests of Alexander the Great to be a fulfillment of this prophecy. Alexander spared the city of Jerusalem and the temple during his conquest.

Zechariah 9:9-17 is about the Messiah King who would come with righteousness and salvation riding on a colt, the foal of a donkey.

The fulfillment of this prophecy was announced when Christ triumphantly entered Jerusalem (Mt 21:1-5). Christ's kingdom would be a universal kingdom of peace, a spiritual kingdom that is not of this world. Jesus told his disciples that they did not belong to the world even though he chose them out of the world (John 15:19).

John 18: 36 "Jesus answered, "My kingdom is not of this world. If my kingdom were of this world, My servants would fight, so that I should not be delivered to the Jews; but now my kingdom is not from here."

The kingdom of Christ is in the hearts of believers, and Christ rules from heaven over their hearts. People of any nation can enter the kingdom of God and find peace with God there. The Kingdom of God, the Kingdom of Heaven, and the Kingdom of Christ are synonymous.

Zechariah 10:8-12: The Lord promises to re-gather Israel, his scattered people, and redeem them. Redemption began when Christ died on the cross. This prophecy also has a dual meaning. As before, some of this prophecy is relevant to the history of the Jews after they returned to Jerusalem from exile, and some of the prophecies predict the ultimate salvation offered by the Messiah.

Zechariah 11:1-3: These verses predict devastation against the Israelites by describing the destruction of its trees. A fire of judgment would consume the ungodly people of the Lord. The Romans slaughtered the Jewish nation, the city of Jerusalem, and the temple in A.D. 70.

A siege was laid on Jerusalem and was followed by the destruction of the city and slaughter of the Jews. God predicted the attack against Jerusalem, but He did not provoke it.

The cause of the destruction was the rejection of the Messiah by the Jewish nation. The Jewish Zealots were responsible for the destruction by rising up in opposition against the Romans.

Zechariah 11:7-17: The prophet spoke of a payment of thirty pieces of silver and of the end of the good shepherd. This is a foreshadowing of the price paid to Judas for betraying Christ, which led to his arrest, trial and crucifixion. This took place about five hundred years after Zechariah wrote about it.

Matthew: 27:3-7 "Then Judas, His betrayer, seeing that he had been condemned, was remorseful and brought back the thirty pieces of silver to the chief priests and elders saying' "I have sinned by betraying innocent blood."

And they said, "What is that to us? You see to it!" Then he threw down the pieces of silver in the temple and departed, and went out and hanged himself. But the chief priests took the silver pieces and said it is not lawful to put them into the treasury, because they are the price of blood. And they consulted together and bought with them the potters field, to bury strangers in."

Zechariah prophesied about Christ, a messianic shepherd, who would be rejected by the Jewish nation but would be embraced by many of the Jewish people and even some of the Gentiles. The national unity of Israel was broken. (11:14: Then I cut into my other staff, bonds that I might break the brotherhood between Judah and Israel.)

The Law of Moses was replaced by the gospel of Christ, and God's people would be those who would have faith in Christ as the Savior. The church, a spiritual temple, replaced the temple built by men.

The people of the Lord's chosen nation of Israel were divided. Christ became the good shepherd of the sheep who would accept Him as the Messiah.

Zechariah presented a picture of the rejection of the Messiah by many of the Jews in the first century. God promised salvation to Israel and restoration of the land, but due to the rejection by the Jews, the Jews became a people without a land and were scattered throughout the world.

The Lord challenged the faith of the Jews in the first century when Christ came and the gospel of Christ replaced the Law of Moses. The Jews were taught to accept Jesus by faith as the Messiah, but many would not accept Christ. In Zechariah 13 Zechariah describes the gospel of Christ as a fountain for the cleansing of sin and for righteousness. The Apostles and the writers of the New Testament replaced the work of the prophets.

The office of the Apostles ceased in the first century, but the written word of God in the New Testament was complete containing the completion of God's plan to redeem people from the guilt of sin through faith in Christ.

Book of Malachi (400 B.C.)

The Hebrew word Malachi means 'My messenger,' and it describes the function of the prophet rather than his name. The one who wrote the book was a messenger of the Lord, and it was written to a people who had become skeptical of the Lord's promises to them. Malachi is the last of the written prophets, in fact the last of any prophet until the time of John the Baptist in the first century A.D. The date of the writing of Malachi was around 420 to 400 B.C.

After the Jews returned from the Babylonian captivity there was prophetic silence until John the Baptist began his ministry in the first century A.D. The people of Judah had the Old Testament scriptures but they were in a state of sin and apostasy. The priests were ignoring the written word of God. The ministries of Zechariah and Malachi focused on bringing the people back to the Lord. In Malachi, chapter one, the Lord denounces the Jews, His beloved people, because the priests were corrupt and offering polluted sacrifices. The people were guilty of infidelity to God.

The descendants of a faithful remnant of God's people still remained in the first century and they were the people through whom Christ would be born.

Malachi 2:15 "But did He not make them one, having a remnant of the Spirit? And why one? He seeks godly offspring. Therefore take heed to your spirit, and let none deal treacherously with the wife of his youth."

The book of Malachi contains several questions asked by the people and the stern warnings by the Lord. Temple services had been resumed, and sacrifices were being offered, but the priests and people had drifted into a casual attitude of indifference toward worshiping the Lord. Blemished sacrifices were being offered, and the people neglected to tithe. The book deals with the sins of Israel and judgment for the guilty but blessings for those who would repent.

Malachi 1:2-5 the Lord expresses His love for Israel (Jacob). The Lord loved Jacob more than He loved his brother Esau, and He demonstrated His love for Israel and His disdain for Edom, the descendants of Esau. Jacob was faithful to the Lord, and Edom was rebellious.

If the people would return to the Lord with all their heart, they would see what the Lord would do, and they would say, "Great is the Lord." The Lord would prove that he is Great in every part of the world.

Malachi 1:6-14 states that the Lord was both Father and Master to the Israelites, but they had failed to show respect for Him as Father and Master. The priests showed contempt for his name when they offered blind, crippled and diseased animals as sacrifices.

The Lord is great and feared among the nations, and He demands and expects the best sacrifices. The Lord is the Father of mankind and a father deserves honor and love, and Israel had failed to honor, respect and love God their Father.

Admonition for the unfaithful priests is the subject of Malachi 2:1-9. The priests also failed to honor the name of the Lord. Regardless of how often or how great the sacrifice is, if a person's heart is not given from an attitude of faith, hope and love the sacrifice is not acceptable.

The Lord made a covenant with Levi: that all priests would be chosen from the tribe of Levi, a practice that continued throughout the Old Testament covenant. The covenant demanded reverence, and the first priests did revere and stand in awe of the Lord, but the priests who had returned to Jerusalem from the exile failed to revere the name of the Lord. Today all of the Lord's people are priests, and each one must personally honor the Lord from a true heart of faith, hope and love when offering spiritual sacrifices.

As well as offering sacrifices, the priests were messengers of the Lord, and the people sought knowledge and instruction from them. The unfaithful priests caused many people to stumble. If the priests and the people were faithful, the Lord would bless them, and all nations would call them blessed.

Today all Christians are priests and they are required to offer sacrifices *Romans 12:1-2 "I beseech you therefore brethren, by the mercies of God, that you present your bodies a living sacrifice, holy and acceptable to God, which is your reasonable service. And do not be conformed to this world, but be transformed by the renewing of your mind, that you may prove what is that good and acceptable and perfect will of God."*

A follower of Christ offers the rest of their life in obedience to Jesus for an example to the world proving the good, perfect and acceptable will of God. The Lord shows compassion to those who fear and honor His name. He makes a distinction between the righteous and the wicked, between those who serve him and those who do not. The Lord said, "Guard yourself in your spirit and do not break faith." The Lord was seeking godly offspring among his people.

Malachi 3:1-4 states that the Lord promised to send his messenger to prepare the way for the Messiah of Israel and the redeemer of all people of faith. The Messiah would be a descendant of David and would inherit his throne.

Throughout the years following King David's reign, the days of the Kingdom of Heaven had been advancing; they had been drawing nearer and nearer to being fulfilled. When the messenger came, the Messiah whom the Jews were seeking. He would come to cleanse and bring judgment on earth.

John the Baptist was the messenger who came to prepare the way for Christ the Messiah to begin His ministry. John was sent first to get the people ready to welcome the Messiah. He was preaching in the wilderness and baptizing people preparing them to receive Jesus by convicting them of sin. John warned people to repent and be baptized to cleanse them of their sins. When Jesus first came to John in the wilderness, Jesus told the crowd that John was the messenger sent by the Lord.

Malachi 3:5-12 states that the Lord's judgment will come against sorcerers, adulterers, those who swear falsely, and those who cheat their employees, those who oppress the widows and orphans, and those who deny justice to aliens. Malachi mentions the same sins that God hates and which the other prophets wrote about.

The Lord accused the Jews of robbing Him when they robbed His people. He promised the Jews that if they would honor Him honestly with the proper prescribed tithe, He would open the floodgates of heaven and pour out so many blessings that they would not have room for it.

The Lord reminded them that He would not change his mind about the promises He had made to them to send a redeemer. The Lord had punished them for their sins, but He had not destroyed them.

In Malachi 4 The Lord declared that the day is coming when all the arrogant and evildoers will burn like a furnace. He was talking about the final judgment when those who do not know God and those who have not obeyed the gospel of Christ will be punished. *2nd Thess 1:6-10 "Since it is a righteous thing with God to repay with tribulation those who trouble you, and to give you who are troubled rest with us when the Lord Jesus is revealed from heaven with His mighty angels, in flaming fire taking vengeance on those who do not know God, and on those who do not obey the gospel of our*

Lord Jesus Christ. These shall be punished with everlasting destruction from the presence of the Lord and from the glory of His power, when He comes in that Day, to be glorified in His saints and to be admired among all those who believe, because our testimony among you was believed."

The second coming of Christ will be a time to reward those who by faith have accepted God and obeyed the gospel of Christ and will be a time of condemnation and punishment for the wicked.

Luke wrote In Luke 1:78-79 (paraphrased) "Because of the tender mercy of our God, by which the rising sun will come to us from heaven to shine on those living in darkness and in the shadow of death, to guide our feet into the path of peace."

The rising sun symbolizes the Messiah (Jesus Christ) who God was sending to bring peace to those who were separated from the fellowship of God because of sin. The sacrifice of Christ made possible peace with God and redemption to those who were guilty of sin. *Malachi 4:2 The Sun of Righteousness shall arise with healing in his wing.*

Christ is the 'Sun of Righteousness' who came to provide salvation for all people of faith.

There was a period of approximately 400 years after Malachi's ministry before John the Baptist, the first New Testament prophet, was born. Jesus was born soon after the birth of John. When both of them were grown, John began his ministry first in order to prepare the way for Jesus' ministry. Jesus began His ministry around 30 to 35 A.D.

The Birth, Life and Ministry of Jesus

This is the story of Jesus of Nazareth and His life and ministry but not every detail of everything Jesus said or did. I have attempted to present the events of the story of Jesus' life in the order in which they occurred in the scriptures, and I do not claim my listing of events to be in exact chronological order due to the difficulty of following the writings of four different authors telling the same story in their own order and style.

Matthew, Mark, Luke and John each told their own view of the life and ministry of Jesus of Nazareth, the Son of God, and Mary, His mother. Jesus Christ is the Messiah, the Anointed of God, the King and Redeemer of all people of faith. Jesus came through David's line of the Jewish people of Israel in the first century.

Malachi was the last of the Old Testament prophets, and he prophesied about the coming of John the Baptist who would come ahead of Jesus to prepare the minds of the people to accept Jesus Christ as the Messiah.

Malachi 4:2,4-6 (Verse 2) "But for you who revere my name, the sun of righteousness will rise with healing in its wings." (Verses 4-6) "Remember the Law of Moses, My servant, which I commanded Him for all Israel, with the statutes and judgments, behold I will send you Elijah the prophet before the coming of the great and dreadful day of the Lord. And he will turn the hearts of the fathers to the children, and the hearts of the children to their fathers, lest I come and strike the earth with a curse."

The prophet in Malachi 3:1-4 states that the Lord promised to send his messenger to prepare the way for Jesus Christ the Divine Seed. The messenger was John the Baptist who would come with power like the prophet Elijah to prepare the way for Christ. John was sent to baptize the people who by faith were willing to accept Jesus Christ as the Messiah and repent of their sins and submit to water baptism.

Jesus Christ was a descendant of King David, and He would come to be a King in the line of David, and the Sun of Righteousness. Jesus' kingdom would be a spiritual kingdom. Throughout the years following King David's reign, the days of the Kingdom of the promised Christ had been drawing nearer and nearer each year to being fulfilled. When the messenger came in the first century, Jesus the Messiah, whom the Jews were seeking, would also come to bring judgment against sinners and a way to be redeemed from the guilt of sin for those who would have faith in Him. The coming of Jesus would fulfill the promises of God from the time of the Garden of Eden to the end of time.

In the first century A.D. the Jewish people, a small nation, was under the power of the Roman Empire and was subject to Roman law. The people were allowed to have their own king, but the king was appointed or approved by the Romans who had power over them. In 37 BC, Herod Antipater governed the Jews by the authority of the Roman Empire.

The Jewish people were obligated in their religion to continue to keep the Law of Moses until the Messiah came.

Most jews lived in Palestine, Judea, Galilee and Samaria at the time Jesus was born. Under the rule of the Romans, the Jews had religious identity and some freedom under the leadership of their priests.

The high priest served as a magistrate. The Jews were allowed to keep their temple in Jerusalem for religious purposes, and they followed, to some extent, a corrupted view of the Law of Moses.

There were two Jewish religious parties who had different views about obeying the Law of Moses. They were the Pharisees and the Sadducees. They were united in the decision to reject Jesus as the Messiah and conspired to put Him to death.

The Pharisees were a major religious party from the second century BC to the second century AD. The Pharisees were middle class and in touch with the common people, and they accepted the written word to be inspired by God. They believed in the resurrection and an afterlife. They also believed in an appropriate punishment or reward based on the individual.

The Sadducees were an upper class group of Jews who were wealthy and influential and were more concerned with politics than religion. The Sadducees denied life after death, the resurrection and the existence of the spiritual world including angels and demons.

The scribes were writers, copyists and the interpreters of the Law. The scribes served as priests and teachers of the Law and were usually associated with the Pharisees. Some scribes became members of the Sanhedrin, a legal administrative body in the Jewish population. The Scribes were professional students of the Law of Moses and its defenders.

The History of The People of Judah After Their Return From Babylonian Exile And As They Wait For The Coming of the Messiah

The empire that had previous been the Babylonian Empire was now the Persian Empire, because in 332 B.C. the Babylonian Empire had fallen to Alexander the Great. Alexander chose Babylon as his capital. Alexander and his army went to Egypt where he was welcomed, and Alexander built a new city in Egypt called Alexandria. Alexander strengthened his army with Persians, and their borders reached to the plains of India in 326 B.C.

Alexander died on June 13th in 323 B.C. Since the invasion of the Assyrians and Babylonians, the Jewish people had not been able to live as an independent nation politically. After the Jews were allowed to leave Babylon, they struggled for several years dominated by the Persian, Greek, and Roman Empires, and they never again became a great nation like they were under David's rule.

Judea was becoming Hellenistic and the people spoke the Greek language in their political, social and religious life. The Jews were allowed to live in Jerusalem and worship in the temple, but there were many who lived a distance from Jerusalem. The Jews who lived a great distance from Jerusalem worshiped in the synagogue, and at least once a year, they went to the temple in Jerusalem to worship and observe the Jewish feasts. When Alexander died, his empire was divided between four generals of his army.

The Herod family had earlier been converted to Judaism. Herod the Great was born in 72 B.C. and He was the Herod on the throne that ruled in Judea at the time of Jesus' birth. Herod later ordered the slaughter of the male children in Bethlehem in order to procure the death of the infant Jesus.

Herod was the name of a family from Idumaea that ruled in Palestine from 40 B.C. to about A.D. 100. The Romans appointed the Herod's kings of Judea.

There were several Herod's that ruled in line and had authority over Judea where the Jews lived. Archelaus was the next Herod after the death of Herod the Great, but the Romans removed him from the throne after ten years.

Herod Antipas was on the throne in Galilee during the time of John the Baptist. Herod Antipas was the king that had John the Baptist beheaded and opposed Jesus. The territory of Judea included Galilee, Samaria and Judea and the cities and towns within them. Jerusalem and Bethlehem were in Judea. Judea ranged from the Sea of Galilee in the north to the Dead Sea all the way to Zoar. The Jordan River flowed from the Sea of Galilee to the Dead Sea. Judea prospered under the reign of Herod Antipas and he increased trade and built fortresses, aqueducts, and theatres.

Herod began the rebuilding of the Temple and acted as protector and spokesman for various Jewish communities scattered about the world. In the age when the existence of the smaller states depended on the will of Rome, Herod kept Judea safe, secure, and prosperous.

The four gospels, Matthew, Mark, Luke and John, all give an account of the history of the birth of Jesus and His ministry, life, death, and resurrection. The Jewish people were a small nation subject to the laws of the Roman Empire as well as Jewish law.

God appointed the time to send His Son to earth and he sent John the Baptist first. *"I will send my prophet, and he will prepare the way before me."* This was God's promise to send John the Baptist to prepare the way for Jesus. John the Baptist came in the first century A.D. and he lived in the wilderness area of the Jordan River. Christ was born in Bethlehem of Judea during Herod's reign in the first century A.D.

Jesus the Son of God

God's Son came to earth born to a virgin woman by the seed of God—making Him both God and human. He lived on earth as the Son of God in a human form and died as the Son of God in human form, thereby becoming a sacrifice for our sin. Jesus lived approximately 33 years on earth. The story of Jesus' birth, ministry, death, burial and resurrection is in Matthew, Mark, Luke and John. The four gospel books Matthew, Mark, Luke and John tell the story of Jesus of Nazareth and His life and ministry.

During the time before and after the first century A.D, the Jewish people were allowed to maintain their temple in Jerusalem and practice their religion based on the Law of Moses. The Jewish temple in Jerusalem was the focal point of Jewish religion, but there were also other meeting places of worship called synagogues scattered throughout the land in places that were a distance from Jerusalem. The people who lived a distance from Jerusalem could go to the Synagogue to worship God on the Sabbath day. Once a year they would all go to the temple in Jerusalem to worship.

The temple in Jerusalem was a focal point for Jesus ministry. There was still a remnant of faithful God-fearing Jews on earth who had been patiently waiting for the Messiah but the religion of the Jews had become corrupted and divided. Jesus was born in Bethlehem a few months after the birth of John. At the time of Jesus birth, Herod the Great was on the throne in Judea.

Most of the story of Jesus in the New Testament took place in Galilee. Joseph and Mary lived in Nazareth of Galilee.

Jesus was a descendant of King David, and He left heaven and was born on earth to become a spiritual King in the line of David over a spiritual kingdom. Throughout the years following King David's reign, the time of the Kingdom of Christ had been drawing nearer and nearer to being fulfilled each year. When the messenger John the Baptist came in the first century the Messiah whom the Jews were seeking also came to bring judgment against sinners and provide a way for those who would have faith in Him to be redeemed from the guilt of sin.

John the Baptist was the messenger that Malachi prophesied would come to prepare the way for Christ. Jesus Christ was the promised Jewish Messiah and the redeemer of all people who accepted Him by faith and obeyed His commandments. John preached about Jesus and he baptized the people who were willing to repent of their sins and accept Jesus as the Son of God. John was called the Baptist, because he baptized people.

John the Baptist was born approximately 400 years after the prophet Malachi's ministry. John the Baptist and Christ were both born during the reign of Herod in the first century A.D. John was born first and his ministry preceded Jesus, because he was to prepare the way for Jesus, the Messiah.

The parents of John the Baptist, Zacharias and Elizabeth, were chosen by the Lord. They were righteous people who obeyed all the commandments and ordinances of the Lord. John's birth was miraculous because Elizabeth was very old and beyond the age to conceive. Zacharias and Elizabeth lived in the hill country of Hebron. They were Levites, and Zacharias was a priest who served in the temple at Jerusalem. His duty was to burn incense in the Holy Place in the temple. Zacharias had been praying for a son for a long time.

Around the first century A.D. it became Zacharias' turn to offer the incense. He was an old man and had waited a long time to take a turn at burning the incense in the Holy Place, so Zacharias and Elizabeth went to Jerusalem for Zacharias to fulfill his priestly duty. He was alone in the Holy Place when an angel of the Lord appeared to him standing on the right side of the altar of incense.

The sight of the angel frightened Zacharias, but the angel told him not to be afraid. The angel told him his prayer had been heard. His wife was to have a son, and they were to call him John.

Luke 1:15-17 "For he will be great in the sight of the lord, and shall drink neither wine nor strong drink. He will also be filled with the Holy Spirit, even from his mother's womb. And he will turn many of the children of Israel to the Lord their God. He will go before Him in the spirit and power of Elijah, 'to turn the hearts of the fathers to the children,' and the disobedient to the wisdom of the just, to make ready a people prepared for the Lord."

The Lord was answering Zacharias' prayer but Zacharias wanted to see a sign for proof since his wife was barren. Gabriel told Zacharias what the sign would be. He would not be able to speak again until the child was born.

When Zacharias came out of the temple, the people waiting outside decided that Zacharias could not speak because he had seen a vision while he was in the temple.

When Zacharias completed his days of service in the temple, he and Elizabeth left Jerusalem and went back to their home in the hill country. Sometime later Elizabeth became pregnant and she hid herself saying that God had taken away her reproach among women. It was a shameful thing among the people of Israel if a woman could not conceive.

Elizabeth gave birth to her son, and on the eighth day they circumcised him. Zacharias was still unable to talk. They wanted to call the child Zacharias after his father, but Zacharias asked for a writing tablet and he wrote, "His name is John." When he wrote the name John for the baby, Zacharias was filled with the Holy Spirit and was able to speak, and he praised God. Zacharias praised God because he realized that God was fulfilling His promise to raise up a savior from the line of David to fulfill the promise made to Abraham to bless all people through God's Own seed.

Zacharias, being filled with the Holy Spirit, prophesied about a horn of salvation from the house of David. The Holy Spirit was speaking of Mary's child Jesus, and prophesying that He is the one the prophets spoke of and the descendant that God promised to Abraham saying that He would bless all people through Him. Mary's son Jesus would be the Messiah whom the Jews had been waiting for since the time of the prophets. Elizabeth and Zacharias' son, John, was a prophet of God who would prepare the way for Jesus. John, who was later called 'the baptist' or 'the baptizer,' lived by himself in the wilderness area near the Jordan River, and he was strong in the Holy Spirit.

The Birth of Christ

Six months after Elizabeth became pregnant with John the Baptist, God sent the angel Gabriel to Nazareth in Galilee to the Virgin Mary. The angel Gabriel announced that Mary was to have a son.

Mary wasn't married, but she was betrothed to a young man named Joseph who was in the birth line of Jesus. Gabriel told Mary she was to call her baby boy Jesus. Gabriel said He would be great and would be the Son of God and he would be given the throne of David and reign forever; there would be no end of His kingdom.

Mary being a virgin was confused not knowing how a virgin could give birth. Gabriel told her that the Holy Spirit would come upon her and she would conceive. Mary believed the Holy Spirit and said,

"Behold the maidservant of the Lord! Let it be to me according to your word." Mary was willing to become the mother of the Son by the Seed of God. Gabriel also informed Mary that her cousin, Elizabeth, was going to have a child in her old age, so Mary went to the hill country to see Elizabeth and tell her what the angel said.

Mary was betrothed to Joseph and at that time betrothed was the same as being legally married even though they had not yet come together as husband and wife. When Joseph learned that Mary was pregnant before they were married he wanted to dissolve the marriage contract secretly. Normally a man would publicly put away a woman under those circumstances, but Joseph was a good man and did not want to expose Mary publicly.

While Joseph was thinking about what to do, an angel from heaven appeared to him and explained that Mary was pregnant from the Holy Spirit of God. The angel said *"Joseph, son of David, do not be afraid to take to you Mary your wife, for that which is conceived in her is of the Holy Spirit. And she will bring forth a Son, and you shall call His name Jesus, for He will save His people from their sins."*

"So all this was done that it might be fulfilled, which was spoken by the Lord through the prophet saying: "Behold, the virgin shall be with child, and bear a Son, and they shall call His name Immanuel." Which is translated, "God with us."(Matt. 1:19-23)

Joseph took Mary as his legal wife, but they did not consummate the marriage until after the birth of their Son Jesus. The name Jesus is a transliteration of the name Joshua and means 'Jehovah is salvation.' Jesus grew up in Nazareth, which was a very small village in Galilee. Joseph and Mary lived in Nazareth after their betrothal. Joseph was a carpenter in Nazareth.

While Mary was pregnant, she went into the hill country to the house of Zacharias to see Elizabeth before Elizabeth's son was born. When Mary saw Elizabeth, she greeted her, and when Elizabeth heard the greeting of Mary, the baby leaped in her womb, and Elizabeth was filled with the Holy Spirit. Elizabeth spoke with a loud voice and said, *"Blessed are you among women, and blessed is the fruit of your womb! But why is this granted to me, that the mother of my Lord should come to me?" For indeed as soon as the voice of your greeting sounded in my ears, the babe leaped in my womb for joy. Blessed is she who believed, for there will be a fulfillment of those things which were told her from the Lord."*

Mary and Elizabeth talked about their sons, and Mary magnified the Lord by singing a song about the Lord and what He had done for her. Mary cited scripture from the prophecies of the Old Testament, including an understanding of the seed of Abraham. Mary's son was to be the Seed of God and He would be a blessing to all people. Mary remained with Elizabeth about three months and then went home to Nazareth.

Before Jesus was born, the Roman emperor Caesar Augustus issued a decree for a census to be taken in the entire Roman world. Everyone was to go to his own hometown to register, so Joseph, being a descendant of David, had to go to Bethlehem, the city of David. Mary was pregnant, but she went with Joseph to Bethlehem in Judea to be registered in the census. While Mary and Joseph were in Bethlehem, the time came for her baby to be born. There were no unoccupied rooms in the local inn, so Joseph and Mary had to stay in a stall where they kept cattle. Mary gave birth to her baby boy, wrapped Him in swaddling cloths, and laid Him in a manger. A manger was a crib in a barn or stable used to feed cattle. In Bible times it was a ledge or projection at the end of the stall where hay or other food was placed. Travelers with animals would use the stalls to feed their animals.

Bethlehem was situated in an area with surrounding fields where shepherds brought their flocks of sheep. The shepherds stayed in the fields day and night and watched over their flocks. On the night Jesus was born, the shepherds were watching over their flocks when an angel of the Lord came and stood before them. The glory of the Lord shone around them frightening them.

The expression that the shepherds were surrounded by the glory of the Lord probably makes reference to a bright light shining around them as the angel spoke of the birth of God's Son. The angel told the shepherds to not be afraid because he was bringing them good news that was joyful. The people of Israel, including the shepherds, had been waiting many years for the Messiah to come. The angel announced that the Savior (Messiah) had been born that very day in Bethlehem. This Messiah was Jesus Christ.

Luke 2:12-14 "And this will be the sign to you: you will find a Babe wrapped in swaddling cloths, lying in a manger." And suddenly there was with the angel a multitude of the heavenly host praising God and saying:

"Glory to God in the highest,
And on earth peace, Good will toward men!"

Then the angels left and returned to heaven, and the shepherds went to Bethlehem to see the baby Jesus. When the shepherds came to Bethlehem they found Joseph and Mary and the baby Jesus and they went out and told others about the birth of the Messiah. The shepherds then returned to the fields glorifying and praising God. (The prophets had foretold the birth of the Son of God many years before Jesus' birth.)

Wise men from the east came to Jerusalem to visit with baby Jesus who was to be the king of the Jews. The Greek word for wise men is magi referring to astrologers. The wise men had been searching the stars for many years for the sign of the Messiah's birth and they knew He would be born in the vicinity of Jerusalem.

At the time of His birth a certain star would be the sign of His birth, and the child was to become the King of the Jews. When the wise men said they were looking for the sign of the King of the Jews, Herod was troubled. He knew about the prophecies of the coming of the Jewish Messiah. So he gathered some of the religious leaders of the Jews together and questioned them about where the Messiah was to be born. They told Herod that Jesus would be born in Bethlehem of Judea quoting the words of the prophet *Micah in 5:2 "But you, Bethlehem Ephrathah, Though you are little among the thousands of Judah, yet out of you shall come forth to Me The One to be Ruler in Israel, whose going forth are from of old, From everlasting."* Herod asked the wise men what time the star had appeared. Then he sent the men to Bethlehem to search for and find the Christ child, because he planned to kill Him.

The wise men from the east saw a bright star in the sky and followed it to the place where Jesus was. The men went into the house and saw the baby with Mary. They worshiped Him and gave Him gifts they had brought with them. Before they left, they were warned in a dream not to return to Herod, because he was looking for the Christ child so he could kill Him. So the wise men left and went home a different way. When Herod learned the wise men had deceived him, he became very angry and ordered all the male children in Bethlehem who were two years of age and younger to be put to death.

An angel of God came to Joseph in a dream and told him to take Mary and the baby Jesus and go to Egypt instead of going home to Nazareth. The angel said to stay in Egypt until he was told that it was safe to go home. Joseph and his family went to Egypt and remained there until Herod died. When Joseph heard that Herod had died, he took Mary and baby Jesus and left Egypt and went back to Nazareth, a town in the region of Galilee.

When the baby was eight days old, they circumcised him and named him Jesus. After Mary's days of purification according to the Jewish law was completed, they took Jesus to the temple in Jerusalem. There was an old man in Jerusalem named Simeon, a devout man who had been waiting for the consolation of Israel by the Messiah for many years. Simeon described the birth of Jesus as God's salvation that was for all people and as a Light to reveal acceptance and salvation of the Gentiles. Jesus Christ, came to provide salvation for all people. Mary, Joseph and Jesus were descendants of the Jewish people in the birth line of King David.

The Jewish people regularly observed several feasts in accordance with their religion. The feasts acknowledged God as the One who provided for His chosen people. The Feast of Unleavened bread, also called the Passover Feast, commemorated their deliverance from bondage in Egypt. The Feast of Weeks was also called the Feast of Harvest and the day of first fruits, later called the feast of Pentecost. The Feast of Tabernacles or Feast of Booths was also called the Feast of Ingathering. The Sabbath was regarded as a feast and was called a Sabbath of rest.

There is no record in the Bible of the early years of Jesus life with His parents in Nazareth. Joseph and Mary did everything that was required by Jewish law after Jesus was born and they returned to their home in Nazareth, and Jesus lived in Nazareth with his parents until He was twelve years old.

Near the beginning of His thirteenth year Jesus went with His parents to the temple in Jerusalem for the Passover Feast. They went with a large group of people from Nazareth to Jerusalem. Joseph and Mary left Jerusalem after the Passover and were on their way back to Nazareth when they discovered that Jesus was not among the people returning with them. Joseph and Mary turned around and went back to Jerusalem to search for Jesus, and after three days they found Him sitting in the temple court listening to the teachers and asking them questions.

Joseph and Mary didn't know what to make of Jesus being among the teachers of the Law. Mary scolded Him telling Him she had been worried. She asked Him why He treated them that way. Jesus seems to have known by that time that He was the Messiah, and He answered, "Didn't you know I had to be in My Fathers house?" Joseph and Mary knew Jesus was a special child given to them by God, but they may not have realized at that time He was the promised Messiah.

The mission of Jesus the Son of God was to be born on earth teach the good news of redemption, then die on the cross, be resurrected and return to heaven. According to Jewish law, a male becomes an adult at the end of his twelfth year. Considered as an adult, he would have the responsibility and duty of an adult, especially the duty and responsibility to learn and practice Jewish law. Jesus was growing in wisdom but it would be several years before He answered the call to officially begin His work as the Messiah. After his baptism at the age of responsibility under the Jewish law Jesus returned to Nazareth and lived with His family in Nazareth and He became strong in the Holy Spirit and filled with wisdom. Jesus was aware that the Holy Spirit was with Him by the favor that God was showing Him.

When Jesus was thirty years of age John the Baptist, baptized Him and Jesus began His ministry.

The gospel of John, John writes that Jesus is the Word that was with God in the beginning. John establishes the divinity of Christ and declares that He participated with God in the creation. John wrote that the evidence of Christ was revealed, but people did not comprehend His existence or His mission.

John 1:1-5 "In the beginning was the Word, and the Word was with God and the word was God. He was in the beginning with God." All things were made through Him, and without Him nothing was made that was made. In Him was life, and the life was the light of men. And the light shines in the darkness, and the darkness did not comprehend it."

Verses 6-8 "There was a man sent from God, whose name was John. This man came for a witness, to bear witness of the Light, that all through Him might believe. He was not that Light, but was sent to bear witness of that Light."

Verse 9-11 "That was the true Light that gives light to every man coming into the world. He was in the world, and the world was made through Him, and the world did not know Him. He came to His own, and His own did not receive Him."

Verse 12 "But as many as received Him, to them He gave the right to become children of God, to those who believe in His name."

Verse 14 "And the word became flesh and dwelt among us, and we beheld His glory, the glory as of the only begotten of the Father, full of grace and truth."

The gospel writers Matthew, Mark, and Luke and John wrote a record of Jesus life and works including His death burial and resurrection. The first chapter of John's gospel records a preamble of the story of the life and ministry of Christ.

Jesus was in the beginning with God during the creation and He had a part in making everything in creation. God sent a man named John who was called the Baptist because he would baptize those who believed in Jesus. John the Baptist came to be a witness for Christ who is the Light. Jesus is called the Light because He came to reveal the knowledge and the fulfillment of righteous plan of God to redeem those who are guilty of sin.

Jesus is the true Light who gives light (knowledge of redemption) to the world. His own people the Jewish people rejected Him but all people who would believe in Him were given the right to become children of God, born of God through faith in Christ. Before Jesus came, there was no hope for redemption. Jesus came to establish a way of redemption that would ultimately lead to His death. By His death He established the forgiveness of sin.

John the Baptist begins Teaching and Baptizing

According to the prophet Malachi, God promised to send a messenger to prepare the way for Jesus ministry. John the Baptist was that messenger. With the birth of John the Baptist the first part of God's redeeming plan was beginning to take place. John was filled with the Holy Spirit of God at an early age and John knew he was a prophet sent by the Lord to prepare the minds of the Jews to accept Jesus of Nazareth as the Messiah. John taught about Jesus and baptized those who accepted Jesus as the Messiah.

(MT 3) John was about thirty years old when he began to preach in the desert area of Judea near the Jordan River and baptizing people. John preached a baptism of repentance for the remission of sin. He lived by himself in a wilderness area and he wore clothing made from camel's hair and ate locusts and wild honey. John told people to repent, because the Kingdom of God was coming to the earth. The kingdom of God was coming in the person of Jesus and would be formally established on earth after the death of Jesus. Baptism means to be immersed in water and repentance means that a person is aware of their sins and feels remorse and they turn to God in obedience and reform their life. Baptism and repentance demonstrates a person's faith in Christ and a conviction to serve God and Christ.

The Jewish people who believed in God had been waiting a long time for the Messiah. Some of the people thought John was the Messiah, but John told them that he was not the Messiah but was sent to baptize people with water in preparation for the Messiah. He told those who came to him for baptism to bear fruit, which meant to follow Christ who was coming after him.

Jews came from Jerusalem and the whole area of the Jordan, and they confessed their sins and John baptized them. Those who believed in Jesus and were baptized by John were to be members of the kingdom of God that would be formally introduced after Jesus' death. Many of the religious teachers, the scribes and Pharisees came to hear John. When he saw them coming, he called them a brood of vipers and asked them, "Who told you to turn away from the wrath of God that is coming?"

John told the people that one mightier than he was coming. John spoke of Jesus, and he told them Jesus would baptize them with the Holy Spirit and with fire. Baptism of the Holy Spirit means the gift of the Holy Spirit would be in them and help them in their life of obedience to God and Christ. People of faith who are baptized receive an indwelling of the Holy Spirit. Baptized with fire means to experience the fiery judgment of God at the end of time. Baptized with fire is a baptism that comes on non-believers who will face the full judgment of God at the end of time. (John 1)

The Jews sent officials of the people to ask John the Baptist who He was? John had stirred a lot of interest with his teaching and baptizing. They probably wanted to find out if he was the Messiah. John emphatically said he was not the Christ (Messiah). They asked if he was Elijah or one of the other prophets. John told them he was someone crying in the wilderness.

John Baptizes Jesus

(MT 3) At the age of thirty Jesus went to the Jordan River where John was teaching people about the Kingdom of God and baptizing them. When John saw Jesus coming to be baptized, he recognized Jesus immediately as the Messiah, and he said, *"Behold the Lamb of God who takes away the sin of the world."* While Jesus was on earth in the flesh, He looked, felt and acted like a person. Jesus understood the weakness of the flesh allowing Him to practice compassion, love and mercy for those who were sinners. When Jesus first came from Galilee to be baptized. John did not want to baptize Him, because he knew Jesus was the Messiah. But Jesus told him to baptize Him to fulfill all righteousness, so John Baptized Him in the Jordan River

John baptized Jesus, and as Jesus was arising from the water the heavens divided and the Holy Spirit came down like a dove and sat on Jesus. Then a voice came from heaven saying, *"You are My beloved Son in whom I am well pleased."* Mark 3:9-11

John 1:32-34 "And John bore witness, saying, "I saw the Spirit descending from heaven like a dove, and He remained on Him. I did not know Him, but He who sent me to baptize with water said to me, 'Upon whom you see the Spirit descending and remaining on Him, this is He who baptizes with the Holy Spirit.' And I have seen and testified that this is the Son of God."

Jesus submitted to baptism as an example to show that baptism was a part of God's righteous plan for people to be redeemed. Jesus was both human and divine and He submitted to baptism as a human example to fulfill all righteousness. God chose to send his Son into the world as the son of man so that he could experience life as a human being experiencing the same weaknesses and temptations that all people experience.

Baptism is an act of faith, a way to demonstrate a person's faith publicly. John called Jesus a lamb metaphorically because He was an innocent person who had a meek and gentle attitude like a lamb. Jesus offered no resistance later when He was taken before the authorities and crucified, like a lamb led to be slaughtered.

Jesus Tempted by Satan

(Matt. 4) After His baptism, the Holy Spirit led Jesus into the wilderness of the Judean desert to be tempted by the Devil. Jesus fasted for forty days before He was tempted because the first temptation would be hunger.

The Devil tempted Jesus by telling Him to perform a miracle and turn the stones into bread to satisfy His hunger. Jesus had the power to turn stones into bread, but He told the devil that life is not sustained by bread alone but by living and obeying the word of God. Jesus said *"It is written, 'Man shall not live by bread alone, but by every word of God."* Jesus had faith that God would sustain Him. The purpose of the temptation was to illustrate the power of faith in God.

Satan tempted Jesus to disobey God by telling Jesus he would give Him all the kingdoms of the world if He would worship him, but Jesus said, *"Get behind Me, Satan! For it is written, 'You shall worship the Lord your God and Him only you shall serve."* Jesus taught that it is not right to deliberately tempt God. Everything Satan asked Jesus to do was against the will of God but Jesus would not disobey His Father leaving us an example of great faith in God.

Satan tried again to get Jesus to doubt God by tempting Him. Satan told Jesus to go up to the highest part of the temple and jump off. A fall from that height would kill or seriously maim anyone. Satan told Jesus the angels would save him from harm, because God had put them in charge of His safety. Jesus didn't doubt that the angels would save Him, but He would not deliberately tempt God. Jesus refused and said, "It has been said, *'You shall not tempt the Lord your God.'*

Jesus' mission was to prove that He was the Messiah who came to save people from the guilt of sin. Jesus performed many miracles recorded in the gospels to prove who He was. Jesus would eventually submit to being sacrificed on a cross for the sins of the world. He would voluntarily go with His accusers without fighting or offering resistance to provide a sacrifice for the sins of all people who would have faith in Him.

Jesus Begins His Ministry

(MT 4) During the course of His ministry, Jesus went through the land of Galilee teaching in the synagogues, preaching the good news of the kingdom and healing people of all kinds of disease. His fame spread throughout Syria, and He healed sick people of various diseases, cast out demons, cured epilepsy and paralytics. A great many people followed Him from Galilee, Decapolis, Jerusalem, and Judea and beyond the Jordan River.

(MT 4) Jesus would select 12 men who were His disciples to travel with Him. These twelve men were later called apostles. (The word apostle means 'one sent on a mission') The apostles would accompany Him during His ministry and would continue to preach the gospel after Jesus death. The men Jesus chose would eventually become leaders in the Kingdom of God (The Church). The disciples called apostles were ordinary men. Peter, Andrew, James and John were fishermen who fished for a living. Matthew was a tax collector.

The men had different positions in life and their personalities varied from impulsive, passionate, thoughtful and pessimistic. Their qualification to become a disciple was to have faith in Jesus and be willing to follow Him faithfully and all but one would remain faithful to Jesus. A disciple is a follower of a person or idea; one who follows their teacher. An apostle was a disciple that was chosen by Jesus during His ministry and sent by Jesus to preach and teach the gospel; the good news that Jesus is the Son of God sent to redeem believers.

The men Jesus chose gave up their occupation and followed Him during His ministry on earth. In the books of (John-1) Jesus chose Peter, Andrew and Philip. (MT-4) James and John. (MK-3) Bartholomew and Thomas Matthew, James the son of Alphaeus, Thaddeus, Simon the Canaanite and Judas Iscariot who would betray Him.

When Jesus heard that John the Baptist had been put in prison, He left Galilee and went to Capernaum on the shore of the Sea of Galilee. Matthew's account says as Jesus walked by the Sea of Galilee, He saw Peter and Andrew casting a net into the Sea. *Matthew 4:19 "Then He said to them, follow Me, and I will make you fishers of men."* Peter and Andrew left their nets and followed Jesus.

The next day Jesus met Philip and told Philip to follow Him. Jesus saw James and John, the sons of Zebedee, in their boat with their father. Jesus called to them, and they left their boat and followed Him.

Following Jesus means to accept Jesus as the Messiah sent by God. Philip began following Jesus and he found Nathanael and told him that Jesus was the one spoken of by Moses and the prophets and Nathanael joined them. Nathanael said he knew Jesus was the Son of God, the King of Israel.

John 1:50-51 "Jesus answered and said to him, because I said to you, 'I saw you under the fig tree,' do you believe? You will see greater things than these." And He said to him, "Most assuredly, I say to you, hereafter you shall see heaven open, and the angels of God ascending and descending upon the Son of Man."

Jesus Family Lives in Capernaum

(JN 4) Jesus and His family lived in Capernaum after leaving Nazereth. In the first chapter of his Gospel, John gives testimony of Christ. (John 2) Jesus disciples followed Him and stayed with Him day and night everywhere He went. Three days after the disciples joined Jesus, they were with Him in Capernaum and went to a wedding in the city of Cana near Capernaum.

Mary, the mother of Jesus, was at the wedding. During the wedding feast Jesus changed water into wine, His first miracle.

The miracle in Cana demonstrated that Jesus was the Son of God, and His disciples believed in Him. *John12-12 "This beginning of signs Jesus did in Cana of Galilee, and Manifested His glory; and His disciples believed in Him. After this He went down to Capernaum."*

Jesus went back to Capernaum called the city of comfort. It was located on the shore of the Sea of Galilee also known as Tiberias or the lake of Gennesaret.

Capernaum was a relatively large and prosperous city a large fishing village and trading center. Jesus often traveled from there to teach and perform miracles, and there is frequent mention of Capernaum in the gospels.

Peter, Andrew, James and John lived in Capernaum near the shore of the Sea of Galilee and they were fishermen when Jesus called them. Jesus made many trips back and forth from and to Capernaum. Jesus taught and healed many people around the area of the Sea as well as many other locations including Jerusalem.

Jesus' mother and brothers had a house in Capernaum, and they went back to Capernaum after leaving Cana. Jesus and His disciples didn't stay long at any place, because Jesus was eager to take his ministry to other places.

Jesus traveled throughout Galilee and taught in the cities, villages, on the mountains, in a boat on the Sea of Galilee and in the synagogues.

Passover feast in Jerusalem

(Gospel of John) Jesus, being a Jew, went to Jerusalem in Judea for the Passover feast. On one occasion while He was in Jerusalem He entered the temple area and found people selling animals and doves for sacrifices. There were also changers of money there. Jesus made a whip from cords and drove them from the temple. To those who sold doves He said *John 2:16 "Take these things away! Do not make My Fathers house a house of merchandise!"* The temple was the Jews place of worship, and Jesus didn't think it was right to make it into a place of merchandise. The Jews at the temple asked Jesus for a sign to prove that He had authority to drive them out, so Jesus told them of a forthcoming sign. He said that if He were put to death, He would be alive again in three days. He was speaking of His forthcoming resurrection. When that took place, they would know He had the authority.

During the time Jesus was on earth, Satan's influence of lying to and deceiving people spread as Satan attempted to destroy the effect of the gospel Jesus was teaching. Some people gladly responded to the gospel, but not all who obeyed remained faithful. Some of the people who heard the word of the gospel wanted to believe, but the cares of the world kept them from becoming faithful believers. The term gospel means the good news of redemption through faith in Christ.

While Jesus was in Jerusalem, He met a Pharisee named Nicodemus. Nicodemus knew Jesus was the Messiah because of the miracles He was performing, and he called Jesus a teacher who came from God, but he didn't know of the Kingdom of God. Jesus seemed to be surprised that Nicodemus, a leader of the Jews, would not have already known about the Kingdom. The prophets of Israel had clearly prophesied about the coming of the Kingdom.

Jesus then taught Nicodemus about the Kingdom of God and how one can become a member. Jesus said to him *"Most assuredly, I say to you, unless one is born again, he cannot see the kingdom of God." John 3:4 "Nicodemus said to Him, "How can a man be born when he is old? Can he enter a second time into his mother's womb and be born?"*

Jesus was speaking of a spiritual birth. When a person acquires faith in Jesus, they are baptized in water and receive the Holy Spirit into their lives. Before baptism, a person is not joined with Christ. After being baptized, they are a new person because their sins are washed away, and they are joined with Christ in a spiritual relationship, because they have Christ's spirit living in them. In this way they are said to be born again, they become a new person, the Holy Spirit comes into them and they are children of God who have been forgiven of their past sins. They are added to the kingdom of God. (John 3) John the Baptist baptized people in Aenon where there was a lot of water. Jesus and His disciples went to Judea and the disciples baptized people there. Jesus was converting people, and his disciples were baptizing more people than John. John said he baptized to help Jesus gain disciples. John said he would be going away. John continued to baptize people until he was arrested and put in prison then later executed.

(Luke 3) When John first began to baptize, people wondered if he was the Messiah, but John told them Jesus was coming and Jesus would baptize with the Holy Spirit and with fire. Later Herod put John in prison and eventually executed him. Jesus came to Galilee and preached the gospel saying His time had come the kingdom of God was near meaning his time to be crucified. The people Jesus and His disciples baptized were forgiven of their sins and were accepted by God as a member of the kingdom of God (Christ) that would be recognized a few years later.

Jesus and the Disciples go to Samaria

(John 4) Jesus left Jerusalem in Judea to go back toward Galilee, but on His way He decided to go to Samaria. We don't know why Jesus decided to go to Samaria, but it is evident that something was drawing Him into that area. I believe the Holy Spirit was sending Him to Samaria, because there were people there who needed the gospel.

The Samaritans were a race that was formed when Jews from the northern kingdom married non-Jews. They weren't all Jewish. The Jews from the southern kingdom despised Samaritans and would not associate with them. Jesus and the disciples came to the city of Sychar in Samaria near a plot of land that Jacob had given to his son Joseph long ago. Jacob's well was there, and since it had been a long walk and Jesus was tired, He set down by a well to rest.

A Samaritan woman came to the well to get water, and Jesus asked her for a drink. Jesus was alone because the disciples had gone to buy food. The woman was surprised that Jesus even spoke to her. The woman thought it was strange that a Jew would talk to her. She said, "How is it that you, being a Jew, would ask me, a Samaitian woman, for a drink?" Jesus said, *John 4:10 "If you knew the gift of God, and who it is who says to you 'Give Me a drink,' you would have asked Him, and He would have given you living water.".* Living water represents the gospel that leads to faith in Christ and eternal life. God's plan of redemption is for people of all nationalities. The woman didn't understand living water, so she told Jesus that the well was deep and He had nothing to draw water with. Then she asked him where He was going to get this living water.

Jesus answered and said to her, "Who ever drinks of this water will thirst again, but who ever drinks of the water that I shall give him will never thirst. But the water I shall give him will become in him a fountain of water springing up to everlasting life." John 4:13-14

Jesus used water in a symbolic sense. The water Jesus spoke about is the Holy Spirit that would be given to Christians; "rivers of living water." According to *John 7: 38-39 "He who believes in Me, as the scripture has said, out of his heart will flow rivers of living water." But this He spoke concerning the Spirit, whom those believing in Him would receive; for the Holy Spirit, was not yet given, because Jesus was not yet glorified."*

The woman could tell that Jesus was a prophet but she did not know He was the Messiah. She told Jesus that her ancestors worshiped on the mountain they were on but the Jews say that Jerusalem is the place to worship.

John 4:21-26 "Jesus said to her, "Woman, believe Me, the hour is coming when you will neither on this mountain, nor in Jerusalem, worship the Father. You worship what you do not know; we know what we worship, for salvation is of the Jews. But the hour is coming, and now is, when the true worshipers will worship the Father in spirit and truth; for the Father is seeking such to worship Him. God is Spirit, and those who worship Him must worship in spirit and truth."

Jesus told the woman that He was the Messiah. Worship is a matter of the heart, and the nation of Israel at one time, including the people who were called Samaritans, worshiped the God of Israel according to the old Law of Moses. God's people worshiped Him in the temple and offered animal sacrifices according to the Law of Moses., but a time was coming when people everywhere would worship God in their hearts instead of a temple. Their hearts would represent God's temple. Jesus let the woman know that now that He had come, all people, including Samaritans, could become God's spiritual people. Many of the Samaritan people believed that Jesus was the Messiah. Worshiping God from the heart does not require material objects or special places like a temple or anything made by the hands of men.

The woman who had come to draw water left her water pot and went to the city to tell the people about the man that knew everything she had ever done. She wondered if He was Jesus the Messiah. The people from the city came to the well to see Jesus and He taught them.

The disciples came back from the city and they were amazed that Jesus had talked to the Samaritan woman. Jesus remained in Samaria two more days, and many of the Samaritans became believers and pleaded with Jesus to stay there. Jesus left there and returned to Galilee in the power of the Spirit. The people of Galilee welcomed Him, because they had been at the feast in Jerusalem and had seen all the things He did there.

Jesus goes to Nazareth

(Luke 4) Jesus went to His hometown of Nazareth. On the Sabbath day He entered the Synagogue and read from the book of Isaiah, chapter 61. *"The Spirit of the Lord is upon Me, Because He has anointed Me To preach the gospel to the poor; He has sent Me to heal the broken hearted, to proclaim liberty to the captives And recovery of sight to the blind, To set at liberty those who are oppressed; To proclaim the acceptable year of the Lord." Luke 4:18-19*

Jesus closed the book and sat down. All the people in the synagogue stared at Him. Jesus said, *"Today this Scripture is fulfilled in your hearing."* Many of the people there were astonished. They wondered where Jesus got such wisdom and knowledge of the things He taught. The people wondered about who Jesus was and some said, *"Is this not Joseph's son."* Some recognized Jesus as the carpenter, the son of Mary. Jesus' brothers and sister were also there.

Jesus began to speak about the people's unfaithfulness, and they were filled with anger towards Him. The people failed to honor Jesus as the Messiah or a prophet, and they became very angry. They ran Jesus out of the city and took Him to the edge of a cliff to throw Him off, but He escaped. Jesus said, *"A prophet is not without honor except in his own country, among his own relatives, and in his own house."*

Because Jesus wasn't accepted in that town, He did not perform many works there. Jesus did not force people to accept Him and his works. He used miraculous works and words of knowledge and wisdom to confirm His identity as the Son of God and taught people to accept him and obey the gospel.

(John 4) After two days, Jesus went to Galilee and was received well by the Galileans who had been in Jerusalem. They had witnessed the things Jesus had done at the feast. He then went to Cana in Galilee, the place where he turned water into wine, but he soon left there and went to Capernaum.

While he was in Capernaum, a nobleman came to him and told Jesus his son was sick and at the point of death.

He asked Jesus to heal Him. Jesus said, *"Unless you people see signs and wonders, you will by no means believe."* Jesus then told him, *"Go your way; your son lives."* The nobleman believed what Jesus said, so he left to go home. On the way home his servants met him and told him his son was well. This was Jesus second miracle.

(MT 4) Jesus went from Capernaum by the Sea, to the region of Zebulun and Naphtali in Galilee and began to preach saying, "Repent and believe in the gospel for the kingdom of heaven is near." Jesus walked near the Sea of Galilee and He saw Peter and Andrew, two of His disciples casting a net in the sea. *Mark 1:17 'Then Jesus said to them, "Follow Me, and I will make you become fishers of men."* They left their nets and followed Jesus. Jesus went a little farther and He saw James and John in their boat mending nets. Jesus called them and they left Zebedee, their father, and followed Jesus. (MK 1) Jesus was in Capernaum on the Sabbath. He taught at the synagogue and the people were amazed, because He taught with authority. Jesus healed a man who had a demon in him. When the demon saw Jesus, he knew Jesus was the Son of God and he asked Jesus if He came to destroy him. Jesus told the demon to come out of the body of the man and the demon left.

Jesus and the disciples left the synagogue and went to Simon Peter's house in Capernaum. Peters mother was sick, so when they told Jesus, He went in to her and healed her. He then took her by the hand and she got up. That evening people brought all who were sick with various diseases, and Jesus healed them. Jesus also cast out many demons.

The next morning Jesus rose early and went to a private place to pray. Jesus often went off by himself to pray and to be away from the crowd for a while. The disciples found Him and told Him that everyone was looking for Him. Jesus then decided to go to other towns close by so He could preach to the people there.

Mark 1:38 "He said to them, "let us go into the next towns, that I may preach there also, because for this purpose I have come forth."

(LK 5) As Jesus stood by the lake of Gennesaret (Sea of Galilee) one day the people crowded in close to Him in order to hear Him teaching the Word of God. While He was there, He saw two boats standing empty by the lake and the fishermen washing their nets nearby. One of the fishermen was Simon Peter, one of His apostles, so Jesus got into Simon Peter's boat and asked him to push out a little way from shore. Jesus sat in the boat and taught the people on shore.

After a while He stopped speaking and asked Peter to go further out into deeper water and let down the nets to catch some fish.

Peter told Jesus they had fished there all night without catching any fish, but he did what Jesus said and let down the nets again. They caught so many fish in the net that Peter had to call for help to get them in the boat. Peter fell to his knees telling Jesus to leave him, because he was a sinful man. Peter was overwhelmed by the miracle Jesus performed and felt unworthy to be in His presence. Jesus told Peter to not be afraid. He said from then on they would all be fishers of men. The twelve disciples became the twelve Apostles and Jesus commissioned them to go out and become fishers of men by preaching the gospel. When the disciples came on shore they left everything and followed Jesus. The word apostle means one sent forth by God. *Hebrews 3:1 "Therefore, holy brethren, partakers of the heavenly calling, consider the Apostle and High Priest of our confession, Christ Jesus, who was faithful to Him who appointed Him, as Moses also was faithful in all his house. For this one has been counted worthy of more glory than Moses, inasmuch as He who built the house has more honor that the house. For every house is built by someone, but He who built all things is God."* Christ is more worthy than Moses because by His own sacrifice He built His own house the kingdom of God on earth. All Christians are members of the Kingdom Of God that Jesus built and they are members of the household of God and are to go forth and teach the gospel to everyone.

(Mark 2, Luke 5) After a few days Jesus went to Capernaum to the house where his mother and brothers lived. As soon as the people heard He was there, many came to see Him. The house soon became so full that no one else could enter. Jesus left Capernaum the next day and again went to a deserted place to rest, but the people found Him and pleaded with Him to stay with them. He told them, *"I must preach the kingdom of God to the other cities also, because for this purpose I have been sent."* (Luke4: 43)

Jesus went throughout Galilee, and in each city on the Sabbath He would go to the synagogue and teach about the kingdom of God. He healed all kinds of sickness and disease, and His fame spread throughout the Roman Empire.

As Jesus and the disciples went from place to place, in one city a man with leprosy came to Jesus, and kneeling down before Him. The man told Jesus he believed Jesus could heal him if He was willing. Jesus was moved with compassion, and because the man had expressed faith in Jesus to heal him, Jesus put out His hand and touched the man saying *"I am willing; be cleansed."* Jesus then told the man to tell no one that he was healed and to go to the priest and make an offering as a testimony. News of the healing spread everywhere, and great multitudes assembled to hear Jesus teach and to be healed. Jesus often became very tired and went into a wilderness area and rested and prayed.

(MK 2, LK 5) on another day Jesus was in Capernaum at the house where his mother and brothers lived, and as soon as people heard He was there, many people came to Him. The house became so full of people no one else could enter.

Jesus was teaching the Pharisees at that time and four men carried a man that was paralyzed to the house. The house was so full of people that they could not bring him inside. The four men uncovered the roof above where Jesus stood, and they lowered the man's bed down into the room. Jesus said to the man *"Son your sins are forgiven you."*

There were some scribes and Pharisees there, and they reasoned in their hearts that Jesus was speaking blasphemies for saying your sins are forgiven. They believed that God was the only one who could forgive sins. They did not believe Jesus was the Son of God even though He demonstrated who he was with miraculous acts including healing.

Jesus knew what they were thinking in their hearts and He said, *"Why do you reason about these things in your hearts? Which is easier, to say to the paralytic, 'Your sins are forgiven you,' or to say, 'Arise, take up your bed and walk? But that you may know that the Son of Man has power on earth to forgive sins"*—He said to the paralytic, *I say to you, arise take up your bed, and go to your house."* The paralytic arose, picked up his bed and carried it. The crowd saw it and was amazed, and they glorified God.

Jesus took advantage of every opportunity He had to convince people that He was the Messiah that had come from God. Many people believed Him but some did not believe and they planned to kill him later.

Jesus Chooses Matthew for an Apostle

Jesus, still in Capernaum, walked to the seashore of the Sea of Galilee. The crowd followed Him and He taught them. As they were walking along Jesus saw Levi Matthew, the son of Alphaeus, at the tax office, because he was a tax collector. Jesus told Matthew Levi to follow Him. He followed Him and became a disciple of Jesus.

The Scribes and the Pharisees observed Jesus eating with tax collectors and sinners, and they asked Jesus' disciples why He would do that. No respectable Jew wanted to be seen with people they thought were sinners, especially tax collectors. Jesus heard their remarks and answered them saying, *"Those who are well have no need of a physician, but those who are sick. I did not come to call the righteous, but sinners to repentance."*

(LK 5) The Pharisees complained about Jesus and the disciples because they did not observe fasting. Fasting is a voluntary abstinence from eating food, and it was a common practice among the Jews. The fast celebrates the Jewish Day of Atonement. The observation of fasting was commanded in the book of Leviticus.

Jesus came to take away the observance of the old Law of Moses and establish the gospel. The Law of Moses could not take away the guilt of sin, because no one could keep the Law perfectly so they were condemned because of sin. There was no provision in the law for the forgiveness of sin.

Jesus often spoke in figurative language, and He taught a parable calling Himself a bridegroom who was celebrating with his friends. The kingdom of heaven was later called the church and the bride of Christ. Jesus celebrates with His disciples who are the first members of the kingdom.

Jesus told them the time is coming when He, the bridegroom, will be taken away—referring to His death. Jesus used figurative language and parables so His disciples would understand but His enemies would not understand.

In the first part of the gospels, Jesus taught many parables. There are no parables recorded in the book of John, but parables taught by Jesus are recorded in the other three gospels. A parable is a brief story that is told to compare a familiar story drawn from nature or everyday events to a story with spiritual significance.

Jesus spoke many parables to attract interest and provoke an inquiry, giving Him an opportunity to teach a spiritual lesson. Jesus told them a parable about making a garment out of new cloth before it is shrunk, or putting new wine in old wineskins.

Jesus taught that the kingdom that was coming would be different than the Law of Moses, which would go away. The kingdom of heaven that Jesus would establish would not be a reformed kingdom adhering to the Law of Moses. The Law would become of no effect when Jesus died. Then the gospel of Christ would be preached, and people would come into the Kingdom of Christ

The Law of Moses was given for a good purpose, but the Jewish people were not able to obey the Law perfectly. They became unrighteous sinners with no way to regain their righteous status. Since Christ became our sacrifice for sin when he was crucified, the sacrifice of Christ makes all followers of Christ righteous through their repentance and prayer. Kingdom of God, Kingdom of heaven, and Kingdom of Christ are all names for the same kingdom, which was later called the church.

Jesus goes to Jerusalem for the Passover

(John 5) On one occasion Jesus went to Jerusalem for the Jewish Passover Feast. While there, He went to the pool called Bethesda near the Sheep Gate. The place where the pool was located had five porches for those who were sick, blind, lame or paralyzed. The people came there to wait for the moving of the water in the pool. There was a belief that an angel would come at a certain time and stir up the water, and the first person in the pool would be healed.

(5: 6-8) On the day Jesus came, there was a man with an infirmity that he had for thirty-eight years. The man had not been able to be the first in the pool, because he had no one to put him in the pool when the water was first stirred. Jesus saw the man and asked him, *"Do you want to be made well?"* The man told Jesus he had no one to put him in the pool when the water stirred. *"Jesus said to him, "rise, take up your bed and walk."* And immediately the man was made well and he took up his bed, and walked. The Jews saw the man walking and carrying his bed and they accused him of unlawfully working on the Sabbath, a ridiculous accusation.

The Jews became aware that Jesus was the one who healed the man on the Sabbath and they persecuted Jesus and looked for an opportunity to kill Him. Jesus answered the undeserved outrage of the Jews saying, *"My Father has been working until now, and I have been working."* Jesus claimed to be the Son of God and He explains that God had always been working for the good and the salvation of mankind and now Jesus was working for the same reason. The Jews wanted to kill Jesus because He healed on the Sabbath and because He claimed that God was His Father.

Jesus continued to teach and explain the unity between Himself and God. Jesus said that His Father would show greater works to do than the work He had already performed. *John 5:21 For as the Father raises the dead and gives life to them, even so the Son gives life to whom He will."* Jesus lets them know that everything He did was because of His father. Jesus claims the same power as God, which identifies Him as the Son of God.

John 5:26-29 "For as the father has life in Himself, so He has granted the Son to have life in Himself, and has given Him authority to execute judgment also, because He is the Son of Man. Do not marvel at this; for the hour is coming in which all who are in the graves will hear His voice and come forth Those who have done good, to the resurrection of life, and those who have done evil, to the resurrection of condemnation."

Jesus revealed that His reason for coming to earth was to die and provide redemption for the guilt of sin.

Jesus performed many miracles and did great works among the people so people would believe He was the Messiah the Son of God.

The Story of Faith, Hope and Love

Jesus came to establish faith so that people would voluntarily submit to God's plan of salvation. The works of John the Baptist and the works of Jesus bear witness that Jesus Christ is the Son of God. The Scriptures from Genesis through Revelation bear witness of Christ.

John 5:24-30 "Most assuredly, I say to you, he who hears My word and believes in Him who sent Me has everlasting life, and shall not come into judgment, but has passed from death into life. Most assuredly, I say to you the hour is coming, and now is, when the dead will hear the voice of the Son of God; and those who hear will live. For as the Father has life in Himself, so He has granted the Son to have life in Himself, and has given Him authority to execute judgment also, because He is the Son of Man. Do not marvel at this; for the hour is coming in which all who are in the graves will hear His voice and come forth—those who have done good, to the resurrection of life, and those who have done evil, to the resurrection of condemnation. I can of Myself do nothing. As I hear I judge; and My judgment is righteous, because I do not seek My own will but the will of the Father who sent Me."

Jesus talked about the witness of John the Baptist who was a witness of the truth. Jesus told them, John was the burning and shining lamp, and people were willing to listen to John for a time. Many of the Jews at first believed what John said about Jesus. Jesus said His works were greater than John's. *John 5:36 "But I have a greater witness than John's; for the works which the father has given Me to finish—the very works that I do—bear witness of Me, that the Father has sent Me."*

When Jesus healed the man on the Sabbath, He was doing the work that God had sent Him to earth to do. Jesus faced the difficulty of establishing the law of liberty, the gospel, while the religious leaders were still teaching the Old Law. Under the Old Law it was unlawful to work on the Sabbath.

As Jesus and the disciples walked through the grain fields one day, the disciples pulled and ate some of the grain, and the Pharisees accused them of unlawfully working on the Sabbath. The charge made by the Pharisees was ridiculous, and Jesus told them the Son of Man is the Lord of the Sabbath. Jesus is the King of the kingdom of heaven, and His gospel is the rule for the life and behavior of His disciples.

Jesus continued to defend Himself by showing that the religious leaders missed the true meaning in the scriptures that people were supposed to live by. They believed the scriptures taught them how to have eternal life.

The scriptures in fact did teach them and they testified that eternal life comes through the Messiah, but they didn't believe Jesus was the Messiah.

Jesus heals in a Jewish synagogue

On another Sabbath Jesus went into the synagogue and saw a man with a withered hand. The Scribes and Pharisees were watching Jesus to see what He would do hoping they could make a charge against Him. Jesus knew their thoughts, and He told the man with the withered hand to stand up. Jesus asked the Scribes and Pharisees if it was lawful, to do good on the Sabbath or to do evil, to save life or destroy life?

Then Jesus told the man to stretch out his hand and Jesus restored his hand. The Scribes and Pharisees went into a rage.

(MK3) The Pharisees planned to kill Jesus but He knew their intentions, so Jesus and His disciples left and went to the Sea of Galilee. A great crowd from Galilee, Judea, Jerusalem, Idumea, Tyre and Sidon came to Him because they heard about the great things Jesus was doing. Jesus healed many and the crowd closed around Him to touch Him. The demons he cast out fell down at His feet saying, *"You are the Son of God."* The demons knew who Jesus was, because they were fallen angels that served Satan. They had left heaven and come to the earth to torment God's people.

Jesus stood with His disciples and a great crowd of people from Judea, Jerusalem and the seacoast of Tyre and Sidon and He healed them. The people tried to touch Him because they saw the power to heal that had come out of Him.

During his ministry Jesus had many disciples, or followers, besides the twelve who became apostles. A disciple is a follower of a certain person or movement. Jesus' disciples were simply those who followed him. We who follow Christ's teaching today are disciples of Jesus Christ.

(LK 6) Jesus went to a mountain to pray, and He prayed all night. The next morning He called His disciples to Him, and he chose twelve men to be His apostles. He gave them special power from the Holy Spirit so they could continue His ministry after he was crucified.

In order to be an apostle, they had to have been an eyewitness of Jesus and especially to have been with Him after His resurrection. They had to have the ability to testify to everything Jesus did. Jesus officially chose the twelve who would serve as apostles. They would continue to follow Him and serve Him and the kingdom of God for the rest of their lives. The apostles were Peter, James, John, Andrew, Philip, Bartholomew, Matthew, Thomas, James the son of Alphaeus, Thaddaeus, Simon the Cananite, and Judas Iscariot. These twelve disciples were called apostles.

The word apostle means one sent on a mission. Jesus sent His apostles on a mission to preach and to teach about Him and His Kingdom after His death. They were there in the beginning of Jesus' Kingdom here on earth.

Jesus Preaches the Sermon on the Mount

Most of Jesus' time on earth was spent in Galilee proper and the area of the Sea of Galilee. The Sea of Galilee was near the middle of Galilee on the far eastern side. The Hebrew word for hill and mountain were sometimes used interchangeably. There are many references to Jesus going up on a mountain to speak to the people so everyone could see him. Some of the larger mountains in Galilee were Mt Hermon, Meron, Gilboa, Lebanon, Tabor, and Carmel, and then there were many smaller mountains.

(Matt. 5 through 8, Luke 6) Jesus went up on the mountain and sat down, and He called His disciples to him and preached what we call the Sermon on the Mount. At the beginning of His sermon He taught them about being blessed if they have certain attitudes toward Him, His kingdom, and their fellow man. We call these blessings the beatitudes. He continued by teaching them many other things concerning living a Christian life. *Mt 8:28 "And so it was, when Jesus had ended these sayings, that the people were astonished at His teaching. For He taught them as one having authority, and not as the scribes."*

Jesus' teaching was recorded in the scriptures for all people in every generation. The work of the apostles ceased after their death, but they left an inspired record in the scriptures. Jesus taught about the proper attitude and behavior expected of a disciple. Mt 5-6-7, Luke 6:20-49 Matthew and Luke give a similar, but not the exact, version of the Sermon on the Mount. Some believe the writers in Matthew and Luke were writing about two different times. It doesn't matter, because Jesus is teaching the word Of God documented by both Matthew and Luke, and both versions are valid scripture. I have chosen to use Matthew's version of the Beatitudes in this document found in Matthew 5:3-12.

"Blessed are the poor in spirit, For theirs is the kingdom of heaven.

Blessed are those who mourn, For they shall be comforted.

Blessed are the meek, For they shall inherit the earth.

Blessed are those who hunger and thirst after righteousness, For they shall be filled.

Blessed are the merciful, For they shall obtain mercy.

Blessed are the pure in heart, For they shall see God.

Blessed are the peacemakers For they shall be called sons of God.

Blessed are those who are persecuted for righteousness sake, for theirs is the kingdom of heaven.

The word blessed means to praise, to make happy by God. Blessed also means to receive the gifts of God, especially the gift of eternal life in heaven. Jesus described those in His kingdom as being blessed. They will be accepted and blessed by God and will be happy.

Jesus taught that God would bless those who were poor in spirit. The poor in spirit learn to depend on God for their everyday needs. They would be willing to have faith in Christ and follow His teaching.

He taught that those who mourn will be comforted. Mourning is an expression of deep grief, especially when someone you love is hurt, seriously ill or dies. Jesus' disciples would experience deep grief when Jesus was tortured and died on the cross. There are other times when people express sorrow and grief over the misfortune of someone else. Sorrow and grief for the misfortune of other people shows that a person has deep feelings for other people. They will be comforted by the Holy Spirit and by the word of God. God will bless them because they are the kind of people God takes delight in.

He taught that those who are meek shall inherit the earth. A meek person has a humble spirit, not haughty, does not boast, does not think too highly of himself, or does not set himself above others.

Inheriting the earth does not mean the earth we now live on. Inheriting the earth refers to entrance into the new heaven and new earth at the end of time.

Isaiah 66:22 "For as the new heavens and the new earth, which I will make shall remain before Me," says the Lord, So shall your descendants and your name remain. And it shall come to pass That from one New Moon to another, And from one Sabbath to another, All flesh shall come to worship before Me," says the Lord."

Those who are hungry and thirsty for righteousness are those who have a desire to constantly learn from God's word. They can be filled, because they feed of God's word every day. Jesus said, *"My Father gives you the true bread from heaven. For the bread of God is He who comes down from heaven and gives life to the world." (John 6:32b-33) "I am the bread of life." (John 6:48)*

Those who show mercy to other people will receive mercy from God. *James 2:13: "For judgment is without mercy to the one who has shown no mercy. Mercy triumphs over judgment."*

Christians are admonished to keep a pure heart, because the pure in heart will see God after the resurrection. *Matt. 12:34b "For out of the abundance of the heart the mouth speaks."* Christians are to keep their hearts pure so that what they speak and do will be acceptable to God. The peacemakers will be called the sons of God. They love everyone and live in peace. *Romans 12:17-18 "Repay no one evil for evil. Have regard for good things in the sight of all men. If it is possible, as much as depends on you, live peaceably with all men. Beloved, do not avenge yourselves but rather give place to wrath; for it is written, 'Vengeance is Mine, I will repay,' says the Lord." V.21 "Do not be overcome by evil, but overcome evil with good."*

Jesus said you are blessed if you are persecuted for righteousness sake. People may be persecuted because they are striving for righteousness. Matthew's account of the teaching of Jesus also compares Jesus' disciples to light.

Jesus said a city that is on a hill couldn't be hid, because everyone can see the lights from the city. Then He said that you wouldn't light a candle and then cover it up with a basket, but instead you would put it out where it could give light.

The life of God's people should be like a light illuminating the gospel of Christ to those around us as they see our godly lives, and are drawn to our godliness in Christ.

Matthew also compared Jesus' disciples to salt. Salt has many good characteristics such as seasoning, and preserving. God's people can by example change the attitudes of people towards faith, hope and love for God and Christ by being good examples of living by the teaching of Christ in obedience to the gospel message, and by promoting the teaching of the Bible. The life of those who live in obedience to the gospel are preserving their life for eternity.

The religious leaders of the Jews in the first century were bad examples of their religion. They mistreated and discouraged people by their own bad example of unrighteousness. Jesus said to those who would be disciples that their righteousness must be greater than the righteousness of the scribes and Pharisees.

(Mt 5) Jesus said He did not come to establish the Law. He came to fulfill the Law. The Law of Moses could not take away the guilt of sin; in fact it caused sin to multiply, because people failed to obey the Law.

Fulfilling the Law of Moses means it would cease to be in effect after the death, burial and resurrection of Jesus. Jesus continues His sermon teaching about murder, adultery, divorce, oaths, retaliation and love.

Matthew 5:43-48 "You have heard that it was said, 'You shall love your neighbor and hate your enemy.' But I say to you love your enemies, bless those who curse you, do good to those who hate you, and pray for those who spitefully use you and persecute you, that you may be sons of your Father in heaven; for He makes His sun rise on the evil and on the good, and sends rain on the just and on the unjust.'

"For if you love those who love you, what reward have you? Do not even the tax collectors do the same? And if you greet your brethren only, what do you do more that others? Do not even the tax collectors do so? Therefore you shall be perfect, just as your Father in heaven is perfect."

People who have faith in Christ can be saved from the guilt of sin if they have faith in Christ, repent and ask God for forgiveness and continue to live a life of faith, hope and love. The sacrifice of Christ will atone for their sin.

(MT 6) Jesus continued His teaching on the mountain with a lesson about charitable deeds. Disciples, by nature, would be inclined to be charitable which is good, and Jesus taught that people must have the right attitude when they give to or do favors for people. Jesus said to not glorify your self before others for praise, because that is like a hypocrite. Jesus advised not to let wealth or the pursuit of wealth, hinder your responsibility to serve God.

Jesus also applied the same advice about praying. Do not pray to attract favorable attention to yourself. Jesus advised to pray in secret. Jesus is not saying you should not pray publicly, but when you do, pray with the proper attitude of humility towards God. Pray that God's will be done in all things, pray for our daily sustenance, pray for our inadequacies, and pray for the moral strength to do the right thing. Ask God for the things you need and He will give you what you need, God in heaven gives good things to those who ask. *Mt 7:12 "Therefore, whatever you want men to do to you, do also to them, for this is the Law and the prophets."*

(MT 7) Jesus said to not judge. That does not mean a disciple should never have an opinion about other People. People make judgments about many things constantly. Jesus was referring to do not make unjust and condemning judgments about other people. God is the judge of all people. People who judge other people need to remember their own sins instead of being hypocritical. Be considerate and kind to other people and let God do the judging.

At this time the Jewish people were still obligated to keep the Law of Moses, so Jesus told them to continue to obey the Law of Moses. He then taught them about a new righteousness that would take the place of the Law of Moses after His death, burial, resurrection and ascension.

Jesus taught about two paths in life that people follow, and He compares them to a path that leads to a narrow gate and a path that leads to a wide gate. The path to the wide gate or way of life leads to destruction, because that path leads to worldly things that are evil and do not serve God, but many people enter that gate. The path to the narrow gate leads to eternal life, because your life is spent in obedience to God, but only a few people enter that gate.

Jesus warns that there will be false teachers that proclaim to be righteous but are actually like wolves that will destroy you by their false teaching. Jesus teaches that not everyone who claims to be righteous is rightcous. Only those who do the will of God will be in the kingdom.

(MT 7) The person who hears Jesus teaching and does what He says is wise like a man who builds his house on rock, which is a solid foundation of the truth of the Word of God. His life will stand up against the storms of life when they come.

Everyone who hears God but does not do what He says is foolish, and his house is built on sand and he will not be able to withstand the storms of life. In the life of everyone there will be some difficult times and some good times, and those who have a solid foundation of faith, hope and love in Christ will be able to withstand the difficult times.

Jesus teaching astonished the people because He taught them as one having authority. When Jesus came down from the mountain, a great many people followed Him and Jesus healed a man with leprosy.

Jesus Goes to Capernaum

(Luke 7) After Jesus came down the mountain, He and the disciples went to Capernaum. There was a centurion, an official in the Roman army, in Capernaum who had a servant who was very sick and about to die. When the centurion heard that Jesus was in Capernaum, he sent some elders of the Jews to ask Jesus to come and heal his servant. Jesus agreed to go with them.

When Jesus and the men came to the house, the centurion came out and asked Jesus not to come into his house, because the centurion felt he was worthy to even ask Jesus.

But he told Jesus that if he would just say the word, his servant would be healed. The centurion had faith and a hope that Jesus would heal his servant. When he said this, Jesus said to the crowd following him, *"I say to you, I have not found such great faith not even in Israel!"(Luke 7:9)* When the men who were with Jesus went into the house, the servant was healed.

Luke 7.11 "Now it happened the day after, that He went into a city called Nain in the plain of Jezreel; and many of His disciples went with Him, and a large crowd." Nain means pleasant or green pastures because it overlooks the Plain of Esdraelon and the valley of Jezreel.

Jesus came near the gate of the city and saw a dead man being carried out. The dead man was the only son of a widow. Jesus had compassion for her and told her not to cry. He then touched the open coffin and told the young man to arise and he set up. The people were afraid, and they glorified God when they recognized Jesus as a prophet of God. The report of Jesus raising a person from the dead was spread throughout Judea and the surrounding area.

(LK 7) The disciples of John the Baptist told John about the things Jesus was doing, so John sent two of his disciples to Jesus to ask Him if He was the Messiah. The men came to Jesus and asked, "Are You the Messiah, or should we keep looking?"

While John's disciples were there, Jesus healed many people of infirmities, evil spirits and other afflictions. Jesus told John's disciples to go tell John that the blind see, the lame walk, the lepers are cleansed, the deaf hear and the dead are raised and the poor have the gospel preached to them.

Jesus did many marvelous things in approximately three years before He ascended to heaven. Jesus did many works in numerous cities but he was not always pleased with the result of His teaching and healing in some of the cities. Many people would not believe in Jesus and follow Him.

Matthew 11:20-24 "Then He began to rebuke the cities in which most of His mighty works had been done, because they did not repent; "Woe to you, Chorazin! Woe to you Bethsaida! For if the mighty works, which were done in you had been done in Tyre and Sidon, they would have repented long ago in sackcloth and ashes. But I say to you, it will be more tolerable for Tyre and Sidon than for you in the day of judgment. And you Capernaum, who are exalted to heaven, will be brought down to Hades; for if the mighty works which were done in you had been done in Sodom, it would have remained until this day. But I say to you that it shall be more tolerable for the land of Sodom in the day of judgment than for you."

Jesus was talking about people who are sinners and will not repent of their sin—warning them about going to a place called Hades. Hades is a place in the heavens where the spirits of the dead go to wait for the second coming of Christ. There is a place in Hades for the spirits of the righteous and a separate place for the spirits of the unrighteous.

Hades is also referred to as hell. Hell was used by Jesus as the hell of fire indicating a place of torture or death. In the Old Testament the word Sheol was translated as grave or pit—a place of both the saved and unsaved spirits. When the New Testament was translated into Greek, Sheol was translated as Hades Thayer's Greek—English Lexicon.

Luke 16:19-31 "there was a certain rich man clothed in purple and fine linen and fared sumptuously every day. But there was a certain beggar named Lazarus, full of sores, who was laid at his gate, desiring to be fed with the crumbs which fell from the rich man's table. Moreover the dogs came and licked his sores. So it was that the beggar died and was carried by the angels to Abraham's bosom.

The rich man also died and was buried. And being in torment in Hades, he lifted up his eyes and saw Abraham afar off, and Lazarus in his bosom. Then he cried and said, 'Father Abraham, have mercy on me and send Lazarus that he may dip the tip of his finger in water and cool my tongue; for I am tormented in this flame.'

"But Abraham said, 'Son, remember that in your lifetime you received your good things, and likewise Lazarus evil things; but now he is comforted. And besides all this, between us and you there is a great gulf fixed, so that those who want to pass from here to you cannot, nor can those from there pass to us."

According to this parable, when people die their spirits go to Hades. There are two places in Hades. One is for the spirit of those who are saved by their faith, hope and love and they are in a place of paradise. Another place for those without faith is a place of torment. When people die, their fate is already determined, and their spirit has no choice or chance to change their destination in hell or paradise. The spirits wait there until the day of God's judgment at the end of time.

Jesus Eats at the House of a Pharisee

(LK 7) One of the Pharisees named Simon invited Jesus to eat with him, so Jesus went to his house and sat down to eat. A woman who was a sinner came to the house when she learned that Jesus was there. She brought with her some expensive fragrant oil and stood at Jesus' feet crying. She then began to wash His feet with her tears and wipe them with her hair. She kissed Jesus' feet and rubbed fragrant oil on them.

The Pharisee saw her and reasoned to himself that Jesus must not be a prophet, because He did not know the woman was a sinner. Otherwise He would not have let her touch Him. But Jesus knew everything about the woman. He knew who she was and what she was.

Jesus told Simon that He had something to tell him. He then told him a parable about two men who each owed a debt to a creditor. One owed a large sum of money and the other one owed quite a bit less. Neither of the debtors had the money to repay the creditor, so the creditor forgave the debt of each man. Jesus asked Simon, "Which one do you think loved the creditor more?" Simon said he supposed the one with the largest debt. Jesus told Simon he had correctly judged. He reminded Simon about how loving and graciously the woman had treated Him, The debt of sin of the woman was great, but her faith in Jesus saved her. *Luke 7:50 Then He said to the woman, "Your faith has saved you. Go in peace."* The redeeming power of Jesus is great enough to nullify the penalty of all kinds of sin.

(LK 8) Jesus and His twelve disciples continued traveling. They went through every city and village and Jesus taught about the kingdom of God. Some of the women who had been healed provided them with food. Mary Magdalene, Joanna, the wife of Herod's steward and Susanna.

Jesus leaves Capernaum

Jesus left Capernaum the next day and went to a deserted place to rest, but the people found Him and pleaded with Him to stay with them. Jesus said, *Luke5: 43 "I must preach the kingdom of God to the other cities also, because for this purpose I have been sent."* Jesus wanted to teach the gospel while He had an opportunity, and each Sabbath He went to the synagogues to teach. He went to Galilee and the surrounding regions teaching about the kingdom of God and healing all kinds of sickness and disease. His fame spread throughout the Roman Empire.

(MT 12) A blind and mute man who had a demon in him was brought to Jesus, and Jesus healed him. The people were amazed and wondered if Jesus could be the descendant of King David. They knew the Messiah was to come from the birth line of David. Jesus was the Messiah they had been expecting for many years.

Jesus healed the man and the Pharisees accused Jesus of casting out demons by the power of Beelzebub. Beelzebub was a false god that was worshiped by the Philistines in the city of Ekron. He was associated with Satan, the ruler of the demons.

Jesus could read the thoughts of people, so He asked them if Satan would cast out his own demons? The demons are Satan's angels. Jesus said a house divided against its self could not stand, implying that he could not be casting out Satan by the power of Satan.

Jesus was casting out demons by the power of God. Jesus told them every sin could be forgiven, even blasphemy against men, but blasphemy against the Holy Spirit would not be forgiven.

Mark 3-28-29 "Assuredly, I say to you, all sins will be forgiven the sons of men, and whatever blasphemies they may utter; but he who blasphemes against the Holy Spirit never has forgiveness, but is subject to eternal condemnation."

Jesus would die so sinful people could be forgiven of sin through faith in Him, but blasphemy against the Holy Spirit would not be forgiven. Blasphemy means speaking evil against the Holy Spirit. The work of the Holy Spirit includes spiritual guidance and comforting God's people.

The Pharisees demanded to see Jesus perform a miracle to prove that He was the Messiah. Jesus called them an adulterous generation. Faith hope and love once established, does not require a sign, and Jesus said only a wicked and adulterous generation would ask for a sign. Jesus said there would be no sign except the sign of Jonah.

Even the Gentiles believed in the story of Jonah. God had sent Israel's prophet Jonah to preach to the people in Nineveh, but Jonah didn't want to obey God, so God punished him. Jonah got aboard a ship trying to run away from God, but God caused a great wind to come up. The waves were high, and Jonah told the frightened crew of the ship to throw him in the sea, and the winds would cease. So Jonah was thrown into the sea and a great whale swallowed him.

In the whale's belly, Jonah prayed to God for forgiveness. After three days and nights in the whale's belly, the whale spit Jonah out on dry land. After that Jonah preached to the people in Nineveh. God saved Jonah's life in a strange way to prove that He is God Almighty.

Jesus was comparing what happened to Jonah to His upcoming death, burial and resurrection. Jesus would be three days and nights in the grave, and then He would come out of the grave and resume His mission on earth.

(MT 12, LK8) On one occasion while Jesus was talking to the people, His mother and brothers came to speak with Him. Someone told Jesus they wanted to speak with Him and Jesus said, *"Who is My mother and who are My brothers?"* Then he pointed to His disciples and said, *"Here are My mother and My brothers! For whoever does the will of My Father in heaven is my brother and sister and mother."* Jesus recognized and loved, His mother and His family but He also loved everyone even the sinners he came to die for.

Jesus Teaches in Parables

The term parable literally means placing beside. A parable puts thoughts side by side similar to an allegory. A parable tells a short story with interesting illustrations of moral and religious truth, a story that is familiar in nature or in every day life. Many of Jesus' parables related to the characteristics of the kingdom of God. They enlightened the knowledge about the kingdom of God for some people but hardened the hearts of those who did not believe the gospel truth.

Jesus spoke in parables to attract interest and provoke an inquiry, giving Him an opportunity to teach a spiritual lesson.

Matthew 13:10-17 "And the disciples came and said to Him, "Why do You speak to them in parables?" He answered and said to them, "Because it has been given to you to know the mysteries of the kingdom of heaven, but to them it has not been given. For whoever has, to him more will be given, and he will have abundance; but whoever does not have, even what he has will be taken away from him."

Therefore I speak to them in parables, because seeing they do not see, and hearing they do not hear, nor do they understand. And in them the prophecy of Isaiah is fulfilled, which says: Hearing you will hear and shall not understand, and seeing you will see and not perceive; for the hearts of this people have grown dull. Their ears are hard of hearing, and their eyes they have closed, lest they should see with their eyes and hear with their ears, lest they should understand with their hearts and turn, so that I should heal them."

Honest people without prejudice and with an honest heart would be able to understand Jesus' parables, but those who were prejudice against Jesus would harden their heart. There were some things about the kingdom that Jesus wanted to teach his disciples without revealing the meaning to His enemies, so He taught in parables and explained the meaning of the parables to His disciples. There are many parables in the book of Luke that reveals Christ's understanding of the attitudes of all kinds of people, as He examines their responses and attitudes toward God and Christ.

Some of Jesus' parables are illustrations about the attitudes and actions of the rich and the poor. The middle class was not wide spread in the first century. There were only a small degree of those who might be classified as the middle class. The majority of the people were poor. Jesus accomplished two purposes with the parables: to point out the improper attitudes of those who were rich, and to express God's attitude towards people. Jesus taught about the attitudes of the various Jewish sects

In order to understand the meaning of a parable a person must not be prejudice but be interested enough to listen and thoughtfully consider what they hear. Parables reveal the truth to those with understanding hearts. Potential believers accept the truth taught in the parable and learn from the parable. Unbelievers would not understand the true meaning of a parable and they would leave Jesus alone.

Jesus taught in parables to reveal the truth to the righteous and conceal it from the wicked. (MT 13) (Luke 8). A great many people came from every city to see and hear Jesus teach in parables. In Matthew 13, Luke 13, 14 and Mark 4 Jesus taught 38 parables. In this document the parables are not necessarily in the order of the time Jesus taught them.

(MT 13-MK 4-LK 8) The Parable of a Sower, Soils, Wheat and the Mustard seed, Parable of leaven, the tares and of Hidden Treasure, The Pearl of Great Price, Parable of the Dragnet, Parable of the Householder. The disciples asked Jesus why He taught people in parables Jesus explained that they knew about the secrets of the kingdom of heaven because it was given to them but it was not given to other people. When the Apostles taught the Holy Spirit inspired them with knowledge and truth.

The parable of the soils is about a farmer that sowed seed in four different types of soil, and he received a different yield from each soil. The seed represents the gospel of Christ that is preached to all people but yields different results from the people hearing the parable.

The parable of the wheat is also about a farmer. The farmer planted good seed in his field, and an enemy planted weed seed among the farmer's good seed. All of the seeds produced plants.

The good seed represents people who hear the gospel and respond to it in a positive way by obeying the gospel and remaining faithful. The plants that grow from the bad seed represent people who hear the gospel message and respond to the message in a negative way refusing to obey the gospel. Jesus said both kinds of people will remain on earth together, but when He comes, He will separate the good people from the bad people and destroy the bad people represented by the weeds.

(Mark 4) The, parable of the soils is a comparison between the people who hear the gospel message and how they respond to it. The soil represents the heart of those who hear. In the parable of the soils, the types of ground represent four types of people with different attitudes toward the gospel message. People who believe the gospel and respond in a positive way are the people with an obedient heart; they represent the good soil. The people represented by the other types of soil will reject the gospel of Christ.

There will always be some people with believing hearts and positive attitudes and there will also be those who have unbelieving hearts.

The parable of the mustard seed compares the kingdom of God to a mustard seed. The mustard seed is a very tiny seed when planted, but it yields a very large plant. The kingdom of God started with Jesus and a few disciples and began to grow and eventually grew into a large kingdom. Jesus predicts that the Kingdom of God (church) will grow and spread out over the earth.

The parable of the leaven is about leaven that is added to dough to make the lump of dough grow larger, one example is yeast. Without the leaven, the dough would not grow larger. The gospel of Christ that is actively taught is leaven that will make the kingdom of God grow larger.

Parable of the hidden treasure *Matthew 13:44 "Again the kingdom of heaven is like treasure hidden in a field, which a man found and hid; and for joy over it he goes and sells all that he has and buys that field."*

The hidden treasure is membership in the kingdom of God, which is so great that a person of faith will do whatever is necessary to gain entrance into the kingdom of God.

Jesus teaches a parable about a lamp that gives light. A lamp that is lit should not be hidden so that its light can shine all around. The light from the lamp represents the Word of God including the gospel of Christ. The advice to those who have knowledge of God's word and accept it and obey Christ should not hide their righteousness and knowledge but let it shine everywhere they are.

Parable of the pearl of great price is like a merchant looking for beautiful pearls. He found one very expensive pearl and he sold everything he had and bought the pearl. The pearl represents membership in the kingdom of God and the merchant represents anyone who is willing to obey the gospel when they learn about it. Membership in the Kingdom of God is more valuable than anything else on earth.

Parable of the dragnet is about casting a net into the sea and catching all kinds of fish. It is about the separation of the saved from the unsaved at the end of time. Some will be good enough for God to keep and some will be thrown into the fire to be burned. The angels at the end of time will separate the good from the bad. Parable of the householder is about the generation that was living during the time Jesus was on earth. The scribe is like the religious members of Judaism. The householder is God who made a covenant with people during Moses time but made a new and better covenant in Christ. The scribes, Pharisees and other religious leaders held on to the old Law of Moses and rejected the gospel of Christ.

Jesus and His Disciples Cross the Sea of Galilee

(MT 8) To avoid the great multitude coming toward Him, Jesus told His disciples to cross the sea in their boat to the other side. Before Jesus could go with them, a scribe came to Him and told Jesus he would follow Him anywhere He went. Jesus said, *"Foxes have holes and birds of the air have nests, but the Son of Man has nowhere to lay His head."* Jesus could not have a permanent place to stay, because He wanted to constantly be teaching. Another person wanted to follow Jesus, but he told Jesus that he must first go and bury his father. Jesus said, *"Follow Me, and let the dead bury the dead."* Jesus' meaning was to let those who will not follow Him bury the dead.

Spiritual matters are more important than other matters and should be given priority. There is nothing more important than obeying the gospel of Christ.

(MT 8) On one occasion Jesus and the disciples were in their boat in the middle of the sea. A great storm came up and the waves of the sea were high. Jesus was asleep in the boat, and His disciples became scared and woke Him saying, "Lord, save us." But Jesus said to them, *"Why are you fearful, O you of little faith?"(Matt. 8:26)* Jesus was disappointed that His disciples would be afraid after all of the things they had witnessed Him do. Jesus got up and said to the wind and waves, *"Peace, be still."* And He calmed the waters. The disciples were amazed that Jesus had the power to make even the sea and the wind obey Him. The disciples didn't yet realize that Jesus had such great power even over the forces of nature, and they wondered at who He was that even the wind and sea obeyed Him.

On the other side of the sea they came to the country of the Gergesenes (also called the Gaderenes) who lived in the large region east of Galilee. The people were residents of Gadara, one of the cities of the Decapolis. Gadara was located east of the Jordan River. Jesus came ashore and a man from the city who had been possessed by demons for a long time came to Him. The man was naked. He didn't live in a house. He lived in the tombs where people were buried. The man fell down in front of Jesus, and in a loud voice said, *"What have I to do with you, Jesus Son of the Most High God?"* The demons in the man knew who Jesus was, because demons are the Devil's fallen angels who lived in heaven at one time. Jesus told the demons to come out of the man. The man was shackled and chained because of the demons, but he broke free from them, and the demons drove him into the wilderness. Jesus asked the demon his names and he said legion, because many demons had entered the man.

God created the angels before the creation of the universe, they are heavenly creatures but have the ability to go between heaven and earth and they serve God day and night. The angels have personalities of their own, Some angels had rebelled against God and took up with Satan the Devil. The angels who serve Satan rebel against God and are called demons, and they are antagonistic towards God's people. Demons have much greater power than humans, but they are subject to God. The demons are enemies of Christ and the Jews who were God's people. During the days of Jesus' ministry, the demons persecuted the Jews and some even lived inside people.

Matthew records an incident of two men who were possessed by demons. These demons saw Jesus and called Him the Son of God. They asked Jesus if He had come to torment them. The demons feared He would cast them out of the two men, and they asked Him to let them go into a herd of pigs that was nearby. Jesus told them to go, and they entered the pigs and the whole herd ran down a slope into the sea.

(MK 5) Jesus and His disciples crossed over the sea again and went back to Capernaum. One of the rulers of the synagogue in Capernaum by the name of Jairus came and fell at Jesus' feet begging Him to come lay His hands on his little daughter who was at the point of death and heal her. Jesus told him to not be afraid but believe in Him and she would be well. Jesus then went with Jairus. He entered the house but only allowed Peter, James and John and the father and mother of the girl to go in the house with Him.

They all wept because they thought the girl was dead, Jesus told them not to weep because she was only sleeping. But they still believed she was dead. Jesus made all of them go outside, and then He took her hand and told her to arise. Her spirit returned to her and she immediately arose. Her parents were astonished at what Jesus had done.

(MK 5) There was a woman there among the people who had been bleeding for twelve years. The doctors weren't able to help her, and she was getting worse. When she saw Jesus, the woman made her way through the crowd and touched His clothes. When she touched His clothes her bleeding stopped. Jesus realized that power had gone out of Him, so He asked who touched His clothing? The woman came and fell down before Jesus and told Him she had touched Him. Jesus told her that her faith made her well.

(MT 9) When Jesus left Jairus house two blind men followed Him and called out to Him saying, "Son of David, have mercy." Jesus went into the house and they came to Him, and Jesus asked them if they thought He could heal them. They said, "Yes Lord" and He touched their eyes and He said, *"According to your faith let it be to you."* Jesus told them not to tell anyone but to spread the news about Him.

A man was brought to Jesus who was possessed of a demon and couldn't speak. Jesus cast the demon out of him and then the man was able to speak.

(MT13) Jesus and His disciples went to Nazareth where He grew up, and on the Sabbath He entered the synagogue and taught the people. Everyone was puzzled by His wisdom and teaching and of the mighty works He was doing. The people of Nazareth recognized Jesus as the son of Joseph and Mary, and they knew His brothers James, Joses, Judas, Simon and His sisters. They thought that Jesus was an impostor who only claimed to be the Messiah. Jesus was rejected in His own hometown, and He said, *"A prophet is not without honor except in His own country, among His own relatives, and in His own house."(Mark 6:4)* He didn't perform many miracles in Nazareth, because the people there didn't believe in Him.

The Twelve Apostles Are Sent Out to Preach

(LK 9) Jesus gave the twelve apostles power and authority over demons and the power to heal diseases. He told them to go and preach about the kingdom of God and to heal the sick. He also told them not take anything with them when they went, not a staff, baggage, bread or money. When they entered a house, they were to stay there while they were teaching. If anyone would not invite them in, they were to go on their way. Jesus was preparing them for the work of an apostle. The apostles would finish their work after Jesus' death.

The apostles obeyed Jesus in every way, and then they returned to Jesus and reported what they had done and taught, and Jesus allowed them to go to a deserted place in their boat so they could rest.

(MK 6) King Herod began to hear about Jesus, because his name was becoming well known, but He thought Jesus was John the Baptist who had come back from the dead. Herod had previously ordered the execution of John the Baptist by having him beheaded.

Jesus and His disciples got in a boat and crossed over the Sea of Galilee to get away from the crowd, but the people saw them leave and ran from the cities and arrived where Jesus and the apostles were going before they got there. When Jesus got there and saw the multitude and He had compassion for them.

(JN 6) Jesus went up a mountain and sat down and started teaching them. It was beginning to be late in the day, and Jesus saw a great multitude of people who had come to hear him. He turned to Philip and asked where they could buy bread to feed the people that followed them because they were in a deserted place. Jesus was testing Philip, because Jesus already knew that He would miraculously supply enough food to feed the five thousand people. Later As the day became longer the disciples asked Jesus to send the people away so they could go to town and get food. But He said, *Luke 9:13 "You give them something to eat."*

One of His apostles, Andrew, told him that there was a boy there with five loaves of bread and two fish, not enough food for five thousand people. Jesus had the people to sit down on the grass, and then He miraculously supplied enough food for everyone. Jesus had the people assemble in groups of fifty. He blessed the small amount of food the disciples had and broke it into pieces and told the disciples give it to the crowd.

Everyone had enough to eat and there were twelve baskets full left over. Jesus told the disciples to pick up the food left over so that nothing would be wasted. The people witnessing the miraculous feeding said Jesus was truly a prophet.

(MK 6, MT 14) After feeding the five thousand, Jesus was afraid the people would attempt to make Him their king by force. He told His disciple to go alone by boat to the other side of the sea, then Jesus went up the mountain by himself to pray.

When evening came Jesus was alone, and the disciples were in their boat. That evening when it became dark the disciples were in the middle of the sea, and a strong wind was blowing. Jesus began walking to the disciples on the water. When he was a distance from the boat, the disciples saw Him and they were afraid because they thought He was a ghost, and they cried out.

Jesus called to them and told them to be of good cheer because it was He, and He told them not to be afraid. Peter asked Jesus to command for him to come to Him on the water, and Jesus told him to come. Peter got out of the boat and began to walk on the water to Jesus, but the waves were washing around him, and he became frightened. He began to sink, and he cried out for Jesus to save him. Jesus put out His hand and helped Peter into the boat and the wind died down. His apostles worshiped Jesus saying, "Truly, You are the Son of God."

(MK 6) They crossed the sea and came to Gennesaret. When the disciples left the boat, the people on shore recognized them. They ran through the territory and began to bring sick people on beds for Jesus to heal. Jesus entered the cities, villages and market places and the people begged Him to let them touch the hem of His garment. Those who touched him were healed.

(JN 6) The next day the people whom Jesus had fed on the mountain went to the place where they had seen His disciples leave in their boats. They saw that Jesus wasn't there, so they left in boats to find Him.

Jesus had already gone into Capernaum by then, so they went to Capernaum and found Him.

Jesus took advantage of an opportunity at that time to teach a lesson about the benevolence of God. He told them that the only reason they were looking for Him was to get more food. He told them to not be more concerned with finding food to eat than being concerned with finding spiritual food that could give them everlasting life. Jesus said he could give them that kind of food, because His Father God had chosen Him for that work. The people wanted to know what they could do to work the works of God?

John 6:29 "Jesus answered and said to them. "This is the work of God, that you believe in Him whom He sent." When Jesus said for them to believe, He was saying to have faith and hope in Him. The people then asked Jesus to perform a miracle so they could believe in Him, and they reminded Him of the fathers of old who miraculously received bread in the wilderness wandering in the Sinai desert. Jesus said, *John 6:32-33 "Most assuredly I say to you, Moses did not give you the bread from heaven, but My Father gives you the true bread from heaven. For the bread of God is he who comes down from heaven and gives life to the world."* Jesus identifies Himself as the true bread from heaven sent by God who could give them eternal life.

Jesus Goes to Capernaum then leaves for Tyre

Jesus and the disciples left Capernaum and went to the area of Tyre and Sidon. Tyre was a seaport on the Phoenician coast and Sidon was not far from there. Jesus secretly entered a house so he could be hidden from the crowd of people for a while. (Sometimes Jesus sought privacy so He could rest.)

Jesus wasn't in the house long before a woman who had a daughter possessed by a demon found out where He was. The woman came and fell at Jesus' feet. She was a Greek, a Syro-Phoenician. The woman asked Jesus to cast out the demon, but Jesus said, *Mark 7:27 "Let the children be filled first, for it is not good to take the children's bread and throw it to the little dogs."* The woman was not satisfied with Jesus' answer and she said, "Lord, even the little dogs eat the crumbs under the table that fall from the children."

Jesus came to His own people the Jews first, even though His sacrifice would be for the redemption of all people. The Jews had been the children of God throughout the old covenant, and the woman and her daughter were Gentiles. The Jews considered gentile people to be no better than dogs. Jesus was a Jew, and God sent Him to the Jews first, because the promise of redemption was to come through the Nation of Israel. *Mark 7:29-30 "Then He said to her, 'For this saying go your way; the demon has gone out of your daughter.' And when she had come to her house, she found the demon gone out, and her daughter lying on the bed."*

(MK 7) Jesus and His disciples left Tyre and Sidon and went through the region of Decapolis to the Sea of Galilee. Decapolis was a Gentile area during that time, but a small Jewish population also lived there. Decapolis bordered Galilee and Perea.

The people brought a deaf mute with a speech impediment to Jesus and begged Him to heal the man. Jesus took him out away from the crowd. Then He put his fingers in the man's ears. He then spat and touched his tongue. Jesus then looked toward heaven and said "*Ephatha,*" meaning 'be opened.' The man was immediately able to hear and he could talk plainly. The people were astonished at what He had done. Jesus told the people not to tell anyone what He had done, however the more He commanded them not to tell anyone, the more they spread the news all over that area.

(MT 15) Jesus left the area of Decapolis and went along the edge of the Sea of Galilee. Then He went up on a mountain there and sat down. A great many people came to where He was and brought the lame, blind, mute, and maimed to him for Him to heal. They put those needing healing at the feet of Jesus, and He healed them and the people were amazed. Jesus called His disciples to come to Him, and He told them He felt sorry for the people because they had been with Him a few days and had nothing to eat.

The disciples were concerned because they were in the wilderness and there was no place to get food. Jesus asked them what food they had and they said seven loaves of bread and a few fish. Jesus told the people to sit down and He gave thanks and broke them. Then He gave the bread and fish to the disciples and they fed the people, and the food did not run out. Jesus miraculously fed the four thousand people and they had seven baskets of food left.

Jesus and His Disciples go to Dalmanutha

(MK 8) Jesus sent the people away and He and the disciples left in a boat and sailed to Dalmanutha on the west shore of the Sea of Galilee south of Capernaum. Mary Magdalene was from Magdala in that same area.

The Pharisees came to where Jesus was, but they still did not believe He was the Messiah, and they were anxious to see if He could perform a miracle. Jesus was disgusted with them because of their unbelief. *"He sighed deeply in His spirit and said, "Why does this generation seek a sign? Assuredly, I say to you no sign shall be given to this generation." (Mark 8:12-13)*

Jesus was so disappointed because of their unbelief that He got into the boat and left Dalmanutha and went to the other side of the Sea of Galilee. His disciples had forgot to bring bread, and they only had one loaf in the boat. Jesus told them, *"Take heed, beware of the leaven of the Pharisees and the leaven of Herod." (Mark 8:15)* The disciples didn't understand what Jesus meant. They thought He was talking about having no bread. Jesus was aware of their thoughts and He said, *"Why do you reason because you have no bread? Do you not yet perceive nor understand? Is your heart still hardened? Having eyes, do you not see? And having ears, do you not hear? And do you not remember? When I broke the five loaves for the five thousand, how many baskets full of fragments did you take up?(Mark 8:17-19.)*

Jesus was very disappointed in the disciple's attitude. It seems as though after all the miracles they had witnessed Him do, they still had little faith and understanding in His power and who He was.

(MK 8) Jesus and the disciples came to Bethsaida on the north shore of the Sea of Galilee. A blind man was brought to Jesus, and the people begged Him to heal the man. Jesus led the blind man out of town and He spit on his eyes, put His hands on him, and asked him if he could see. The man said he could see men like trees walking. Jesus put His hands back on the man's eyes and his eyesight was restored. Jesus then sent him away but told him not to tell anyone that Jesus had healed him.

The scriptures don't tell us why Jesus at times did not want the person He had healed to tell anyone about it. He may have been so physically tired at times that He needed to rest.

(MT 16-MK8-LK 9) Jesus and His disciples left Bethsaida and travel to the towns in Caesarea Philippi located at the foot of Mt Hermon, the main water source for the Jordan River. Jesus asked His disciples who the people thought He was? Some thought He was John the Baptist, Elijah, Jeremiah or one of the prophets. Jesus asked them who they thought He was. Peter said to Jesus, *"You are the Christ."*(Messiah). Jesus blessed Peter and told him that it was God who had revealed to Peter who He was.

Matthew 16:18-20 "And I say to you that you are Peter, and on this rock I will build My church, and the gates of Hades shall not prevail against it. And I will give you the keys of the kingdom of heaven, and whatever you bind on earth will be bound in heaven, and whatever you loose on earth will be loosed in heaven."

Jesus did not say the church would be built on Peter but on Peter's confession that Jesus is the Messiah. The church would be built on the fact that Jesus was the Messiah. Jesus then told Peter and the disciples that whatever they taught would be solid like a rock meaning it would be true and confirmed forever, because they taught by the inspiration of the Holy Spirit of God.

The word church describes the kingdom of God when the kingdom was formally presented in Jerusalem after Jesus ascension to heaven. Confessing ones faith in Jesus and obeying the gospel message is the only way for entrance into the kingdom. Jesus said the church would be built regardless of what anyone did to try to prevent it being built.

(MK 9) Jesus and the disciples left Caesarea Philippi and went through Galilee, Jesus did not want anyone to know where He was, because He wanted a private time with the disciples so He could tell them about His death. *Mark 9:31 "The Son of Man is being betrayed into the hands of men, and they will kill Him. And after He is killed, He will rise the third day."*

This must have been a shock to the disciples after seeing the great power Jesus had already exhibited. They probably wondered what would become of them if Jesus died. Jesus had already hinted of His death, and the disciples were puzzled when Jesus said He would rise on the third day. The faith of the apostle continued to grow as they traveled with Jesus and witnessed His miracles, but the things He told them puzzled them at times.

The disciples asked Jesus who in the kingdom would be the greatest? Jesus told them that a member of the kingdom would be like a little child. Little children look to their parents with humility and accept what their parents tell them. Those who are in the kingdom must look to God and Christ with the humble attitude of faith, hope and love and accept what the scriptures teach them.

The Kingdom of God is to be ruled by God through His word revealed in the scriptures, not by the weakness and whims of men who take upon themselves the authority to rule over them spiritually. When Jesus spoke about the greatest in the kingdom, the disciples, no doubt, thought of authority, possibly pomp and splendor, but Jesus had a surprising answer that did not include any of those things.

Jesus said one must change and become as a little child. One enters the kingdom with faith, hope, love and humility when they give their lives to God and Christ. Entering the kingdom of God involves a change of heart from worldly priorities to accepting Christ and the authority of His word with all of their heart. We should love the Lord our God with all our heart, soul, and mind. The love that the Father has lavished on us, Is very great because we are His children.

Christian association with one another depends on a proper relationship of love. Disciples are united in one body as brothers and sisters of Christ. Jesus asked the question "Who is my mother, and my brothers?" Then He said that whoever does the will of His Father in heaven is His brother, His sister and His mother."

If anyone says, "I love God," and yet he hates his brother, he is a liar. He who does not love his brother whom he has seen cannot love God whom he has not seen. Believers are many in number, yet we are one body in Christ, and individually members one of another. Jesus said that if God's people love one another, God lives in us and His love is perfected in us.

1st Corinthians 13:1-7 "Though I speak with the tongues of men and of angels, but have not love, I have become a sounding brass or a clanging cymbal. And though I have the gift of prophecy, and understand all mysteries and all knowledge, and though I have all faith, so that I could remove mountains, but have not love, I am nothing.'

"And though I bestow all my goods to feed the poor, and though I give my body to be burned, but have not love, it profits me nothing. Love suffers long and is kind; love does not envy; love does not parade itself, is not puffed up; does not behave rudely, does not seek its own, is not provoked, thinks no evil; does not rejoice in iniquity, but rejoices in the truth; bears all things, believes all things, hopes all things, endures all things."

The proper attitude for brothers and sisters in Christ is faith, hope and love. These three are all important, but 1st Corinthians 13 says that the greatest of these three is love.

The religious leaders claimed to honor God, but at the same time they failed to obey His commandments. They honored Him with lip service, which God didn't accept, because they failed to obey His commandments. The Word of God had not effect on them because of their traditions.

Jesus called all the people to come hear Him and told them that the food they ate would not defile them. He told them it is the things that come out of the mouth that defiles blasphemy, lies and evil thoughts. Jesus is talking about being defiled morally in the eyes of God.

Mark 7:20-23 "And He said. "What comes out of a man, that defiles a man. For from within the heart of men, proceed evil thoughts, adulteries, fornications, murders, thefts, covetousness, wickedness, deceit, lewdness, an evil eye, blasphemy, pride, foolishness. All these evil things come from within and defile a man."

Jesus called all the people to come hear Him and told them that the food they ate would not defile them. Jesus said that it is the things that come out of the mouth that defiles; blasphemy, lies and evil thoughts. Jesus is talking about being defiled morally in the eyes of God.

Mark 7:20-23 "And He said. "What comes out of a man, that defiles a man. For from within the heart of men, proceed evil thoughts, adulteries, fornications, murders, thefts, covetousness, wickedness, deceit, lewdness, an evil eye, blasphemy, pride, foolishness. All these evil things come from within and defile a man."

Jesus Reveals His Suffering and Death

From that time Jesus began to reveal to His disciples that He would have to go to Jerusalem and suffer at the hands of the elders, chief priests and scribes, and be killed but He would be resurrected on the third day.

(MT 16) The Pharisees did not believe Jesus was the Messiah they thought He was an impostor. They wanted to see Jesus perform a miracle to prove He was the Messiah. Jesus had already proved Himself many times and He was disturbed by their unbelief and He would not show them another miracle.

Jesus told them they would see a miracle like Jonah who was in the belly of the whale for three days and nights then was spit out alive. Jesus was referring to His death burial and resurrection. He was in the grave for three days and nights. Jesus would be seen again after His resurrection and before He ascended to heaven.

When Jesus died, was buried and resurrected it was time for the Kingdom of God to come because people with faith in Christ were forgiven of the guilt of sin and would become members of the kingdom. It would not be long before the kingdom would be formally inaugurated in the city of Jerusalem and soon after be called the church.

From that time forward Jesus began to reveal that He would be put to death and resurrected on the third day. Peter did not Believe Jesus when He said he would be killed and Jesus privately rebuked Peter and told him he did not understand the things of God and was thinking like a man.

Jesus tells the disciples about the cost of following Him and said they must first deny their own self and take up the cross and follow Him. The cross represents the suffering associated with being a disciple of Christ. The disciples would suffer many things during their mission to establish the church on earth, (Kingdom of God).

Matthew 16:27-28 "For the Son of man will come in the glory of His Father with His angels, and then He will reward each according to his works. Assuredly, I say to you, there are some standing here who shall not taste death till they see the Son of Man coming in His kingdom."

(MK 8) Jesus began to teach His disciples about what lies ahead for Him in the future. Jesus tells them He will suffer many things and be rejected by the religious leaders. Be killed and resurrected after three days. This was a lot for the disciples to believe and Peter spoke openly and rebuked Him. Jesus turned around looked at the disciples and began rebuking Peter. Mark 8:33 *"Get behind Me, Satan! For you are not mindful of the things of God, but the things of men."*

Mount of Transfiguration

(MT 17-MK 9-LK 9) Six days after Jesus teaching about coming back in glory Jesus took Peter, James and John up on a high mountain and he was transfigured as they were watching Him. His face was shining like the sun and His clothes became as white as light. Moses and Elijah two of the greatest prophets of all times were there with Him. Peter told Jesus it was good to be there and he suggested making three tabernacles one for each of Jesus, Moses and Elijah. Suddenly a bright light shone above them and the voice of God said, *"This is My beloved Son, in whom I am well pleased. Hear Him."*

The message meant that the time for hearing Moses and Elijah had ceased and now everyone should obey the teachings of Jesus. The disciples were scared and they fell to the ground but Jesus told them to get up and do not be afraid. The scribes taught that before the Messiah came John the Baptist would come first. Jesus told them Elijah had already come. Jesus was speaking of John the Baptist who came before Jesus. He came with power and prophecy like Elijah.

Eight days after the vision Jesus took Peter, James and John up on a high mountain to pray probably Mt Hermon or Mt Tabor. God identified Jesus as his Son and gave His approval of Jesus ministry.

The disciples were afraid and they fell face down to the ground but Jesus touched them and told them not to be afraid. When they looked again Jesus was the only one they saw, Moses and Elijah had disappeared.

The disappearance of Moses and Elijah meant their work was completed and now people must follow Jesus. Jesus told the disciples not to tell anyone about what they had seen until after Jesus was resurrected. The disciples still did not understand the complete truth about everything that would take place in Jesus life as the Messiah, the Redeemer.

Jesus told the disciples not tell anyone about the things they saw until He rose from the dead. The disciples wondered what rising from the dead meant. They asked Jesus about Elijah and wanted to know why the scribes taught that Elijah must come before the Messiah.

Mark 9:12 "Then He answered and told them, "Indeed, Elijah is coming first and restores all things. And how is it written concerning the Son of Man, that He must suffer many things and be treated with contempt? But I say to you that Elijah has also, and they did to Him whatever they wished, as it is written of him."

Jesus told them that John the Baptist fulfilled the prophecy of the coming of Elijah. John ministered in the same way and spirit and power of Elijah when he prepared the people to accept Jesus as the Messiah sent by God.

They asked Jesus a question about Elijah because they saw him before in a vision with Christ and Moses. Elijah had come in the first century in the person of John but the religious leaders, didn't know him. The disciples then understood that Jesus was talking about John the Baptist who came before Jesus.

(MT 17) Jesus and the disciples caught up with the multitude and Jesus cast a demon out of a boy. The demon caused the boy to have epileptic fits and he often fell into the fire or the water.

The disciples had tried to cast out the demon but they were not able. Jesus cast the demon from him. Jesus referred to that generation of people as faithless. The disciples privately asked Jesus why they could not cast out the demon and he told them they did not have enough faith.

Matthew 17:20-21 So Jesus said to them, "Because of your unbelief; for assuredly I say to you, if you have faith as a mustard seed, you will say to this mountain, 'Move from here to there.' And it will move; and nothing will be impossible for you. However, this kind does not go out except by prayer and fasting."

While they were in Galilee Jesus told the disciples about His upcoming death. Jesus told them He was going to be betrayed and given to men who would kill Him. He said after His death He would be resurrected on the third day. The disciples were very sorrowful after hearing that Jesus would die.

Jesus and the Disciples go back to Capernaum

(MT 17) Jesus and the disciples go back to their home base in Capernaum. The men who received the taxes for the temple asked Peter if Jesus had paid the temple tax and Peter told him yes. Jesus knew what Peter was thinking and he asked him do the kings of the earth take taxes from their sons or from strangers? Peter answered from strangers.

Jesus replied then the sons are free. Jesus implies that the sons are not obligated to pay taxes but to keep from offending anyone for the sake of His ministry, Jesus told Peter to go to the sea and put in a fish hook and open the mouth of the first fish he caught and he would find a piece of money. Jesus told him to pay the taxes for Him and for your self.

Jesus paid the tax to avoid trouble with the religious leaders. Jesus knew the disciples had been arguing and He knew what they argued about but He asked them what they argued about when they were on the road. The disciples had argued about who would be the greatest in the kingdom and they did not answer Jesus. Jesus said those who desire to be first will be last of all and he will be the servant of all. There is to be equality in the Kingdom of God (church).

(MT 18) Jesus set a child by them and told them that they would not enter heaven unless they become like a child. Jesus was talking about the humility of a little child.

Little children are not concerned with being great or worried about social status they are happy to be accepted and to accept God and those who are caring for them. Those who strive to be great by their own ambitions cause many problems within the church. Their attitudes need to be like the humble attitude of little children.

Matthew 18:2-5 "Then Jesus called a little child to Him, set him in the midst of them, and said, "Assuredly, I say to you, unless you are converted and become as little children, you will by no means enter the kingdom of heaven. Therefore whoever humbles himself as this little child is the greatest in the kingdom of heaven. Whoever receives one little child like this in My name receives Me."

Jesus used the scriptures they knew and claimed to follow in order to shame them because they did not honor the very scriptures they quoted.

The religious leaders of that time honored God with lip service, which God did not accept because at the same time they claimed to honor Him they failed to obey His commandments. They made the Word of God have no effect by their traditions.

The religious leaders of that time honored God with lip service, which God did not accept because at the same time they claimed to honor Him they failed to obey His commandments. They made the Word of God have no effect by their traditions.

Jesus called all the people to come Him hear Him and told them that the food they ate would not (LK 18) Jesus was talking to tax collectors and sinners and the Pharisees and scribes complained. The religious leaders and notable people thought they were too good to even speak to people who collected taxes and they criticized and shunned them. Jesus came to bring salvation to all people and He taught everyone that would listen to Him.

Jesus taught a parable about lost sheep comparing them to people who are lost because of sin. Sheep are docile and need someone to lead them in the right direction and protect them from their enemies. Sinners have the same need and Jesus is the Good Shepherd that guides sinful people to a life of righteousness so they will not be lost.

Luke 15:7 "I say to you that likewise there will be more joy in heaven over one sinner who repents that over ninety-nine just persons who need no repentance." Everyone was a sinner when Jesus came and like a good shepherd Jesus provided a way of salvation for everyone, God in heaven sent Jesus to shepherd those who would follow Him.

The Feast of Dedication the same as the Feast of Lights took place during the time of the feast of tabernacles and it was celebrated for eight days.

Jesus went to Solomon's porch in the temple at that time and the Jews surrounded Him. They asked Jesus how long He was going to keep them in suspense about who He was.

They wanted Jesus to positively declare whether He was the Messiah. Jesus had plainly shown them that He was the Messiah several times by His works and they did not believe Him. Jesus said the works He did in His Fathers name were witness that He was the Messiah. Jesus told them they did not believe because they were not of His sheep. Jesus sheep symbolized the people who would believe in Him and follow Him. Jesus was the good Shepherd of those who accepted Him and His teaching and obeyed Him.

Jesus goes to Jerusalem

(LK 9) Jesus knew ahead of time everything that was going to happen to Him. When it was near the time for Jesus to face the danger awaiting Him and knowing He would be arrested, He went on His way to Jerusalem. Jesus was leaving from Galilee and going to Samaria.

Jesus sent messengers before Him and they went into a Samaritan village to prepare for Him but the Samaritans did not receive Jesus because they knew He was on His way to Jerusalem.

James and John asked Jesus if they could do as Elijah had done and call fire down on them. Jesus rebuked them telling them they did not understand what manner of spirit they were of. The disciples of Jesus were not taught to be people who were of a mean spirit ready to retaliate every time someone offended them. Jesus rebuked them and He told them He did not come to destroy people's lives, He came to save them and they went to another village.

Jesus teaches the disciples about the cost of discipleship. On the road to Jerusalem one of the disciples said to Jesus, *"Lord I will follow you wherever you go."* Jesus said, *"Foxes have holes and birds of the air have nests, but the Son of Man has nowhere to lay His head."*

Jesus told another disciple to follow Him and He said he had to bury his father first. Jesus said, *"Let the dead bury their own dead, but you go and preach the kingdom of God."* Jesus emphasizes the importance of the mission of the twelve men He chose to be apostles. The apostles main concern would be the preaching of the gospel for the rest of their life.

The Jews under the Law of Moses came to Jerusalem every year to observe their annual feasts. There were seven annual feasts the, Passover of seven days including the weekly Sabbath and unleavened bread, first fruits, Pentecost, the day of Atonement, the first day of booths, and the eight day of booths. On the way to Jerusalem Jesus entered a village and was met by ten lepers and they stood at a distance. People were afraid of leprosy because it was a painful disease and there was no known cure. The lepers shouted out to Jesus and asked Him to have mercy on them. *Luke 17:14 "So when He saw them, He said to them "Go show yourselves to the priests." And so it was that as they went, they were cleansed."*

One of them that had been healed returned to Jesus and Glorified God with a loud voice. He was a Samaritan and he fell down at Jesus feet and thanked Him. Jesus asked him "Were there not ten cleansed? Jesus said where are the other nine? A foreigner was the only one that that gave God the glory for healing him. Jesus used the scriptures they knew and claimed to follow in order to shame them because they did not honor the very scriptures they quoted.

Jesus in the Temple

(JN 7) Jesus brothers left for Jerusalem during the time for the feast and Jesus secretly went to Jerusalem. Jesus went to the temple and taught and the people were amazed because of His wisdom and knowledge they knew he had never studied. Jesus told them the things he taught came from God who sent Him. Jesus asked them why they wanted to kill Him and the people said he had a demon. They thought a demon gave Jesus His power to perform miraculous signs. Jesus asked them if they were angry because He healed a man on the Sabbath? Jesus told them not to judge by appearance but to use righteous judgment.

The people were discussing among themselves about who Jesus was and where He came from. Jesus told them that they knew Him and knew where He was from then He told them God sent Him.

The people were divided in their opinion of Jesus. Some accepted Him as a great prophet others said He is the Messiah but some wondered if the messiah would come from Galilee instead of Judea. They knew the scripture said He would come from Bethlehem. Jesus remarks stirred up those who were talking about Him and they wanted to seize Him but no one touched Him. Many of the people were convinced that He was the Messiah but they still wondered if the Messiah would have done more signs than Jesus. The Pharisees heard the people discussing the things Jesus said and they sent officers to arrest Him. Jesus predicted His death.

John 7:33-34 "Then Jesus said to them, "I shall be with you a little longer, and then I go to Him who sent Me. You will seek Me and not find Me, and where I am you cannot come."

Jesus told them that He would not be here much longer before He would go to God who sent Him. They would look for Him and would not be able to find Him because they could not go where He was going. Jesus was talking about the time when He would be crucified, buried, resurrected and would ascend to heaven. The Jewish Sanhedrin council and the people were confused about who Jesus was.

During the last day of the feast Jesus stood up and said, *"If anyone thirsts, let Him come to Me and drink. He who believes in Me, as the scripture has said, out of his heart will flow rivers of living water."*

(JN 7) Jesus was speaking about the Holy Spirit that would be given to those who believed in Jesus. Living, flowing waters is an endless stream of water figuratively representing the spiritual life of a disciple in whom the Holy Spirit dwells.

The evidence of the living waters is found in Acts chapter two on the day of Pentecost when the Holy Spirit gave power to the disciples. *Acts 2:1-4 "When the day of Pentecost had fully come, they were all with one accord in one place. And suddenly there came a sound from heaven, as of a rushing mighty wind, and it filled the whole house where they were sitting. Then there appeared to them divided tongues, as of fire and one sat upon each of them. And they were all filled with the Holy Spirit and began to speak with other tongues as the spirit gave them utterance."*

(JN 8) Everyone left the temple to go home and Jesus went to the Mt of Olives. Jesus came to the temple again early the next morning and the scribes and Pharisees brought a woman to Him that had committed adultery.

Jesus said, *John 8:7 "He who is without sin among you, let him throw a stone at her first."*

Those who were asking Jesus what to do were convicted by there own conscience because they knew they were sinners and they left. Jesus told the woman He did not condemn her. This does not mean Jesus approved of her sin. His time for judgment had not come. Judgment and condemnation belongs to God. Jesus left the temple and hid because He had aroused the anger of the people in the temple by His answers to their questions and they picked up stones to throw at Him. They asked Jesus what He thought they should do? Jesus did not answer them directly instead He wrote on the ground *"He who is without sin among you, let him throw a stone at her first."* Jesus told the woman He did not condemn her and told her to go and sin no more.

Jesus spoke to the people again and told them He was the light of the world and whoever follows Him will not walk in darkness but have the light of life. Light is used figuratively meaning Jesus has the real truth and knowledge and can enlighten their minds and teach them the way of righteousness. Jesus continued to talk to those who are in the temple. Jesus tells them His judgment is true because God is with Him in His judgment and He bears witness of Him. God bore witness of Jesus from the beginning and through the scriptures. Jesus told them they did not know God for if they did they would know Him. The scriptures had for many years taught about the coming of the Messiah but the Jews failed to believe. Jesus said he was going to God and they could not come. The people who refuse to accept Jesus will never see God. Jesus warned them that if they die and are still guilty of sin they would die in their sins. Jesus hinted that after they kill Him they would then realize who He was.

Some of the people in Jerusalem did not know Jesus and they wondered if Jesus was the one the scribes and the Pharisees wanted to kill?

They reasoned that Jesus was not the Messiah because they knew where Jesus was from. Jesus cried out from within the temple *"You both know Me, and you know where I am from; and I have not come of Myself, but He who sent Me is true, whom you do not know. "But I know Him, for I am from Him, and He sent Me."*

The officers of the temple had apparently taken Jesus but they had not delivered Him to the officials. The officers were beginning to believe that Jesus was the Messiah and they said no man had ever spoken like Jesus. The members of the Sanhedrin the highest tribunal of the Jews were upset and they asked if any of the rulers or Pharisees had believed in Him? Then they cursed the crowd.

Nicodemus a cautious Pharisee believed Jesus would receive unlawful treatment reminded them that Jesus must receive a fair hearing under the Law he asked if the law would judge a person before they hear them? They asked Nicodemus if he was also from Galilee and said no prophet had ever come from Galilee. Everyone left the temple and went home.

Jesus used the words living water when He sat at a well and ask a Samaritan woman for a drink. Jesus told the woman He would give her living water. The living water promised by Jesus is the Holy Spirit that dwells in those who believe and accept Christ.

Ephesians 1:13-14 In Him you also trusted, after you heard the word of truth, the gospel of your salvation; in whom also, having believed, you were sealed with the Holy Spirit of promise, who is the guarantee of our inheritance until the redemption of the purchased possession, to the praise of His glory."

The Holy Spirit was not given to all believers at that time but later after Jesus Death, burial and resurrection the Spirit would indwell all believers. There is a difference in the measure of the Spirit that would be given.

For those special people directly chosen by Christ like the disciples who became Apostles the Spirit was given in a generous amount in order to for them to accomplish their mission of preaching the gospel.

In the early days of the church, certain members of the kingdom were given temporary gifts of the Holy Spirit so they could lead and teach the members of the church before the scriptures were completely written. The special gifts eventually ceased to be given because the Bible scriptures were completed and the redemption plan of God was completely documented. It is up to each individual person to have faith in God and Christ in their hearts and continue to obey the scriptures that are available to them.

Jesus spoke plainly and bluntly to his accusers the leading members of Judaism telling them that they do not know Him because they don't know God.

They knew there was a God that created everything but they failed to know Him in a personal way and they failed know Jesus as the Son of God and have faith in Him. Jesus told them he was going away meaning He was going back to heaven. Jesus told them they could not go there because they are of this world.

Jesus enemies had no spiritual insight or yearning for heaven. Jesus knew they would still be guilty their when they died because they would not accept Him as God's Son.

And He told them if they did not believe in Him they would die in their sins. To the Jews who did believe in Jesus He said.

John 8:31 "If you abide in My word, you are My disciples indeed. And you shall know the truth, and the truth shall make you free."

The sinful Jews still thought they would be saved because they were Abraham's descendants and they thought that made them children of God. They waned to know why Jesus said they would be made free.

John 8:34-36 *Jesus answered them, "Most assuredly, I say to you, whoever commits sin is a slave of sin, And a slave does not abide in the house forever, but a son abides forever. Therefore if the Son makes you free, you shall be free indeed."*

Abraham was highly commended by God because Abraham was faithful to obey God in everything God told him. Abraham would be saved because of his faith in God.

The Jews insisted that they were God's children but Jesus told them if they were God's children they would not be trying to kill Him. God's children would not be trying to kill God's Son. Jesus accused the Jews of being the children of the devil because the devil had always been a murderer. The Jews who killed Jesus were murders and did not belong to God. *John 8:47 "He who is of God hears God's words; therefore you do not hear, because you are not of God."*

The Jews then accused Jesus of having a demon and Jesus said he did not have a demon and He honors His Father, but they dishonor Him. Jesus says again, those who obey His word will never see death. Jesus is referring to spiritual death. The Jews continue to ridicule Jesus and they call attention to His age and with sarcasm saying have You seen Abraham?

Jesus tells them that He existed before the time of Abraham. The Jews picked up stones to kill Him but Jesus went out of the temple and disappeared.

Jesus Heals a Blind Man

(JN 9) Jesus saw a blind man who had been blind since birth. The disciples thought blindness and other defects were caused by sin but Jesus knew that sin is not the cause of birth defects. Jesus told them the works of God are revealed in Him and He must do those works while He is still here. The miracles Jesus performed were works that proved that He was the Son of God. People cannot perform real miracles unless they get their power from God. Jesus spit on the ground and mixed the spittle with the clay and anointed the blind man's eyes. He told him to go wash in the pool of Siloam a public pool of rain, water used by the people of Jerusalem. The man washed in the pool and he was able to see.

When the self, righteous legalistic minded Pharisees found out about the miracle they said Jesus was not from God because He broke the law of the Sabbath. The Pharisees could not be convinced to believe that Jesus was from God and they told the man who was healed of blindness that he was born with sin and they threw him out of the synagogue. No one is born of sin because sin is a deliberate act of disobedience to God's commands.

Jesus heard what the Jews did to the man and He looked for him and found him. Jesus asked him if he believed in the Son of God? The man did not know who the Son of God was and Jesus said, *John 9:37 "You have both seen Him and it is He who is talking with you."*

Then the man told Jesus he believed Him and he worshiped Him. The man learned that Jesus was a prophet and the Son of God. Jesus taught the disciples a parable about Himself as the Good Shepherd.

There is a doorway that leads into the Shepherd's flock and the call goes out for sheep to enter His flock through the door. The doorway represents obedience to the Shepherd's message.

The sheep represent the people who have faith in Jesus and Jesus Himself is the Good Shepherd. No one can enter heaven unless they believe in the shepherd and follow Him. Jesus only accepts those sheep that love Him and obey his voice into His fold.

The shepherd guides His sheep by His voice and from then on and they are to follow no one else.

Jesus portrays a good shepherd as one who loves His sheep and knows their voice and understands their needs and He provides for their protection against their enemies. He leads them into places of food and water. He watches over them even as they sleep.

If the sheep stray from the flock he hunts for them until He finds them and brings them back into the fold. The Shepherd loved His sheep enough to sacrifice himself for them.

God is the Father of the Good Shepherd Jesus Christ and He loves the Shepherd because He gives His life for the Sheep. The teaching of Jesus caused a division among the Jews, some accused Him of having a demon and being out of His mind but others realized that Jesus words were not the words of a demon and a few like the disciples followed Him.

Jesus Selects Seventy Disciples to Teach

(LK 10,11,12,13) Jesus appointed seventy disciples besides the twelve and sent them out two by two to all of the places where He would be going. He told them the harvest was very great and there was only twelve workers.

The seventy would be teaching about Jesus and the gospel. Jesus warned the seventy or as some say seventy-two that they will be like sheep among wolves.

Being like sheep means they will be defenseless against the Jews who oppose Jesus. The disciples would be on the move constantly teaching about Jesus and there would not be time for them to do anything else.

The time was becoming short before Jesus would be arrested and Jesus wanted many people to know about Him and his gospel before his arrest.

Jesus gave the seventy disciples power from the Holy Spirit so they would be able to teach the gospel message and to confirm the authority of their message. The apostles were, inspired by the Holy Spirit meaning the Spirit would give them the very words to speak as they taught. They were to tell those they taught that the kingdom of God was coming soon and they would be able to recognize the kingdom.

The Jewish people were familiar with the story about Sodom and Gomorrah in the Old Testament about how God destroyed the people of that city. Jesus warned the people that in the Day He returns from heaven it will be a worse time for the unrighteous than it was on the day Sodom and Gomorrah was destroyed.

Jesus pronounced a woe on the cities of Chorazin and Bethsaida, cities in Galilee a few miles from Capernaum. After Jesus left Nazareth at the beginning of His ministry His Home base was in the city of Capernaum where his mother and brothers and some of the disciples lived. The people in that area knew about many of the great things Jesus did but many still did not believe in Him. Jesus then pronounced a woe on Capernaum the town that had seen and felt the mighty power of Jesus but still had not accepted Jesus as the Messiah. Jesus said Capernaum would be brought down to Hades meaning they will be condemned on the great judgment day of God at the end of time. Jesus told the seventy that the people who reject their message about Him are rejecting God.

Luke 10:17-20 "And He said to them, I saw Satan fall like lightning from heaven. Behold I give you the authority to trample on serpents and scorpions, and over all the power of the enemy, and nothing shall by any means hurt you, but rather rejoice because your names are written in heaven."

The statement Jesus made about Satan was directly connected with the Disciples report of success when they preached the gospel in the areas where Jesus sent them. The gospel message had a clear and successful impact on the hearts and minds of many of the people they taught. They exposed the influence of the lies and deceit in the doctrines of the Devil.

Jesus often spoke in figurative language teaching some people and hiding the truth from others. The power of the influence of God's Word in the gospel is the best way to overcome the influence of evil and it is God's way.

The influence of Satan to corrupt the minds of people causes them to ignore the commands of God. God gave Adam and Eve a command that they must not eat of the tree of the knowledge of good and evil in the Garden of Eden. The knowledge of good represents obeying God's commandments and the knowledge of evil represents those who ignore God's commandments.

People are free to make their own decisions to obey or disobey. Satan works against the will of God and tempts people to sin but people are always free to make up their own mind to obey or disobey God. The good influence of God's word, and the evil influence of Satan still exists today and will exist until Christ returns to destroy Satan at the end of time.

After the death of Christ people would be able to have redemption from the guilt of sin but they would always be engaged in a spiritual battle for the rest of their life.

In Ephesians 6 Paul states that God's people are engaged in a spiritual battle against the forces of darkness and wickedness.

The only defense against the evil spiritual forces is the armor of God, the truth, and faith in Christ that leads to righteousness *Colossians 3:1-17 "And whatever you do in word or deed, do all in the name of the Lord Jesus, giving thanks to God the Father Through Him."* Jesus rejoiced because many of the people He preached the word of God to obeyed the gospel and the influence of the word of God destroyed the influence of Satan's evil. Jesus compared it to lightning falling from the sky.

Luke 23-24 "Blessed are the eyes which see the things you see; for I tell you that many prophets and Kings have desired to see what you see, and have not seen it and to hear what you hear, and have not heard it."

A lawyer tested Jesus by asking Him what he could do to have eternal life? Jesus asked him a question about what the Law of Moses said. The lawyer quoted from Deuteronomy where it says to love the Lord with all your heart, soul, strength and mind and to love your neighbor like you love yourself. Jesus told him that was the right answer and if he did that he would have eternal life. Anyone with that kind of love will be redeemed because their love will prompt them to have faith in Christ and obey Him.

Jesus and the Disciples Continue to Travel

Jesus and His disciples continued to travel and they entered another village and a woman named Martha welcomed Jesus to her house.

Martha had a sister named Mary and Mary sat at Jesus feet and listened to Him teach about the kingdom. Martha was busy serving and Mary was not helping her, she was sitting at Jesus feet listening to Him.

Martha asked Jesus if he cared that Mary had left her to do all the serving. Martha wanted Jesus to tell Mary to help her.

Luke 10:41-42 "And Jesus answered and said to her, "Martha, Martha, you are worried and troubled about many things. But one thing is needed, and Mary has chosen that good part, which will not be taken away from her."

Mary was doing what was right at the time because she was dedicated to listening to Jesus. Jesus did not say that either one of the women were not doing the proper thing, He suggested that Mary was doing a good thing by devoting her attention to hearing him teach. Spiritual matters are more important that other activities in a person's life.

(LK 11) One of the disciples asked Jesus to teach them how to pray. "So He said to them, *"When you pray, say: Our Father in Heaven Hallowed be your name. Your kingdom come. Your will be done on earth as it is in heaven. Give us this day our daily bread. And forgive us our sins, for we also forgive everyone who is indebted to us. And do not lead us into temptation, But deliver us from the evil one."*

Jesus taught a parable about a friend that was persistent in asking for a favor. The lesson Jesus is teaching in the parable is that people should be persistent in their prayers to God. If God does not answer the first time you pray keep praying until God answers.

The parable of the good Father is about God the Father who is willing to give His children good gifts including the gift of the Holy Spirit to help them understand the Word of God and live according to God's will.

(LK 11-12) Jesus teaches several parables to instruct the apostles how to conduct themselves as Disciples of Christ. They would be faced with many problems from those who do not believe especially from the religious leaders of the Jews. In order to serve Jesus the disciples must fear God and trust Jesus with implicit trust even in the midst of persecution. Jesus warned of persecution from the Pharisees when they learned about all the things the disciples were doing and what they were teaching.

Jesus told the disciples not to fear the Pharisees. Instead fear God who not only can kill but can also cast into hell. Jesus assures them that God will protect and provide for them if they do His will. If people will confess their faith in Jesus He will confess them before the angels and before His Father.

Jesus said it was possible for people to be forgiven of sin but if anyone speaks evil of the Holy Spirit they will not be forgiven. Blasphemy of the Holy Spirit is a sin that will not be forgiven. In 1st Corinthians 2 Paul wrote that God has revealed through the Spirit the things God has prepared for His people.

1st Corinthians 2:10-12 God has revealed them to us through His Spirit. For the Spirit searches all things, yes the deep things of God. For what man knows the things of a man except the spirit of the man which is in him? Now we have received not the spirit of the world, but the Spirit who is from God that we might know the things that have been freely given to us by God."

Jesus warns the disciple of a time that He will be killed. He warns them about the persecution they will suffer after He is gone. He says there will be much division among the people when He goes away.

Jesus Warns to be Ready For His Returns

As Jesus continues teaching in Luke Jesus tells them He will return and He advises them to prepare for the time of His return. Jesus said, for no one knows the day or hour when He will return. He exhorts them to do the things He teaches them and to judge everyone according to their own faithfulness to Him and the gospel.

(LK 13) Jesus teaches about repentance a term that implies a change of ones purpose, mind and heart. Repentance in the Bible makes reference to sorrowfully regretting the guilt of sin and changing one's mind to serve God instead of sin. Jesus said, unless you repent you will all perish. When Jesus sent the twelve disciples to preach they told people to repent.

Mark 6: 12 "So they went out and preached that people should repent. And they cast out many demons, and anointed with oil many who were sick, and healed them."

Jesus told a parable about a fig tree that had not been producing fruit for three years. The owner of the tree asked if he should cut it down. Jesus told them to fertilize it then if it does not produce fruit cut it down. Jesus compares the fig tree to people that do not repent and obey the Gospel. Teach and encourage them and if they still refuse to accept Jesus leave them alone. Jesus referred indirectly to the people of Israel. God gave them many opportunities to repent and accept Christ as the Messiah but most of them refused to accept Christ.

(JN 10) During the winter when it was time for the Feast of Dedication Jesus went to Solomon's porch at the temple and the Jews gathered around Him. The Feast of Dedication is now known as Hanukkah and is a memorial to the dedication of the temple by Judas Maccabeus several years earlier.

The Jews were very anxious to know if Jesus was truly the Messiah. They asked Him how long He would keep them in suspense. They said if you are the Christ tell us in a way that we can understand. Jesus spoke to them in parables and they did not always understand Him.

The Jews accused Jesus of blasphemy because they said you are a man but you claim to be God. Jesus argued from Psalm 82 where God talks to a group of beings and He calls them gods and sons of the Most High. That was an example of mortals or angels being referred to as gods. Jesus asks how could He be accused of blasphemy if He referred to Himself as a Son of God. All of those that obey the gospel are children of God.

John10: 37-38. "If I do not do the works of My Father, do not believe in Me; but if I do, though you do not believe Me, believe the works, that you may know and believe that the Father is in Me, and I in Him."

The people wanted to arrest Jesus, but He escaped from them and went to the area of the Jordan where John the Baptist had previously done his baptizing. The people there believed in Jesus and they agreed that everything John said about Him was true.

Jesus Travels Toward Jerusalem

Jesus went through other towns and villages towards Jerusalem and He taught as he traveled. Jesus told the people they must do something now while they are living before they can go to heaven, if they wait it may be too late. That same day the Pharisees came to Jesus and warned Him to leave because Herod wanted to kill Him.

Jesus was not afraid of Herod and He had not completed His work among the people but Jesus decided to leave. He did not want to die outside of the city of Jerusalem. Jesus was resigned to the fact that He was going to suffer and die. Jesus had the power to prevent His death but He came for the purpose of dying for the sins of the people and it was not yet the right time.

Luke 13:34-35 "O Jerusalem, Jerusalem, the one who kills the prophets and stones those who are sent to her! How often I wanted to gather your children together, as a hen gathers her brood under her wings, but you were not willing! See!'

"Your house is left to you desolate; and assuredly, I say to you, you shall not see Me until the time comes when you say, 'Blessed is He who comes in the name of the Lord!'"

Jesus did everything He could to convince His own people that He was the Messiah but many Jews especially the religious leaders rejected Him and eventually were responsible for His death not knowing that they were dooming themselves to eternal destruction.

Jesus went to the house of a Pharisee and there were other guests at the house besides Jesus.

Jesus taught them by asking questions with obvious answers in order to teach about relationships among the members of the Kingdom of God. The kingdom would be established soon and God's people would be governed by the gospel of Christ

Jesus went to the house of a Pharisee and there were other guests there. Jesus began teaching by asking questions that had obvious answers so He could capture their attention and teach them about proper relationships among the members of the kingdom of God. Jesus noticed as they arrived that they chose the best seats.

Jesus teaches Pharisees and Lawyers

Luke 16:14-17 "Now the Pharisees who were lovers of money, also heard these things, and they derided Him. And Jesus said to them, "You are those who justify yourselves before men, but God knows your hearts. For what is highly esteemed among men is an abomination in the sight of God. The Law and the prophets were until John.'

"Since that time the kingdom of God has been preached, and everyone is pressing into it. And it is easier for heaven and earth to pass away than for one tittle of the law to fail."

Jesus told them that a new law from God was coming that was not like the Law of Moses. Jesus taught them about the gospel of Christ and He said those who exalt themselves, will be humbled.

Then Jesus told a parable about a certain man that was rich and had everything he wanted every day. Jesus made a comparison between a rich man and a beggar named Lazarus.

Lazarus was full of sores, and was laid at the rich man's gate hoping he would be fed with the crumbs from the rich man's table. The dogs were the only ones that cared about Lazarus and they came and licked his sores. When the beggar Lazarus died the angels took him to Abraham's bosom.

The rich man also died and was buried but he was in torment in Hades. He could see Abraham far off and Lazarus was in his bosom. The rich man cried out and said, *'Father Abraham have mercy on me and send Lazarus that he may dip the tip of his finger in water and cool my tongue; for I am tormented in this flame.'*

But Abraham said to the rich man remember that in your lifetime you received good things, and Lazarus evil things; but now he is comforted. And besides all this, between us and you there is a great gulf fixed, so that those who want to go from here to you cannot, nor can those there come to us."

The moral in this story is you cannot depend on what you possess materially in this life to claim a place in heaven. The Lord judges people by what is in their heart. You must have faith, hope and love in and for God and Christ regardless of whether you are rich or poor.

According to the parable when people die their spirit goes to Hades a place reserved for the spirits of the dead. There are two places in Hades one for those who are saved because of their faith, and it is a place of paradise. There is also a place of torment for those who have no faith. When a person dies, their fate has already been determined.

Jesus Goes to Bethany to Raise Lazarus

(JN 11) Lazarus lived in Bethany near Jerusalem the town where Mary and Martha lived. Martha sent a message to Jesus that Lazarus was dead. She was hoping Jesus would restore his life. Jesus was a close friend of the family and knew they believed in Him. Jesus told the disciples they were going to Judea again.

The disciples did not believe they should go back to Judea but Jesus told them His friend Lazarus was dead and He was going to raise him from the dead. Jesus had told Martha He had the power to raise Lazarus from the dead.

Jesus said those who believe in Him would not die. Jesus was referring to the spirit of people. Lazarus spirit continued to live after his body died and his spirit was in Hades. Martha confessed her faith in Christ to raise Lazarus and she went to call her sister Mary. Martha called to her sister Mary and told her the teacher had come and he was asking for her. The Jews in the house with Mary were comforting her as she grieved for her brother.

They followed Mary when she left the house to go to the tomb where Lazarus was buried. When Mary came to Jesus she wept and fell down at His feet. When Mary arrived at the place where Jesus was she fell at His feet and told Him if He had been there Lazarus would not have died. Mary and the Jews that came with her were crying and Jesus was deeply moved. Jesus loved Mary, Martha and Lazarus. Jesus was disturbed in his spirit and He asked where Lazarus was buried.

Jesus told them that Lazarus will rise again and said, "let us go to Him." When Jesus arrived at the tomb He could tell that Lazarus had been dead for four days. Since Jerusalem was close to Bethany many women from there had joined Martha and Mary to console them.

And she confessed her faith in Christ by saying, "Lord if You had been here, my brother would not have died. But even now I know that whatever You ask of God, God will give You." Martha thought Jesus meant Lazarus would live after the resurrection at the end of time.

John 11:25-26 "Jesus said to her, "I Am the resurrection and the life. He who believes in Me, though he may die, he shall live. And whoever lives and believes in Me shall never die. Do you believe this?"

The tomb was a cave and there was a stone covering the entrance. Jesus told them to move the stone and Martha said Lord by now there is a bad smell for he has been dead for four days. Jesus reminded them that He told them before that they would see the glory of God after their death.

At the gravesite Jesus prayed to His Father God and called for Lazarus to come out of his grave. Lazarus emerged from the grave wearing his grave clothes and he was still bound up. Jesus told the people there to unbind him and let him go.

Some of the Jews that had come with Mary to Lazarus tomb saw Jesus raise Lazarus from the dead and they believed in Him but some told the Pharisees. The Pharisees and priests had a council together and discussed what they should do about Jesus. They wanted to do something against Him because everyone might believe in Him then the Romans would take away their freedom as a nation. Caiaphas was the high priest that year and he suggested that Jesus should die for the nation.

Caiaphas did not have the authority to kill Jesus but he prophesied that Jesus would die for the nation and He would unite the people as one.

From then on the Jews plotted to kill Jesus so He no longer walked publicly among the Jews. Jesus went to a city called Ephraim and stayed there with His disciples.

The time for the Jewish Passover was near and many of the Jews went to Jerusalem to celebrate the Passover. They looked for Jesus in the temple wondering if He would come to the Passover. They were looking for Him so they could arrest Him.

(LK 17) Jesus went toward Jerusalem and he passed through Samaria and Galilee. He entered a village and was met by ten lepers. The lepers were a distance from Jesus but when they saw Him they knew Him and shouted at Him saying "Jesus, Master, have mercy on us!" Jesus told them to go and show themselves to the priests. The lepers were healed and one of them a Samaritan with a loud voice glorified God. Jesus rebuffed the others who were Jewish by saying.

Luke 17:17-19 So Jesus answered and said, "Were there not ten cleansed? But where are the nine? Were there any found who returned to give glory to God except this foreigner?" And He said to Him, "arise, go your way. Your faith has made you well."

The Pharisees asked Jesus when the kingdom of God would come they were referring to the kingdom of God on earth. They thought the kingdom would have all of the visible characteristics of an earthly kingdom. Jesus told them the kingdom (church) would not be visible because it is within the spirit of people and cannot be seen. You cannot tell if a person is a member of the kingdom by a visual observation. The Pharisees were probably puzzled by Jesus answer and Jesus tells them a second time. The Kingdom of God is within the hearts of the members.

Jesus goes to Judea

(MT 19) Jesus and the disciples leave Galilee and go beyond the Jordan River in Judea and a great crowd of people followed Him and He healed them. The Pharisees came to test Him by asking Him questions about the law.

They first asked about marriage and divorce. Jesus answered that the reason God made people both male and female was so they could live together as a family. Jesus said people should not separate the union of man and wife that God joins together.

The Pharisees asked Jesus why Moses commanded a certificate of divorce? Jesus told them Moses permitted divorce because of the hardness of their heart. Hardness of the heart is stubbornness, a weakness that keeps people from doing what is right and sometimes keeps a person from obeying God.

Matthew 19:8-9 "He said to them, "Moses because of the hardness of your hearts, permitted you to divorce your wives, but from the beginning it was not so. And I say to you, whoever divorces his wife, except for sexual immorality, and marries another, commits adultery; and whoever marries her who is divorced commits adultery."

The disciples reasoned among themselves that it would be better not to marry at all but Jesus told them that not everyone would be able to remain single and everyone should use their own judgment about getting married. God honors marriage and has from the beginning of time.

Little children were brought to Jesus so he could put His hands on them and pray for them. The disciples did not agree with bringing children to Jesus but Jesus said let them come to Him.

(MK 10) 13-16 Then they brought little children to Him, that He might touch them; but the disciples rebuked those who brought them. "But when Jesus saw it, he was greatly displeased and said to them, "Let the little children come to Me, and do not forbid them; for of such is the kingdom of God. Assuredly, I say to you, whoever does not receive the kingdom of God as a little child will by no means enter it." And He took them up in His arms, laid His hands on them and blessed them."

Little children are innocent and without sin because they do not know or understand their moral obligations until they are taught as they mature. God does not punish those who are not morally accountable for their actions due to their age or ability to think and reason clearly.

The Rich Young Ruler

A rich young man came to question Jesus about what to do to have eternal life? Jesus asks him why he called Him good and told the young man no one but God was good and to have eternal life he must keep God's commandments. The young man asked which of the commandments? *Matthew 19:18-19 Jesus said, "'You shall not murder,' 'You shall not commit adultery', 'You shall not bear false witness,' 'Honor your father and your mother,' and, 'You shall love your neighbor as yourself.'"*

The young man said he had always done those things and what else must he do? Jesus told him in order to be perfect, sell the things you have and give to the poor.

Follow Me then you will have treasure in heaven. The young man went away unhappy because he had many possessions. Jesus told His disciples it was hard for a rich man to come into the Kingdom of God, but it is possible.

The disciples left everything to follow Jesus and they wondered what they would gain by giving up their life to follow Him. *Matthew 19:28-30 "So Jesus said to them, "Assuredly I say to you, that in the regeneration, when the Son of Man sits on the throne of His glory, you who have followed Me will also sit on twelve thrones, judging the twelve tribes of Israel.'*

"And everyone who has left houses or brothers or sisters or father or mother or wife or children or lands, for My name's sake, shall receive a hundredfold, and inherit eternal life. But many who are first will be last, and the last first."

Regeneration is the rebirth of the spirit and it is accomplished by faith, hope and love. When people are reborn spiritually their priority in life is to serve God. *John 1:12-13 "But as many as received Him, to them He gave the right to become children of God, to those who believe in His name: who were born, not of blood, nor of the will of the flesh, nor of the will of man, but of God."* Those who are reborn will reign with Christ in eternal life. In the book of James Peter said God gives us new birth through the resurrection of Jesus Christ.

The parable of the laborers taught by Jesus in Matthew 20 is about the grace of God that is freely given to people from every culture if they are willing by faith to come into the kingdom of God. In the kingdom there is equality with God among the members. No person or laborer is worthy of the kingdom but by the grace of God and the sacrifice of Christ anyone can become a laborer in the kingdom of God by faith in Christ.

Jesus and the Disciples go to Jerusalem

(LK 18) Jesus and the disciples begin a journey to Jerusalem. The events the prophets predicted about Jesus would soon begin to take place. Jesus spoke privately to the twelve disciples (Apostles). Jesus tells the twelve that he will be arrested and given to the Gentiles. They will spit on Him mock Him and insult Him. Then they will beat him and kill Him but on the third day He will be resurrected. An ordinary person would have avoided Jerusalem but Jesus was dedicated to accomplishing God's will.

(MT 20) The mother of James and John came to Jesus with her sons and Jesus asked her what she wanted. She told Jesus she wanted her sons to sit on each side of Jesus in the Kingdom. Jesus told her she did not understand what she was asking and it was not within His authority to grant what she asked. The other disciples were not pleased with the request of James and John and Jesus taught about the proper relationship among the disciples. The Members of the kingdom (church) will not be given authority over one another. Those who will be great in the kingdom are those who serve the other members. Jesus is an example for the members of the church, He did not come to be served but to serve and to become a sacrifice for the many.

(LK 18) Jesus and the disciples continued on their way to Jerusalem and they came near Jericho and saw a blind man sitting by the road begging. The blind man heard the multitude following Jesus and he asked what was happening.

He was told that Jesus of Nazareth was going by and he cried out saying Jesus the Son of David have mercy on me. The people in front of the multitude told him to be quiet but he cried out louder. Jesus stopped walking and commanded that the blind man be brought to Him. Jesus asked him what he wanted and he asked that his sight be restored.

Luke 18:42-43 "Then Jesus said to him, "Receive your sight; your faith has made you well.""

Jesus came into Jericho and He saw a rich tax collector named Zacchaeus. Zacchaeus wanted to see Jesus but he was short and could not see over the crowd. Zacchaeus climbed into a sycamore tree so he could see and Jesus looked up and saw him and told him to hurry and come down from the tree. Jesus told Zacchaeus He wanted to stay at his house. Zacchaeus hurried down the tree. The Jews complained because they said Jesus was going to the house of a sinner.

The Jewish people did not like tax collectors they hated them because they often took a large portion of the money they collected for themselves. Zacchaeus was a Jew and Jesus called him a son of Abraham. Jesus said He came to seek and save the lost.

Luke 19:9-10 "And Jesus said to him, "Today salvation has come to this house, because he also is a son of Abraham; for the Son of Man has come to seek and to save that which was lost." Jesus came to save all people but He went to the Jews first, the descendants of Abraham.

Jesus and Zacchaeus left Jericho and a large crowd followed them. They came to two blind men sitting near the road. The men heard Jesus and shouted have mercy on us, O lord, Son of David! Jesus called to them and asked what they wanted Him to do for them. They said they wanted their eyesight restored. Jesus had compassion for them and He touched their eyes and immediately their eyesight was restored.

(JN 14) Six days before the Passover Jesus was on His way to Jerusalem and He came to Bethany and ate with Martha, Mary and Lazarus. Mary anointed Jesus feet with some expensive oil. Judas Iscariot complained saying the ointment could have been sold and the money used to help the poor. Judas did not care about the poor he wanted the ointment to be sold and the money put in the common box because He carried the box and sometimes used the money for himself. *John 12:7-8 But Jesus said let her alone; she has kept this for the day of My burial. For the poor you have with you always, but Me you do not have always."*

(JN 12) Many of the Jews knew Jesus was at Martha's house and they came there to see Jesus and to see Lazurus whom Jesus raised from the dead. The chief priests planned to kill Jesus and Lazarus because many Jews began to believe in Jesus after He raised Lazarus from the dead.

The Triumphal entry into Jerusalem

Jesus and the disciples came to Bethpage near Jerusalem and the Mt of Olives. Jesus sent two disciples to a village where they would find a donkey and a colt tied. He told them to bring them to Him and if anyone said anything tell him the Lord has a need, and then he will let you have the donkey and the colt. This was done in fulfillment of an Old Testament prophecy in Zechariah 9:9:

> *"Rejoice greatly, O daughter of Zion!*
> *Shout O daughter of Jerusalem!*
> *Behold your king is coming to you;*
> *He is just and having salvation,*
> *Lowly and riding on a donkey,*
> *A colt, the foal of a donkey."*

After Jesus and the disciples reached Jerusalem Jesus taught in the temple during the day and at night. He went to the Mt of Olives early in the morning then return to the temple. During the Passover feast a Great crowd of people came to Jerusalem for the feast.

They heard that Jesus would be coming there and they took palm branches and went to meet Him crying

> *"Hosanna to the Son of David!*
> *'Blessed is He who comes in the name of the Lord!'*
> *The King of Israel!'*
> *Then Jesus found a young donkey, sat on it as it is written:*
> *"Fear not, daughter of Zion;*
> *Behold, your King is coming,*
> *Sitting on a donkey's colt."(John 12:13-15)*

The disciples did as Jesus requested and they laid their clothes on the donkey and colt and set Jesus on them. A large crowd of people spread their clothes on the road and some cut branches from the trees and spread them out on the road. Matthew 21:9 "Then the multitudes who went before and those who followed cried out, saying:

> *"Hosanna to the Son of David!*
> *'Blessed is He who comes in the name of the Lord!'*
> *Hosanna in the highest!"*

The Pharisees said among them selves, you are accomplishing nothing. Look the world has gone after Him. Jesus was very popular with the people. Jesus came near the city of Jerusalem and He wept. *Luke 19:41-44 "If you had known, even you, especially in this your day, the things that make for your peace! But now they are hidden from your eyes. For days will come upon you when your enemies will build an embankment around you and close you in on every side, and level you, and your children within you, to the ground; and they will not leave in you one stone upon another, because you did not know the time of your visitation."*

The religious leaders rejected Jesus because they did not believe He was the Messiah. Jesus knew what was going to happen to Him soon, His death and burial and he wept over the city of Jerusalem. Jesus was aware of the cruel things they would do to Him but He had compassion for the people causing Him to weep.

Jesus entered Jerusalem and went into the temple and looked around but the time was late so He went to Bethany with the disciples. Bethany was a small village on the other side of the Mt of Olives and the village where Mary, Martha and Lazarus lived it was not far from Jerusalem.

Jesus and the disciples go back to Jerusalem and Jesus went to the temple and drove out those who were buying and selling things in the temple. He turned over the tables of the changers of money and the seats of those who sold doves. Jesus did not believe it was right bring merchandise in the temple.

Mark 11:17 "Then He taught saying, *"Is it not written, 'My house shall be called a house of prayer for all nations?'* But you have made it a den of thieves'" The people were astonished at Jesus teaching and the Scribes and chief priests were afraid of Jesus because of the people and they discussed how they might kill Him. Then the blind and the lame came to Him in the temple and he healed them. The chief priests and scribes watched the wonderful things Jesus did and heard those who followed Jesus crying out "Hosanna to the Son of David!" The priests and scribes were angry and said do you hear what they are saying? Jesus said, *"Yes, Have you never read, 'Out of the mouth of babes and nursing infants You have perfected praise?"*

When evening came Jesus went into the city of Bethany to spend the night. The next day when Jesus came out of Bethany he was hungry. He saw a fig tree with leaves still on it and thought there might be some figs but there were no figs. Jesus knew what was waiting for Him in Jerusalem and He took His frustration out on the tree. *"Let no one eat fruit from you ever again."* Jesus went into the city of Jerusalem and went into the temple. The chief priests and elders of the people made a bold stand against Him while He taught, they asked him where he received authority to do the things He was doing? Jesus answered them by asking a question. Where did John get authority to baptize? Was it from Heaven or from men?

They were afraid to answer Jesus because if they said from heaven then Jesus would say, why didn't you believe him? If they said from men the people would attack Him because the people believed John was a prophet. The chief priest said we do not know.

MT 21 Jesus taught a parable about two sons that worked in their father's vineyard. The parable was meant to show the hypocrisy of the religious leaders and the attitudes of those who will obey the gospel. The Father in the parable represents God and the vineyard represents the people that respond to the message of the gospel.

The owner of the vineyard said to the oldest son go work in the vineyard. The first son had said he would not go to work but later he repented and went to work in the vineyard. The second son said he would go but he changed his mind. Jesus asks which son obeyed his father and the people said the first. In this parable Jesus is rebuking the Jewish leaders for pretending to be righteous leaders of God's people but they did not keep the commandments of God.

The first son represents the followers of Christ and the second son represents the Jews who failed to accept Christ. Jesus came to His own people first and they rejected him. Today Jesus calls out for all people to accept Him by faith, with hope and love.

(MT 21) Jesus teaches a parable about a landowner who planted a Vineyard put a hedge around the vineyard to keep out those who are undesirable, built a watchtower and leased it to tenants then he went away. God is the landowner, the vineyard is the nation of Israel and the tenants are the leaders of Israel. God the owner of the vineyard cared for the people of Israel and sent leaders and prophets to advise and help Israel (the tenants) but the people killed, beat and stoned those sent to help them. God sent His Son Jesus and they were conspiring to kill Him.

The Jews that would not accept Christ as the messiah tried many times to trap Jesus into saying or doing something against the government so they could have Him arrested. The enemies of Christ sent a Jewish group that was in the favor of Herod to trap Jesus. They told Jesus they believed He was teaching the way of God truthfully and that He was not prejudiced. Then they ask Him a question to trap Him. They ask Jesus if it was lawful to pay taxes to Caesar, or to refuse to pay? Jesus knew they were trying to trick Him to say something that they could have Him arrested for.

Matthew 22:18-22 "But Jesus perceived their wickedness, and said, "Why do you test Me, you Hypocrites! Show me the tax money" So they brought Him a denarius. And He said to them, "Whose image and inscription is this?"

"They said to Him, Caesar's." And He said to them, "Render to Caesar the things that are Caesar's, and to God the things that are God's." When they had heard these words, they marveled and went their way."

Jesus was leaving the temple and one of the disciples asked Him, what kind of stones were in the structure of the temple? Jesus had a surprising answer, He told them the temple was going to be destroyed. The Jewish temple was a large magnificent building with beautiful stones. Jesus was sitting on the Mount of Olives with a view of the temple when He made those comments. Jesus told them that the days would come when the temple would be destroyed and He told them there would be signs before the temple was destroyed.

James, John and Andrew asked Him in private what kind of sign there would be before the temple would be destroyed. Jesus answered.

Luke 21:20-24 "But when you see Jerusalem surrounded by armies, then know that its desolation is near. Then let those who are in Judea flee to the mountains, let those who are in the midst of her depart, and let not those who are in the country enter her. For those are the days of vengeance, that all things that are written may be fulfilled."

Luke is writing about Jesus prediction of the destruction of Jerusalem in A.D. 70 when the temple was literally destroyed. Luke said there will be great distress and people will be killed with the sword of the Gentiles. Jesus told them to pay careful attention that no one deceives them. He said many things would happen before the destruction of Jerusalem but do not be troubled. He said they would hear rumors about war but do not be troubled by them. He said there would be earthquakes, famines, and other troubles before the destruction of the temple.

Jesus said those things were bound to happen but they were just the beginning of trouble. A Jewish historian named Flavius Josephus recorded the events of the destruction in Jewish history. The Jews began a revolt against the Romans in 66 A.D. Nero was the Emperor of Rome during the revolt and Nero the leader of the Roman army was sent to Jerusalem. He gave his son Titus the position of leader of the Roman army and in A.D. 70 The Roman General Titus completely destroyed Jerusalem and the temple fulfilling Jesus predictions.

Jesus told the disciples they would have much trouble. He was referring to their persecution because of preaching the gospel. They would be brought before councils and beaten in the synagogues. They would be arrested and brought before rulers and Kings because they were Jesus disciples. He said the gospel must be preached first before the trouble appears.

The Apostles would begin their preaching in earnest after the death of Christ and would be preaching when the Romans destroyed Jerusalem. Preaching the gospel would be the first priority of the apostles of Jesus. Jesus told them the Holy Spirit would be with them and the Spirit would tell them where to go and what to say. Jesus said there would be a time of trouble for all people. He told them they would be hated because they believed in Him but if they endured to the end they would be saved.

(MK 13) The second coming of Jesus will take place at the end of time. We are still waiting for the second coming of Christ. Jesus describes what will take place when He returns. The sun will become dark and the moon will not shine. The stars will fall and the powers of heaven will be shaken. Matthew writes that Jesus coming will be a spectacular sight and the carnage on earth will be great. Then the sign of Christ will be appear in heaven. People will be able to see Christ coming from the heavens with His angels on clouds with power and glory. Christ will send His angels ahead with the loud sound of a trumpet. Christ will gather all those who are saved for eternal life and they will ascend to heaven.

(MT 24) Jesus said, no one except God, not even the angels know when Jesus will return to earth. People will be busy with their daily activities not knowing it is the time for the lord to return. Some will be taken for heaven when He comes and some will be left for destruction. Jesus advised everyone to be spiritually prepared for the day when He returns.

(LK 21) In Luke's account before the time of the second coming there will be great tribulation on earth. Nations will be at war and there will be great earthquakes, famines and pestilences, fearful sights and great signs from heaven. John describes in more detail in the book of Revelation.

Jesus told a parable about a fig tree, you can tell by looking at the tree and know by the beginning of the budding of the tree that it is almost summer time but no one knows when Jesus will return. He said when you see the things beginning to happen that I just told you about then you will know by those things that His return is beginning to take place.

The time for the second coming of Jesus is not known and will not be known until people see Him coming in the clouds with His angels. However the people living in Jerusalem in A.D. 70 would be able to see the signs of the beginning of Jerusalem's destruction by the Romans. The events of the destruction of Jerusalem in A.D 70 would take place in their generation.

Jesus taught a parable about the kingdom of heaven comparing it to ten virgins. The virgins prepared themselves to meet the bridegroom. Five of the virgins were wise and the other five were foolish. They were all waiting for the wedding procession.

The Old Testament prophets portrayed the Messiah as a husband of the people and Jesus and John the Baptist both said the Messiah was the bridegroom. The bride of Christ represents the kingdom of God (church), which represent the virgins that are wise and are waiting for Jesus to come for them. *John 3:27-29 John answered and said, "A man can receive nothing unless it has been given to him from heaven. You yourselves bear me witness that I said, 'I am not the Christ,' but 'I have been sent before Him.' He who has the bride is the bridegroom; but the friend of the bridegroom, who stands and hears him, rejoices greatly because of the bridegroom's voice.*

The five foolish virgins represent the people who will not be prepared for the return of Jesus at the end of time. Jesus will say to the foolish virgins when He comes that He does not know them. They will not be admitted into the new heaven and new earth with the bridegroom. Jesus said watch, meaning to be ready spiritually at all times because no one knows the day or the hour when Jesus will return.

Jesus teaches a parable about the talents of those who are in the kingdom of God. Members of the kingdom must remain faithful and use their talents during the time they are waiting for the bridegroom to return. The Lord expects each one to be ready for the second coming of Jesus and each one will be judged according to the way they have used their talents.

Jesus taught directly to the Jewish people because they were God's people that had been waiting for the Messiah to come. For many years God had singled them out as His people that were chosen to be the first to receive the gospel.

(MT 26) Jesus talked to His disciples about the time for the Passover feast in Jerusalem. Sometime after the feast He would be arrested, tried and crucified. During the day Jesus taught in the temple and at night He went to the Mt of Olives. In the mornings Jesus would return to teach in the temple.

The life of the Jewish people revolved around the temple activities and the Jewish feasts that had been established many years before the first century. There were several feasts during each year. The seven main feasts were Passover, Un-leavened Bread, Day of First fruits and The Feast of Pentecost, the Feast of Trumpets, The Day of Atonement and the Feast of Tabernacles.

Some Greeks came to Jerusalem and approached Philip from Bethsaida about seeing Jesus. Philip told Andrew, then they told Jesus. Jesus taught the Greek people and He told them that the time had come for Him to be glorified. Glorified meant His time to be crucified.

Jesus compared His death to a grain of wheat that produces nothing unless it is put in the ground and dies. When it is planted it produces new life. Jesus sacrifice on the cross would provide new life for those who would have faith, hope and love.

Jesus said, *"He who loves His life, will lose it."* Jesus speaks figuratively. If a person loves their life on earth more than serving God they will lose eternal life in heaven. *"He who hates his life in this world will keep it for eternal life."*

(MK 14) Two days later it was time for the Passover and the feast of Un-leavened bread and the Chief priests and the scribes were still discussing how they could kill Jesus. They were afraid to kill Him during the feast time because they were afraid of what the people would do to them. They were looking for a way to turn the people against Jesus.

Before the feast of Passover, Jesus knew the time had come for His arrest His trial and death. Satan had entered Judas Iscariot, the disciple who would betray Jesus. Judas went to the chief priests and captains and asked them what they would pay him if he identified Jesus, so they agreed to give him 30 pieces of silver. From that time on Judas looked for an opportunity to betray Jesus. God had determined that Jesus would die for the sins of the world and then ascend to heaven. This was God's plan.

(LK 22, MT26, MK 14) When the day of unleavened bread came, it was time to kill the animal for the Passover meal. Jesus sent Peter and John to go and prepare the Passover, and they asked Him where they should go. Jesus told them to go to Jerusalem. He told them that as they entered the city, they would see a man carrying a pitcher of water. Jesus said to follow the man into the house and say to the master of the house that the Teacher asks where the guest room was where they could eat the Passover meal. Jesus said, "He will show you a large upper room already furnished." The disciples went as Jesus said and prepared the Passover meal. When the evening came, Jesus and His disciples sat down to eat.

(This section of the story about Jesus' last days on earth before His ascension are difficult to put in exact chronological order, because the events were written by four different authors after the facts. However all of the events are true and reliable scripture. I have placed the events according to my own understanding and I do not claim to be exact.)

The Lord's Supper

(Matt. 26:26-29) As they were eating, Jesus took the bread, blessed it and broke it. He then gave it to his disciples and said, *"Take, eat; this is My body."* The bread represented His body that would soon be broken when He was crucified.

Then He took the cup and gave thanks and gave it to them saying for all of them to drink it. He said, *"This is my blood of the new covenant, which is shed for many for the remission of sins. But I say to you, I will not drink of this fruit of the vine from now on until that day when I drink it new with you in My Father's kingdom."*

Jesus said the cup represented His blood of the new covenant, which would be shed for many. The new covenant of God meant redemption for the guilt of sin accomplished by the death of Christ for those who would have faith, hope and love in Christ.

1st Corinthians 11:23-25 For I received from the Lord that which I also delivered to you: that the Lord Jesus on the same night in which He was betrayed took bread; and when He had given thanks, He broke it and said,' "Take, eat; this is my body which is broken for you; do this in remembrance of Me" In the same manner He also took the cup after supper, saying, "This cup is the new covenant in My blood. This do, as often as you drink it in remembrance of Me."

Luke 22:15-18 "Then He said to them, "with fervent desire I have desired to eat this Passover with you before I suffer; for I say to you, I will not longer eat of it until it is fulfilled in the Kingdom of God." Then He took the cup, and gave thanks, and said, "Take this and divide it among yourselves; for I say to you, I will not drink of the fruit of the vine until the kingdom of God comes."

Jesus got up after the meal and laid His clothes aside and girded Himself with a towel, poured water in a basin and washed the disciples feet to teach them to love one another and maintain equality among themselves and the members of the kingdom. When He came to Simon Peter, Peter asked Him if He was going to wash his feet? Peter could not accept the washing of his feet by Jesus.

Jesus told Peter that he didn't understand at that time why He was washing His feet but later he would know. Jesus taught His disciples to love one another and accept each other with humility. Peter told Jesus He would never wash his feet but Jesus said, *"If I do not wash you, you have no part with Me"*

(JN 13) Jesus told Peter that He himself was clean, but He said, "Not all of you are clean." Jesus was referring to being spiritually clean. Jesus then told the disciples that He did not mean all of them were unclean, but Jesus was referring to Judas who would betray Him. Judas was unclean spiritually, but Jesus did not reveal his name.

Jesus washed the disciples feet and sat down again and said to them, *"Do you know what I have done to you? You call Me teacher and Lord, and you say well, for so I am. If I then, your Lord and Teacher, have washed your feet, you also ought to wash one another's feet. For I have given you an example, that you should do as I have done to you. Most assuredly I say to you, a servant is not greater than his master; nor is he who is sent greater than he who sent him."(John 13:12-16)*

(Matt. 26) As they were eating, He told them one of them would betray Him. The disciples were filled with sorrow and each one began to ask Him if they were the one. Jesus answered saying, "It is the one who dips his hand with Me in the dish." Jesus said, "Woe to the man who betrays Me. It would be good if he had never been born." Judas asked if he was the one, and Jesus replied, *"You have said it."* Jesus dipped a piece of bread and gave it to Judas Iscariot and Satan entered Judas.

Jesus told Judas to do it quickly. None of the other disciples understood why Jesus said what He did to Judas, but Judas knew what Jesus meant and he left and went out into the night waiting for an opportunity to betray Jesus.

(JN 13) After Judas left to betray Jesus, Jesus and the other disciples went out into the night. Jesus told the disciples now was the time that He was going to be glorified and God would be glorified in Him.

Jesus was talking about the time for His death. Jesus sacrificial death glorified God because God gave His only Son to die for the guilt of sin. Jesus would be glorified because He willingly submitted to death for the sins of the people.

John 12:23-25 "But Jesus answered them saying "The hour has come that the Son of Man should be glorified. Most assuredly, I say to you, unless a grain of wheat falls into the ground and dies, it remains alone; but if it dies, it produces much grain. He who loves his life will lose it, and he who hates his life in this world will keep it for eternal life. If anyone serves Me let him follow Me; and where I am, there My servant will be also. If anyone serves Me, him My Father will honor. Now My soul is troubled, and what shall I say? 'Father, save Me from this hour? But for this purpose I came to this hour. Father, glorify My name."

Jesus prayed for Himself, for His Disciples, and then for all Believers:

John 17:1-5 (paraphrase) Jesus looked up and prayed to God. *"Father, the hour has come. Glorify Your Son, that Your Son also may glorify You."* He continued praying saying that God had given Him authority over all people, and asking God to give eternal life to as many as God had given Him. He said that eternal life was knowing God and Jesus Christ, the one whom God had sent. Jesus then said that He had completed the work God had given Him to do, and asked God to glorify Him with the glory He had before the creation of the world.

John 17:6-19 (paraphrase) Jesus then prayed for His Disciples. He told God that he had manifested God's name to the men whom God had given Him out of the world and they had kept His word. Jesus said that he had given them the words that God had given Him, and they had received them believing that they came from God. They also believed that Jesus Christ came from God and was sent by God. Jesus then prayed that God would keep them that they might be one as He and God are one. He prayed that He had kept them while He was here on earth, and none of them was lost except for the "son of perdition" (Judas) that the scripture might be fulfilled. He prayed that they might have His joy fulfilled in them selves. He told God the world hated them because they were not of the world, and prayed to (v.17) *"sanctify them by Your truth. Your word is truth."* (V.19) *And for their sakes I sanctify Myself, that they also may be sanctified by the truth."*

Jesus then prayed for all believers. He` prayed that all those who believe in Him through the word may be one *"as You, Father, are in Me, and I in you."* He said the glory that God had given Him, He had given to us that we may all be one just as They are one: *I in them, and You in Me; that they may be made perfect in one, and that the world may know that You have sent Me, and have loved them as You have loved Me.* Then Christ prayed that he desired that we (believers) might be with Him where He is that we may behold His glory and that the love with which God loves Christ may be in us.

A New Commandment

Jesus called the disciples little children at that time because, like children, they did not understand what was about to take place. They did not yet know of the grief and sorrow that was in store for Jesus and for them.

After His death Jesus would not be with them in person, and where He was going was a place they could not come to Him. Without the presence of Jesus to comfort and protect the disciples, they would need to remember what He had taught them and lean on each other for support.

John 13:34-35 "A new commandment I give you, that you love one another; as I have loved you, that you also may love one another. By this all will know that you are My disciples, if you have love for one another"

During the time Jesus was with the disciples He told them what would happen in the future, but they did not understand Him. In His teaching Jesus had emphasized the coming of the Kingdom. The disciples argued about which of them would be the greatest in the kingdom. He explained to them that the kingdom of God would not be like the kingdoms of the Gentiles. The Kingdoms of men have kings that have authority over the people.

Jesus said it would not be so in the kingdom of God (Church). He said there would not be human authority over the church. Jesus is the only King and the only authority in the kingdom. Men called elders had limited authority when the church was in its infancy. The leaders in the church were given spiritual wisdom by the Holy Spirit for a limited time until the gifts of the Holy Spirit ceased to be given. After that the kingdom members would depend on the scriptures. All Christians have an indwelling of the Holy Spirit.

In the kingdom of God (the church) whoever is the greatest will be like the least member and the one who governs will be no different in authority from the one who serves. Jesus taught equality among the members of the kingdom. The apostles were given a greater measure of the gifts of the Holy Spirit to build up and spread the gospel in the first century.

Luke 22:28-29 "But you are those who have continued with Me in My trials. And I bestow upon you a kingdom, just as My Father bestowed upon Me, that you may eat and drink at My table in My kingdom, and sit on thrones judging the twelve tribes of Israel."

Jesus said to let the greatest be like the youngest and the one who governs like the one who serves. Later the kingdom was to be governed with mutual understanding of the Word of God and cooperation of the members. Jesus used Himself as an example of one who served.

Jesus Predicts Peters Denial

Jesus spoke to Simon Peter and told him that Satan had asked for him so that he could sift him like wheat. Satan wanted to corrupt Peter, because Peter was strong and influential, but Jesus told him that He prayed that Peter's faith would not fail. He told Peter to strengthen the other disciples. Peter was strong in faith and in his determination to serve Jesus saying he would go with Jesus to prison and even to death. Peter was convinced that he would never deny Jesus. However, Peter was as human as anyone else, and He would later deny that he knew Christ.

Jesus knew what Peter would do. *Luke 22:33-34 Then, He said "I tell you Peter the rooster shall not crow this day before you will deny three times that you know Me."*

Jesus then said it was time for Him to be glorified on earth and in heaven, glorified by the things that were about to take place. Those things would prove He is the Son of God and the Redeemer of mankind.

After His death, burial and resurrection Jesus would ascend to heaven and would be glorified by sitting at the right hand of God. Jesus said God would also be glorified at that time, because His plan for redeeming mankind will have been fulfilled and Christ would be on the throne beside God with authority over his kingdom.

Jesus gave the disciples a commandment to love one another the way He loved them. In this way everyone would know they were His disciples. Peter asked Jesus where He was going, so Jesus told the disciples that they could not go where he was going at that time, but later they would follow Him.

Peter asked why he couldn't go with Jesus. He said he would lay down his life for Jesus' sake. Jesus answered him, *"Will you lay down your life for My sake? Most assuredly, I say to you the rooster shall not crow till you have denied Me three times."* Jesus was going back to heaven, but Peter and the other apostles must remain on earth to preach the gospel and establish the church (kingdom).

Peter made the statement that even if it meant his death He would never deny Jesus, and all of the disciples agreed to the same thing. After they sang a hymn, they went to the Mt of Olives. Jesus told them that very night that they would all be made to stumble.

Mark 14:27-31 "Then Jesus said to them, "All of you will be made to stumble because of Me this night, for it is written: 'I will strike the Shepherd, And the sheep will be Scattered.' "But after I have been raised, I will go before you to Galilee." Peter said to Him, "Even if all are made to stumble, yet I will not be." Jesus said to him, "Assuredly I say to you that today, even this night, before the rooster crows twice, you will deny Me three times." But he spoke more vehemently. If I have to die with you, I will not deny You!" And they all said likewise.

Jesus told the disciples to be prepared when they preached the gospel after His death. He had told them they did not need to carry anything the first times he sent them out, but now they must carry a moneybag, a knapsack and a sword. The disciples would be met with resistance from the Jews, and they would need a sword for defense. Christ promised the disciples that He would prepare a place in heaven for them and come back for them. He will come back at the end of time.

(JN 14) Jesus told the disciples not to worry; they believed in God then believe in Him. He told them that there are lots of rooms in God's house. Thomas did not know where Jesus was going, and he was concerned about how He would know the way. The apostles were not able to see the future.

Philip asked Jesus to show him God, and that would be enough proof for him. Jesus told Philip that by now he should have known who God was. It was hard for the disciples to understand the bad things that Jesus predicted. Jesus said the things He taught did not come from Him; they came from God. He said that God lived in Him. Jesus told Philip if he would believe in Him he would be able to do the things He did.

Jesus told the disciples He would pray to God, and God would give them a helper that would be with them forever. The Helper He spoke of was the Holy Spirit who would inhabit the disciples during their ministry. There was a disciple named Judas who was not Judas Iscariot, the one who betrayed Jesus. Judas asked Jesus how He and the other disciples would recognize Jesus without the world knowing Him. Jesus told Judas that those who loved Him and kept His word would know Him and His Father, because they would come to those who believed in Him and teach them all things. God, Christ and the Holy Spirit are one in unity. When the Holy Spirit comes to the people of faith, it is like God, Christ and the Holy Spirit in one.

Luke 12:12-12 For the Holy Spirit will teach you in that very hour what you ought to say." John 14:26-27 "But the Helper, the Holy Spirit, whom the Father will send in My name, He will teach you all things, and bring to your remembrance all things that I said to you." Peace I leave with you, My peace I give to you; not as the world gives do I give to you. Let not your heart be troubled, neither let it be afraid."

Jesus quoted from scripture in Zechariah that predicted they would scatter and return home. Jesus tells them that after He is resurrected He will go to Galilee ahead of them. Peter declared that he would not stumble even if the others did. Peter was trying to be strong but later he denied Jesus. Jesus had told him, before the rooster crows that night Peter you will deny Me three times.

(JN 14) Jesus comforts the disciple with encouraging words. He tells them not to be troubled but to believe in Him. Jesus told them He was going back to His Fathers house and He would prepare a place for them there and then come back for them. There was already a place in heaven reserved for Jesus beside God His Father and there would also be a place there for Jesus' apostles. Jesus prayed for the disciples and promised them that he would come back to them after his death.

John 14:13-18 "And whatever you ask in my name, that I will do, that the Father may be glorified in the Son. If you ask anything in My name, I will do it. If you love Me, keep My commandments. And I will pray the Father, and He will give you another Helper, that He may abide with you forever—the

Spirit of truth, who the world cannot receive, because it neither sees Him nor knows Him but you know Him, for He dwells with you and will be in you. I will not leave you orphans; I will come to you."

Jesus promised that God would not leave them alone when they preached the gospel. He would give them the Holy Spirit to be with them to guide them and help them. The Holy Spirit is promised to everyone in the kingdom. The Holy Spirit was with God and Christ in the beginning and He will be with God's people forever.

A disciple named Judas, not Judas Iscariot, asked Jesus how he would let Himself be known to them and not to the world? Jesus told him that if anyone loves Him they will keep His word and His father will love them and come to them. Both He and the Father will live with them. Jesus said to the disciples that those who don't love Him and do not obey Him do not belong to Him.

Jesus said He would not talk with them much longer, because the ruler of the world (Satan) was coming. It was very near the time of Jesus' arrest. Satan was the instigator of the death and the suffering that Jesus would be subjected to.

(JN 17) When the time for Jesus' arrest was near, Jesus prayed that He had fulfilled His mission to Glorify God and to give eternal life to as many as God had given Him. Jesus asked God to keep His disciples from the evil one so that they might be one as He and God are one. Jesus wanted unity among the apostles as they continued their work after His death.

Jesus prayed that the members of His kingdom would also be united as brothers and sisters and would love and serve each other. Jesus said He had kept all but one referring to Judas Iscariot.

John 17:24-26 "My Father, I desire that they also whom You gave Me may be with Me where I am, that they may behold My glory which You have given Me; for You loved Me before the foundation of the world. O righteous Father! The world has not known You but I have known You; and these have known that You sent Me. And I have declared to them Your name, and I will declare it, that the love with which You loved Me may be in them, and I in them."

Satan ruled the hearts of the people of the world through the influence of lies and deception. Jesus told the disciples it was time to go and they sang a hymn and went to the Mt of Olives.

Jesus went with the disciples to a garden called Gethsemane east of Jerusalem beyond the Kidron Valley near the Mt of Olives. Jesus needed to pray in private about the tribulation of suffering that would come to Him soon. He was about to be arrested, tortured, and condemned to die. Jesus experienced sorrow and He was distressed. He was the Son of God on earth, and at that time He was also human. He felt human emotions and desires as well as His Divinity.

He told the disciples, except for the sons of Zebedee, to remain where they were. Then He took Peter, James and John on further. He then told them to wait for him there, and He went off to a place by Himself to pray.

Matthew 26:38-39 "Then He said to them, "My soul is exceedingly sorrowful, even to death. Stay here and watch with Me." He went a little farther and fell on His face, and prayed saying. "O my Father, if it is possible, let this cup pass from Me; nevertheless, not as I will but as you will."

Jesus came back to the disciples after He prayed and found them asleep. Jesus said to Peter, "Could you not watch with Me one hour?" Jesus was deeply disturbed by the coming events when He told the disciples to watch.

In the Greek, the word 'watch' meant to stay awake and pray for Him. Jesus was about to be arrested. He said His spirit was willing; He wanted to obey God's will, but His flesh was weak. His human side wanted to avoid torture, humiliation and death. His will to obey God was stronger than His human side to avoid death. He knew what was going to happen to Him, and because of His faith in God and His love for people He was willing to die, to establish redemption for sin.

When Jesus found Peter, James, and John asleep, He went away a second time to pray. He prayed to God that He would not have to experience the grief and pain of the cross, but He said He would do whatever God willed for Him.

Jesus came back and found them still sleeping, so He left a third time to pray. When He returned, He asked them if they were still sleeping. He then told them that the time had come for Him to be betrayed into the hands of sinners.

The Arrest of Jesus

The arrest and trial of Jesus is difficult to construct in chronological order from the material in the four gospels. The four gospels containing the events were written from four different viewpoints. The reports of the gospels are brief and their chronology sometimes seemed to be a matter of conjecture. One of the difficulties is the fact that the reports were given mainly in the popular language at that time then was translated into Greek from the Hebrew and we read about it in English.

(JN 18) Jesus and the disciples went over the Brook Kidron north of Jerusalem. The brook flows past the temple mount on its way to the Dead Sea. There was a garden there and they entered the garden called Gethsemane on the night before Jesus' crucifixion. Jesus had often gone there with the disciples. Judas knew Jesus and the disciples were there, so he came with troops and officers sent by the chief priests and Pharisees. They came with lanterns, torches and weapons. Jesus could have miraculously escaped but He committed Himself to be sacrificed for the redemption of sin. Jesus stepped forward and asked them whom they wanted, and they said Jesus of Nazareth. Luke wrote that Judas came and kissed Jesus. That was a sign that Judas had agreed to with the chief priests to identify Jesus if they would give him money. When Jesus identified Him self, those who came to arrest Him fell back on the ground. Jesus said since they wanted Him, to let His disciples go. The mob seized Jesus, and Peter drew his sword and cut off the ear of Malchus, the high priest's servant. *John 18: 11 "So Jesus said to Peter, "Put your sword into the sheath. Shall I not drink the cup which My Father has given Me?"*

Jesus knew He was going to die. That is why He came to earth and He offered no resistance. (LK 22) Jesus touched the ear of the servant and restored his ear. Jesus asked the chief priest and captains of the temple why they came out against him like He was a thief. Jesus told them this was their hour and the power of darkness (ignorance). It was their hour to do what they wanted to do, but the time was coming when Jesus would be resurrected.

(MK 14) The crowd and the religious leaders had come for Jesus with swords and clubs like He was a robber. Jesus told them He had taught in the temple every day and no one attempted to take Him. The disciples all left Jesus and walked away frightened.

Jesus was arrested and tied up without any real proof of a crime against Him. They took Him to Annas, a former high priest, and Peter went with the crowd following at a distance. (LK 22) Annas then sent Jesus to the high priest Caiphas, and Caiphas told them that it was a good thing for one man to die for the people inferring they should put Jesus to death.

Simon Peter went into the courtyard and sat down by the fire. As he was warming himself by the fire, a servant girl saw Peter and accused him of being with Jesus. Peter denied being with Jesus and said, "I do not know Him." Later someone else saw Peter and said he was with Jesus. Peter said he was not with those who were with Jesus. About an hour later someone else accused Peter of being with Jesus because he was a Galilean. For the third time Peter denied knowing Jesus, and while he was speaking a rooster crowed. Jesus had told Peter before that he would deny Him three times before the rooster crowed. Peter remembered what Jesus had said, and He cried. Peter was strong in faith and he was ashamed of his weakness in denying that he knew Jesus.

The disciples were afraid for Jesus, but they could do nothing because of the Jewish and the Roman authorities. The high priest questioned Jesus about His teaching and about the disciples. Jesus told him He had done nothing secretly and had openly taught in the synagogues and the temple. Jesus told the high priest how he knew about the things that He had said. An officer slapped Jesus with the palm of his hand and said, "Do you answer the high priest like that?" Jesus replied, "If I have spoken evil, then bear witness of the evil; but if I spoke well, why do you strike Me?"

The multitude led Jesus to Pilate, the Roman Governor, and accused Jesus of crimes against Rome. Pilate asked Jesus if he was the King of the Jews. Jesus answered him and said, "It is as you say." Pilate said he found no crime against Jesus, but the multitude became furious and accused Jesus of stirring up the people. When Pilate found out that Jesus was from Galilee, he sent Him to Herod.

Pilate could release one person that had been arrested, so the chief priests of the Jews urged Pilate to release a criminal named Barrabbas. Pilate wanted to please the crowd, so he released Barabbas instead of Jesus. Pilate asked them what he should do with Jesus, and they shouted, "Crucify Him." Crucifixion is a very cruel and painful way to kill. Jesus was sentenced to be beaten and later He was crucified.

The soldiers led Him into the Praetorium where they had assembled the whole garrison. They dressed Jesus in purple; made a crown of thorns and put it on His head, and saluted Him saying, "Hail, the King of the Jews." Jesus was beaten, spat on, hit on the head with a reed, and then they bowed down in mockery, pretending to worship Him. When they were through mocking Him, they put a scarlet robe on Him and led Him away to be crucified. For a full description of the events, read all four gospel accounts in Matthew 27, Mark 15, Luke 22 and John 18,19.

The Religious Sanhedrin tries Jesus.

At the time of Christ the Sanhedrin was the name of the highest Jewish tribunal and they assembled in Jerusalem. They had a wide jurisdiction in civil matters of Jewish law and some degree of authority in criminal matters. Capital matters required confirmation from the Roman authorities. (John 18) Pilate told the Jews to take Jesus and judge Him by their law.

There were two divisions of the Sanhedrin, but the religious Sanhedrin was the highest tribunal of the Jews in Jerusalem. They had authority to order arrests and the power to judge any case except one that required capital punishment. The Romans were the only authority over capital punishment. (JN 18) The Jewish troops arrested Jesus, tied Him up, and took Him to Annas, the father-in-law of Caiphas the high priest. Annas had been a high priest a few years earlier and was deposed, but the Jews considered the priesthood to be a lifetime office and still valued the opinion of Annas. Caiphas had previously said it was a good thing for one man to die for the people. He also said that it was good to let one person go free.

Peter and one of the other disciples followed Jesus into the courtyard of the high priest. Peter stayed outside waiting by the door. The high priest knew the disciple and he spoke to the girl who guarded the gate to have Peter come inside.

The men holding Jesus made fun of Him and beat him. They blindfolded him, hit Him in the face, and told him to prophesy! They said, "Tell us who hit you in the face." They accused Jesus of being evil and said, "If you are the Christ, tell us." Jesus said to them, *"If I tell you, you will by no means believe. And if I also ask you, you will by no means answer Me or let Me go. Hereafter the Son of Man will sit on the right hand of the power of God." (Luke 22:67-69)*

Then they asked Him if He was the Son of God, and He affirmed that He was. The officials believed that Jesus was an impostor. The chief priests, the elders and the council wanted someone to testify against Jesus, so two false witnesses came forward and accused Jesus of saying that He was able to destroy the temple and build it again in three days. Jesus was referring to His body when He said that. He predicted His death, burial and resurrection.

Jesus then remained silent and the high priest said to Jesus, "Do You have nothing to say?" Jesus still remained silent, so the high priest put Him under oath and told Him to tell them if He was the Christ, the Son of God. *"Jesus said to them, 'It is as you said. Nevertheless, I say to you, hereafter you will see the Son of Man sitting at the right hand of the power, and coming on the clouds of heaven."(Matthew 27: 64)*

Jesus had said before that He was going to return to heaven after He was resurrected, and now He tells them He will come back. Jesus would be resurrected soon after His death. The high priest was so angry he was beside him self. He tore his clothes and accused Jesus of blasphemy. Jesus never blasphemed, but He always spoke the truth and glorified God.

Those trying Jesus agreed that He deserved to die, and they spat in His face and slapped Him. Jesus was then ordered to the residence of the provincial governor. The next morning all the chief priests and the elders conspired to kill Him. They bound Him and led Him to Pontius Pilate. (MT 27)

Judas Iscariot was very remorseful after Jesus was condemned, and he brought the thirty pieces of silver to the chief priests and the elders and confessed that Jesus was innocent, but they said they did not care.

When Jesus stood before Pilate, He was asked if He was the king of the Jews. Jesus told him He was, but He said nothing when the chief priest and elders questioned Him. When Pilate heard Jesus was from Galilee, he sent him to Herod who had jurisdiction over Galilee.

Herod was glad to see Jesus, because he had wanted to meet him for a long time. Herod had heard much about Jesus. He was hoping to see Him perform a miracle. When he questioned Jesus, He remained silent even though the chief priests and scribes were accusing Him. Herod and his soldiers treated Jesus with contempt and made fun of Him. They dressed him in a beautiful robe and sent him back to Pontius Pilate. (MK 15) The next morning when Jesus was taken to Pilate, Pilate asked him if He was the King of the Jews. Jesus answered that He was, and the chief priest accused Him of being guilty of many things, but Jesus said nothing. Pilate asked Him why He did not answer but Jesus still remained silent.

Pilate found nothing against Jesus. He thought the chief priest's were jealous of Him, and that was why they arrested Him. There was a custom to release one prisoner every year, and Pilate was willing to let Jesus go free. He gave the chief priest the choice of choosing the person that would be set free to honor their custom. They could have chosen Jesus, but the chief priest encouraged the crowd to choose a prisoner named Barabbas to release instead of Jesus, so Barabbas was chosen.

(John's account of Jesus' arrest and trial in John chapters 18 and 19.)

The first Jewish trial was before Annas, second Jewish trial before Caiphas, second Roman trial before Pilate. The Chief priests took Jesus to Pilate because they did not have the authority to give Jesus the death penalty.

Pilate asked what he should do with Jesus, the one called the king of the Jews. They shouted out, "Crucify him!" Pilate still did not want to do any thing to Jesus, but they shouted louder, "Crucify Him!" (JN 18, 19) Pilate asked Jesus what crimes He had committed. *Jesus answered, "My kingdom is not of this world. If My kingdom were of this world, My servants would fight, so that I should not be delivered to the Jews; but now My kingdom is not from here.' Pilate therefore said to Him, "Are you a king then?" Jesus answered, "You say rightly that I am a king. For this cause I was born, and for this cause I have come into the world, that I should bear witness to the truth. Everyone who is of the truth hears My voice." (John 18:36-37)*

When Jesus said His kingdom was not of this world, He did not mean His kingdom would not be in the world. The kingdom was established in the world, but it is in the hearts of the believers. The phrase 'not of the world' means it is not a worldly kingdom. The kingdom of God is a spiritual kingdom. Pilate told Jesus he had the power to do anything he wanted to with Him, even the power to crucify Him.

Jesus told Pilate he would have no power unless God gave it to him. The Jews knew Pilate wanted to release Jesus, but they insisted that He be charged with a crime. They told Pilate, "If you let Him go you are no friend of Caesar."

Caesar was the supreme ruler of the Roman Empire. Pilate brought Jesus and set Him in the judgment seat in a place called the pavement. In Hebrew it is Gabbatha and was probably a part of the public square where the mob of people gathered. They led Jesus towards the place where the cross was.

The cross was heavy, and Jesus was weak because of the things He suffered, so when they saw a Cyrenian named Simon they had him to carry the cross for Jesus. A great many people followed them on their way to where the cross would be placed in the ground for the crucifixion. Some of the women who were following them were mourning, and Jesus spoke to them.

Luke 23:28-31 "But Jesus turning to them said, "Daughters of Jerusalem, do not weep for Me, but weep for yourselves and for your children. For indeed the days are coming in which they will say, 'Blessed are the barren wombs that never bore, and breasts which never nursed! Then they will begin to say to the mountains, "Fall on us! And to the hills, "Cover us! For if they do these things in the green wood, what will be done in the dry?"

Jesus warned of an event coming in the future that would be much worse than what was happening at that time. There were two future events coming that would be much worse: the destruction of Jerusalem that would come in A.D. 70, and the tribulation that would come at the end of time.

(John 19) They came to a place called Golgotha or Place of the Skull and gave Jesus some sour wine mingled with gall (Myrrh). Jesus tasted it but would not drink it. The soldiers placed Him on the cross and divided His garments among them. (Psalms 22) They cast lots to determine what each one would take. The chief priests, scribes, and elders mocked Him and said,

"He saved others; Himself He cannot save. If He is the King of Israel let Him now come down from the cross, and we will believe Him. He trusted in God; let Him deliver now if He will have Him; for He said, 'I am the Son of God."

By then it was the third hour (9A.M.). Written above Jesus head was an inscription that read, **Jesus of Nazareth, The King of the Jews.** Two criminals were also crucified at that time—one on Jesus' left and one on His right. One of the criminals blasphemed Jesus mocking Him saying, "If you are the Christ, save yourself and save us." The other criminal rebuked them for mocking Jesus, and he said, "Do you not fear God?" Then he asked Jesus to remember him when He comes into His kingdom. Jesus told him that day he would be in Paradise with him. The chief priest, Scribes and elders mocked Him saying, "He saved others but He cannot save Himself. If He is the king of Israel, let Him now come down from the cross, and we will believe Him. He trusted God; let Him deliver Him now if He will have Him; for He said, 'I am the Son of God.'" The robber who was crucified with Him reviled Him, and the people who passed by the cross blasphemed Him and mocked Him. There were women looking on from away off who had followed Jesus and ministered to Him in Galilee.

When it was the sixth hour (noon) it was dark all over the earth until the ninth hour (3 p.m.) *Mark 15: 34 "And at the ninth hour Jesus cried out with a loud voice, saying, Eloi, Eloi, Lama sabachthani?" Which is translated, "My God, My God, why have You forsaken Me?"*

Some who were standing there heard Jesus and they said, "Look. He is calling for Elijah." Someone ran and filled a sponge full of sour wine, and put it on a reed and told Jesus to drink. Jesus cried out with a loud voice and said, *"Father, into your hands I commit My Spirit,"* and then He took His last breath. Then the sun was darkened and the veil of the temple was torn in two. The earth quaked, the rocks were split, and graves were opened. Bodies of the saints who were dead were resurrected and came out of the graves.

The women who followed Jesus watched from a distance. Among them were Mary Magdalene, Mary the mother of James the less and of Joses, and Salome and many other women.

The Centurion who was standing there said, "Truly this Man was the Son of God!" Jesus bore the sins of the world in His own body, and at that moment God had abandoned Him.

The veil of the temple is the curtain that separated the Holy place from the Most Holy place signifying that access to God would now be available to all people, not to Jews only.

(JN 19) Because it was the day of preparation they did not want the bodies left on the cross on the Sabbath, so they asked Pilate if they could break their legs and carry them away. They broke the legs of the two criminals so they would die sooner, but when they came to Jesus He was already dead, so they didn't break His legs. One of the soldiers stuck his spear in Jesus side and blood and water poured out.

Zechariah 12:10 "And I will pour on the house of David and on the inhabitants of Jerusalem the Spirit of grace and supplication; then they will look on Me whom they pierced. Yes, they will mourn for Him as one mourns for his only son, and grieve for Him as one grieves for a firstborn.

The Burial of Jesus and the Empty Tomb

A man named Joseph from Arimathea asked Pilate for the body of Jesus that he might prepare him for burial. He was a friend of Jesus, a good man who was waiting for the kingdom of God and didn't agree with the decision to kill Jesus. Joseph was wealthy and a member of the Sanhedrin.

Joseph took Jesus down from the cross, and a man named Nicodemus brought a large mixture of myrrh and aloes to prepare the body. They wrapped His body with strips of linen cloth with spices and put it in a burial tomb that was cut out of the rocks. Tombs of that kind hewn from rock were very large. The tomb, which was in a garden, was a new one where no one had been buried. After the body was prepared, Joseph and Nicodemus placed Jesus' body on a stone ledge in the tomb and rolled a stone in front of the tomb that would serve as a door.

It was Friday, the day of preparation, and the Sabbath was about to begin.

Mary Magdalene and another Mary followed Joseph and saw where he buried Jesus. They went home and prepared spices and perfume for Jesus' body. They would have to wait until after the Sabbath to go back to the tomb, because of the law of the Sabbath to not do any work on that day. The Sabbath day was on Saturday.

Jesus Resurrection

(MT-MK) Early in the morning of the first day of the week there was a great earthquake and an angel came from heaven and rolled back the large stone that sealed the tomb. The angel sat on the stone. His face shone like lightning and his clothes were as white as snow. The men guarding the tomb were so frightened they shook and could not move.

When the women arrived and saw the angel, the angel told them to not be afraid. The angel then told them that Jesus was no longer in the grave. The angel showed the women the place where Jesus had been laid and said, "Go quickly and tell His disciples He is in Galilee." The women ran to tell the disciples.

(LK 24) Luke said there were two angels, and they asked the women why they were looking for the living among the dead. They told the women that Jesus was resurrected. The angels reminded them that Jesus had told them that he would be crucified and then be resurrected on the third day. The women left the tomb and told the eleven disciples about Jesus resurrection. (Judas had hanged himself previously after he had betrayed Jesus.)

(JN 20) When Mary Magdalene saw that Jesus was not in the tomb, she ran and found Peter and John, the disciple whom Jesus loved. Mary told them someone had removed Jesus from the tomb, and she didn't know where they had put Him. Peter and John then ran towards the tomb. John got there first and looked in, then Peter came from behind him and went into the tomb.

Peter saw the burial clothes and noticed that the handkerchief that had been on His head was not with the other clothes. John arrived and entered the tomb and saw that Jesus was not there, and He remembered the scriptures that said He would rise again from the dead, so he believed Jesus was alive.

Mary was standing outside the tomb crying, because when she looked in the tomb she didn't see Jesus' body. Instead she saw two angels sitting there. The angels asked her why she was crying. She told them that someone had taken away her Lord, and she didn't know where they had taken Him. She turned to leave when she saw someone standing there. It was Jesus, but she didn't recognize Him and thought he was the gardener. Jesus asked her why she was crying. Mary thought the man she was talking to had taken Jesus' body away. When Jesus called her Mary she recognized Him. *John 20:17 'Jesus said to her, "Do not cling to Me, for I have not yet ascended to My Father; but go to My brethren and say to them, I am ascending to My father and your Father, and to My God and your God."*

Mary Magdalene told the disciples that Jesus had talked to her. She told them that He said to not be afraid but to go and tell His brethren (disciples) to go to Galilee and they would see Him.

Two travelers were walking on the road that went to Emmaus, which was about seven miles from Jerusalem. They were talking about the amazing things that happened in the last few days. Jesus came near them and walked along with them. Miraculously their eyes were restrained so they could not recognize Him and they did not know who He was.

(LK 24) Jesus could see that they were sad, and He asked them what they were talking about. They told Him they were talking about Jesus of Nazareth the mighty prophet. They told about Jesus' arrest, His being condemned to die, and His crucifixion. They were disappointed because they thought Jesus was going to redeem Israel.

This was the third day since His death, and the women had told them that He was not in the tomb and that they saw two angels who said He was alive. *Luke 24:25-27 "Then He said to them, "O foolish ones, and slow of heart to believe in all that the prophets have spoken! Ought not the Christ to have suffered these things and to enter into His glory?"* Jesus then began with Moses and explained from all of the prophets and scriptures the things that were taught about Him self.

As they were coming near a village, Jesus planned to go farther, but the travelers talked Him into going home with them. Jesus sat at the table with them to eat and he broke bread and blessed it and gave them some. They had not been allowed to recognize Jesus before, but now their eyes were opened and they recognized Him. Then Jesus vanished from their sight and they were disappointed. Their hearts were excited when He was with them and talking with them and explained the scriptures.

The two travelers left home and returned to Jerusalem. They found the disciples and told them the Lord had risen. They told them about the things that happened on the road and said the Lord had indeed risen.

The disciples were meeting behind locked doors because they were afraid of the Jewish leaders when suddenly Jesus appeared among them and said, *"Peace to you."* They thought they were seeing a spirit.

Luke 24:38 "And he said to them, "why are you troubled? And why do doubts arise in your hearts? Behold My hands and My feet, that it is I Myself. Handle Me and see, for a spirit does not have flesh and bones as you see I have."

Jesus showed them His hands and His feet where the nails had pierced them when they nailed Him to the cross. Jesus asked them for some food, so they gave Him broiled fish and honeycomb and He ate.

The writings of Mark are close to the same as Luke, but he adds that later Jesus appeared to the eleven disciples, sat at the table with them, and rebuked them for not believing.

Mark 16:15-18 "And He said to them, "Go into all the world and preach the gospel to every creature. He who believes and is baptized will be saved; but he who does not believe will be condemned. And these signs will follow those who believe: In My name they will cast out demons; they will speak with new tongues; they will take up serpents; and if they drink anything deadly, it will by no means hurt them; they will lay hands on the sick, and they will recover."

(JN 20) When Jesus appeared to the disciples, Thomas was not with them, and he didn't believe them. He said that he wouldn't believe it was Jesus unless he could see the nail marks in His hands and feet and His side where He was pierced.

Later when the disciples were together and Thomas was with them behind locked doors, suddenly Jesus appeared among them again. Thomas had doubted Jesus resurrection before and for that reason Jesus told him to look at His hands and put his hand in His side. Thomas then called Jesus Lord and God. Jesus said Thomas believed because He saw the evidence of His crucifixion. He said that those who believe without seeing Him are blessed.

Jesus appeared to the disciples one more time at the town of Tiberius on the western shore of the Sea of Galilee. The disciples who saw Him were Simon Peter, Thomas the twin, Nathaniel from Cana in Galilee, the sons of Zebedee and two other disciples. Peter told them he was going fishing and they all said we are going with him.

At dawn the next morning they had fished all night. Jesus was standing on the shore and called to them asking if they had caught any fish. However, they did not recognize Him. Jesus told them to cast their net on the right side of the boat. When they did, the net was filled with fish and was so heavy and they couldn't draw it in. The disciples then recognized Jesus, and John told Peter it was Jesus.

When Peter realized it was Jesus, he put on his outer garment that he had taken off to work and jumped into the water to go to Jesus. The other disciples came to Jesus in the boat dragging the net full of fish, because they were not far from the shore. When they arrived on shore, they saw a fire and fish on the coals and some bread.

Jesus told them to bring some of the fish they caught. Peter dragged the net full of one hundred and fifty three fish, but the net had not broken. Jesus then told them to come eat breakfast, so they came ashore and ate. This was the third time the disciples had seen Jesus after His resurrection. After they ate breakfast, Jesus questioned Peter.

John 21:15-18 "So when they had eaten breakfast, Jesus said to Simon Peter, "Simon, son of Jonah, do you love Me more than these?" He said to Him, "yes, Lord; you know that I love you." He said to him, "Feed My lambs." He said to him a second time, "Simon, son of Jonah, do you love Me?" And he said to Him, "Lord You know all things; You know that I love you." He said to him, "Tend My sheep." Jesus said for the third time Simon, son of Jonah, do you love Me?" Peter was grieved because He said to Him the third time, "Do you love Me?" And he said to Him, "Lord, You know all things; You know that I love You." Jesus said to him, "Feed My sheep. Most assuredly, I say to you, when you were younger, you girded yourself and walked where you wished; but when you are old, you will stretch out your hands and another will gird you and carry you where you do not wish."

Jesus would soon ascend to heaven and He asked Peter to look after the other disciples. Peter had a strong will and he demonstrated his love for Jesus and his willingness to obey Him many times. Jesus indicated that as the disciples grew older they would need someone with strength to lead them. Peter assured Jesus that he loved Him.

Peter saw John, the disciple whom Jesus loved, behind them. (John was the one who had asked Jesus at the last supper who would betray Him.) Peter said to Jesus, Lord what about this man? Peter was asking about John. Jesus told Peter, if He willed that John remained till He returned, what concern is that to him. Jesus told Peter to follow Him. A rumor spread that Jesus had said the disciples would not die. Jesus had said if it was His will. Jesus' words were taken out of context; everyone is subject to death.

The Ascension

The last words of Jesus recorded in Matthew's gospel:

Matthew 28:18-20 And Jesus came and spoke to them, saying, "All authority has been given to Me in heaven and on earth. Go therefore and make disciples of all the nations, baptizing them in the name of the father and of the Son and of the Holy Spirit. Teaching them to observe all things that I have commanded you; and lo, I am with you always, even to the end of the age."

The disciples received their instructions to make disciples for Christ from among all people in every nation. The teachings of Christ were God's redeeming message to sinful people everywhere until Jesus and the angels return to earth and escort the resurrected disciples to the new heaven and new earth.

Some of the last words of Jesus that are recorded in Mark's gospel are considered the Great Commission.

Mark 16:15-16 "God into all the world and preach the gospel to every creature. He who believes and is baptized will be saved: but he who does not believe will be condemned."

The last words recorded in Mark's gospel say that Jesus was received into heaven where He sat down at God's right hand. The apostles preached the gospel everywhere, and the Lord helped them by confirming their word with miraculous signs.

In Luke the 24th chapter, Jesus promised to send the apostles power from the Holy Spirit. He told them to wait in Jerusalem until they were given that power from heaven. Jesus reminded them of some of the things He had previously told them, the things that must be fulfilled according to the Law of Moses, the prophets, and Psalms.

Jesus gave the apostles the ability to understand the scriptures about Him. He emphasized that His death was necessary for the remission of sins and that the gospel should be preached in His name all over the world beginning in Jerusalem. The apostles were witnesses of all these things. The things that took place in the first century were openly exposed; nothing was done in secret.

The last words of Jesus in the book of Luke: *Luke 24:49 "behold, I send the Promise of My Father upon you; but tarry in the city of Jerusalem until you are endued with power from on high."*

Jesus then led the apostles to Bethany, lifted up His hands to heaven and blessed them. While He was blessing them, He was carried up into heaven.

Jesus performed many miracles that were witnessed by His disciples (followers) that are not in the scriptures, but those that were written, were written so that people would have faith in Christ and have eternal life.

Acts of the Apostles

Tradition claims that Luke wrote the book of Acts of the Apostles. The Book of Acts is a record of the apostle's work of preaching the gospel after Jesus' death to formally establish the Kingdom of Christ.

Jesus said, *"I will build My church and the gates of Hades shall not prevail against it."* Satan worked against the establishment of the church but he was not able to prevent its establishment. The church will continue on earth until the end of time when it will be taken into heaven.

The church is God's spiritual kingdom and is the same as the Kingdom of God, the Kingdom of Christ, and the Kingdom of Heaven that Jesus promised would be established throughout His ministry. The word church is derived from the Greek word 'ekklesia' and means 'a calling.'

The word church was used in reference to a body of people that are called to an assembly to worship. The Kingdom of God is universal. The church can be a local group or any number of groups in other areas that are members of the Kingdom of God. Since the death of Christ, there is redemption of sin for any individual who has faith, hope and love and has been baptized in water like Jesus as a sign of their faith in Jesus.

Before Jesus ascended, He met with the apostles and told them not to leave Jerusalem. The formal establishment of the Kingdom of God on earth (the church) was going to take place in Jerusalem, and He told them what to expect: *"But you shall receive power when the Holy Spirit has come upon you; and you shall be witnesses to Me in Jerusalem, and in all Judea and Samaria, and to the end of the earth."*

The apostles were to receiving Jesus' promise to give them miraculous power from the Holy Spirit to help establish the church. He said, *"You have heard from Me; for John truly baptized with water, but you shall be baptized with the Holy Spirit not many days from now."* The disciples asked Jesus if he would at that time restore the kingdom to Israel? Jesus told them they did not need to know what God had put in His own authority.

The physical kingdom of Israel was not being restored, but a spiritual kingdom of God and Christ was going to be established in Jerusalem on the first Day of Pentecost after Jesus ascended to heaven. After Jesus' ascension, He sat down beside God on the throne, and Jesus will rule over the Kingdom of God (made up of the church) until the end of time when He returns to earth.

(Acts 2) After Jesus' ascension, the apostles went back to Jerusalem as Jesus had instructed them to do and went to the upper room where they and the women had been staying. Mary, the mother of Jesus, and his brothers went with them. There were about a hundred and twenty people from various places that assembled there that day.

Peter began to speak to them about Judas who had a place among the apostles, but had betrayed Jesus and guided those who had arrested Him. He was remorseful and returned the money and confessed that he had sinned. He then went out and bought a field where he hanged himself and fell headfirst and burst open and his insides fell out. When Peter told about Judas' death, they agreed that they should find someone to replace him, because there were originally twelve apostles. The one they were to choose must be one who had been with them from the baptism of John until the day Jesus was crucified. He also must have witnessed His resurrection. The apostles cast lots to choose between Justus and Mathias, and Mathias was chosen. The apostleship would cease sometime after the establishment of the church and the death of the

Apostles. After the death of the apostles, men who were given gifts of leadership by the Holy Spirit led the church. Today the church is lead by the understanding of the scriptures. The spiritual gifts ceased after the first century.

The Holy Spirit Guides the Apostles as They Lead the Church

Acts 2:1-12 "When the day of Pentecost had fully come, they were all with one accord in one place. The Apostles and some other of Jesus disciple were together waiting for the Holy Spirit. 2. And suddenly there came a sound from heaven, as of a rushing mighty wind, and it filled the whole house where they were sitting."

Verse 3. "Then there appeared to them divided tongues, as of fire, and one sat upon each of them."

Verse 4 "And they were all filled with the Holy Spirit and began to speak with other tongues, as the Spirit gave them utterance".

The Holy Spirit could have come silently, but he came in a way to attract a lot of attention to the presence of God's Spirit so that all would know that this was an event from God. The people heard the sound and saw something that looked like tongues of fire that sat on each of the Apostles; a sign that the Holy Spirit of God was enabling them to preach and teach. There were people (Jews) from every nation and language who were in Jerusalem to attend the feast that day. The Holy Spirit told them what to say, and when they spoke everyone heard in their own language.

The term 'other tongues' simply means other languages. The Bible describes the event of speaking in tongues in reference to the existence of the many languages of the people that were present. Speaking in tongues was a temporary gift of the Holy Spirit that ceased when the tongues and other miraculous gifts was no longer necessary. That demonstration by the Holy Spirit was only temporary as a sign for beginning of the church. Miraculous gifts of the Holy Spirit would cease later.

The twelve Apostles stood up to speak and every person heard them in their own language. The speaking of the Apostles and possibly the other disciples in the room must have sounded strange and confusing to the crowd of people that heard them speak. The miracle of the languages attracted the attention of the crowd of people. Some of the people in the crowd began to say that the apostles were drunk, because they couldn't understand the languages other than their own.

Peter took the lead and began to preach about Jesus. He told the people about the fact that Jesus was the Son of God and that Jesus had proven who he said he was.

Acts 2:14-17 "But Peter standing up with the eleven, raised his voice and said to them, Men of Judea and all who dwell in Jerusalem, let this be known to you and heed my words. For these are not drunk as you suppose since it is only the third hour of the day. But this is what was spoken by the prophet Joel: 'And it shall come to pass in the last days, says God, That I will pour out My Spirit on all flesh; Your sons and your daughters shall prophesy, Your young men shall see visions, Your old men shall dream dreams."

Prophesying, seeing visions and dreaming dreams were promised only to the descendants of those Jews on the day of Pentecost and took place as evidence that God had sent His Holy Spirit as He promised. The Holy Spirit was given in a measure that was great enough that those who were gifted with the Spirit would be able to speak and teach the word of God that was given to them.

Gifts of the Spirit in that measure were temporary for a few years to help the Apostles and church leaders form and educate the members of the kingdom with spiritual truth and guidance, but the Spirit in that measure ceased to be given in the first century and the inspired written word of God in the New Testament taught and guided the church and will continue to do so until Christ returns.

Peter and the other Apostles stood before the crowd of people and declared that the things that were happening were a fulfillment of the prophesy of Joel. The prophet Joel (Joel 2:28-32) predicted many years earlier that God would send the Holy Spirit to the descendants of the Jews who lived during Joel's time. The descendants of those Jews were in Jerusalem that Pentecost day when Peter preached. Joel prophesied that God said He would pour out His Spirit on all nationalities of people. On the day Peter preached, there were men of every nation there in Jerusalem.

Peter accused them of the crucifixion of Christ by lawlessness. The people who heard Peter speak were convicted in their hearts of the death of Jesus. The people realized that they were sinful and they asked Peter what they could do about forgiveness for their sin.

Acts 2:36-39 "Therefore let all the house of Israel know assuredly that God has made this Jesus whom you crucified, both Lord and Christ." Now when they head this they were cut to the heart, and said to Peter and the rest of the apostles, Men and brethren, what shall we do?" Then Peter said to them, "Repent and let every one of you be baptized in the name of Jesus Christ for the remission of your sins; and you shall receive the gift of the Holy Spirit. For the promise is to you and to your children, and to all who are afar off, as many as the Lord our God will call."

About three thousand people who believed Peter's message were baptized and were added to the Kingdom of Christ (church). All of the Disciples of Christ continued to fellowship the apostles and learn more about the doctrine of Christ and His Kingdom.

The Church Begins to Grow

Acts 2:42-45 "And they continued steadfastly in the apostles doctrine and fellowship, in the breaking of bread and in prayers. Then fear came upon every soul, and many wonders and signs were done through the apostles. Now all who believed were together and had all things common and sold their possessions and goods, and divided them among all, as anyone had need."

The Disciples of Christ grew to a large number of people in Jerusalem. Many of them had come to Jerusalem for the feast and lived other places. The members of the church banded together as one community in Jerusalem and sold their possessions so that everyone could have what they needed to live. The sharing in common among the church members was a freewill offering from their heart for there was a common need and common bond between the church members.

Acts 2:46-47 "So continuing daily with one accord in the temple, and breaking bread from house to house, they ate their food with gladness and simplicity of heart, praising God and having favor with all the people. And the Lord added to the church daily those who were being saved."

The Church Suffers Persecution

Acts 4:1-4 "Now as they spoke to the people, the priests, the captain of the temple, and the Sadducees came upon them, being greatly disturbed that they taught the people and preached in Jesus the resurrection from the dead. And they laid hands on them and put them in custody until the next day for it was already evening. However many of them who heard the word believed; and the number of the men came to be about five thousand."

The Holy Spirit gave the apostles the power to heal as well as preach, so the miraculous power of the Holy Spirit helped the church in its infancy during the first century.

The religious leaders of the Jews began a campaign of harassment and persecution against the church. Peter and John were healing and preaching that through Jesus there was a resurrection of the dead. When the priests heard them, they arrested them and threw them in prison. When they were brought before the council, the members of the council threatened Peter and John and forbid them to preach in the name of Jesus. (The Sanhedrin was abolished in A.D 70.)

Acts 4:18-22 "So they called them and commanded them not to speak at all or teach in the name of Jesus. But Peter and John answered and said to them, "Whether it is right in the sight of God to listen to you more than to God you judge.'

"For we cannot but speak the things which we have seen and heard." So when they had further threatened them they let them go, finding no way of punishing them, because of the people since they all glorified God for what had been done. For the man was over forty years old on whom this miracle of healing had been performed.'

The one accord of the Christians was to praise and worship God, and to conduct their lives in a way that would glorify God and teach the gospel to other people. The apostles and the other church members accepted everyone who repented and was baptized.

We find that as the church grew and spread to other places the members of the church met regularly on the first day of the week to break bread, a common expression for eating the Lord's supper, in memory of the last supper of Christ and his apostles the night He was arrested. Christians everywhere continued to meet regularly on the first day of the week to pray, observe the memorial of the Lord's supper, sing praises to God, and to fellowship and worship.

The rulers of the Jews continued to threaten the life of the apostles but the apostles stood firm in their faith and God protected them. The church continued to grow and exert an influence for Christ.

(Acts 6 & 7) The apostles selected some men who were well respected and full of the Spirit and wisdom to help with the work of the church. One of those chosen was a young man named Stephen who was strong in the faith. He was empowered with the Holy Spirit and had the ability to speak mightily for the Lord.

Some men accused Stephen of blasphemy and brought false accusations against him. Because of the lies and accusations, the rulers of the Jews arrested Stephen and brought him before the council. As Stephen stood before them, his face began to glow like the face of an angel. When they asked him if the accusations were true, Stephen began to preach to them about how God had made a promise to Abraham to bless all nations through him and how it was fulfilled in Jesus Christ.

The Jewish leaders became irate at Stephen. Stephen, full of the Holy Spirit, looked up and saw into heaven. He saw Jesus the Son of Man standing at the right hand of God in heaven, and he told the people what he saw. The crowd ran at Stephen, dragged him out of the city, and began to stone him. Just before Stephen died from the stoning, he prayed, "Lord, receive my spirit" and asked God not to charge the men with the sin they had committed in stoning him. Then Stephen died.

As they were stoning Stephen, they laid their coats at the feet of a young man named Saul who had been persecuting the followers of Christ. There was a great persecution against the church in Jerusalem at that time. Saul and those he led entered the house of Christians and took them to prison. After Stephen's death, in his eagerness to kill more of the Lord's followers, he decided to go to Damascus.

On the way to Damascus, suddenly and light from heaven shone all around him, and he fell to the ground. Then he heard a voice say, *"Saul, Saul, why are you persecuting Me?* Saul said, *"Who are you, Lord?"* The voice replied, *"I am Jesus, whom you are persecuting. It is hard for you to kick against the goads."*

The Lord Jesus told Saul to go into the city and someone would tell him what to do. When Saul arose from the ground he couldn't see, so the men with him had to guide him. Saul spent three days and nights without sight, and during that time he didn't eat or drink anything.

A disciple of Christ named Ananias was in Damascus, and the Lord told Ananias to go to a certain street to the house of Judas and ask for Saul. Ananias had heard about the way Saul had been persecuting Christians, and he was afraid to go at first. But the Lord said, *"Go, for he is a chosen vessel of Mine to bear My name before Gentiles, kings, and the children of Israel. For I will show him how many things he must suffer for My name's sake."(Acts 9:15)*

Saul had been praying, and he saw Ananias in a vision coming to him and putting his hand on him to restore his sight. Ananias did as the Lord had instructed him. When he got to the house where Saul was he put his hands on Saul and told him that Jesus sent him to restore his sight. He also told Saul that he would be filled with the Holy Spirit. Saul's sight was immediately restored and he was baptized.

After that Saul spent some time with the disciples of Jesus at Damascus. Saul's purpose in life made a dramatic change when he was commissioned by the Lord to preach the gospel. Saul's name was later changed to Paul.

As a Roman citizen Paul was free to travel throughout the empire preaching the gospel. Paul traveled more that seven thousand miles preaching Christ. The life and ministry of the Apostle Paul greatly advanced the gospel of Christ. Before Paul was confined he made three missionary journeys and some of the Christian brothers assisted him. He preached in Cyprus, Greece, Crete and Rome and converted many Gentile people to Christ and established Christian churches. Paul portrayed the church as the body of Christ and those who were outside the church as being under the judgment of God.

With the inspiration of the Holy Spirit, Paul wrote fourteen of the New Testament books. Eventually Paul was arrested and sent to Rome and he lived there two years living in his own rented house. Paul was allowed to teach the gospel in confinement and he did so freely. Many people came to hear Paul and he welcomed all who came.

The gospel message was to be taught throughout the world. The apostles of Christ, including Paul, spoke by direct inspiration of the Holy Spirit. Direct inspiration of the Holy Spirit ceased after the first century, because God's message of faith, hope and love was documented in the scriptures and had spread to many regions of the civilized world. The gospel of Christ taught in the Bible teaches everything that needs to be known about God's plan of redemption and faith, hope and love including obedience to the gospel message that converts people to Christ.

The church will continue to exist in the minds and hearts of the people who understand the scriptures and remain faithful to Christ and the scriptures. In his sermon at Jerusalem, the Apostle Peter, spoke of the gift of the Holy Spirit, which was the gift of direct inspiration to teach the gospel message of Jesus Christ. Direct inspiration of the Holy Spirit was given to the apostles. Other Christians have an indwelling of the Holy Spirit but they are not divinely inspired with power and knowledge as the apostles were.

When the persecution of the church in Jerusalem became severe the members, except for the apostles, left Jerusalem and went throughout Judea and Samaria. Some of those who left the Jerusalem church began to preach the gospel and baptize the believers, forming small church groups everywhere they went.

In spite of several centuries of influences on the gospel of Christ and the church, the pattern for New Testament Christianity will forever exist. Christian men and women who are dedicated to serving the Lord and have love and compassion for other people will continue to spread the gospel message even though they might be persecuted in various ways.

Today Christians do not have direct inspiration from the Holy Spirit as the apostles did, but they have a measure of the Holy Spirit. People who have the intelligence and the desire to know about God, Christ and the church can read the New Testament and accept Christ by faith in obedience to baptism. They then become members of the Kingdom of God.

There are many churches belonging to the Kingdom of God that have been established by men and women who follow the pattern of the church in the New Testament and are willing to accept those who are already Christians as well as those who want to learn more about the gospel and become Christians.

All authority in the kingdom belongs to God and Christ, but advice from members who are wise, competent, well versed in the scriptures, and able to teach and are sincere can help guide those who become members of the kingdom to grow in faith, hope and love. May God and His Holy Spirit bless and help the churches to the end of time.

Colossians 3:12-17 "Therefore as the elect of God, holy and beloved, put on tender mercies, kindness, humility, meekness, longsuffering; bearing with one another, and forgiving one another, if anyone has a complaint against another; even as Christ forgave you, so you must do. But above all these things put on love, which is the bond of perfection.'

"And let the peace of God rule in your hearts, to which also you were called in one body; and be thankful. Let the word of Christ dwell in you richly in all wisdom, teaching and admonishing one another in psalms and hymns and spiritual songs, singing with grace in your hearts to the Lord. And what ever you do in word or deed, do all in the name of the Lord Jesus, giving thanks to God the Father through Him."

The church will remain on earth until the end of time when Christ returns, despite persecution. The New Testament pictures a continuing conflict between the forces of God and the evil forces of the devil. The church that began on the day of Pentecost after Jesus' resurrection will continue to struggle against the forces of evil. There have been evil people on earth since the time of the creation, and that evil will continue until the end of time.

Christianity is the world's largest religion today, and it began with the Israelites (Jews) in Palestine in the first century and spread from Jerusalem into Syria, Assyria, Mesopotamia, Phoenicia, Asia Minor, Jordan and Egypt. In the 4th century Christianity became the state religion of Armenia, Georgia and the Roman Empire.

Christianity is a common religion in Europe. Today Christianity is the largest religion in the United States. According to the encyclopedia today there are approximately 34,000 separate Christian groups around the world.

All Christian religions believe in one God but Christianity is a divided religion with many groups and churches that have their own understanding of the scriptures.

Islam is considered to be the second largest religion today and they do not accept Jesus Christ as the Son of God. The members of Islam are called Muslims, and they are divided between Sunni—80 percent and Shia—20 percent. Hinduism is the world's third largest religion and Buddhism is listed as the fourth largest. Neither group accepts Christ as the Son of God.

The Book of Revelation

Preparatory Introduction

Revelation is the last book in the Bible, and it reveals the last part of God's plan of redemption describing the future and final events of the kingdom of God on earth.

The meaning of the word revelation is to reveal things that are hidden such as an unveiling of future events. The literature of Revelation is called **eschatology**, because it describes the last and final events of God's plan of redemption including a time of great tribulation, the final judgment of God on Satan and the sin of wicked and evil people.

The Book of Revelation is called an **apocalypse**, because it reveals future events. The future events were revealed to the apostle John by dreams and supernatural visions of the past, present, and the future. Apocalypses are written in figurative language using symbolism and metaphors. The only way we can understand the events in Revelation is to understand the meaning of the figurative language in the book.

John used apocalyptic literature in Revelation to hide the meaning of future events from the enemies of the church. The church of the first century was familiar with figurative and apocalyptic literature. Many of the books in the Bible include that type of literature, especially the books of prophecy. The time of the future events in an apocalypse are always viewed as imminent, because the time for their beginning is unknown. The enemy of God's people in Revelation is called the Antichrist who is empowered and controlled by Satan.

The Antichrist will be a political and religious person who will appear during the end time in opposition to God and Christ, and he will claim to be God. The Antichrist will cause great tribulation and death among the people of the earth and will persecute the church.

Paul in his second letter to Timothy said a time is coming when there will be a falling away from faith in God and many people will not accept the teachings of Christ. Paul was speaking of a time still in the future.

During that time of falling away the Antichrist led by Satan will corrupt the minds of the people on earth and many will accept the doctrines of the Antichrist. The time of the great tribulation on earth is referred to as the **end time** a short period of time on earth before Christ returns. Christ will return to earth to destroy the works of Satan and the Antichrist.

Revelation consists of seven sections which run parallel to each other and depict the church and the spiritual condition of the world from the first coming of Christ to His second coming at the end of time.

Revelation is written as seven different independent sections that tell the same story about the end times in each section. Each section is independent of and different from the other sections even though each section describes events that take place from the first coming of Christ to the second coming of Christ.

Revelation 20:1-6 *"Then I saw an angel coming down from heaven, having the key to the bottomless pit and a great chain in his hand. He laid hold of the dragon, that serpent of old, who is the Devil and Satan, and bound him for a thousand years; and cast him into the bottomless pit, and shut him up, and set a seal on him, so that he should deceive the nations no more till the thousand years were finished. But after these things he must be released for a little while."*

The abyss where Satan is imprisoned is referred to in *Luke 8:30-31 "Jesus asked him, saying, "What is your name?" And he said legion, "because many demons had entered him. And they begged him that he would not command them to go out into the abyss."*

Revelation 9:1-2 Then the fifth angel sounded: And I saw a star fallen from heaven to the earth. To him was given the key to the bottomless pit (abyss). And he opened the bottomless pit, and smoke arose out of the pit like the smoke of a great furnace."

Revelation 11:7 When they finish their testimony, the beast (Satan) that ascends out of the bottomless pit (abyss) will make war against them, overcome them, and kill them."

Revelation 17:8 The beast that you saw was, and is not, and will ascend out of the bottomless pit (abyss) and go to perdition" (hell). Satan had come to earth to persecute Jesus and God had him put in the Abyss. He was on earth then he was not.

Jude 6-9 *"And the angels who did not keep their proper domain, but left their own abode, He has reserved in everlasting chains under darkness for the judgment of the great day; as Sodom and Gomorrah, and the cities around them in a similar manner to these, have given themselves over to sexual immorality and gone after strange flesh, reject authority, and speak evil of dignitaries. Yet Michael the archangel, in contending with the devil, when he disputed about the body of Moses, dared not bring against him a reviling accusation, but said, "The Lord rebuke you!"* Michael is an Archangel who is the protector of God's people and he protects them from Satan and the demons. The angels (demons) who left heaven and came to earth to torment God's people were put in the bottomless pit. (Chains, darkness) until the judgment time when they will be released from the Abyss for a little time before they are destroyed.

"And I saw thrones and they sat on them, and judgment was committed to them. Then I saw the souls of those who had been beheaded for their witness to Jesus and for the word of God, who had not worshiped the beast or his image, and had not received his mark on their foreheads or on their hands. And they lived and reigned with Christ for a thousand years. But the rest of the dead did not live again until the thousand years were finished. This is the first resurrection. Blessed and holy is he who has part in the first resurrection. Over such the second death has no power, but they shall be priests of God and Christ, and shall reign with Him a thousand years."

The 7th and last section of Revelation is chapters 20,21 and 22. Section 7 begins with the beginning of the Christian age in the first century after the crucifixion, resurrection and ascension of Christ, and ends with the events of the second coming of Christ at the end of time. Revelation explains God's message about the future times in a way that the average student of the Bible can understand and accept.

This part of the book was not written to criticize anyone's belief but for Christians of all churches to reason together for a better understanding of these future events. No one knows what time in the future the persecution and tribulation will begin, but Christians need to know about these future events and be ready, for they will test your faith when they appear and the end times may begin tomorrow. Sometime after the ascension of Christ and most likely near the end of the first century Satan was bound (in the Abyss) for a period of time symbolized by 1000 years. The fact that Satan was bound means he could not use his power against the church (The Kingdom of Christ).

The word millennium makes reference to one thousand years and is the term used for the time period that Satan is bound during the Christian dispensation. The Christian dispensation began with the first coming of Christ and the kingdom of Christ (church) will remain on earth until Christ returns. Christians in the kingdom look forward to the second coming of Christ and the new heaven and new earth.

The millennium is a symbolic term designating the time from the binding of Satan in the first century (Abyss) to the time Satan is set free to return to the earth at the **end time** to cause great tribulation against God's people. We are now living during the millennium that will exist until Satan is set free to roam the earth again. Christ will return to earth and destroy Satan at the end of the millennium an unknown length of time symbolized by one thousand years.

Binding Satan with a great chain symbolizes restraining the power of Satan to keep him from deceiving the nations. The Greek word for bound is *horothesia* meaning the fixing of a boundary. The Greek word for chain is *halusis* and denotes a chain or bond for binding the body, or any part of it. (Vines) Satan was to be imprisoned so that he would no longer have access to the earth and deceive the nations until he is released during the end time.

The angel from heaven that bound Satan with the great chain had the keys to the bottomless pit. The bottomless pit referred to in the book of Revelation is the abyss and it describes a place of immeasurable depth also called the underworld. The Abyss is located somewhere in the great expanse of space we call the heavens. God gave judgment to the souls of the people who sat on thrones in heaven who had been beheaded on earth, because they would not renounce their faith in Jesus even when threatened with death. These were the martyrs during the first century.

A short time before the second coming of Christ the millennium will expire, Satan will be released from the abyss and go to earth and attempt to deceive the nations and the church.

There will be a great persecution of the church that will challenge the faith of all Christians. Many books have been written to interpret the book of Revelation, and there are many theories about the future persecution and the great tribulation at the **end time** and end of time.

Revelation was written to reveal the events of the persecution and tribulation and to encourage and comfort Christians when the end times come. Satan will be the instigator of the tribulation, and those who are spiritually unprepared may become victims of Satan's evil intent to destroy their faith. The Antichrist, empowered by Satan, will come before the second coming of Christ, and he will be responsible for the persecution and tribulation.

The spirit of mankind does not die—life extends beyond the grave, and at the end of time God will deal justly with all people of every time period. According to Matthew's gospel, people will be divided into two groups—the righteous and the unrighteous. Jesus and the angels will come to the earth to take vengeance on Satan, the Antichrist and the unrighteous people. Those who are still living will be able to see Christ and the angels descend on the clouds of the sky in glory with great power at the end of time. Christ's coming will be a time of grief and sorrow for the unbelievers and the unrighteous, but it will be a time of joy and comfort for God's people.

The earth will be destroyed at the end of time, but God has prepared a new heaven and new earth in which the righteous will live. The righteous will be caught up in the clouds to meet the Lord in the air, and they shall ever be with the Lord. Then the earth and everything in it will be destroyed with a consuming fire.

Since Revelation reveals events of the future that are still pending it is easier to understand the future events if we divide them into sections. The book of Revelation is divided into seven sections and each section covers the same time period but reveals some events not revealed by the other sections. One must read every section for the complete description of all events.

1ˢᵗ John chapter 4 John explains that the antichrist denies the divinity of Christ. John 5: 6-8 says there are three things that determine the real Christ—the Holy Spirit, water baptism, and the blood shed on the cross.

1ˢᵗ John 5:18-19 *"We know that whoever is born of God does not sin; but he who has been born of God keeps himself and the wicked one does not touch him." We know that we are of God, and the whole world lies under the sway of the wicked one."* In 2ⁿᵈ Thessalonians the 2ⁿᵈ chapter, Paul writes about the antichrist and identifies him as the man of sin, also known as the Lawless One, who will appear at the end time.

The end time is a short period of time represented figuratively by Daniel as three and one half years, 42 months, 1260 days, or a time, times and half a time. The end time and the end of time are in the future but the end time could begin to take place at any time.

1ˢᵗ John 2:18 "Little children, it is the last hour; and as you have heard that the antichrist is coming, even now many antichrists have come, by which we know that it is the last hour.

The last hour figuratively refers to the last days. We are presently living in the last hour and the Anti-Christ could appear at any time. There were many people in the first century that denied the divinity of Christ and there are many now but John in revelation is referring to the antichrist that will come during the end time before Christ returns. Today we are living in the time described as the last hour and during this time the days of the end time will occur. The end time is the time defined figuratively as three and one half years of tribulation before the antichrist on earth. Revelation completes the record of the redeeming plan that began in the book of Genesis.

There are several references to the end time in other books of the Bible, but Revelation specifically focuses on the future events of the end times. God made sure the church would be prepared for the end time. He inspired the Apostle Paul to write two letters to the church in Thessalonica. These two letters prepare us to understand the events of the end time. In 1ˢᵗ Thessalonians Paul emphasized the second coming of Christ at an unknown time and warned the church to be ready at all times.

2ⁿᵈ *Thessalonians 2:1-4: Now brethren concerning the coming of our Lord Jesus Christ and our gathering together to him, we ask you, not to be soon shaken in mind or troubled either by spirit or by word or by letter, as if from us, as though the day of Christ has come. Let no one deceive you by any means; for that Day will not come unless the falling away comes first, and the man of sin is revealed, the son of perdition, who opposes and exalts himself above all that is called God or that is worshiped."*

In the first chapter of 2ⁿᵈ Thessalonians, Paul explained that he knew the end time was coming, but he did not know when it would begin. Paul wrote about a great apostasy during the end time that will take place before Christ comes back. He wrote that during that time many people will fall away from their faith in God and will follow a world leader called the Lawless One who is the Antichrist, the man of sin who is corrupted by the power of Satan. Satan will be on earth during the end time and will give power to the Lawless One who will help him establish his evil empire and persecute the church. Paul wrote about the attitude of people during the last days before the return of Christ.

2ⁿᵈ *Timothy 3:1-7 "But know this, that in the last days perilous times will come: For men will be lovers of themselves, lovers of money, boasters, proud, blasphemers, disobedient to parents, unthankful, unholy, unloving, unforgiving, slanderers, without self-control, brutal, despisers of good, traitors, headstrong, haughty, lovers of pleasure rather than lovers of God, having a form of godliness but denying its power. And from such people turn away! For of this sort are those who creep into households and make captives of gullible women loaded down with sins, led away by various lusts, always learning and never able to come to the Knowledge of the truth."*

Daniel wrote about the time of trouble during the end time that is followed by the second coming of Christ.

Daniel 12:1-3 "At that time Michael shall stand up, The great prince who stands watch over the sons of your people; and there shall be a time of trouble, such as never was since there was a nation, Even to that time. And at that time your people shall be delivered everyone who is found written in the book. And many of those who sleep in the dust of the earth shall awake, some to everlasting life some to shame and everlasting contempt. Those who are wise shall shine like the brightness of the firmament, and those who turn many to righteousness like the stars forever and ever."

The idea has been presented that Christ will return to earth, establish His kingdom the church here on earth for a thousand years before the end of time. That theory is not correct Because Christ has already established the kingdom, which is the church a spiritual kingdom. When Christ returns the church ascends to heaven where a place for the church will exist.

Christ has continually reigned over the church since it's beginning. In the first century the church, which is the kingdom of Christ was established on the first Pentecost day and recorded in Acts chapter two. The church has been the kingdom of Christ on earth ever since that day and Christ has reigned over the church from heaven. Christ's reign on earth ends at the end of time when the church will leave this earth bound for a new heaven and new earth.

A Christian's citizenship is in heaven: *Philippians 3:20-21 "For our citizenship is in heaven, from which we also eagerly wait for the Savior, the Lord Jesus Christ, who will transform our lowly body that it may be conformed to His glorious body, according to the working by which He is able even to subdue all things to Himself."*

To reign with Christ means to be in fellowship with Christ—belonging to Christ as a member of His kingdom. Christ reigns from heaven in the hearts of every person who believes He is God's Son beginning from the time of their obedience to the gospel.

The church is viewed as being here now and in heaven in the future, and all Christians already reign with Christ in His kingdom. Christ will come with the angels without any prior warning, but there will be no doubt about what is taking place when He returns.

Everyone will see and hear Him as He descends in the clouds. Those who are members of the church will quickly realize what is happening and know that their redemption is near, and they will anticipate being caught up in the air to meet the Lord.

Luke 21:25-28 "And there will be signs in the sun, in the moon and in the stars; and on the earth distress of nations, with perplexity, the sea and the waves roaring; men's hearts failing them from fear and the expectation of those things which are coming on the earth, for the powers of the heavens will be shaken.'

"Then they will see the Son of Man coming in a cloud with power and great glory. Now when these things begin to happen, look up and lift up your heads, because your redemption draws near."

Matthew 24: 27-31 "For as the lightning comes from the east and flashes to the west, so also will the coming of the Son of Man be. For wherever the carcass is, there the eagles will be gathered together. 'Immediately after the tribulation of those days the sun will be darkened, and the moon will not give its light; the stars will fall from heaven, and the powers of the heavens will be shaken.'

"Then the sign of the Son of Man will appear in heaven, and then all the tribes of the earth will mourn, and they will see the Son of Man coming on the clouds of heaven with power and great glory. And He will send His angels with a great sound of a trumpet, and they will gather together His elect from the four winds from one end of heaven to the other."

Section one is an introduction to the book of Revelation and a greeting to seven of the existing churches of Asia near the end of the first century. In Matthew 16:18 Jesus said, "I will build My church." The word church is from a Greek word that means those who are called out. Jesus made reference to all people everywhere who are called by the gospel message to faith and obedience to Christ.

Revelation teaches that the tribulation in the future that is classified as the end time will be caused by the Antichrist, a man who will oppose and exalt himself above God and demand to be worshiped as God. 2nd Thessalonians, The events of the end time when the Antichrist is on earth will test the faith of Christians. God will allow the tribulation during the end time for the purpose of causing the unrighteous people to obey the gospel of Christ.

The duration of the end time is a time that is symbolized by three and one half years. In Revelation 1:18 Jesus said He is the One who has the keys to Hades and of death—meaning Jesus is the only one who has the authority to determine where the spirits will go when the body is dead. After death, the spirits of people go to two separate places to wait for God's final judgment. God determines whether we are righteous or unrighteous at the time of our death. Hades is the place where the spirits of the dead go to wait for the return of Christ. Hades is somewhere in the heavens.

Luke 16:19-31 Jesus tells a parable about a rich man and a man named Lazarus, a beggar. After physical death, all righteous spirits go either to a place of paradise, the place where Lazarus' spirit went. Or to a place of torment, the spirits of the unrighteous go to a place of torment reserved for them. And the spirits of the redeemed go to a place of paradise in Hades. When they died, the rich man's spirit went to a place of torment and Lazarus' spirit went to a place of paradise in Hades.

Christians understand that God is sovereign over all things, but God is not the source of all tragedy. The majority of human suffering is caused by our sin when we disregard God's laws of nature and His moral laws. Sometimes we might not understand when bad things happen, but we should not blame God. We believe that God is perfect in every way. He is Just and Holy, and so is His will. C.S Lewis said, "God whispers to us in our pleasures, speaks in our conscience, but shouts in our pains. It is His megaphone to rouse a deaf world." Bad things are allowed to happen to remind us that God made us; we are responsible to Him and he sees us when we are good or bad.

Section one introduces the reader to the Apostle John who wrote the book. John was the only Apostle who was still living near the end of the first century, and he was still preaching the gospel of Christ. By that time most, if not all, of the other apostles had been put to death for preaching the gospel.

The Roman Empire ordered John to stop preaching the gospel, but he continued to preach. Instead of killing John, the Romans exiled him to the Island of Patmos to isolate him and to put an end to his witnessing for Christ. However, God provided a way for John to continue preaching by enabling him to write Revelation. The barren island of Patmos afforded John, by the inspiration of the Holy Spirit, the opportunity to write Revelation without any trouble from Rome. John wrote Revelation in the first century A.D. about 50 years after the formal establishment of the church.

Chapters 1 through 3

Chapter 1:1-3 *"The Revelation of Jesus Christ, which God gave Him to show his servant things which must shortly take place. And he sent and signified it by His angel to His servant John, who bore witness to the word of God, and to the testimony of Jesus Christ, to all things that he saw. Blessed is he who reads and those who hear the words of this prophecy, and keep those things which are written in it; for the time is near.'*

John was to hear and see things in visions. Visions are defined as the power of seeing things that are not actually present. The things John saw were seen in his mind. John would see events that will take place in the future at the end time and it would not take long for him to see all of the events.

Once the future end time events begin, they will happen in rapid succession. The symbolic time for the end time is three and one half years.

The statement *the time is near* relates to being ready at all times, because no one knows when the end time will begin.

Verses 4-8 *"John, to the seven churches which are in Asia: Grace to you and peace from Him who is and who was and who is to come, and from the seven spirits who are before His throne, and from Jesus Christ the faithful witness, the firstborn from the dead, and the ruler over the kings of the earth.'* *"To Him who loved us and washed us from our sins in His own blood, and has made us kings and priests to His God and father, to Him be glory and dominion forever and ever. Amen. Behold, He is coming with the clouds, and every eye will see Him, even they who pierced Him. And all the tribes of the earth will mourn because of Him. Even so Amen I am the Alpha and Omega, the Beginning and the End says the Lord, who is and who was and who is to come, the Almighty. I, John both your brother and companion in the tribulation and kingdom and patience of Jesus Christ, was on the Island that is called Patmos for the word of God and for the testimony of Jesus Christ. I was in the Spirit on the Lord's Day and I heard behind me a loud voice, as of a trumpet, saying, "I am the Alpha and the Omega"*

The revelation John received came from Christ who had been given all power and authority over heaven and earth. Christ was the beginning of redemption and He is the end, He is coming back to rescue those who are redeemed. Christ began His reign as the King of Kings and Lord of Lords when He ascended to heaven in the first century and sat down beside God on the throne of God. At the end of time He will be back to claim His own.

Alpha is the first letter in the Greek alphabet and Omega is the last letter. Jesus is the first in the establishment of the church, because the kingdom of Christ on earth began with Him. Jesus is the last, because entrance into the kingdom will end when Jesus returns and takes the church to heaven. Christ is the King of Kings and Lord of Lords who reigns over the church spiritually. All Christians participate in His reign.

1st Corinthians 15:20-28 *"Now Christ is risen from the dead, and has become the first fruits of those who have fallen asleep. For since by man came death, by Man also came the resurrection of the dead. For as in Adam all die, even so in Christ all shall be made alive. But each one in his own order. Christ the first fruits afterward those who are Christ's at His coming. Then comes the end, when He delivers the kingdom to God the Father, when He puts an end to all rule and all authority and power for He must reign till He has put all enemies under His feet. The last enemy that will be destroyed is death. For "He has put all things under His feet." But when He says "all things are put under Him," it is evident that He who put all things under Him is excepted. Now when all things are made subject to Him, then the Son Himself will also be subject to Him who put all things under Him, that God may be all in all."*

At the end of time there will be a resurrection of the dead, and everyone will be able to see Christ coming with His angels. Many will mourn at His coming, because they will not be prepared for heaven.

Verses 9-11 *I, John, both your brother and companion in the tribulation and kingdom and patience of Jesus Christ, was on the Island called Patmos for the word of God and for the testimony of Jesus Christ. I was in the Spirit on the Lord's Day and I heard behind me a loud voice, as of a trumpet, saying, "I am the Alpha and the Omega, the First and the Last."*

And "what you see, write in a book and send it to the seven churches which are in Asia: to Ephesus, to Smyrna, to Pergamos, to Thyatira, to Sardis, to Philadelphia, and to Laodicea."

John wrote Revelation for all the churches during the Christian dispensation, but the churches in Asia would be the first to receive the letters.

He wrote a personal message from Christ for each of the seven churches. The seven churches had spiritual problems that needed to be addressed at that time, so Christ included a special message for them in Chapters 2 and 3 of Revelation.

Then he wrote to all of the churches that will exist before the end time. John's spiritual experience of receiving the revelation began on the first day of the week known as the Lord's Day.

The Lord's Day is the day we call Sunday, a regular day of assembly for the church. It is, most likely, that John was the only Christian on the barren Island, and he was regularly observing a day of worship to God when he heard a loud voice. The voice John heard was the voice of Christ instructing him to write the book of Revelation. John wrote about the past, present, and future of God's people.

John states that those who read the prophecy of Revelation will be blessed by the message, a message of hope and victory for Christians. Persecuted Christians in the first century were anxiously waiting for the day of Christ's return hoping that His coming would be soon, because they were suffering persecution from the Roman Empire.

The seven churches in Asia near Patmos were located in what is now Turkey. John wrote while he was in the Spirit—meaning his mind was under the influence of the Holy Spirit empowering him to see visions and hear voices from heaven. John claimed that he was bearing witness to the word of God and Christ. The Holy Spirit is responsible for revealing the word of God to mankind, and he inspired John as well as all of the other writers of the Bible.

Verses 12-16 "Then I turned to see the voice that spoke with me. And having turned I saw seven golden lamp stands, and in the midst of the seven lamp stands one like the Son of Man, clothed with a garment down to the feet and girded about the chest with a golden band. His head and hair were white like wool, as white as snow, and His eyes like a flame of fire; His feet were like fine brass, as if refined in a furnace, and His voice as the sound of many waters; He had in His right hand seven stars, out of His mouth went a sharp two edged sword, and His countenance was like the sun shining in its strength."

The seven golden lamp stands represent the seven churches in Asia. The glorious figure in the midst of the churches was Christ, the Son of Man and the Son of God with supreme authority. Christ is the Savior, Redeemer, High Priest, and King of the church. Christ is the One who Christians identify with and look to in all of phases of their life. Christ had a sharp two-edged sword in His mouth. A two-edged sword has the ability to cut with either side. Christ could speak with tender words of love, acceptance and praise, or He could speak harsh words of condemnation depending on the person or group to which he was addressing. *Hebrews 4:12: "For the word of God is living and powerful and sharper than any two edged sword, piercing even to the division of soul and spirit and of joints and marrow, and is a discerner of the thoughts and intents of the heart."*

God knows everything about the people He created. He even knows the very thoughts and intents of our heart at all times and God's word has the power to control the attitudes and intents of our heart if we are willing to accept His word.

Verses 17-18 *"And when I saw Him, I fell at His feet as dead. But He laid His right hand on me saying to me, "Do not be afraid; I am the First and the Last. I am He who lives, and was dead, and behold I am alive forevermore. Amen. And I have the keys of Hades and of Death."*

John was overwhelmed when he saw the glorious figure of Christ, and he fell down unable to speak. Christ calmed his fear by laying His hand on him and explaining who he was. John was very familiar with the life and experiences of Christ when He was on earth, and he readily recognized Him.

After Christ was resurrected and ascended to heaven, he was given all power and authority, and He now holds the keys to Hades, the abode of departed spirits. The word key is used figuratively—meaning the authority to judge and determine who and what part of Hades a person is assigned to at death.

Christ demonstrated His power over life and death by His resurrection and His glorious appearance to John. The time of Christ's return is not known and will not be known until He can be seen coming with the angels at the end of time. Before He comes, the events of the end time will begin, therefore every generation needs to always be ready to face the troubling events of the end time.

Luke 12:40 "Therefore you also be ready, for the Son of Man is coming at an hour you do not expect."

Verses 19-20 *"Write the things which you have seen, and the things which are, and the things which will take place after this. The mystery of the seven stars which you saw in My right hand, and the seven golden lamp stands; The seven stars are the angels of the seven churches, and the seven lamp stands which you saw are the seven churches."*

The Lamp stands represent churches and the stars represent the messengers of the churches. Stars give light and guidance and are used in a figurative sense to identify those members in the church who publicly make known God's word.

The word *stars* could have been translated messengers. Christ was referring to the person who would receive the letter and publicly present the message to the church.

John heard a voice behind him that sounded like a trumpet, and he was instructed to write down on a scroll what he would hear and see in the visions and then send it to the seven churches of Asia.

The angels in heaven were instrumental in showing John the nature of things that would take place in the future. The Holy Spirit enabled John to see visions of Christ and visions in heaven and on earth. John could hear words spoken by Christ and by the angels and other celestial beings in heaven.

Christ's loud voice was like rushing waters, indicating a loud voice of authority. Christ held a sword that was sharp on both sides. The sword represents the divine judgment of Christ and His authority. John began to write what Christ told him to write about the churches of Asia.

Some of the churches were faithful to the gospel of Christ, but most had serious problems that needed to be addressed and corrected. Christ extended His grace and peace to all of the churches, even to those with problems, but He warned the churches about the consequences of failing to remain faithful, and He admonished them to repent. John's letters to the seven churches of Asia was for the churches of the first century that were already in existence. John was a brother and companion in the persecution that was occurring at that time. That is why he was on Patmos. Christ addressed the good and the bad associated with each of the seven churches.

The church in Ephesus lacked love. The church in Smyrna was being persecuted, the church in Pergamos was compromising the truth and was engaging in sin taught by Balaam, the church in Thyatira was corrupted by allowing false doctrine to be taught and practiced, the church in Sardis was spiritually dead and needed to repent. The church in Philadelphia was commended that church was faithful to Christ. The church in Laodicea was lukewarm and needed to be strengthened spiritually.

The Church in Ephesus

Chapter 2:1-7 *"To the angel of the church of Ephesus write, 'These things says He who holds the seven stars in his right hand, who walks in the midst of the seven golden lamp-stands: "I know your works, your labor, your patience, and that you cannot bear those who are evil. And you have tested those who say they are apostles and are not, and have found them liars, and you have persevered and have patience, and have labored for My name's sake and have not become weary. Nevertheless I have this against you, that you have left your first love. Remember therefore from where you have fallen; repent and do the first works, or else I will come to you quickly and remove your lamp-stand from its place—unless you repent. But this you have, that you hate the deeds of the Nicolaitans, which I also hate. He, who has an ear, let him hear what the Spirit says to the churches.*

To him who overcomes I will give to eat from the tree of life, which is in the midst of the Paradise of God."

The church in Ephesus was located in a place of idolatrous citizens and strangers. The temple of the Greek goddess Artemis, also known as the temple of Diana, was located in Ephesus. The church in Ephesus had both Jewish and Greek members. A disciple of Christ named Apollos came from Alexandria to the church in Ephesus. Apollos had a thorough knowledge of the scriptures and was a teacher in the church. He may have been the messenger (public speaker) in this church. Priscilla and Aquila had also worked in the church at Ephesus.

Christ knew that many of the members of the church in Ephesus were faithful and worked hard at doing things that demonstrated their faith. He commended the church for the good things they were doing, but Christ was disappointed, because their love for Him had grown weak. He told them to repent and turn back to the same attitude of love and enthusiasm they had when they first obeyed Christ. If they didn't return to their former love, Christ threatened to come and remove the church.

In order to please Christ, churches must possess and demonstrate faith, hope, and love, and actively work to strengthen those attitudes. Christ commended the church for hating the false doctrine of the Nicolaitans. The Nicolaitains were Christians who had been taught to engage in immoral sexual activities by Nicholas of Antioch. In the first century, there were many false religious teachers, some in the church.

The Church in Smyrna

Chapter 2:8-11: *"And to the angel of the church in Smyrna write, 'These things says the First and the Last, who was dead, and came to life: "I know your works, tribulation, and poverty (but you are rich); and I know the blasphemy of those who say they are Jews and are not, but are a synagogue of Satan. Do not fear any of those things, which you are about to suffer. Indeed, the devil is about to throw some of you into prison, that you may be tested, and you will have tribulation ten days. Be faithful unto death, and I will give you the crown of life. He who has an ear let him hear what the Spirit says to the churches. He who overcomes shall not be hurt by the second death."*

Jesus praised the church in Smyrna because they were spiritual. The church was blessed, because of their faith, hope, and love. Jesus said they were about to experience suffering for ten days caused by Satan and possibly would be put to death.

Christ promised the church that if they would remain faithful, they would not die a second time. Jesus was referring to their spirit that would remain alive after physical death.

The Church in Pergamos

Chapter 2:12-17: *"And to the angel of the church in Pergamos write, 'These things says He who has the sharp two-edged sword:' "I know your works, and where you dwell, where Satan's throne is. And you hold fast to My name, and did not deny My faith even in the days in which Antipas was My faithful martyr who was killed among you, where Satan dwells.'*

"But I have a few things against you, because you have there those who hold the doctrine of Balaam, who taught Balak to put a stumbling block before the children of Israel, to eat things sacrificed to idols, and to commit sexual immorality. Thus you also have those who hold the doctrine of the Nicolaitans, which thing I hate.'

"Repent, or else I will come to you quickly and will fight against them with the sword of My mouth. He who has an ear, let him hear what the Spirit says to the churches.'

"To him who overcomes, I will give some of the hidden manna to eat. And I will give him a white stone, and on the stone a new name written which no one knows except him who receives it."

The words of the letter to the church in Pergamos came from Christ, the one who has the two edged sword, a sword of righteousness and of judgment. The sword symbolizes the ability and willingness of Christ to redeem the righteous and punish the sinners. The sword of Christ's mouth is the word of God proclaimed by the Holy Spirit of God, and it cuts both ways, either to redeem or to condemn.

Pergamos was a Roman Province in what is now modern Turkey. The idolatrous doctrines of Satan infiltrated the church there. There were several pagan cults and temples in Pergamos—Zeus, Athena, Dionysus and Asclepius. Idolatry is a work of Satan, and Satan's throne was firmly established in Pergamos. Domitian was the Emperor of Rome when John wrote Revelation. Domitian claimed to be divine, and everyone was ordered to worship him. The influence of Satan ruled the population of the ungodly, and they persecuted the people of God.

Some members of the church in Pergamos practiced the teaching of the Nicolaitains. Nicolaitains practiced sexual immorality and ate food sacrificed to idols in worship. Christ threatened to use judgment against the sinful church with the sword of his mouth if they did not repent.

Some of the members in Pergamos were guilty of the sins of Balaam a false prophet in the Old Testament. Balaam taught Balack, the king of Moab, and the Midianite women how to lead the Israelites into sin by teaching them that it was okay to eat meat sacrificed to idols and to commit immoral sexual acts.

1ˢᵗ Peter 5:8-9: "Be sober, be vigilant; because your adversary the devil walks about like a roaring lion, seeking whom he may devour. Resist him, steadfast in the faith, knowing that the same sufferings are experienced by your brotherhood in the world."

Christians armed with the word of God can resist the temptation to sin. Christ said that He would give hidden manna to those who overcome the temptation to sin. Manna is the food God gave the Israelites in the wilderness to keep them alive physically. The word of God is the manna for Christians that can keep them faithful to Christ and alive spiritually.

Some church members in Pergamos faithfully followed the teachings of Christ, and Christ commended them for their faithfulness. Antipas, a citizen of Pergamos, was a Christian who refused to deny Christ and was put to death for that reason, therefore Antipas became a martyr. Christ promised to give everyone who remained faithful to Him a white stone with a new name written on it.

Stones were used at that time among the people to vote for the guilt or innocence of a person. A white stone represented innocence. Drawing a black stone meant they were guilty. Christ used that illustration to promise eternal life to those who were faithful to Him.

The Church in Thyatira

Chapter 2:18-29: *"And to the angel of the church in Thyatira write, 'These things says the Son of God, who has eyes like a flame of fire, and His feet like fine brass: "I know your works, love, service, faith, and your patience; and as for your works, the last are more than the first.'*

"Nevertheless I have a few things against you, because you allow that woman Jezebel, who calls herself a prophetess, to teach and seduce My servants to commit sexual immorality and eat things sacrificed to idols. And I gave her time to repent of her sexual immorality, and she did not repent.'

"Indeed I have cast her into a sickbed, and those who commit adultery with her into great tribulation, unless they repent of their deeds. I will kill her children with death, and all the churches shall know that I am He who searches the minds and hearts. And I will to each one of you according to your works. "Now to you I say, and to the rest in Thyatira, as many as do not have this doctrine, who have not known the depths of Satan, as they say, I will put no other burden. But hold fast what you have till I come. And he who overcomes, and keeps My works until the end, to him will I give power over the nations-

'He shall rule them with a rod of iron;

They shall be dashed to pieces like the potters vessels'-

As I also have received from My Father; and I will give him the morning star. He who has an ear, let him hear what the Spirit says to the churches."

Thyatira was a city between Pergamos and Laodicea. The church in Thyatira was faithful to the Lord in their attendance and in the acts of worshiping Christ. They had many commendable works such as love, service, faith, and patience, and they were commended for growing spiritually. Even with all of these virtues there was a serious problem with a member named Jezebel who claimed to be a prophetess. Jezebel was sick spiritually and near spiritual death.

A prophet or prophetess is a person who claims to speak for God. Jezebel was not a legitimate prophetess, but some members of the church actually believed she was a prophetess and followed her teaching. She taught that it was proper to indulge in illicit sex and to eat food sacrificed to idols. Those who were guilty of the sins of Jezebel were referred to as Jezebel's children, because she was the one who taught them to sin, and they followed her teaching. Jezebel may have been her real name, or Christ may have identified the woman as Jezebel comparing her to Jezebel of the Old Testament, the evil and immoral wife of King Ahab.

Instead of the church rejecting Jezebel as a false teacher, the church permitted her to continue to teach. She was warned to repent and stop teaching immorality. If she would not repent, Christ threatened to punish her by casting her on a bed of suffering.

A bed of suffering was some kind of affliction of which Jezebel would not recover. Her punishment was most likely spiritual death, a separation from the grace of God. She would not be forgiven if she didn't repent, therefore she would be dead spiritually and have no hope of eternal life.

The church was warned that those who committed adultery with Jezebel would suffer intensely unless they repented. The penalty for failing to repent was to be struck dead spiritually with no hope of redemption.

The members who remained faithful to the teachings of Christ were admonished to hold on to the way they were living and acting.

Christians are alive in Christ, but if they sin and fail to repent they become dead spiritually and will experience the second death.

Christ promises Christians if they continue to be faithful and do His will, they will triumph over the unbelievers and ungodly who will be punished. Christ received authority from God to punish the ungodly, and He will carry out the judgment by destroying the ungodly when he returns at the end of time.

Individual Christians will receive what they are justly due when they die. They will be rewarded according to their works of faith, hope and love. *1st Corinthians 13:12-13 "For now we see in a mirror dimly, but then face to face. Now I know in part, but then I shall know just as I also am known. And now abide faith, hope, and love, these three; but the greatest of these is love."*

Christ warned the church members that were following Jezebel, the terms of His judgment. Christ tells members that were not following Jezebels teaching that he will not burden them with anything else, and said to continue in their works. Those who remained faithful would be given power over the nations. Some Bible versions use the word *authority* instead of power. The power or authority given by Christ to the redeemed at the end of time will be to share in the glory of Christ's victory and they will enter a new heaven and new earth where there is no unrighteousness or death. Christ alone has the power and authority to punish the nations, symbolized by a rod of iron.

The battle is between good and evil. Satan fights for evil and Christ fights for righteousness, and in the end Christ wins, and Christians share in His righteous victory.

Christ will *rule the nations with a rod of iron*. The nations symbolize the unrighteous. The rod of iron symbolizes the punishment described by the statement *dashed to pieces*. The rule with a rod of iron will come on the unrighteous at the end of time. In First Corinthians, Paul gives a synopsis of the events of the kingdom of Christ at the end of time.

1st Corinthians 15:20-28 "But now Christ is risen from the dead, and has become the first fruits of those who have fallen asleep. For since by man came death, by Man also came the resurrection of the dead. For as in Adam all die, even so in Christ all shall be made alive. But each one in his own order: Christ the first fruits, afterward those who are Christ's at His coming. Then comes the end, when He delivers the kingdom to God the Father, when He puts an end to all rule and all authority and power.'

"For He must reign till He has put all His enemies under His feet. The last enemy that will be destroyed is death. For "He has put all things under His feet." But when He says "all things are put under Him," it is evident that He who put all things under Him is excepted. Now when all things are made subject to Him, then the Son Himself will also be subject to Him who put all things under Him, that God may be all in all."

The kingdom (church) began after the resurrection and ascension of Christ in the first century. Christ returned to heaven to rule or reign spiritually over the kingdom we call the church. God allows Christ to reign over the kingdom until the end of time. Christ will return to earth at the end of time to destroy Satan and will *punish with a rod of iron.*

The Church in Sardis

Chapter 3:1-6 *"And to the angel of the church in Sardis write, These things says He who has the seven Spirits of God and the seven stars: "I know your works, that you have a name that you are alive, but you are dead. Be watchful, and strengthen the things, which remain, that are ready to die, for I have not found your works perfect before God. Remember therefore how you have received and heard; hold fast and repent'*

"Therefore if you will not watch, I will come upon you as a thief, and you will not know what hour I will come upon you. You have a few names even in Sardis who have not defiled their garments; and they shall walk with Me in white, for they are worthy.' "He who overcomes shall be clothed in white garments, and I will not blot out his name from the Book of Life; but I will confess his name before My Father and before His angels. He who has an ear let him hear what the Spirit says to the churches."

The church in Sardis thought it strong in faith, but the letter from Christ stated that the church was in danger of dying. He was speaking of a spiritual death. The church was actually weak in faith and their spiritual death was imminent unless they strengthened their faith. They needed to wake up spiritually.

The church was evidently lacking in faith, hope, and love, as well as other Christian virtues. The church may have been going through a form of habitual worship of sacraments and deeds without the proper attitudes of the heart and spirit, or the Christians in Sardis may have been involved in sinful activity while outwardly appearing to be righteous.

Christians who are strong in faith are spoken of figuratively as being dressed in clean white clothes. John said some were wearing soiled clothes indicating that they were living in sin. White clothes are a symbol of righteousness, and wearing soiled clothes is a symbol of sinfulness. Christ called for those in sin to repent and walk in righteousness with Him.

The Church in Philadelphia

Verses 7-13 *"And to the angel of the church in Philadelphia write: 'These things says He who is holy, He who is true, He who has the key of David, He who opens and no one shuts, and shuts and no one opens I know your works. See, I have set before you an open door, and no one can shut it; for you have a little strength, have kept My word, and have not denied My name.'*

"Indeed I will make those of the synagogue of Satan, who say they are Jews and are not, but lie—indeed I will make them come and worship before your feet, and to know that I have loved you. Because you have kept My command to persevere, I also will keep you from the hour of trial, which shall come upon the whole world, to test those who dwell on the earth. Behold, I am coming quickly! Hold fast what you have that no one may take your crown.'

"He who overcomes, I will make him a pillar in the temple of My God, and he shall go out no more. I will write on him the name of My God and the name of the city of My God, the New Jerusalem, which comes down out of heaven from My God. And I will write on him My new name. He who has an ear let him hear what the Spirit says to the churches."

Verses 7-9 Christ addresses the angel of the church in Philadelphia. Christ said He is holy and true and has the key of David.

The key of David symbolizes the authority to rule as a king over the kingdom of God. Christ says He is the only One who can save or condemn. As the ruler of God's kingdom on earth, Christ has absolute authority. Jesus commended the faithful church members at Philadelphia and assured them that the Jews from the Synagogue had no power over their salvation or over the church.

Christ promised to make those of the synagogue of Satan to come and worship at the feet of the faithful in the Kingdom of Christ. Christ also promised to keep the church safe from the hour of trial that some day would come upon the whole world.

The hour of trial symbolizes the tribulation and suffering during the **end time** and the end of time. The synagogue of Satan represents the unrighteous that will receive eternal punishment at that time. Christ says He is coming and those who are counted among the faithful will receive a crown and become a pillar in heaven. They will be identified as those who belong to God and will enter the New Jerusalem in heaven. John received this revelation from the Holy Spirit. Revelation 21.

The Church in Laodicea

Verses 3:14-22 *"And to the angel of the church of the Laodiceans write, 'These things says the Amen, the Faithful and True Witness, the Beginning of the creation of God: I know your works, that you are neither cold nor hot. I could wish you were cold or hot. So then, because you are lukewarm, and neither cold nor hot, I will vomit you out of My mouth.'*

"Because you say, 'I am rich, have become wealthy, and have need of nothing—and do not know that you are wretched, miserable, poor, blind, and naked—I counsel you to buy from Me gold refined in the fire, that you may be rich; and white garments, that you may be clothed, that the shame of your nakedness may not be revealed; and anoint your eyes with eye salve, that you may see.'

"As many as I love, I rebuke and chasten. Therefore be zealous and repent. Behold, I stand at the door and knock. If anyone hears My voice and opens the door, I will come in to him and dine with him, and he with Me. To him who overcomes I will grant to sit with Me on My throne, as I also overcame

and sat down with My Father on His throne. He who has an ear, let him hear what the Spirit says to the churches."

Christ said He knew all about the life of the church. The church is described as being lukewarm and in danger of being rejected by Christ if they do not repent. Lukewarm means showing little or no enthusiasm spiritually. Their works of faith, hope, and love was at a near standstill.

The church in Laodicea believed they were a strong church, but the letter from Christ convicted them of being *'wretched, pitiful, poor, blind and naked,'* a description of their spiritual condition. When Christ counseled them to buy gold refined in the fire, He was talking about strengthening their spiritual condition. When He admonishes them to anoint their eyes with salve, He is talking about the eyes of their heart. Salve is used to help the healing process of the sick, and the word of God is salve for the Christian that is sick spiritually.

Section 2—Chapters 4 through 7

Chapter 4—The Throne Room in Heaven

John received information about the seven churches in Asia. He saw an open door in heaven. The open door was an invitation for John to look into God's throne room where Christ, the angels, the elders, and the four living creatures receive their assignments.

The open door and the expression of being in the Spirit means John had been given the ability from the Holy Spirit to see visions. John would be seeing visions of things that would take place during the end time Paul wrote about in 1st and 2nd Thessalonians.

Chapter 4:1-3 *"After these things I looked, and behold, a door standing open in heaven. And the first voice, which I heard was like a trumpet speaking with me saying "Come up here, and I will show you things which must take place after this. Immediately I was in the Spirit; and behold, a throne set in heaven, and One sat on the throne. And He who sat there was like a jasper and a sardius stone in appearance; and there was a rainbow around the throne, in appearance like an emerald."*

A New Commandment

John heard a loud voice from heaven saying, *"Come up here."* John didn't physically go to heaven—he was able to see and hear things in heaven in a vision. He saw things that are never seen on earth, and the only way to describe those things was to figuratively compare them to earthly objects.

John saw the Majesty of God in resplendent glory in the throne room in heaven, God the Almighty Creator, who makes decisions and assigns duties to the other occupants of Heaven. John, being under the influence of the Holy Spirit, was able to see these things and write what he saw. The voice John heard was loud and clear like the sound of a trumpet.

The decisions made in the throne room will affect the troubling events of the end times coming in the future.

Verses 4-5 *"Around the throne were twenty-four thrones, and on the thrones I saw twenty-four elders sitting, clothed in white robes; and they had crowns of gold on their heads. And from the throne preceded lightnings, thunder, and voices. Seven lamps of fire were burning before the throne, which are the seven Spirits of God."*

John saw a representation of God and His throne. Thrones represent authority, and those who are on thrones receive authority from God to carry out His commands. John saw twenty-four thrones surrounding God's throne. Twenty-four elders were sitting on the 24 thrones.

Most likely, the elders are angelic creatures in heaven who serve God. The term elder means someone who is old in age and has acquired wisdom. The vision of elders on thrones represents God's ability to know the events of the future.

God who produces and controls the lightning and thunder has the wisdom to determine future events and the power to carry them out. John also saw the Holy Spirit and described him as the seven spirits of God. Seven lamps of fire symbolize the Holy Spirit. Lamps are symbols of knowledge, and the Holy Spirit is assigned to distribute the knowledge of God's word.

The seven burning lamps symbolize the power of the Holy Spirit to enlighten the minds and hearts of people with the word of God. The number seven is a symbol of a complete number or perfection. Seven is the word *shebah* in Hebrew and means complete, full, perfect. The Holy Spirit is complete in every way to serve God and to take the word of God to people. The Holy Spirit of God with supernatural power is instrumental in accomplishing all things determined by God.

Verses 6-11 *"Before the throne there was a sea of glass, like crystal. And around the throne were four living creatures full of eyes in front and in back. The first living creature was like a lion, the second living creature had a face like a man, and the fourth living creature was like a flying eagle. The four living creatures, each having six wings, were full of eyes around and within. And they did not rest day or night, saying: "Holy, holy, holy, Lord God Almighty, Who was and is and is to come!" Whenever the living creatures give glory and honor and thanks to Him who sits on the throne, who lives forever and ever, the twenty-four elders fall down before Him who sits on the throne and worship Him who lives forever and ever, and cast their crowns before the throne, saying: "You are worthy, O Lord, to receive gory and honor and power; for You created all things, and by Your will they exist and were created."*

The expanse that looked like glass in front of the throne of God was transparent like crystal. Being transparent signifies that things can be seen on either side front or back when looking through the crystal. God's intentions and actions are clearly seen in heaven and are broadcast to the people of the earth. The actions and the intentions of God from the beginning of time to the end of time can be understood by investigating the word of God in the Bible. John was going to see visions and hear about what was to be in the future plans of God.

In the center of the throne and surrounding the throne were four symbolic winged creatures called living creatures. Creature refers to something that is created and is under the influence and control of the creator. The Cherubim on earth were symbolic representations of winged creatures that live in heaven. They were represented on earth as statue like figures. Cherubim guarded the tree of life in the Garden of Eden. Cherubim were placed at either end of the mercy seat of the Ark of the Covenant. Cherubim decorated Solomon's temple, and they were carved around the walls of the temple. Read more about Cherubim in Ezekiel chapters 1 and 10. In the first chapter of Ezekiel, Ezekiel saw visions of God and he saw the four living creatures in heaven, and he gave a description of their appearance.

Most likely, the creatures John saw in heaven are Cherubim. The Cherubim magnify the power and holiness of God. Cherubim visibly remind one of God's glory, majesty and power.

God deserves great honor, respect, and the worship that is due Him from all creatures in heaven and on earth. The living creatures continually praise, honor and give thanks to God. They are an example for all of God's creation to continually glorify praise, honor, obey and give thanks to the Lord God Almighty.

John saw and received information about events that would take place soon. The word *soon* in the Greek could be translated *immediately*. John was immediately able to see the terrifying future events of the end times. These were not events that were about to happen right away but would come in the future during the end time. In a vision John was allowed to see Christ receive a scroll that contained events of the future of the church during the end time.

Christ and the Apostles spoke of the time when the church and the people on earth will experience a great tribulation caused by Satan and a world leader called the Lawless One who is Antichrist. Paul described the Lawless One as the man who will claim to be God and the man of sin who opposes God and exalts himself above God. This will take place on earth during the end time, and many will fall from the faith because of Satan and the Lawless One.

2nd Thessalonians 2:1-4 "Now brethren concerning the coming of our Lord Jesus Christ and our gathering together to Him, we ask you, not to be soon troubled, either by spirit or by word or by letter, as if from us as though the day of Christ had come.'

"Let no one deceive you by any means; for that day will not come unless the falling away comes first, and the man of sin is revealed, the son of perdition, who opposes and exalts himself above all that is called God or is worshiped, so that he sits in the temple of God, showing himself that he is God."

God's providential protection of the church will keep it from disappearing from the earth during the end time. In the Bible the church is symbolized by the following terms—golden lamp stands, Jerusalem, the Holy City, the New Jerusalem, 144,000 (those with the name of Christ and God written on their forehead), a woman, the bride of Christ, the kingdom of God, the kingdom of Christ, and the temple of God, which is the redeemed.

Chapter 5—The Lamb Receives a Scroll

Chapter 5:1-3 "And I saw in the right hand of Him who sat on the throne a scroll written inside and on the back, sealed with seven seals. Then I saw a strong angel proclaiming with a loud voice, "Who is worthy to open the scroll and to loose its seals?" And no one in heaven or on the earth or under the earth was able to open the scroll, or to look at it.'

John saw God sitting on His throne holding a scroll containing future events that would take place at the end time including the redemption of the saints.

The scroll was sealed—meaning no one could open the scroll and read the contents without being authorized by God. The seals on the scroll symbolize God's control over the events of the end times. When the first seal is opened, God has granted His permission to read from the scroll.

Verses 4-5 "The scroll contained information about the events that were to take place at the end times but the scroll was sealed so that no one could reveal its contents. The saints in heaven and on the earth were anxious to know the contents because it contained the coming judgments of God and the redemption of the saints on earth.'

"So I wept much, because no one was found worthy to open and read the scroll or to look at it. But one of the elders said to me, "Do not weep. Behold, the Lion of the tribe of Judah, the Root of David, has prevailed to open the scroll and to loose its seven seals.'

The saints in heaven are the spirits of the redeemed. They are martyrs anxious to know what was written in the scroll, because it reveals the judgments of God for the future of the redeemed on earth. The elders around God's throne knew that Jesus was the only one worthy to open and read the scroll, because He died on the cross as a worthy sacrifice to provide redemption. They sang a new song about the worthiness of Christ.

Verses 6-10 "And I looked, and behold, in the midst of the throne and of the four living creatures, and in the midst of the elders, stood a Lamb as though it had been slain, having seven horns and seven eyes, which are the seven Spirits of God sent out into all the earth.

"Then He came and took the scroll out of the right hand of Him who sat on the throne.' *"Now when he had taken the scroll, the four living creatures and the twenty-four elders fell down before the Lamb, each having a harp, and golden bowls full of incense, which are the prayers of the saints. And they sang a new song, saying'*

"You are worthy to take the scroll, and to open its seals; for you were slain and have redeemed us to God by Your blood out of every tribe and tongue and people and nation, and have made us kings and priests to our God; and we shall reign on the earth."

The Holy Spirit of God was sent throughout the earth with the word of God. The Holy Spirit works through the spirit of Christians. The spreading of the word of God by the Holy Spirit teaches faith in Christ, which produces love, joy, peace, longsuffering, kindness, goodness, gentleness and self-control. The redeemed are made worthy by the sacrifice of Christ and are the children of God who will eventually live eternally in heaven with Christ and God.

Christ proved His worthiness by sacrificing His life in order to redeem those who would have faith in Him. Christ is compared to a lamb that has been sacrificed. The church is the kingdom of God on earth, and it has been since the establishment of the church in the first century, and Christ reigns over the church as the spiritual leader, King and High Priest. Christians receive the honor of kings and priests of God, because they share in the royalty of Christ. The definition of priest is *one who offers sacrifices*. All Christians are priests, because we present ourselves, both body and spirit, to God as living sacrifices. Christians also share in the reign of Christ on earth now.

Romans 12:1 "I beseech you therefore brethren to present your bodies a living sacrifice, holy, acceptable to God, which is your reasonable service."

The phrase *we shall reign on earth*, has the same meaning in Revelation that Paul applied to the word *reign* in Romans.

The word reign makes reference to Christians prevailing over and having power over sin and death. To reign on earth means to exist on earth with power over sin and death. The members of the kingdom are kings and priests in the eyes of God. Grace reigns, or exists, through the righteousness of those who have faith in Christ. God's grace gives eternal life through the death of Jesus Christ. The word exist or existed can be substituted for the word reign.

Romans 5:17-21 "For if by the one man's offense death reigned through the one, much more those who receive abundance of grace and of the gift of righteousness will reign in life through the one Jesus Christ. Therefore, as through one man's offense judgment came to all men, resulting in condemnation, even so through one man's righteous act the free gift came to all men resulting in justification of life. For as by one man's disobedience many were made sinners, so also by one Man's obedience many will be made righteous. Moreover the law entered that the offense might abound.' "But when sin abounded, grace abounded much more, so that grace might reign through righteousness to eternal life through Jesus Christ our Lord."

Death existed and had power through Adam's sin, because all people sin. Eternal life exists, because the grace of God reigns through righteousness to those who are made righteous by faith in Christ. Christians belong to the family of God as brothers and sisters of Christ, and as a family we share in the reign of Christ.

Ephesians 3: 14-21 "For this reason I bow my knees to the Father of our Lord Jesus Christ, from whom the whole family in heaven and earth is named. That He would grant you, according to the riches of His glory, to be strengthened with might through His Spirit in the inner man, that Christ may dwell in your hearts through faith; that you being rooted and grounded in love, may be able to comprehend with all the saints what is the width and length and depth and height—to know the love of Christ which passes knowledge; that you may be filled with all the fullness of God. Now to Him who is able to do exceedingly abundantly above all that we ask or think, according to the power that works in us, to Him be glory in the church to all generations, forever and ever. Amen."

Verses 11-14 "Then I looked, and I heard the voice of many angels around the throne, the living creatures, and the elders; and the number of them was ten thousand times ten thousand, and thousands of thousands, saying with a loud voice: "Worthy is the Lamb who was slain to receive power and riches and wisdom, and strength and honor and glory and blessing!'

"And every creature which is in heaven and on the earth and under the earth and such as are in the sea, and all that are in them, I heard saying: Blessing and honor and glory and power be to Him who sits on the throne and to the Lamb forever and ever!" Then the four living creatures said, "Amen!" and the twenty-four elders fell down and worshiped Him who lives forever and ever."

The living creatures, the angels, and the elders sang a new song about Christ, because He came to give His life, reign in righteousness and He is worthy to open the scroll and reveal its contents. The song is a new song, because it had never been sung before the death of Christ. The angels praised Christ for being worthy to reign in heaven and on earth.

Philippians 2:5-10 "Let this mind be in you which was also in Christ Jesus, who being in the form of God, did not consider it robbery to be equal with God, but made Himself of no reputation, taking the form of a bondservant, and coming in the likeness of men. And being found in appearance as a man, He humbled Himself and came obedient to the point of death, even the death of the cross. Therefore God has highly exalted Him and given Him the name which is above every name, that at the name of Jesus every knee should bow, of those in heaven, and of those on earth, and of those under the earth, and that every tongue should confess that Jesus Christ is Lord, to the glory of God the Father."

Chapter Six: Opening the Seals of the Scroll

Chapter 6:1-2 *"Now I saw when the Lamb opened one of the seals; and I heard one of the four living creatures saying with a voice, like thunder, "Come and see." And I looked, and behold, a white horse. He who sat on it had a bow; and a crown was given to him, and he went out conquering and to conquer:"*

When each seal was opened, the contents of the seal revealed judgments from God that would come upon the earth in succession during the time of Jesus' first coming until His second coming."

The first seal was opened, and John saw a white horse. The rider had a bow and He was given a crown, and He went out to conquer sin and death. The crown signifies that the rider had the right, as a king, to exercise His authority. Christ is the rider on the white horse who came in the first century to fight a spiritual battle against sin and establish His kingdom called the church. The battle is symbolized by a bow, an instrument of peace. Christ taught the gospel of peace between God and mankind to His Apostles.

They preached the gospel after His ascension and established redemption for everyone who obeys the gospel of Christ. The opening of the other five seals of the scroll will reveal events of the Christian dispensation including the future events at the end time during the great tribulation. Christ continued to open the seals of the scroll, and each time a seal is opened, a colored horse was seen revealing an event of tribulation.

Verses 3-4 *"When He opened the second seal, I heard the second living creature saying, "Come and see." Another horse, fiery red, went out. And it was granted to the one who sat on it to take peace from the earth, and that people should kill one another; and there was given to him a great sword."*

When the second seal of the scroll was opened, John saw a red horse. The rider on the red horse had a large sword, a machaira a type of sword that is used for killing. The red horse symbolizes carnal warfare during the end time.

Satan will be set free from the bottomless pit at the beginning of the end time and give power to the Lawless One (Antichrist), and he will rule over a world empire. He will cause warfare and distress among the nations.

There will be much bloodshed—symbolized by the red horse and the sword. Satan will give the Lawless One power over the people on earth, and the church will suffer great persecution. Paul's letters to the church in Thessalonica explain what will happen during the end time when Satan and the Lawless One takes control of the people on earth. Satan will be out of the Abyss and will be free to influence the people on earth. There will be a rebellion caused by Satan against God, Christ, and the church.

2nd Thessalonians 2:1-5 "Now brethren concerning the coming of our Lord Jesus Christ and our gathering together to him, we ask you, not to be soon shaken in mind or troubled, either by spirit or by word or by letter, as if from us, as though the day of Christ had come. Let no one deceive you by any means; for that Day will not come unless the falling away comes first, and the man of sin is revealed, the son of perdition, who opposes and exalts himself above all that is called God or that is worshiped, so that he sits as God in the temple of God, showing himself that he is God.

God will let Satan out of the Abyss on purpose to give power to the man of sin called the Lawless One (Antichrist). He will claim to be God and will cause great tribulation for the people on earth. Many people will turn to God, repent, and obey the gospel before Christ returns as a consequence of the tribulation. God is a God of grace and love, but not everyone will embrace God's grace and love until they experience the terrible events of the end time.

The tribulation of the end time will punish the enemies of God and will cause some people to repent and obey the gospel. God's judgments are righteous but His justice demands punishment.

Paul continued to write to the church about the second coming of Christ at the end of time and warned the church that it will suffer persecution before Christ returns.

2nd Thessalonians 1:3-10 "We are bound to thank God always for you brethren, as it is fitting, because your faith grows exceedingly, and the love of every one of you all abounds toward each other, so that we ourselves boast of you among the churches of God for your patience and faith in all your persecutions and tribulations that you endure, which is manifest evidence of the righteous judgment of God, that you may be counted worthy of the kingdom of God for which you also suffer; since it is a righteous thing with God to repay with tribulation those who trouble you, and to give you who are troubled rest with us when the Lord Jesus is revealed from heaven with His mighty angels, in flaming fire taking vengeance on those who do not know God, and on those who do not obey the gospel of our Lord Jesus Christ.'

"These shall be punished with everlasting destruction from the presence of the Lord and from the glory of His power, when He comes in that Day, to be glorified in His saints and to be admired among all those who believe, because our testimony among you was believed."

Verses 5-6 "When He opened the third seal, I heard the third living creature say, "Come and see." So I looked, and behold, a black horse, and he who sat on it had a pair of scales in his hand. And I heard a voice in the midst of the four living creatures saying, "A quart of wheat for a denarius, and three quarts of barley for a denarius; and do not harm the oil and the wine."

When the 3rd seal is opened, John sees a black horse with a rider that symbolizes famine and economic depression. The depression and famine John described will negatively affect the life of the people on earth. During the end time the Lawless One (Antichrist) will be responsible for the famine and economic depression. The Lawless One (Antichrist) will be given power from Satan, and with the help of Satan He will control the life of the people on earth.

Verses 7-8 *"When He opened the fourth seal, I heard the voice of the fourth living creature saying, "Come and see." So I looked, and behold, a pale horse. And the name of him who sat on it was Death, and Hades followed with him. And power was given to them over a fourth of the earth to kill with sword, with hunger, with death, and by the beasts of the earth."*

The rider on the pale horse is named death, and many people will die during the end time. More than a fourth of the people on earth will die because of the famine, bloodshed, diseases and beasts. We have wars, natural disasters, storms, earthquakes, famines, disease, and other forces in nature that may take place at anytime, but at the end time they will be much worse.

The Fifth Seal is Opened—The Martyrs

Verses 9-11 *"When He opened the fifth seal, I saw under the altar the souls of those who had been slain for the word of God and for the testimony, which they held. And they cried with a loud voice, saying, "How long, O Lord, holy and true, until You judge and avenge our blood on those who dwell on the earth?" Then a white robe was given to each of them; and it was said to them that they should rest a little while longer, until both the number of their fellow servants and their brethren, who would be killed as they were, was completed."*

The martyrs in heaven will be anxious for God to send Christ to destroy the evil forces on earth and bring the church to heaven.

John saw the martyrs in heaven, and some of them were those who were killed during the end time. During the end time Christians will be persecuted, and some will be put to death because they are Christians, and they become martyrs.

The word *martyr* and *witness* are translated from *martus* or *martur*, which means one who bears witness by his death. The martyrs were killed, because they would not deny Christ. John saw their spirits under God's altar calling out for Him to avenge their death. Each of the martyrs received white robes, which are symbols of righteousness. The martyrs were anxious for God to bring forth His final judgment against Satan and the unrighteous people of the earth who murdered them. But they must wait until the end of time when Christ returns.

The Sixth Seal is Opened—Great Earthquake

Verses 12-14 *"I looked when He opened the sixth seal, and behold, there was a great earthquake; and the sun became black as sackcloth of hair, and the moon became like blood. And the stars of heaven fell to the earth, as a fig tree drops its late figs when it is shaken by a mighty wind. Then the sky receded as a scroll when it is rolled up, and every mountain and island was moved out of its place.*

The sixth seal reveals visions of God's final judgment on earth at the end of time.

In verse 12, the sixth seal was opened, and John saw visions of a great earthquake and the upheaval of the sun, moon and stars. Upheaval of the earth and the universe are common figurative expressions in the Bible having to do with the end of time.

Earthquakes are mentioned in Chapters 6, 8, 11, and 16 of Revelation as events of the end times.

The events in chapter 6 of Revelation are very similar to Matthew 24 depicting the second coming of Christ.

Matthew 24:27-31 "For as the lightning comes from the east and flashes to the west, so also will the coming of the Son of Man be. For wherever the carcass is, there the eagles will be gathered together.

"Immediately after the tribulation of those days the sun will be darkened, and the moon will not give its light; the stars will fall from heaven, and the powers of the heavens will be shaken.'

"Then the sign of the Son of Man will appear in heaven, and then all of the tribes of the earth will mourn, and they will see the Son of Man coming on the clouds of heaven with power and great glory.'

"And He will send His angels with a great sound of a trumpet, and they will gather together His elect from the four winds, from one end of heaven to the other."

Jeremiah, Joel, and Zechariah all used the terms that are used in chapter 6 to describe the events of the end of time. Earthquakes happen naturally, but during the end of time the greatest earthquake ever will come from an act of God at the final judgment.

Darkness will fill the earth and Islands will disappear. The Earthquake will cause unbelievers and the ungodly to fear God, because they will realize that the wrath of God has come.

Verses 15-17 *"And the kings of the earth, the great men, the rich men, the commanders, the mighty men, every slave and every free man, hid themselves in the caves and in the rocks of the mountains, and said to the mountains and rocks, "Fall on us and hide us from the face of Him who sits on the throne and from the wrath of the Lamb! For the great day of His wrath has come, and who is able to stand?"*

At the end of time the unrighteous will be filled with fear and call to the mountains and rocks to fall on them and deliver them from God's wrath. Most likely some will repent but not all of the unrighteous.

The whole earth will be in chaos and turmoil, and everyone who is left on earth will realize that the final judgment of God has come. There will be great anguish for the unrighteous, but the righteous will shout with joy.

These things take place at the end of time, but God's redeemed will be safe.

Chapter 7—The One Hundred and Forty-Four Thousand

Section two ends in Chapter 7 with events of the end of time. The souls that are saved before and during the end time will be in heaven.

Chapter 7:1-8 *"After these things, I saw four angels standing at the four corners of the earth holding the four winds of the earth, that the wind should not blow on the earth, on the sea, or on any tree. Then I saw another angel ascending from the east, having the seal of the living God. And he cried with a loud voice to the four angels to whom it was granted to harm the earth and the sea, saying, "Do not harm the earth, the sea, or the trees till we have sealed the servants of our God on their foreheads.'*

"And I heard the number of those who were sealed. One hundred and forty-four thousand of all the tribes of the children of Israel were sealed: Of the tribe of Judah twelve thousand were sealed; of the tribe of Reuben twelve thousand were sealed; of the tribe of Gad twelve thousand were sealed;' "of the tribe of Asher twelve thousand were sealed; of the tribe of Naphtali twelve thousand were sealed; of the tribe of Manasseh twelve thousand were sealed; of the tribe of Simeon twelve thousand were sealed; of the tribe of Levi twelve thousand were sealed; of the tribe of Issachar twelve thousand were sealed; of the tribe of Zebulun twelve thousand were sealed; of the tribe of Joseph twelve thousand were sealed; of the tribe of Benjamin twelve thousand were sealed."

Before the events at the end of time begin to take place, God's people are identified symbolized by the seal of God. They will be identified to signify their safety during the events of destruction. The total number that will be sealed is symbolized by 144,000 not the literal number.

In chapter 14 the 144,000 are standing on Mt Zion with God's name written on their foreheads, and John identifies them as the redeemed from the earth. The reason John identified the redeemed at the end of time with the twelve tribes of Israel is because when he wrote Revelation, the church was predominantly Jewish and could identify with the symbolic descriptions he used. The redeemed will be from many cultures from all over the earth.

After the things that take place during the end of time, John writes about seeing the redeemed in heaven. Each section ends with events of the end of time. God holds back His destroying angels until the end of time after the redeemed are safe in heaven. After John saw the great earthquake at the end of time, John looked into heaven and saw the redeemed from every nation, tribe, and language including those who came out of the great tribulation during the end time.

Verses 9-17 *After these things I looked, and behold, a great multitude which no one could number, of all nations, tribes, peoples, and tongues., standing before the throne and before the Lamb, clothed with white robes, with palm branches in their hands, and crying out with a loud voice, saying, "Salvation belongs to our God who sits on the throne, and to the Lamb! All the angels stood around the throne and the elders and the four living creatures, and fell on their faces before the throne and worshiped God, saying: "Amen! Blessing and glory and wisdom, Thanksgiving and honor and power and might, Be to our God forever and ever. Amen."*

"Then one of the elders answered, saying to me, "Who are these arrayed in white robes, and where did they come from?" And I said to him, "Sir, you know." So he said to me. "These are the ones who come out of the great tribulation, and washed their robes and made them white in the blood of the Lamb. Therefore they are before the throne of God, and serve Him day and night in His temple. And He who sits on the throne will dwell among them. They shall neither hunger anymore; nor thirst anymore; the sun shall not strike them, nor any heat; for the Lamb who is in the midst of the throne will shepherd them and lead them to living fountains of waters. And God will wipe away every tear from their eyes."

Before the destruction of the earth takes place, the dead will be resurrected, and then all who are saved from the beginning of time and from every nation including those from the Old Testament period will be taken to a new heaven and new earth.

John saw the angels, the elders, and the living creatures in heaven where the 144,000 and every being was worshiping God. An elder in heaven asked, *Who are those in the white robes?* because they were newcomers to heaven.

John said to him that the saints in white are the ones who came to heaven during the great tribulation. John was talking about the great tribulation that Satan will cause at the end time. John was seeing things in heaven after the events of the end of time. Those clothed in white identify the redeemed of all time inclusive of all the saved before and during the end of time, and they were the righteous cleansed by the blood of the Lamb. The scene was in the throne room of God where all of the heavenly beings were, including the angels.

The redeemed of the earth will join the heavenly host at the end of time to praise God. Christ will be there, for he is the Shepherd that will lead them to a new heaven and new earth. God will spread His tent over them. The word for tent in Greek is the same as tabernacle or temple—all referring to God's dwelling place.

The seventh trumpet will sound at the end of time and the inhabitants of heaven, including the redeemed from the earth, will worship God and thank Him, because He has used His great power against Satan and the forces of evil. The time had come for judging the dead and rewarding the redeemed. Christ returns to the earth with the angels to bring the redeemed to heaven.

Section 3 Chapters 8 through 11

Beginning in chapter 8, when the seventh seal of the scroll is opened more events of the end time, were revealed. There is a period of silence in heaven for a short time indicative of a break in the time before the other events come upon the earth. Seven angels, each with trumpets, signal the beginning of an event during the end time. The first trumpet sounds, and hail and fire mingled with blood will be thrown to the earth, a symbol of destruction and death.

The Second trumpet sounds, and something like a great mountain on fire is thrown into the sea killing a third of the creatures in the sea and destroying a third of the ships. The third trumpet sounds, and a great star falls on a third of the rivers and springs of water—a symbol of poisoned water. The fourth trumpet sounds, and a third of the sun, moon, and stars are darkened affecting the normal amount of light on earth.

Chapter 9—The fifth trumpet sounds, and a star falls from heaven. A mighty angel comes to the earth and lets Satan out of confinement in the Abyss (bottomless pit). Demons terrorize the people of the earth. The sixth trumpet sounds and four angels kill a third of the people on earth.

Chapter 10—A mighty angel with a little book declares that the mystery of God would be finished when the seventh angel sounds his trumpet for the end of time. John eats the little book, a symbol of learning the contents of the book.

Chapter 11—God gives power to two witnesses to prophesy for 1,260 days during the end time. The two witnesses may be two prophets who can communicate with God. The two witnesses are symbolized by two olive trees and two lamp stands. The two witnesses have power to stop the rain, turn the waters to blood and strike the earth with plagues. The power of the two witnesses comes from God, and they will have the ability to invoke the power Of God to perform miracles to protect the church.

Satan will be on earth, and he will make war against the two witnesses and kill them. Killing the two witnesses means to silence them for a while. The two witnesses will be resurrected, and they will ascend to heaven.

Then a great earthquake killing seven thousand people. The ability of the witnesses to call on God will be restored after they are resurrected. The seventh trumpet sounds at the end of time, and the inhabitants of heaven, including the redeemed from the earth, worship God and thank Him, because has He used His great power against Satan and the forces of evil. The time had come for judging the dead and rewarding the redeemed. Section 3 ends with chapter 11.

Chapter 8:1-7 *"When He opened the seventh seal, there was silence in heaven for about half an hour. And I saw the seven angels who stand before God, and to them were given seven trumpets. Then another angel, having a golden censer, came and stood at the altar.'*

"He was given much incense that he should offer it with the prayers of all the saints upon the golden altar, which was before the throne. And the smoke of the incense, with the prayers of the saints, ascended before God from the angel's hand. Then the angel took the censer, filled it with fire from the altar, and threw it to the earth. "And there were noises, thunderings, lightnings, and an earthquake. So the seven angels who had the seven trumpets prepared themselves to sound."

"The first angel sounded: and hail and fire followed, mingled with blood, and they were thrown to the earth. And a third of the trees were burned up, and all green grass was burned up."

The time of opening the seventh seal is near the end of time, and events become increasingly worse with time. The events will cause pain and sorrow on the earth. In chapter 8, the incense and prayers of the saints ascended before God, then the angel filled the censer with the incense and prayers mixed with fire and threw it to the earth causing noises, thundering, lightning, and an earthquake—sign's that God was answering the prayers of the saints with judgments against Satan and the unrighteous people of the earth.

Each time an angel sounds a trumpet an event of God's wrath takes place. The angels will hold back the four winds of the earth—winds from the east, west, north and south—waiting for the sound of the trumpet. The winds are symbols of God's destroying power. The four angels are given the power to harm the land and the sea. Thunder is associated with the voice of God, and lightning is regarded as an instrument of the judgment of God. God gave His approval to send a judgment against the unrighteous on earth to warn them to repent.

The first angel sounds his trumpet, followed by hail and fire mingled with blood burning up a third of the trees and all of the green grass on earth. Hail, fire, and blood symbolize death and great damage to one third of the earth.

Verses 8-9 *"Then the second angel sounded: And something like a great mountain burning with fire was thrown into the sea, and a third of the sea became blood. And a third of the living creatures in the sea died, and a third of the ships were destroyed."*

John saw and heard the second angel blow his trumpet, and he saw the results of the judgment. Something similar to an enormous mountain that is on fire—possibly a huge meteorite—will fall into the sea. There will be blood in a third of the sea, and one third of the living things in the sea will die, and many ships will be destroyed. Only one third of the area of the seas will be affected. The purpose of the object thrown into the sea will be to inflict great damage upon the earth to punish the unrighteous and to cause as many as will to repent. God makes known that He is real and He demonstrates His great power during the end times.

Verses 10-11 *"Then the third angel sounded: And a great star fell from heaven, burning like a torch, and it fell on a third of the rivers and on the springs of water. The name of the star is Wormwood.*

A third of the waters became wormwood, and many men died from the water, because it was made bitter."

The large star was on fire like a torch when it fell from the sky, and it fell on a third of the rivers and springs of fresh water. The star was called wormwood. Wormwood is a perennial bitter herb that is toxic and is used in a figurative sense to describe something bitter or extremely unpleasant suggesting sorrow and bitterness resulting from the death and destruction of the falling star. Falling stars and meteorites are common occurrences even now, but the one John writes about will be much greater in power. It will be huge, and it will cause the fresh water to be bitter and poisoned from contamination. The water will cause many people to die.

Verse 12 *"Then the fourth angel sounded: And a third of the sun was struck, a third of the moon, and a third of the stars, so that a third of them were darkened. A third of the day did not shine, and likewise the night.*

The sounding of the fourth angel's trumpet signals a plague that will obscure a third of the light that normally illuminates the earth—the light that comes from the sun, moon, and stars. This plague means there will be a time of darkness upon the earth during the day as well as the night. The darkness will, most likely, cause great fear and cause a cease of most activities on earth. The darkness is a sign of the great woe that will be caused by the blowing of the other three trumpets.

Verse 13 *"And I looked, and I heard an angel flying through the midst of heaven, saying with a loud voice, "Woe, woe, woe to the inhabitants of the earth, because of the remaining blasts of the trumpet of the three angels who are about to sound!"*

John continued to look and listen, and he heard an angel flying through heaven. The angel was crying out with a loud voice saying, "Woe! Woe! Woe!" to the people on earth.

The definition of a woe is something that causes great grief, trouble, or distress. There are three remaining trumpet judgments, and there is grief, trouble, and distress associated with each one.

The events of the three woe judgments that are coming will be much worse than the other judgments. The angel will call out to the inhabitants of the earth to warn them to repent because of the severity of the plagues that will follow the last three trumpet blasts.

God has forever warned mankind of the consequences of disobedience, but most people ignore Him and continue to disobey Him.

Some versions of the Bible use the word eagle instead of angel. Eagle and vulture are translated from the same Greek word. The vultures will have a feast on the dead bodies caused by the judgments.

When the next three angels blow their trumpets, Satan and his demons will be allowed to come out of the bottomless pit and cause a great tribulation of the people on earth during the end time.

According to the woes in John's visions, the end times will last much longer than an instant of time, because several things will take place in succession.

In between the events, the unbelievers and ungodly people will have an opportunity to turn to God and Christ and repent before the final destruction. There will be three more trumpets of judgment, the 5th, 6th and 7th, signaling the three woes that will let the people of the earth know that the events of the end of time are taking place.

The sounding of the 7th trumpet announces the last days of God's judgment at the end of time.

The Fifth Trumpet Sounds

The 5th angel is the first of the angels representing the three woes mentioned in chapter 8:13. The first woe represents an event much worse than any previous event. The angel sounds his trumpet, and Satan is released from the Abyss.

Chapter 9:1-2 *"Then the fifth angel sounded: And I saw a star fallen from heaven to the earth. To him was given the key to the bottomless pit. And he opened the bottomless pit, and smoke arose out of the pit like the smoke of a great furnace. So the sun and the air were darkened because of the smoke of the pit.'*

The release of Satan from the Abyss is the first of the three woes. When the fifth angel blew his trumpet, John saw a star fall out of heaven. The word *star* in the Bible is often used to designate an angel. The star in verse 1 is Michael, the Arch Angel, the protector of God's people. Michael is given the key to the Abyss to let Satan and his demons out of the Abyss

The Abyss is suggested as a place of conscious existence, a place other than the earth. It's a place God has prepared for spirits who are waiting for the final judgment of God. The verb *tartaro* is not Sheol, Hades, nor hell, but it is the place where those angels who sin are confined to be reserved until the judgment. The region is described as pits of darkness. (Vines Expository Dictionary)

Luke 8:30-31 Jesus asked him, saying, "What is your name?" And he said "Legion", because many demons had entered him. And they begged Him that He would not command them to go into the abyss."

Heaven is so vast that it consists of many areas called the heavens. There is the highest heaven where God and Christ are, and the Abyss is somewhere in the heavens below the highest heaven.

Romans 10:6-7 But the righteousness of faith speaks in this way, "Do not say in your heart, 'Who will ascend into heaven?' (that, is to bring Christ down from above) or, "'Who will descend into the abyss?'" (that is, to bring Christ up from the dead).

The Bible reveals that there is more than one place in heaven. The Bible speaks of at least three heavens and there may be more than three. The word hell is used fourteen times in the New Testament, and it is described as a place of torment. There are four words that are all translated hell: the Hebrew word Sheol, the Greek words Hades, Gehenna, and Tartarus. Sheol signifies the grave or the state of death and the world of the dead. Sheol is parallel to the Hebrew words for pit or hell. Sheol is a place of consciousness for the spirits of the dead. Gehenna is the final destiny of those who reject God and is described as a place of unquenchable fire. *Mark 9:45 "And if your foot causes you to sin, cut it off. It is better for you to enter life lame, rather than having two feet, to be cast into hell, into the fire that shall never be quenched."*

There is a clear description of Hades in Luke 16:19-31. Hades is described as a place in the heavens where departed spirits of the dead go. Hades consists of two separate places. There is one place for the spirits of the righteous and a separate place for the spirits of the unrighteous. Spirits cannot go from one place to the other. The spirits of the righteous are in a place of paradise, and the spirits of the unrighteous are in a place of torment.

Revelation 20:1-2 "Then I saw an angel coming down from heaven, having the key to the bottomless pit and a great chain in his hand. He laid hold on the dragon, that serpent of old, who is the devil and Satan, and bound him for a thousand years; and he cast him into the bottomless pit, and shut him up, and set a seal on him, so that he should deceive the nations no more till the thousand years were finished. But after these things he must be released for a little while."

Being in the Abyss meant Satan and the demons were not capable of using their evil power. They were like prisoners confined to one area. With instructions from the throne, Michael will let Satan and his demons out of the Abyss, and Satan will use his power to torment people on earth and empower the Lawless One (Antichrist) to rule on earth.

God will allow this event to take place, because the time for the second coming of Christ will be near, and many of the people on earth will not have repented of their unrighteous ways and obeyed the gospel of Christ. The purpose of the torment is not just to punish but also to cause repentance.

Verses 3-4 *"Then out of the smoke locusts came upon the earth. And to them was given power, as the scorpions of the earth have power. They were commanded not to harm the grass of the earth, or any green thing, or any tree, but only those men who do not have the seal of God on their foreheads."*

Where there is fire there is smoke, and when the Abyss is opened, smoke comes out. This act of God's judgment allows Satan and the demons to torment the people on earth during the end time to cause them to repent, and some will probably repent.

The creatures from the Abyss will be Satan's demons and not literal locusts, but they will come in great numbers like locusts and will have power to harm mankind. The demons are symbolized by locusts because of their great number and destructive power like a swarm or plague of locusts. These demons will harm people on earth causing pain compared to the sting of a scorpion.

Verses 5-6 *"And they were not given authority to kill them, but to torment them for five months. Their torment was like the torment of a scorpion when it strikes a man. In those days men will seek death and will not find it; they will desire to die, and death will flee from them."*

The normal life of a locust is five months, and the demon's time to torture people will be limited to five months since their purpose is not to kill people but to cause the unrighteous to repent. The reason God will not allow the demons to kill the people is because He wants them to turn to Christ and obey the gospel of Christ. God is giving them a chance to repent before the end of time.

Verses 7-12 *"The shape of the locusts was like horses prepared for battle. On their heads were crowns of something like gold, and their faces were like the faces of men. They had hair like women's hair and their teeth were like lions teeth. And they had breastplates like breastplates of iron, and the sound of their wings was like the sound of chariots with many horses running into battle.'*

"They had tails like scorpions, and there were stings in their tails. Their power was to hurt men five months. And they had as king over them the angel of the bottomless pit, whose name in Hebrew is Abaddon, but in Greek he has the name Apollyon. One woe is past. Behold, still two more are coming after these things."

The locusts represent Satan's demons that were let out of the Abyss." The king of the demons is Satan, the angel of the bottomless pit.

Satan's name in Hebrew is Abaddon. In Greek he has the name Apollyon. Abaddon and Apollyon mean destroyer.

A figurative description is given to illustrate the appearance of the demons. The appearance of the demons will look like an army with armor, and they will make a loud noise. The demons will be animal-like creatures resembling horses and humans with large teeth. Their appearance will be terrifying and unlike anything ever seen on earth before. The sight of them will probably be almost as bad as their sting. They will appear like horses prepared for battle. On their heads will be crowns like gold, and their faces will be like the faces of men.

They will have hair like women's hair, probably long, and their teeth will be like lions' teeth large and fierce looking. Their breastplates will look like breastplates of iron, and the sound of their wings will be like the sound of chariots with many horses running into battle. They will have tails like scorpions, and they will hurt people for five months.

The torture caused by the demons will be so severe that people will long to die. The demons are commanded not to harm the grass of the earth, or any green thing, or any tree but only those men who do not have the seal of God on their foreheads. The seal of God on the forehead symbolizes some kind of identification showing they are Christians and must not be harmed in any way.

The Sixth Trumpet Sounds

Verses 13-15 *"Then the sixth angel sounded: And I heard a voice from the four horns of the golden altar which is before God, saying to the sixth angel who had the trumpet, "Release the four angels who are bound at the great river Euphrates." So the four angels who had been prepared for the hour and day and month and year, were released to kill a third of mankind."*

The first woe was a plague of demons symbolized by locusts. After the first woe, the sixth of the seven angels will blow his trumpet. The 6th trumpet sounds and the second woe proceeds. A voice from the horns of God's altar will be heard, and the sixth angel will be instructed to turn loose the four angels that are waiting at the Euphrates River for their instructions to kill a third of the earths population. Those who are killed will not be Christians. They will be from among the unrighteous and may be from the army of the empire of the lawless one.

The order came from the golden altar in heaven, possibly from the voice of Christ. Four angels had been prepared and waiting for the time they would be sent to kill a third of the unrighteous people on earth. Christ gives the okay for the Angels to act.

The Angels were already at the Euphrates River waiting for the time of the sixth angel to sound his trumpet. Angels from heaven symbolized by an army of horsemen will carry out the plague that follows the sound of the sixth trumpet.

Verses 16-19 *"Now the number of the army of the horsemen was two hundred million; I heard the number of them. And thus I saw the horses in the vision: those who sat on them had breastplates of fiery red, hyacinth blue, and sulfur yellow; and the heads of the horses were like the heads of lions; and out of their mouths came fire, smoke, and brimstone.*

By these three plagues a third of mankind was killed—by the fire and the smoke and the brimstone, which came out of their mouths. For their power is in their mouth and in their tails; for their tails are like serpents, having heads; and with them they do harm."

An army of two hundred million on horseback does not make reference to an army of humans and must refer to a supernatural army. There are a countless number of angels, and it is reasonable to believe that the horsemen are literal angels that had been bound at the Euphrates River for that purpose. The word 'bound' indicates the angels were prevented to act by the power of God and could not act until God allowed them to. With the approval of God, they were to kill a third of the number of the unrighteous people on earth. Christians should not fear because God's angels will not harm them.

The release of the angels will be the answer to the prayers of the saints (Christians) who are suffering persecution from Satan and an evil generation.

The large number of unrighteous people killed will be a warning sign from God. There are references in the Old Testament when God's angels were sent to kill.

2nd Kings 19:35 "And it came to pass on a certain night that the angel of the Lord went out, and killed in the camp of the Assyrians one hundred and eighty-five thousand."

John saw a vision of the troops in the army, which symbolizes an army of ferocious creatures that kill people.

There was smoke, fire, and suluphur coming out of their mouths. The creatures will have tails that can inflict injury.

This plague is sent against the unbelieving and ungodly people of the earth with the purpose to make them repent, but many still will not repent.

The Euphrates River may be a symbolic reference that would be understood by the Jewish Christians in the first century.

In the Old Testament, the enemies of Israel traditionally gathered at the Euphrates River in advance of assaulting God's people. The river was a natural boundary between Israel and her enemies.

The fact that the Euphrates River is mentioned doesn't necessarily mean this event will occur at the Euphrates River.

The place where the battle begins is not important, because God is the only one who will have complete control of the events of the end time and the end of time.

Revelation gives readers a mental picture of the great amount of evil and idolatry that will exist during the end time.

The army of horsemen will not harm Christians at the end time. Some of the unrighteous at the end time that did not repent were not killed and they continued to engage in sexual immorality and idolatry.

The unwillingness of some to repent after witnessing the torture by the horsemen is a testimony to the depth of their wicked character.

Verses 20-21 *"But the rest of mankind, who were not killed by these plagues, did not repent of the works of their hands, that they should not worship demons, and idols of gold, silver, brass, stone and wood, which can neither see nor hear nor walk. And they did not repent of their murders or their sorceries or their sexual immorality or their thefts."*

The Mighty Angel and The Little Scroll

Chapter 10:1-7 *"I saw still another mighty angel coming down from heaven, clothed with a cloud. And a rainbow was on his head his face was like the sun, and his feet like pillars of fire. He had a little book open in his hand. And he set his right foot on the sea and his left foot on the land, and cried with a loud voice, as when a lion roars. When he cried out, seven thunders uttered their voices. Now when the seven thunders uttered their voices, I was about to write; but I heard a voice from heaven saying to me, "Seal up the things which the seven thunders uttered, and do not write them." "The angel whom I saw standing on the sea and on the land raised up his hand to heaven and swore by Him who lives forever and ever, who created heaven and the things that are in it, the earth and the things that are in it, and the sea and the things that are in it, that there should be delay no longer, but in the days of the sounding of the seventh angel, when he is about to sound, the mystery of God would be finished, as He declared to His servants the prophets."*

John saw a mighty angel like the angel in chapter nine. Mighty may refer to an Arch Angel, possibly Michael or Gabriel.

Michael is an Arch Angel that is spoken of as being like God. He is the guardian of God's people, and was an intercessor for Israel. The name Gabriel means the strength of God or man of God. Gabriel is one of the Arch Angels that stands before the throne of God. The angel was holding an open book in his hand and is seen in a vision, not a literal sighting.

The term seven is sometimes used symbolically for fullness and is often associated with the voice of God. The little book revealed the mystery of the events God planned for the end of time. The angel John saw was standing on the land and the sea, because the coming events would be great and affect both the land and the sea. John was told to eat the little book that was open in the hands of the angel. He was to fully digest or memorize what was revealed and not to write anything down. The events of the end of time would be revealed and written down later.

When the seventh angel sounds his trumpet, the events of the end of time will take place and the mystery of God's plan for the end of time and the second coming of Christ will be completed. After several partial judgments there will be one final judgment, and everything on earth, including the atmosphere above the earth, will be destroyed with fire. There will be no more time for repentance after the seventh angel sounds his trumpet.

The sounding of the 7th trumpet will take place in chapter 11:15-19 at the end of time.

2nd Peter 3:10-13 "But the day of the Lord will come as a thief in the night, in which the heavens will pass away with a great noise, and the elements will melt with fervent heat; both the earth and the works that are in it will be burned up. Therefore, since all these things will be dissolved, what manner of persons ought you to be in holy conduct and godliness, Looking for and hastening the coming of the day of God, because of which the heavens will be dissolved, being on fire, and the elements will melt with fervent heat? Nevertheless we, look for new heavens and a new earth in which righteousness dwells."

Verses 8-11 *"Then the voice, which I heard from heaven, spoke to me again and said, "Go, take the little book which is open in the hand of the' "angel who stands on the sea and on the earth. So I went to the angel and said to him, "Give me the little book. And he said to me, "Take and eat it; and it will make your stomach bitter, but it will be as sweet as honey in your mouth." Then I took the little book out of the angel's hand and ate it, and it was as sweet as honey in my mouth. But when I had eaten it, my stomach became bitter. And he said to me, "You must prophesy again about many peoples, nations, tongues, and kings."*

The little book revealed the events of the mystery of God's plan for both the redeemed and the unrighteous. John ate the book, and it tasted sweet like honey. The little book was sweet because it contained messages of hope and victory for the church but it was sour in his stomach because the contents of the book revealed events of great tribulation during the end times.

John learned that he would be prophesying to many people all over the earth. The book of Revelation contains the words of the prophecy revealing the mystery of the destiny of the whole creation during the final judgment of God. The judgments of God during the end times will come one at a time over a period of a few years. People who are still alive after each judgment will have an opportunity to repent and accept Christ.

Daniel wrote that Michael, the great angel who is the protector of God's people, would come to earth to help the church. Daniel prophesied that the dead will be resurrected, and everyone whose name is written in the book of life will be delivered.

Daniel 12:1-3 "At that time Michael shall stand up, The great prince who stands watch over the sons of your people; And there shall be a time of trouble, Such as never was since there was a nation, Even to that time. And at that time your people shall be delivered, Every one who is found written in the book. And many of those who sleep in the dust of the earth shall awake, some to everlasting life, Some to shame and everlasting contempt. Those who are wise shall shine Like the brightness of the firmament, And those who turn many to righteousness Like the stars forever and ever."

John was told that he must continue to prophesy about events involving many people of all nationalities and rulers.

Chapter 11: The Two Witnesses

Chapter 11 is the last chapter in section three and ends with the second coming of Christ at the end of time. It describes the great persecution against the church that will take place during the end times when the world is being controlled and devastated by Satan and the Lawless One (Antichrist) whom Paul wrote about in second Thessalonians.

Chapter 11 begins by presenting a limited view of the end time when nations are at war, and the nation represented by the Lawless One (Antichrist) will have control and rule over a worldwide empire opposed to God and Christianity.

2nd Thessalonians 2:1-4 Now brethren, concerning the coming of our Lord Jesus Christ and our gathering together to him, we ask you, not to be soon shaken in mind or troubled either by spirit or by word, or by letter, as if from us, as though the day of Christ had come. Let no one deceive you by any means; for that day will not come unless the falling away comes first, and the man of sin is revealed, the son of perdition, who opposes and exalts himself above all that is called God or that is worshiped, so that he sits as God in the temple of God, showing himself that he is God."

The events that occur during the end times will not begin until after the man of sin who is called the Lawless One (Antichrist) rises up claiming to be God.

He will rule over the whole earth for a little while. Satan and his demons will be the power behind the empire of the Lawless One (Antichrist). The lawless one (Antichrist) will persecute the church and attempt to turn everyone against the true God of creation.

Luke 21:8-11 "And He said: Take heed that you be not deceived. For many will come in My name saying 'I am He' and the time has drawn near.' 'Therefore do not go after them. But when you hear of wars and commotions, do not be terrified; for these things must come to pass first, but the end will not come immediately. Then He said to them, "Nation will rise against nation, and kingdom against kingdom. And there will be great earthquakes in various places, and famines and pestilences; and there will be fearful sights and great signs from heaven."

Chapter 11:1-2 *"Then I was given a reed like a measuring rod. And the angel stood, saying, "Rise and measure the temple of God, the altar, and those who worship there. But leave out the court, which is outside the temple, and do not measure it, for it has been given to the Gentiles. And they will tread the holy city underfoot for forty-two months.*

The Romans destroyed the Jewish temple in Jerusalem in A.D. 70, and the temple John writes about is symbolic of the church. The Holy Spirit dwells in every member of the church, the temple of God. The name Gentiles here represents those who are not members of the church.

Ephesians 2:19-22 "Now therefore, you are no longer strangers and foreigners, but fellow citizens with the saints and members of the household of God, having been built on the foundation of the apostles and the prophets, Jesus Christ Himself being the chief cornerstone, in whom the whole building, being fitted together, grows into a holy temple in the Lord, in whom you also are being built together for a dwelling place of God in the Spirit."

Unbelievers will persecute the church, treading on the holy city. Holy city here metaphorically represents the church. John was told to measure the temple in heaven, the altar, and those who worship there.

Measuring the temple, the altar, and the worshipers meant to count the number of members in the church. The word altar means to sacrifice. Worshipers of God brought their animal sacrifices and offered them on the altar in the literal temple in Jerusalem. Since the death of Christ, God requires living sacrifices from the heart of the worshipers.

All Christians are priests who offer sacrifices. *Romans 12:1 "I beseech you therefore, brethren, by the mercies of God, that you present your bodies a living sacrifice, holy acceptable to God, which is your reasonable service."*

Verses 3-5 *"And I will give power to my two witnesses, and they will prophesy one thousand two hundred and sixty days, clothed in sackcloth. "These are the two olive trees and the two lamp stands standing before the God of the earth. And if anyone wants to harm them, fire proceeds from their mouth and devours their enemies. And if anyone wants to harm them, he must be killed in this manner."*

During the end time the church will have two witnesses who will prophesy, meaning they will speak for God. The witnesses will be in mourning, because of the persecution of the church. At the end time God will give miraculous power to witnesses to defend Christianity. God will protect the church with the witnesses, which is symbolized by fire proceeding from their mouth.

The fire from their mouth could symbolize their ability to preach in a powerful way to turn people to obey Christ and also to reinforce the faith of the church.

Fire could also mean powerful prayer that would be answered with miraculous action from God against their enemies. The 42 months is a figurative time, the same as 1260 days or three and one half years, the length of time for the end time.

Verse 6 *"These have power to shut heaven, so that no rain falls in the days of their prophecy; and they have power over waters to turn them to blood, and to strike the earth with all plagues, as often as they desire."*

Zechariah prophesied about the end time before Christ came to earth and he saw a vision similar to what John wrote about. An angel told Zechariah that the lamp stand and the olive trees are symbols of the word of the Lord and the Holy Spirit of God. The word of God and the Holy Spirit are the two witnesses.

Zechariah 4:1-6 "The angel who talked with me came back and wakened me, as a man who is wakened out of sleep. And he said to me "What do you see?" So I said, "I am looking, and there is a lamp stand of solid gold with a bowl on top of it, and on the stand seven lamps with seven pipes to the seven lamps.'

"Two olive trees are by it, one at the right of the bowl and the other at its left." So I answered and spoke to the angel who talked with me saying, "What are these my Lord?" Then the angel who talked with me answered and said to me, "Do you not know what these are?" And I said "No, my Lord." So he answered me and said to me, "This is the word to Zerubbabel: Not by might nor by power, but by My Spirit says the Lord of hosts."

The Holy Spirit and the word of God at the end time will be reminiscent of the prophets of Israel as they used the inspiration of the Holy Spirit to proclaim God's word. The security of the church will not depend on the church members or their power but on the power of the Lord.

The testimony of the word of God is not by the might and power of the one who testifies but by the Spirit of God. The Holy Spirit and the word of God will protect the church during the end time.

Those who testify for God and righteousness will be preaching the word of God and prayer to defend the church and God will answer their prayers.

Verses 7-8 *"When they finish their testimony, the beast that ascends out of the bottomless pit will make war against them, overcome them, and kill them. And their dead bodies will lie in the street of the great city, which spiritually is called Sodom and Egypt, where also our Lord was crucified.'*

Satan is the beast from the Abyss (bottomless pit). When those who testify for God have completed their testimony, Satan and the demons will be out of the bottomless pit, and they will attack those who are witnesses for the word and kill them. Satan will put an end to the witnessing for a time.

There may be any number of people proclaiming the word of God at that time. The number two is most likely a symbolic number for all those who are proclaiming the word. According to verses 5 and 6, the witnesses will have great power. Their power comes from God when the church prays for help but Satan will temporarily prevent the proclamation of the Holy Spirit inspired word of God by killing the witnesses. No one, not even Satan can literally kill the Holy Spirit and the word of God, but Satan can cause the death of those who proclaim the word of God and cause the witnessing to cease for a while.

The news of the death of the two witnesses will be a time of celebration for Satan and those who follow him. The dead bodies of the witnesses will lie in the street of the great city that is identified figuratively as Sodom and Egypt. The dead bodies symbolically represent those who were witnessing. Sodom and Egypt are symbolic examples of the great evil that will exist on earth during the end times.

Both Sodom and Egypt were known for their gross immorality and all kinds of evil and wickedness symbolizing the type of people at the end of time.

The bodies of the witnesses will not receive a decent burial; their bodies will be left on the street in a world that is opposed to God. People of the world will look at the bodies lying in the street, but no one will bury them. The people in an anti-God world full of evil will celebrate the death of the two witnesses.

Verses 9-10 *"Then those from the peoples, tribes, tongues, and nations will see their dead bodies, three-and-a-half days, and not allow their dead bodies to be put into graves. And those who dwell on the earth will rejoice over them, make merry, and send gifts to one another, because these two prophets tormented those who dwell on the earth.'*

The two prophets who proclaimed the word of God had tormented the unrighteous with their preaching, and they were killed.

Verses 11-14 *"Now after the three-and-a-half days the breath of life from God entered them, and they stood on their feet, and great fear fell on those who saw them. And they heard a loud voice from heaven saying to them, "Come up here. And they ascended to heaven in a cloud, and their enemies saw them. In the same hour there was a great earthquake, and a tenth of the city fell.'*

"In the earthquake seven thousand people were killed, and the rest were afraid and gave glory to the God of heaven. The second woe is past. Behold the third woe is coming quickly."

Three and a half days figuratively represents the length of time the bodies of God's witnesses lay dead in the street. Then a voice from heaven calls them to come up here, strongly suggesting that those who were witnesses for the word of God become martyrs. The Christians who die during the great tribulation of the end time will also become martyrs. The resurrection of the witnesses is a miraculous sign for all to see the saving power of God. Then there will be a terrible earthquake, and a tenth of the evil population of the world will die as a result of the great earthquake, which is a sign of God's great wrath against Satan and the unrighteous for harming His witnesses.

The Seventh Trumpet

Verses 15-19 *"Then the seventh angel sounded: And there were loud voices in heaven saying, "The kingdoms of this world have become the kingdoms of our Lord and of His Christ, and He shall reign forever and ever! And the twenty-four elders who sat before God on their thrones fell on their faces and worshiped God saying: "We give you thanks, O Lord God Almighty, the One who is and who was and who is to come, because you have taken your great power and reigned. The nations were angry, and your wrath has come, and the time of the dead that they should be judged, and that You should reward your servants the prophets and the saints and those who fear your name, small and great, and should destroy those who destroy the earth. Then the temple of God was opened in heaven, and the ark of His covenant was seen in His temple, And there were light-nings, noises, thunderings, an earthquake, and great hail."*

When the seventh and last angel blows his trumpet, it will be a sign that it is time for the mystery of God to be completed at the end of time. The third woe will take place and the full wrath of God will come upon all of those who refuse to accept Christ. Verse 15 is looking forward to and anticipating the second coming of Christ when the entire number of the redeemed will ascend to heaven and all of the kingdoms of men will be destroyed.

Christ God and the church will reign forever in heaven. The population of heaven gives thanks to God in anticipation of God using His great power to complete the end of time when all the faithful people of God are rewarded. Then the temple of God is opened in heaven, and the ark of His covenant is seen in His temple (the redeemed church) a sign that God and Christ have used their great power to save the redeemed.

They will destroy the unrighteous at the end of time. The martyrs and the Ark of the Covenant are witnesses of the faithfulness of God and His word and His judgments. In the book of Daniel, an angel told Daniel that the events at the end will be for a time, times, and half a time: 3 and 1/2 years, 1260 days or 42 months the length of the end time. Christ will rescue his church from the wrath that will come upon the earth.

When the angel blew his trumpet, John heard loud voices and saw a vision in heaven. He saw the Ark of the Covenant, the meeting place where the Lord reveals His will to His servants. John saw the coming judgment of God symbolized by lightning, thunder, an earthquake and a hailstorm. This is an indication that the coming wrath of God will be very severe. The power of God and Christ will have taken control of the nations on earth that were under the dominion of Satan and the Lawless one. The nations that are allied with Satan will be angry because of God's judgments. God will send a great earthquake to reveal himself to the people in an effort to make them repent before the final and total destruction of the earth. The survivors of the earthquake will be terrified, and some will turn to God, glorify Him, and repent because of the resurrection of the two witnesses and the earthquake.

The mystery of God will be accomplished, and those who are on earth at that time will understand the true meaning of John's message. There will be great distress upon the earth at the end time and end of time, because Satan, the Antichrist, and the Lawless One (Antichrist) will be on earth. God doesn't want anyone to perish; He wants everyone to have faith in Christ and repent of sin. God does everything he can to reach the hearts of people, even if He must use drastic and punishing measures to convince them.

For more about the Antichrist-Lawless One, read the second chapter of Paul's second letter to the church in Thessalonica and the twelfth chapter of Daniel. Daniel wrote that during the end times many people would be made pure. They will be made spotless and be refined because of the judgments of God that caused them to repent and obey the gospel. Daniel prophesied that the dead will be resurrected, and everyone whose name is written in the book of life will be saved.

After the resurrection of the dead God will judge the people on earth and reward His servants, the prophets, and all the faithful will ascend to heaven with Jesus and the angels. After the faithful have been removed from the earth there will be great anguish for those who are left. The unbelievers and ungodly will have one last opportunity to repent during that time. The events in section 3 ends with events of the **end time** and the end of time. Section 4 reveals more **end time** events.

Section 4 Chapters 12 through 14

Section 4 begins with the birth of the church and ends with the second coming of Christ to reap the grapes of wrath at the end of time. The central theme of section 4 is the ultimate victory of Christ and the church over Satan and his evil forces. Chapters 12 through 14 portray a spiritual war between Christ and Satan featuring the beast out of the sea, the beast out of the earth, the false prophet, and the Lawless One (Antichrist). The focus is on the events of the end time and the end of time. Chapter 12 is a Synopsis of the beginning of Christianity in the first century. Satan is cast out of heaven to earth. A Jewish woman named Mary from the nation of Israel named gives birth to the Messiah named Jesus. Jesus came to provide redemption for mankind from the guilt of sin. Satan called the dragon attempted to prevent Jesus from accomplishing God's plan of redemption. From the beginning of time Satan had the freedom to go back and forth between heaven and earth. Satan and his angels the demons persecuted the Jewish people living in the region where Mary lived in the first century.

Satan knew God was sending the Messiah to earth and he was waiting for Christ to be born so he could kill him.

Chapter 12:1-4 *"Now a great sign appeared in heaven: a woman clothed with the sun, with the moon under her feet, and on her head a garland of twelve stars. Then, being with child, she cried out in labor and in pain to give birth.' "And another sign appeared in heaven: behold, a great, fiery red dragon having seven heads and ten horns, and seven diadems on his heads. His tail drew a third of the stars of heaven and threw them to the earth. And the dragon stood before the woman who was ready to give birth, to devour her child as soon as it was born.'*

In the language of Revelation a sign is a person or an event that looks beyond itself and can represent more than one thing. The woman in verse 1 is a sign of the people belonging to God, first the nation of Israel, the Jewish nation and later in the first century the church, the people of God. Mary, the mother of Jesus, was an ordinary Jewish woman chosen by God to give birth to Jesus the Messiah, Who is the redeemer of mankind. After the church was established the woman represents the church, which is the kingdom of Christ on earth.

John saw a sign in heaven, an enemy of God, Christ and the church. The enemy was Satan the fiery red dragon who sent demons from heaven to earth to torment people. Satan is God's adversary and the enemy of God's people.

The Jews who remained faithful to God had been waiting for the coming of the Messiah for hundreds of years. Satan was waiting for the Messiah so he could kill Him while he was still an infant and prevent Christ from establishing redemption.

Verse 5 *"She bore a male Child who was to rule all nations with a rod of iron, and her Child was caught up to God and His throne."*

Mary the Jewish woman bore Jesus the Christ child who would provide redemption and eventually rule all unrighteous nations with a rod of iron. Christ came as a Messiah to die on the cross and redeem mankind from the guilt of sin and to establish His spiritual kingdom the church.

Jesus the Son of Mary was caught up to the throne of God in heaven after His death, burial and resurrection. Jesus will return to earth at the end of time and will rule all nations with a rod of iron. Rule with a rod of iron means to punish the unrighteous nations.

When Satan was on earth Christ was born, He conducted His ministry of redemption, died on the cross, ascended to heaven and assumed all authority in heaven and on earth.

Satan and his demons are cast into the Abyss affording the opportunity for the establishment and growth of the kingdom of God, which is the church. God can imprison and releases Satan from the Abyss anytime He chooses to.

The kingdom of Christ on earth was established during the first century. John the Baptist told the people in the first century to repent because the kingdom was at hand Mt 3:2. Jesus said in Luke 11:20 that the kingdom has come upon you. Christ will not return to earth to set up an earthly kingdom, the kingdom is here now. When Christ returns to earth He will gather up the church and the church will be given a place in a new heaven and a new earth. The kingdom later called the church was formally established in the first century. Christ reigns; over His kingdom the church now and has reigned since the church was established.

Verse 6 *"Then the woman fled into the wilderness where she had a place prepared by God, that they should feed her there one thousand two hundred and sixty days."*

In this section John Moves from events of the first century after the establishment of the church to events of the end time lasting 1260 days the length of the end time. During the end time Satan and the demons will be released from the Abyss and cause great tribulation on earth and persecute the church. The, woman in verse 6 represents the church that will be attacked by the evil forces of Satan at the end time and will go into the wilderness where she will be safe.

The wilderness represents a condition of safety the church is protected by God and she can worship God without being killed. Jesus will return at the end of time to reward the church with eternal life. Satan and the demons will be destroyed and Christ will punish the unrighteous nations with a rod of iron.

Verses 7-9 *And war broke out in heaven: Michael and his angels fought with the dragon; and the dragon and his angels fought, but they did not prevail, nor was a place found for them in heaven any longer. So the great dragon was cast out, that serpent of old, called the Devil and Satan, who deceives the whole world; he was cast to the earth, and his angels were cast out with him."*

Verses 7 through 9 explain why Satan and his angels were cast out of heaven and were on earth during the life and ministry of Christ. There was a war in heaven between the Arch Angel Michael and his angels with Satan and his angels called demons. Michael is the protector of God's people and Michael and his angels prevailed over Satan and the demons and they were cast out of heaven.

Satan and the demons were cast out of heaven at the beginning of the Christian age and they attempted to prevent Christ from fulfilling His mission to provide redemption. Satan and his demons were banned from that part of heaven forever.

Verses 10-11 *"Then I heard a loud voice saying in heaven, "Now salvation, and strength, and the kingdom of our God, and the power of His Christ have come, for the accuser of our brethren who accused them before our God day and night has been cast down. And they overcame him by the blood of the Lamb and by the word of their testimony, and they did not love their lives to the death.*

John hears a voice from heaven saying Satan had been cast down referring to throwing Satan and his angels out of heaven. This was a victory for Christ and the church because Satan and his angels were no longer in heaven fighting against God's plan of redemption. Satan and his angels attempted to thwart God's plan of redemption on earth after they were thrown out of heaven but Christ sacrificed His life and guaranteed redemption.

Verses 12-17 *"Therefore rejoice, O heavens, and you who dwell in them! Woe to the inhabitants of the earth and the sea! For the devil has come down to you, having great wrath, because he knows that he has a short time. But the woman was given two wings of a great eagle, that she might fly into the wilderness to her place, where she is nourished for a time and times and half a time from the presence of the serpent.'*

"So the serpent spewed water out of his mouth like a flood after the woman, that he might cause her to be carried away by the flood. But the earth helped the woman, and the earth opened its mouth and swallowed up the flood, which the dragon had spewed out of his mouth.' The dragon was enraged with the woman, and he went to make war with the rest of her offspring who keep the commandments of God and have the testimony of Jesus Christ."

Spewed water like a flood is figurative language that describes Satan's attempt to destroy the church like a flood destroys anything in its path. Satan was not able to destroy the church in the first century and he will not be able to destroy the church at the end time, because God and the earth will help the church. The earth may refer to those who are not Christians but will sympathize with the church and will help her escape from the wrath of Satan. Sometime after the church was established Satan was imprisoned in a place in the heavens called the Abyss and bottomless pit. Later during the end time Satan will be free to roam the earth again and he will persecute the church.

The Beast From the Sea

Chapter 13:1-4 *"Then I stood on the sand of the sea. And I saw a beast rising up out of the sea, having seven heads and ten horns, and on his horns ten crowns, and on his heads a blasphemous name. "Now the beast I saw was like a leopard, his feet were like the feet of a bear, and his mouth like the mouth of a lion." The dragon gave him his power, his throne and great authority. And I saw one of his heads as if it had been mortally wounded, and his deadly wound was healed. And all the world marveled and followed the beast. So they worshiped the dragon who gave authority to the beast; and they worshiped the beast, saying, "Who is like the beast? Who is able to make war with him?'*

Chapter 12 took us to the end time when Satan and his demons will be on the earth. Chapter 13 describes some of the events that will take place during the 1260 days (three and one half years or 42 months) of the end time. John saw a beast coming out of the sea. The beast is a symbol of a powerful world empire that comes from among the world of unrighteous humanity. The beast John saw was like a leopard, bear, and lion. Beasts are used in scripture to represent world empires. In the 7th chapter of the book of Daniel, Daniel saw a vision of four beasts that represented the Babylonian, Persian, Greek, and Roman empires. Beasts represent evil world empires, because they like beasts are powerful and viscous without any regard for their victims.

Satan accomplishes his evil through human agencies such as nations and empires, and he spreads deception and evil among the people. The empire that is represented by the beast will be an evil empire ruled by an unrighteous individual from among the unrighteous people on earth that Paul called the man of sin and the Lawless One (Antichrist). The world empire of the Lawless One (antichrist) will be a powerful empire that controls several smaller nations. Satan will be the power that creates and controls the empire during the end time when he is out of the Abyss. The beast John saw had seven heads and ten horns with crowns. The heads, horns, and crowns are symbols of rulers and authorities under the control of a great power and authority like an evil world empire. Paul wrote about the Lawless One (Antichrist) in his second letter to the church in Thessalonica.

2nd Thessalonians 2:1-4 "Now brethren, concerning the coming of our Lord Jesus Christ and our gathering together to Him, we ask you, not to be soon shaken in mind or troubled, either by spirit or by word or by letter, as if from us, as though the day of Christ had come. Let no one deceive you by any means; for that day will not come unless the falling away comes first, and the man of sin is revealed, the son of perdition, who opposes and exalts himself above all that is called God or that is worshiped, so that he sits as God in the temple of God, showing himself that he is God."

Satan will be let out of the Abyss at the end time, and Satan will give power to the beast the Lawless One (antichrist) and he will declare that he is God, and many people will worship him. Some will fall away from a belief in the true God at that time.

2nd Thessalonians 2:5-8 "Do you not remember that when I was still with you I told you these things? And now you know what is restraining, that he may be revealed in his own time. For the mystery of lawlessness is already at work; only He who now restrains will do so until He is taken out of the way. And then the lawless one will be revealed, whom the Lord will consume with the breath of His mouth and destroy with the brightness of His coming.'

The lawlessness is already at work refers to the descendants of a people that already existed but would not gain their power until the end time. Paul said the second coming of Christ was being restrained now because he will not return until after the coming of the Lawless One (Antichrist). At the time Paul wrote the letters to the church in Thessalonica the second coming of Christ was being restrained by God and is being restrained now. God will prevent Christ's second coming until He is ready for Him to return at the end of time after the Lawless One (antichrist) has wielded his power and influence throughout the earth at the end time.

2nd Thessalonians 2:9 "The coming of the lawless one is according to the working of Satan, with all power, signs and lying wonders, and with all unrighteous deception among those who perish, because they did not receive the love of the truth that they might be saved. And for this reason God will send them strong delusion, that they should believe the lie, that they all may be condemned who did not believe the truth but had pleasure in unrighteousness."

Satan will be let out of the Abyss, then the beast of the sea Paul called the Lawless One (antichrist) will come into power. Satan is the one who gives him his power. The people of the earth will be deceived by the great power Satan gives the Lawless One (Antichrist) and their demonstration of great power will deceive the people on earth.

Verses 5-10 *"And he was given a mouth speaking great things and blasphemies, and he was given authority to continue for forty-two months. Then he opened his mouth in blasphemy against God, to blaspheme His name, His tabernacle, and those who dwell in heaven. It was granted to him to make war with the saints and to overcome them. And authority was given him over every tribe, tongue and nation. All who dwell on the earth will worship him, whose names have not been written in the Book of Life of the Lamb slain from the foundation of the world. If anyone has an ear, let him hear. He who leads into captivity; he who kills with the sword must be killed with the sword. Here is the patience and the faith of the saints."*

The Lawless One (antichrist) will claim to be God, and he will speak against God and worship Satan. Lawlessness has always existed since the Garden of Eden when Satan first deceived Adam and Eve but there will be extreme wickedness during the end time. Satan was free in the beginning to roam heaven and earth, but God had him thrown into the abyss. Satan will come out of the abyss when God lets him out at the end time to torment the people on earth. Satan will then take control of the people of the earth except for the members of the church. God will allow the

Lawless One (Antichrist) to go to war with the church. The church will survive during the end time, because the Church will have God's protection.

God has a two-fold reason to allow the events of the end time. One is a last resort to cause unrighteous people to repent and accept Christ and the second reason is to punish the unrighteous that will not repent. The mystery of the type of lawlessness that will exist during the end time was already at work symbolically by the Roman Empire when John wrote. There were already men in Rome who claimed to be God and demanded their subjects to worship them.

Satan and The Lawless One (antichrist) will blaspheme God's name and attempt to turn the population of the world against God and Christ. There will be a great rebellion on earth against God, Christ, and the church at that time. All of the world, except those who choose to obey God and confess faith in Christ, will marvel at the beast and will worship Satan.

"Then I saw another beast coming up out of the earth, and he had two horns like a lamb and spoke like a dragon. And he exercises all the authority of the first beast in his presence, and causes the earth and those who dwell in it to worship the first beast, whose deadly wound was healed.'

John saw another beast, and he came out of the earth. The beast out of the earth will already be on earth and he will have an evil nature like the beast out of the sea. He will claim to be a true prophet. The beast out of the earth will join the Lawless One (antichrist). The antichrist will accept the beast out of the earth and allow him to have authority, because he will have the power to create false miracles. He will claim to be a true prophet, but he will be a false prophet. His two horns represent his power and authority.

The false prophet will be a demon that prophesies for the Lawless One (Antichrist) that claims to be God.

"And I saw three unclean spirits like frogs coming out of the mouth of the dragon, out of the mouth of the beast, and out of the mouth of the false prophet." Revelation 16:13

The beast out of the earth is a demon that is allied with Satan, and he speaks with lies and deceit. He will appear to be religious and have the nature of a gentle harmless person, but he will be a demon that supports the Lawless One. He speaks like Satan the dragon, because he is controlled and supported by Satan. During His ministry, Jesus warned His disciples that there would be false prophets. Jesus said, *"Watch out for false prophets, for they come to you in sheep's clothing, but on the inside they are ferocious wolves."* The false prophet will promote the worship of the beast with false miracles, signs, and wonders and, he will have extraordinary power to deceive the people of the world.

Verses 13-15 *"He performs great signs, so that he even makes fire come down from heaven on the earth in the sight of men. And he deceives those who dwell on the earth by those signs which he was granted to do in the sight of the beast, telling those who dwell on the earth to make an image to the beast who was wounded by the sword and lived. He was granted power to give breath to the image of the beast that the image of the beast should both speak and cause as many as would not worship the image of the beast to be killed."*

The signs the false prophet performs will look so real that people will be deceived and believe the Lawless one is God. One of the false miracles of the false prophet and the Lawless One (Antichrist) will be to claim that the Lawless One was wounded and was dead, and the false prophet brought him back to life.

Anyone who would not believe the lie and not worship the beast would be killed.

Verses 16-18 *"He causes all, both small and great, rich and poor, free and slave, to receive a mark on their right hand or on their foreheads, and that no one may buy or sell except one who has the mark or the name of the beast, or the number of his name. Here is wisdom. Let him who has understanding calculate the number of the beast, for it is the number of a man. His number is 666."*

The Lawless One (antichrist) and the false prophet will require everyone be identified as a loyal follower of the Lawless One. People will be identified by a mark on their forehead or right hand.

Since we are reading from a source of figurative language we cannot know for sure ahead of time what the mark is or the name of the beast or the number of his name. To have the mark of the beast means to be loyal to the beast and worship him.

The beast identifies his followers with the mark so everyone can see that they belong to the beast. What the mark looks like is not important everyone that is living during the end time will know the significance of the mark when they see it.

Revelation 14:9-10 "Then a third angel followed them saying with a loud voice, "if anyone worships the beast and his image, and receives his mark on his forehead or on his hand, he himself shall also drink of the wrath of God, which is poured out full strength into the cup of His indignation."

Angel warned that if anyone followed the beast and received his mark, they would be punished by the wrath of God.

The church and the people of the world will not be able to ignore or defeat the power of the beast. Only Christ, at the end of time, will be able to destroy Satan, the Lawless One (antichrist) and the false prophet.

The end time will be a time that tests the faith of everyone on the earth. Speaking figuratively, God will give Satan and the beast forty-two months to deceive the people and persecute the church.

This is the same length of time predicted by the prophet Daniel for the trampling of the holy city (the church) and for the ministry of the two witnesses in chapter 11.

Daniel 12-7 "Then I heard the man clothed in linen, who was above the waters of the river, when he held up his right hand and his left hand to heaven, and swore by Him who lives forever, that it shall be for a time, times, and half a time; when the power of the holy people has been completely shattered, all these things shall be finished."

The man clothed in linen represents either Gabriel or Michael who swore before God that the tribulation at the end time would last for a time, times and half a time, which is 1260 days, three and one half years or 42 months. After the end time the beast and the false prophet will be destroyed in a lake of burning sulfur at the end of time.

The Lamb And The One Hundred Forty-four Thousand

Chapter 14 is the last chapter in section 4. John begins the chapter by writing about the earliest days of Christianity, then he gradually merges into the end times with a scene of Christ and the redeemed singing a new song; a song of victory for Christ and the redeemed.

Three angels will make a public declaration of the gospel. An angel flies in the midst of heaven preaching the gospel to the people on earth encouraging them to obey the gospel, because the time for the final judgment of God had come. Another angel proclaims that Babylon, the symbol of evil has fallen. A third angel warns the people on earth that they will suffer the wrath of God if they continue to worship the beast. The **end time** merges into the end of time, and Christ returns to earth with His angels, and they destroy the unrighteous.

Revelation 14:1-5 "Then I looked and behold, a Lamb standing on Mount Zion, and with Him one hundred and forty-four thousand, having His Father's name written on their foreheads. And I heard a voice from heaven, like the voice of many waters, and like the voice of loud thunder.' "And I heard the sound of harpists playing their harps. They sang as it were a new song before the throne, before the four living creatures, and the elders; and no one could learn that song except the hundred and forty-four thousand who were redeemed from the earth.' "These are the ones who were not defiled with women, for they are virgins. These are the ones who follow the Lamb wherever he goes.

These were redeemed from among men, being first fruits to God and to the Lamb. And in their mouth was found no deceit, for they are without fault before the throne of God."

Christ is the Lamb and the one hundred and forty four thousand represent the redeemed in heaven, and they are identified as God's people. God's name is written on their forehead, because they belong to Him.

These are the faithful that remained true to God. Mt Zion is symbolic of the temple that was built on Mt Zion in Jerusalem figuratively representing God's people, the church. Name written on the forehead is symbolic of God's knowledge of everyone that belongs to Him. The temple was the place where God met with His people. In Revelation the temple figuratively represents the church, God's redeemed people in heaven. There were many redeemed who were already in heaven from both covenants when John wrote. The martyrs and all of the redeemed were represented figuratively as one hundred and forty four thousand.

John heard a loud sound like the sound of many waters and loud thunder. The sound came from the temple in heaven from the voices of the redeemed. The redeemed are the only ones who can learn and sing a new song. The song is new to them, because it had not been sung before. It was a song of complete victory over Satan and the forces of evil. The expression *were not defiled with women* means they were not idolaters; they had remained true to God and Christ.

The Lamb and the 144,000 figuratively represent all of the redeemed in heaven during the end time, a short time before the end of time when their fellow brothers and sisters in Christ would join them. In the interim, the gospel would continue to be preached.

Verses 6-8 *"Then I saw another angel flying in the midst of heaven, having the everlasting gospel to preach to those who dwell on the earth—to every nation, tribe, tongue, and people—saying with a loud voice, "Fear God and give glory to Him, for the hour of His judgment has come; and worship Him who made heaven and earth, the sea and springs of water." And another angel followed saying, "Babylon is fallen, is fallen, that great city, because she has made all nations drink of the wine of the wrath of her fornication."*

When Christ returns to earth, many of the unrighteous will still be on earth, and an angel will be preaching the gospel warning the unrighteous of the coming of God's judgment. Babylon is used as a symbol for evil and the angels are declaring that now is the time all evil will be destroyed, including Satan the empire of the Lawless One (Antichrist), the beast out of the earth, and all of the unrighteous people left on earth.

Verses 9-13 *"Then a third angel followed them, saying with a loud voice, "If anyone worships the beast and his image, and receives his mark on his forehead or on his hand, he himself shall also drink of the wine of the wrath of God, which is poured out full strength into the cup of His indignation. He shall be tormented with fire and brimstone in the presence of the holy angels and in the presence of the Lamb. And the smoke of their torment ascends forever and ever; and they have no rest day or night, who worship the beast and his image, and whoever receives the mark of his name. Here is the patience of the saints; here are those who keep the commandments of God and the faith of Jesus. Then I heard a voice from heaven saying to me, "Write: Blessed are the dead who die in the Lord from now on." "Yes," says the Spirit, that they may rest from their labors, and their works follow them."*

At the end of time, Christ will come and *reap the earth* and everyone will see the coming of Christ and the angels. Reaping the earth represents rewarding the righteous and destroying the unrighteous. Everyone is warned not to follow the evil and unrighteous example of Babylon.

The saints are told to be patient, and if they are killed, they will find rest with God. The saints have a place of paradise waiting for them in a new heaven. The unrighteous will suffer, and they will be tormented forever if they do not repent and obey the gospel.

Luke 21:25-28 "And there will be signs in the sun, in the moon and in the stars; and on the earth distress of nations, with perplexity, the sea and the waves roaring. Men's hearts failing them from fear and the expectation of those things, which are coming on the earth, for the powers of the heavens will be shaken. Then they will see the Son of Man coming in a cloud with power and great glory. Now when these things begin to happen, look up and lift up your heads, because your redemption draws near."

Verses 14-16 "Then I looked, and behold, a white cloud, and on the cloud sat One like the Son of Man, having on His head a golden crown, and in His hand a sharp sickle. And another angel came out of the temple, crying with a loud voice to Him who sat on the cloud, "Thrust in Your sickle and reap, for the time has come for You to reap, for the harvest of the earth is ripe." So he who sat on the cloud thrust in His sickle on the earth and the earth was reaped."

The crown is a sign of the King of Kings and a symbol of His authority to fulfill the wrath of God at the end of time. The sickle represents the destruction of the unrighteous people on the earth.

The earth will be ripe for reaping, because the people have become so evil that God will not wait any longer, and He will send Christ and the angels to reap the earth.

Verses 17-18 "Then another angel came out of the temple that is in heaven, he also having a sharp sickle. And another angel come out from the altar, who had power over fire, and he cried with a loud cry to him who had the sharp sickle saying, "Thrust in your sharp sickle and gather the clusters of the vine of the earth, for her grapes are fully ripe.' "So the angel thrust his sickle into the earth and gathered the vine of the earth, and threw it into the great winepress of the wrath of God. And the winepress was trampled outside the city, and blood came out of the winepress up to the horses' bridles, for one thousand six hundred furlongs."

John's visions give a figurative view of the execution of God's wrath poured out on the unrighteous by Christ and the angels at the end of time. Section 4 ends with events of the end of time. **In section 5,** more events of the end time will take place beginning with chapter 15. **Section 5** ends with chapter 16 when the 7th bowl of wrath is poured out.

Section 5

Chapters 15 through 16

Chapter 15 introduces the bowl judgments that will be poured out during the end time. John begins chapter 15 with a vision in heaven of seven angels who have the seven last plagues that will come upon the earth during the end time. They are seven bowls of God's wrath, one bowl for each angel. Pouring out the bowls of wrath reveals the final judgments that come when the end time merges with the end of time. When the seventh angel completes delivering God's wrath against the unrighteous, the judgment of God is completed.

John saw those who had remained faithful to Christ during the end time. They hadn't worshiped the beast or any image of the beast, and they were in heaven. They had become martyrs. The sea of glass is a place for worship that is in front of God's throne. All of those who gained a victory over the beast were standing on the sea of glass waiting for the trumpet blasts to signal the angels to act, and they sang the song of victory like the song that Moses sang when the Israelites were delivered from Egypt. When the seventh bowl is poured out, the islands and mountains disappear. Great hail falls upon the earth. The statement *will rule them with a rod of iron* symbolize the destruction with force against the unrighteous from the bowls of wrath at the end of time.

The Bowl Judgments

Chapter 15:1-8 *"Then I saw another sign in heaven, great and marvelous: seven angels having the seven last plagues, for in them the wrath of God is complete. "And I saw something like a sea of glass mingled with fire, and those who have the victory over the beast, over his image and over his mark and over the number of his name, standing on the sea of glass, having harps of God. They sang the song of Moses, the servant of God, and the song of the Lamb, saying: Great and marvelous are Your works, Lord God Almighty! Just and true are Your ways, O King of the saints! Who shall not fear You, O Lord, and glorify Your name? For You alone are holy. For all nations shall come and worship before You, For Your judgments have been manifested.'*

"After these things I looked, and behold, the temple of the tabernacle of the testimony in heaven was opened. And out of the temple came the seven angels having the seven plagues, clothed in pure bright linen, and having their chests girded with golden bands. "Then one of the four living creatures gave to the seven angels seven golden bowls full of the wrath of God who lives forever and ever. The temple was filled with smoke from the glory of God and from His power, and no one was able to enter the temple till the seven plagues of the seven angels were completed."

Angels are instrumental in carrying out the last plagues of God's wrath on a world of unrighteous people. John sees the redeemed in heaven they had been victorious over Satan and the unrighteous. They were in heaven where they would be safe from the plagues and the beast. They were the martyrs who died because they would not deny Christ, and they were redeemed.

When the redeemed sing the song of victory, the song will praise God as the Almighty King of the saints, the Only Holy and Righteous One. John saw the temple of the tabernacle of the testimony, and it was opened. (A testimony is a statement used for evidence or proof.).

In the Old Testament, the tabernacle in the wilderness and the temple in Jerusalem were testimonials for God and the places where God met with His people.

In the Christian dispensation the church is the temple of God, and the church meets with God spiritually in the hearts of Christians producing praise, prayer, worship, and song. John saw seven angels with the seven final plagues of God's wrath come from the midst of the redeemed. The angels were dressed in clothes that symbolized righteousness.

God will be righteous in taking action against Satan, the false prophet, the beast, and the ungodly people on earth. The angels each received a bowl of God's wrath from one of the living creatures in heaven. The temple was filled with smoke so that no one could enter, symbolizing the protection of the church, which is God's temple. The pouring out of the bowls of wrath will not harm the church.

God's Bowls of Wrath Poured On The Earth

First Bowl—Loathsome Sores

Chapter 16:1-2 *"Then I heard a loud voice from the temple saying to the seven angels, "Go and pour out the bowls of the wrath of God on the earth." 2 So the first went and poured out his bowl upon the earth, and a foul and loathsome sore came upon the men who had the mark of the beast and those who worshiped his image.'*

Second Bowl—The Sea Turns to Blood

Verse 3 *"Then the second angel poured out his bowl on the sea, and it became blood as of a dead man; and every living creature in the sea died."*

Third Bowl—The Waters Turn to Blood

Verses 4-7 *"Then the third angel poured out his bowl on the rivers and springs of water, and they became blood.*

And I heard the angels of the waters saying: "You are righteous, O Lord, The One who is and who was and who is to be. Because you have judged these things. "For they have shed the blood of saints and prophets, And you have given them blood to drink. For it is their just due. And I heard another from the altar saying, "Even so, Lord God Almighty, true and righteous are your judgments."

Fourth bowl—Men are Scorched

Verse 8-9 *"Then the fourth angel poured out his bowl on the sun, and power was given to him to scorch men with fire. And men were scorched with great heat, and they blasphemed the name of God who has power over these plagues; and they did not repent and give Him glory."*

Fifth Bowl—Darkness and Pain

Verses 10-11 *"Then the fifth angel poured out his bowl on the throne of the beast, and his kingdom became full of darkness; and they gnawed their tongues because of the pain. They blasphemed the God of heaven because of their pains and their sores, and did not repent of their deeds."*

Sixth Bowl—Euphrates Dried Up

Verse 12-16 *"Then the sixth angel poured out his bowl on the great river Euphrates, and its water was dried up, so that the way of the kings from the east might be prepared. And I saw three unclean spirits like frogs coming out of the mouth of the dragon, out of the mouth of the beast, and out of the mouth of the false prophet. For they are spirits of demons, performing signs, which go out to the kings of the earth and of the whole world, to gather them to the battle of that great day of God Almighty. "Behold, I am coming as a thief. Blessed is he who watches and keeps his garments, lest he walk naked and they see his shame." And they gathered them together to the place called in Hebrew, Armageddon."*

Seventh Bowl—The Earth Utterly Shaken

Verse 17-21 *"Then the seventh angel poured out his bowl into the air, and a loud voice came out of the temple of heaven, from the throne saying, "It is done! "And there were noises and thunderings and lightnings; and there was a great earthquake, such a mighty and great earthquake as had not occurred since men were on the earth. Now the great city was divided into three parts, and the cities of the nations fell. And great Babylon was remembered before God, to give her the cup of the wine of the fierceness of His wrath.' 20 Then every island fled away, and the mountains were not found. 21 And great hail from heaven fell upon men, each hailstone about the weight of a talent. Men blasphemed God because of the plague of the hail, since that plague was exceedingly great."*

The loud voice to begin the bowl judgments came from the authority of God. God's judgment against the earth will be completed when the last bowl is poured out at the end time. No one can enter the temple (the church) until after the angels have completed their mission. When the mission is complete, the three angels in chapter 14 have the everlasting gospel to preach on earth to all people telling them to fear God and give him glory, for the hour of His judgment has come.

This will be the last chance for those who are still living to obey the gospel. Once the process of the bowl judgments starts, it will not be interrupted. No one can prevent God from completing the plan He had from the beginning to punish the unrighteous and reward the righteous with a new heaven and a new earth.

John still looking into heaven heard a voice coming from the temple telling the seven angels with the bowls of wrath to go ahead and pour out the bowls on the earth. The first angel will pour out his bowl when the end time is close to merging into the end of time. There is not a sharply defined beginning and ending of the separation between the end time and the beginning of the end of time. There is no exact length of time prescribed for the end of time but it will take place quickly once it begins.

Before the actual destruction of the earth by fire, there will be a period of great suffering for the unrighteous and those who worship the Lawless One. The angels preaching the gospel of

Christ are trying to persuade the unrighteous to accept and obey Christ before the day of the end of time, because there will not be another chance (chapter 14:6-11). Satan and the demons will have been released from the Abyss to persecute and torture the people on earth. Satan and the demons will remain on the earth until they are destroyed at the second coming of Christ; they will be on the earth during the bowl judgments.

When the first angel pours out his bowl, sores will break out on the people who are identified with the mark of the beast. The sores will cause great pain in one last effort to make the unrighteous repent. The sores are not meant to kill but are a sign that God's wrath is beginning. The bowls are poured out one at a time to inflict maximum suffering, and the lapse of time between pouring out each bowl will give people an opportunity to repent. The second and third bowls are poured out, and they affect the sea and the sources of fresh water. Every creature in the sea dies. The term *sea* is used metaphorically to represent the sea of unrighteous humanity on earth that will die when the second angel pours out his bowl.

The statement *blood to drink* means many people will die during the end times. Life can no longer be sustained in the sea or on the portion of land that was affected by the first three bowls. People cannot survive without water. The angel who will be responsible for damaging the water will praise God for his righteous judgment. The angels will proclaim that God is righteous in everything He does. The heat of the sun will scorch the unrighteous, but they will not repent. Instead they will blaspheme God. Suffering is intended to help people realize their need for God and repent, but some people will blame God and curse Him.

In chapter 1 of Romans, Paul writes about the guilt of mankind and God's wrath against unrighteousness.

Romans 1:18-21 "For the wrath of God is revealed from heaven against all ungodliness and unrighteousness of men, who suppress the truth in unrighteousness, because what may be known of God is manifest in them, for God has shown it to them. For since the creation of the world His invisible attributes are clearly seen, being understood by the things that are made, even His eternal power and Godhead, so that they are without excuse, because, although they knew God they did not glorify Him as God, nor were thankful, but became futile in their thoughts, and their foolish hearts were darkened."

It is evident that tribulation and punishment from the wrath of God will come upon the unrighteous at the end times including those who persecute the church.

2ⁿᵈ Thessalonians 1:3-10 "We are bound to thank God always for you brethren, as it is fitting, because your faith grows exceedingly, and the love of everyone of you all abounds toward each other, so that we ourselves boast of you among the churches of God for your patience and faith in all your persecutions and tribulations that you endure, which is manifest evidence of the righteous judgment of God, that you may be counted worthy of the kingdom of God, for which you also suffer; since it is a righteous thing with God to repay with tribulation those who trouble you, and give you who are troubled rest with us when the Lord Jesus is revealed from heaven with His mighty angels, in flaming fire taking vengeance on those who do not know God, and on those who do not obey the gospel of our Lord Jesus Christ."

The tribulation and persecution that Christians endure comes from the actions of the unrighteous, but faithful Christians do not deny their faith in God and Christ. When God repays the unrighteous with tribulation, it is a righteous punishment. The manifestations of God have existed from the beginning of time and there is no excuse for anyone to ignore God and Christ and God's redeeming plan. God could end everything on earth within a moment during the end time but instead He punishes in measured sections of time to encourage repentance so people will obey the gospel. Those who die from God's wrath will be evil, ungodly people who deserve to die. John heard another voice confirming what the angel said. *"Even so, Lord God Almighty, true and righteous are your judgments." (Revelation 16:7.)* The voice came from the altar, and could have been from the saints who were under the altar.

God's judgments will be just, because the evil people who suffer from his judgments are like those who killed his saints, prophets, and apostles. They will be receiving what they deserve.

The fourth bowl affects the heavenly bodies, and when the fourth bowl is poured out on the sun, it will cause intense heat that will scorch people, and they will curse God.

The depravity of people at the end time is evidenced by the fact that no amount of suffering keeps them from cursing God. The judgments of God will be terrible, but the people who are scorched by the sun will be of the worst kind. They will be those who speak evil of God and refuse to repent even after being warned over and over again. The fifth angel pours out his bowl of God's wrath on the kingdom of the beast, and it becomes full of darkness.

The unrighteous will blaspheme God because of the pain and the sores, but they still will not repent. The Euphrates River dries up when the sixth angel pours out his bowl. The demons perform miraculous signs to stir up the unrighteous people against God. The seventh angel pours out his bowl of wrath fulfilling God's wrath against Satan, the demons, and the unrighteous people on earth. God doesn't pour out his wrath on those who are righteous.

The angel will make a direct hit on the beast, which figuratively is the evil empire of the Lawless One, the false prophet and Satan. In Chapter 8: 13, an angel flew through heaven and in a loud voice he said, *"Woe, woe, woe to the inhabitants of the earth, because of the remaining blasts of the trumpets of the three angels who are about to sound."*

The woes were to be announced by the fifth sixth, and seventh trumpet blast. Woe means great grief, trouble, and distress. The forces of God will attack the beast and his followers, but they will stubbornly refuse to repent, and the sixth angel will pour out another bowl of God's wrath.

The sixth bowl of wrath involves warfare between the forces of God, Christ, and the angels against Satan, the demons, the empire of the Lawless One (Antichrist), and the false prophet at the end of time. The forces of evil will gather together for a final battle before they are destroyed. John writes about the last and final battle against evil symbolized as Babylon the Great, the mother of evil.

Babylon figuratively represents all evil regardless of time. The ancient city of Babylon situated on the banks of the Euphrates was an enemy of God's people at one time. The Euphrates River in ancient times was the place where the enemies of God's people gathered to invade Israel. The Euphrates River is used figuratively to represent the location of the last and final battle (Armageddon) against all evil on earth.

The word Armageddon is found nowhere outside the Bible and it is mentioned only once in Revelation 16:16. The word Armageddon symbolizes Christ's war against the forces of evil at the end of time. The kings of the earth, Satan and the demons will unite with the lawless one to war against God in the battle of Armageddon on *the great day of God Almighty.*

The place of the battle of Armageddon is symbolic, so it doesn't matter where the battle is located. We do know what the outcome will be, because it has already been decided. God and the church will be victorious and that will be the day when the forces of God destroy all evil on the earth, a great day for God Almighty and the church.

Christians who have remained faithful will be blessed and will not be harmed, but the unrighteous will suffer from the judgments sent by God. The term *It is done* means God's final act of judgment will be completed when the seventh bowl is poured out ending the plagues. The result of pouring out the seventh bowl is recorded in Revelation 16:18-21. When Christ said He was coming as a thief, He meant that no one knows the time when the Lord will come until they see Him coming in the clouds. Verses 18 through 21 describe the great battle when Christ returns. When the seventh angel blows his trumpet, God's mysterious plan will be completed. The fifth, sixth, and seventh bowls have been poured out by the angels symbolizing the battle of Armageddon, the last battle between good and evil.

Section 6

Chapters 17 through 19

In chapters 16 God remembered Ancient Babylon and her great evil, and the seventh bowl of God's wrath was poured out. The evil Empire of the Lawless One (Antichrist) will be like Ancient Babylon. Babylon was a type of evil. Types refer to a person or thing having the characteristics of a kind, class, or group. Anti-types are copies of an earlier type. Ancient Babylon is a type and the Roman Empire and the empire of the Lawless One (Antichrist) are anti types of the evil demonstrated by Ancient Babylon.

Chapters 17 Explains why the wrath of God was directed against Babylon and her antitypes. Babylon the symbol of all kinds of evil is described as a prostitute, the mother of harlots and the sinful abominations of the earth. Chapter 18 portrays the fall of Babylon the Great. During the end of time Christ will return and will destroy the antitype of Babylon, the Empire of the Lawless One (Antichrist).

God will destroy all traces of her evil. Chapter 19 portrays the Second coming of Christ with the angels at the end of time to strike down the evil nations symbolized by the phrase '*He Himself will rule them with a rod of Iron.*'

Revelation makes use of many types and anti-types and features Ancient Babylon in order to describe what the empire of the Lawless one (Antichrist) and the morals and attitudes of people will be like during the **end times**. The world Empire of Babylon is called the great harlot, therefore the Empire of the Lawless One (Antichrist) at the end time will be a great harlot that corrupts the morals of many people symbolized by sitting on many waters. The greater part of the population of the earth will be under the control of The Lawless One (Antichrist) who will be under the control of Satan.

Chapter 17—The Great Harlot Who Sits On Many Waters

Chapter 17: 1-6 *"Then one of the seven angels who had the seven bowls came and talked with me saying to me, "Come, I will show you the judgment of the great harlot who sits on many waters, with whom the kings of the earth committed fornication, and the inhabitants of the earth were made drunk with the wine of her fornication. So he carried me away in the Spirit into the wilderness. And I saw a woman sitting on a scarlet beast that was full of names of blasphemy, having seven heads and ten horns. The woman was arrayed in purple and scarlet, and adorned with gold and precious stones and pearls, having in her hand a golden cup full of abominations and the filthiness of her fornication. And on her forehead a name was written: MYSTERY, BABYLON THE GREAT, THE MOTHER OF HARLOTS AND OF THE ABOMINATIONS OF THE EARTH. I saw the woman, drunk with the blood of the saints and with the blood of the martyrs of Jesus. And when I saw her, I marveled with great amazement."*

The woman on the scarlet beast first represents Ancient Babylon, then Rome, and finally the Empire of the Lawless One (Antichrist) who will be guilty of every kind of evil and is yet to come.

Verses 7-8 *"But the angel said to me, "Why did you marvel? I will tell you the mystery of the woman and of the beast that carries her, which has the seven heads and the ten horns. The beast that you saw was, and is not, and will ascend out of the bottomless pit and go to perdition. And those who dwell on the earth will marvel, whose names are not written in the Book of Life from the foundation of the world, when they see the beast that was, and is not, and yet is."*

The Empire of the Lawless One (Antichrist) is represented as a woman. The beast that carried and supported the woman is Satan. Satan supported Ancient Babylon, then the Roman Empire, and at the end time Satan will support the Lawless One (Antichrist). The evil empires are represented by a woman the beast that carries them is Satan. The term beast is used to represent Satan the false prophet and the evil empires.

The seven horns and ten heads represent the great power of empires like the worldwide Empire of the Lawless One (Antichrist).

Satan is the power behind the empires called beasts and the beast that John saw in his vision. Satan was at one time in heaven, then was on earth, then was cast into the Abyss, and is not now on earth. Ancient Babylon was the first beast. The Roman Empire was the second beast and the Empire of the Lawless One will be the third and last beast. The beast that John saw was Satan that controlled the Babylonian Empire, and the Roman Empire. Satan is not on earth now because God put him in the Abyss but he will be released from the Abyss at the end time and give power to the Lawless One (Antichrist).

Verses 9-14 *"Here is the mind which has wisdom: The seven heads are seven mountains on which the woman sits. There are also seven kings. Five have fallen, one is, and the other has not yet come. And when he comes, he must continue a short time. The beast that was, and is not, is himself also the eighth, and is of the seven, and is going to perdition." "The ten horns which you saw are ten kings who have received no kingdom as yet, but they receive authority for one hour as kings with the beast. These are of one mind, and they will give their power and authority to the beast.' These will make war with the Lamb, and the Lamb will'* *"overcome them, for He is Lord of lords and King of kings; and those who are with Him are called, chosen, and faithful."*

The woman in verses 9 and 10 is the Roman Empire that was supported by Satan. Rome, the capital of the Roman Empire, was built on seven hills. At the time John wrote, he and other Christians would recognize that the Empire of the Lawless One (Antichrist) would be an anti type of the Roman Empire.

The seven kings were those who once ruled the Roman Empire. Five kings were in the past, one was ruling when John wrote, and there was one more to come. The one to come will be the Lawless One (Antichrist) who will be an anti-type of the evil rulers of the Roman Empire.

The empire of the Lawless One (Antichrist) is the harlot that was yet to come. The beast *that was* represents Ancient Babylon and the Roman Empire as a harlot. The Roman Empire was, is not now, but is coming back as the Lawless One (Antichrist), an anti-type of the Roman Empire.

Ten kings who have not yet received a kingdom will be allied with the Lawless One (Antichrist) for a very short time and war against Christ. Christ will be victorious. The ten kingdoms will be kingdoms in existence when the Lawless One is in power.

The kings that were allied with the Lawless one will, in time, come to hate the Lawless One (Antichrist), and they will make her desolate and naked, eat her flesh, and burn her with fire, because God will turn them against her. The nations on earth that turned against the Antichrist will help the church.

Verses 15-18 *"Then he said to me, "The waters which you saw, where the harlot sits, are people, multitudes, nations, and tongues. And the ten horns that you saw on the beast, these will hate the harlot, make her desolate and naked, eat her flesh and burn her with fire. For God has put it into their hearts to fulfill His purpose, to be of one mind, and to give their kingdom to the beast, until the words of God are fulfilled. And the woman whom you saw is that great city which reigns over the kings of the earth."*

Chapter 18 John describes the destruction of the Lawless One (Antichrist) and the attitudes of the people who loved her in her beginning and will still love her at the end.

God Summons His People to Come Out of Babylon

In chapter eighteen John saw an angel coming from heaven with great authority. He was a mighty angel with a loud voice that cried out, "Babylon the Great has fallen." Babylon the Great fell many years earlier, but John is speaking of the anti-type of Babylon, the Empire of the Lawless One (Antichrist) at the end time. Ancient Babylon was destroyed because of her evil ways and her persecution of God's people. Ancient Rome fell for the same reason, and the empire of the Lawless One (Antichrist) is destined to fall as well at the end of time.

The Angel saw the destruction of the empire of the Lawless One (Antichrist) at the end of time ahead of time so he could warn God's people. The story of Revelation continues as God makes an appeal for his people to come out of Babylon before it is too late. The expression *coming out of Babylon* means to come out of the sin of Satan and the Lawless One. The destruction of the evil forces symbolized by Babylon of the past, present, and future will be exposed to God's wrath at the end of time. The anti-type forces of evil will receive a double punishment.

The empire of the Lawless One will receive back double all of the anguish, grief and tribulation she was guilty of imposing on God's people and the people of the earth. God's people will be glad to see the great evil empire punished, but the rulers of the earth and those that profited from her, especially the greedy, will mourn because of the loss of wealth and luxury. They will be terrified when they learn of her punishment knowing that they must face the judgment of God. Those who profit from evil are those who become wealthy from the guilt of the seven sins God hates.

Proverbs 6:12-19 "A worthless person a wicked man walks with a perverse mouth. He winks with his eyes he shuffles his feet he points with his fingers. Perversity is in his heart he devises evil continually.'

"He sows discord therefore his calamity shall come suddenly. Suddenly he shall be broken without remedy.' "These six things the Lord hates, Yes seven are an abomination to Him; A proud look, A lying tongue, Hands that shed innocent blood, a heart that devises wicked plans, Feet that are swift in running to evil, a false witness who speaks lies, and the one who sows discord among brethren."

The Fall of Babylon The Great

John saw a mighty angel come down from heaven, probably Michael who came down to protect God's people. The angel shouted with a loud voice to all of the nations of earth who are guilty of her evil deeds. Chapter 18 pictures the great evil that will exist on earth at the end time and declares that it will be destroyed.

Chapter 18:1-5 *"After these things I saw another angel coming down from heaven, having great authority, and the earth was illuminated with his glory. And he cried mightily with a loud voice saying, "Babylon the great is fallen, is fallen, and has become a dwelling place of demons, a prison for every foul spirit, and a cage for every unclean and hated bird! For all the nations have drunk of the wine of the wrath of her fornication, the kings of the earth have committed fornication with her, and the merchants of the earth have become rich through the abundance of her luxury. And I heard another voice from heaven saying, "Come out of her, my people, lest you share in her sins, and lest you receive of her plagues. For her sins have reached to heaven, and God has remembered her iniquities."*

The fate of the empire of the Lawless One (Antichrist) is the same as ancient Babylon. God warns everyone who partakes of her evil to come out of her evil ways and repent because God is going to destroy all evil during the end time. The expression *coming out* would mean repenting of sin and accepting the grace of God through faith in Christ.

Verses 6-8 *"Render to her just as she rendered to you, and repay her double according to her works; in the cup, which she has mixed, mix double for her. In the measure that she glorified herself and lived luxuriously, in the same measure give her torment and sorrow; for she says in her heart, 'I sit as queen, and am no widow, and will not see sorrow.' Therefore her plagues will come in one day—death and mourning and famine. And she will be utterly burned with fire, for strong is the Lord God who judges her.'*

The World Mourns Babylon's Fall

God will repay all evil at the end of time with a judgment of fire.

Verses 9-20 *"The kings of the earth who committed fornication and lived luxuriously with her will weep and lament for her, when they see the smoke of her burning, standing at a distance for fear of her torment saying, "Alas, alas, that great city Babylon, that mighty city! For in one hour your judgment has come.' And the merchants of the earth will weep and mourn over her, for no one buys their merchandise anymore: Merchandise of gold and silver, precious stones and pearls, fine linen and purple, silk and scarlet, every kind of citron wood, every king of object of ivory, every kind of object of most precious wood, bronze, iron, and marble; and cinnamon and incense, fragrant oil and frankincense, wine and oil, fine flour and wheat, cattle and sheep, horses and chariots, and bodies and souls of men. The fruit that your soul longed for has gone from you, and all the things which are rich and splendid have gone from you, and you shall find them no more at all. The merchants of these things, who became rich by her, will stand at a distance for fear of her torment, weeping and wailing, and saying, 'Alas, alas, that great city that was clothed in fine linen, purple, and scarlet, and adorned with gold and precious stones and pearls!"*

"For in one hour such great riches came to nothing. Every shipmaster, all who travel by ship, sailors, and as many as trade on the sea, stood at a distance and cried out when they saw the smoke of her burning saying, 'What is like this great city. They threw dust on their heads and cried out, weeping and wailing and saying, 'Alas, alas, that great city, in which all who had ships on the sea became rich by her wealth!

For in one hour she is made desolate.' "Rejoice over her, O heaven, and you holy apostles and prophets, for God has avenged you on her!"

Fall of Babylon

The fall of the Empire of the Lawless One (Antichrist) that was involved in all kinds of evil will be destroyed and will become desolate within one hour. Verses 21-24 *"Then a mighty angel took up a stone like a great millstone and threw it into the sea saying, "Thus with violence the great city Babylon shall be thrown down, and shall not be found anymore.*

The sound of harpists, musicians, flutists, and trumpeters shall not be heard in you anymore.'

"No craftsman of any craft shall be found in you anymore, and the sound of a millstone shall not be heard in you anymore. The light of a lamp shall not shine in you anymore, and the voice of bridegroom and bride shall not be heard in you anymore. For your merchants were the great men of the earth, for by your sorcery all the nations were deceived. And in her was found the blood of prophets and saints, and of all who were slain on the earth."

The empire will have confidence that nothing will ever be able to harm her, but the plagues from the wrath of God will overtake her, and she will be destroyed by fire from the mighty judgment of God. The people of the earth who made money by doing business with her will mourn when they see her destruction. In John's Revelation he states that her destruction will be a time of rejoicing for Christians, including the apostles and prophets, because of the way she treated God's people. John saw the symbolic description of the death of all the evil forces that were anti-types of Babylon the Great at the end of time. A powerful angel picked up an enormous boulder, threw it into the sea, and stated aloud, *"With the same violence the great city of Babylon will be thrown down and will never be found again."*

Heaven Celebrates Babylon's Defeat

Chapter 19:1-3 *"After these things I heard a loud voice of a great multitude in heaven, saying, "Alleluia! Salvation and glory and honor and power belong to the Lord our God! For true and righteous are His judgments, because He has judged the great harlot who corrupted the earth with her fornication; and He has avenged on her the blood of His servants shed by her." Again they said, "Alleluia! Her smoke rises up forever and ever!"*

Babylon, the great harlot, symbolizes the epitome of all kinds of evil. After her fall, the inhabitants of heaven will celebrate her destruction.

"Alleluia! For the Lord God Omnipotent reigns! Let us be glad and rejoice and give Him glory, for the marriage of the Lamb has come, and His wife has made herself ready." And to her it was granted to be arrayed in fine linen, clean and bright, for the fine linen is the righteous acts of the saints.' Now I saw heaven. Then he said to me, "Write: 'Blessed are those who are called to the marriage supper of the Lamb!'" And he said to me, "These are the true sayings of God." And I fell at his feet to worship him.

But he said to me, "See that you do not do that! I am your fellow servant, and of your brethren who have the testimony of Jesus. Worship God! For the testimony of Jesus is the spirit of prophecy."

John heard them say, *"The wedding of the Lamb has come, and his bride is ready."* Christ is the bridegroom, and the faithful church is the bride. The time for the wedding of Christ and the church comes when Christ returns at the end of time. The church that remains faithful will be waiting for the bridegroom and the new heaven and new earth.

Christ Returns on A White Horse—End of Time

Verses 11-16 *"Now I saw heaven opened, and behold, a white horse. And He who sat on him was called Faithful and True, and in righteousness He judges and makes war. His eyes were like a flame of fire, and on His head were many crowns. He had a name written that no one knew except Himself. He was clothed with a robe dipped in blood, and His name is called The Word of God. And the armies in heaven, clothed in fine linen, white and clean, followed Him on white horses. Now out of His mouth goes a sharp sword, that with it He should strike the nations. And He Himself will rule them with a rod of iron. He Himself treads the winepress of the fierceness and wrath of Almighty God. And He has on His robe and on His thigh a name written: KING OF KINGS AND LORD OF LORDS."*

John continued to look into heaven, he saw a rider on a white horse. The rider was named *Faithful and True.* Christ is the rider on the white horse. White is a symbol for righteousness, and Christ and the white horse both symbolize righteousness and justice. Christ had crowns on his head, signifying that he is a ruler with authority. Christ is Sovereign over heaven and earth. He has all authority and power. Christ had on a bloody robe, and he was called *The Word of God.* The bloody robes symbolized the death and destruction of the unrighteous. The angels from heaven will follow Christ, dressed in white robes and riding on white horses.

They are His army. Everything that John saw indicated a great battle on earth that would involve great bloodshed. Christ and his army of angels are going to strike down the nations. There will be a sharp sword in the mouth of Christ, a symbol of the word of God, which gives Him authority to punish the nations of ungodly people, and on His thigh will be written: KING OF KINGS AND LORD OF LORDS. This signifies His supreme authority

The Beast and His Armies Defeated

Verses 17-21 *"Then I saw an angel standing in the sun; and he cried with a loud voice, saying to all the birds that fly in the midst of heaven, "Come and gather together for the supper of the great God, that you may eat the flesh of kings, the flesh of captains, the flesh of mighty men, the flesh of horses and of those who sit on them, and the flesh of all people, free and slave, both small and great.' "And I saw the beast, the kings of the earth, and their armies, gathered together to make war against Him who sat on the horse and against His army. Then the beast was captured, and with him the false prophet who worked signs in his presence, by which he deceived those who received the mark of the beast and those who worshiped his image.' "These two were cast alive into the lake of fire burning with brimstone. And the rest were killed with the sword, which proceeded from the mouth of Him who sat on the horse. And all the birds were filled with their flesh."*

Christians are invited to the wedding supper of the Lamb. When Paul wrote the second letter to the church in Corinth, he told the members that he promised them one husband. Christ is that husband the church will be presented to Christ as a pure virgin bride. The church is united with Christ spiritually now, but at the end of time the church will be with Christ in person. At the end of time, Christ and all of the faithful will come together, and the church will take her place in the new heaven and the new earth. John was about to worship the angel that revealed these events to him, but the angel would not let him. God and Christ are the only ones who are worthy to receive worship.

Section 7

Chapters 20-22

Chapter 20:1-3 Christ will deal with Satan and the judgment at the end of time. *"Then I saw an angel coming down from heaven, having the key to the bottomless pit and a great chain in his hand. He laid hold of the dragon, that serpent of old, who is the Devil and Satan, and bound him for a thousand years; and he cast him into the bottomless pit, and shut him up, and set a seal on him, so that he should deceive the nations no more till the thousand years were finished. But after these things he must be released for a little while."*

The first three verses of chapter 20 begin with the first century when Satan was put in the Abyss. Chapter 20 ends with the great judgment of God at the end of time. The thousand years that Satan was bound in the Abyss is called the millennium, a figurative term denoting the period of time from the first century to the second coming of Christ. The exact length of that time is literally unknown by anyone but God. Satan was put in the Abyss where he is now, but at the end time near the end of the millennium, he will be released and will begin his reign of terror on the earth against the church until he is destroyed at the end of time.

1st Corinthians 15:20-28 "But now Christ is risen from the dead, and has become the first fruits of those who have fallen asleep. For since by man came death, by man also came the resurrection of the dead. For as in Adam all die, even so in Christ all shall be made alive. But each one in his own order: Christ the first fruits, afterward those who are Christ's at His coming. Then comes the end, when He delivers the kingdom to God the Father, when He puts and end to all rule and all authority and power. For He must reign till He has put all enemies under His feet. The last enemy that will be destroyed is death. For "He has put all things under His feet." But when He says "all things are put under Him," it is evident that He who put all things under Him is excepted. Now when all things are made subject to Him, then the Son Himself will also be subject to Him who put all things under Him, that God may be all in all."

Christ reigns during the Christian dispensation, and all Christians reign with Christ. At the end of time Christ will deliver the church to God and the rule of Christ will end. *Romans 5:17-18 "For if by the one man's offense death reigned through the one, much more those who receive abundance of grace and of the gift of righteousness will reign in life through the One, Jesus Christ."*

Reign means to exist or to prevail. Christians will live on earth until Christ returns and they will prevail over death in the resurrection. Christ, the King of Kings reign over the church on earth now until the time of His return, then He will deliver the church to God in heaven. The Bible does not mention a kingdom existing for one thousand years. The one thousand years, also called the millennium, is figurative language meaning a long period of time of which the literal length is not known until Christ returns. Christ began His millennial reign when He ascended to heaven and sat down at the right hand of God.

Matthew 28:18-20 "And Jesus came and spoke to them, saying, "All authority has been given to me in heaven and on earth. Go therefore and make disciples of all the nations, baptizing them in the name of the Father and of the Son and of the Holy Spirit."

Verses 4-6 *"And I saw thrones and they sat on them, and judgment was committed to them. Then I saw the souls of those who had been beheaded for their witness to Jesus and for the word of God, who had not worshiped the beast or his image, and had not received his mark on their foreheads or on their hands.' "And they lived and reigned with Christ for a thousand years. But the rest of the dead did not live again until the thousand years were finished. This is the first resurrection. Blessed and holy is he who has part in the first resurrection.'*

"Over such the second death has no power, but they shall be priests of God and of Christ, and shall reign with Him a thousand years."

The thrones were in heaven, and those on the thrones were martyrs who were given authority to judge. The spirits of the martyrs go directly to heaven at the time of their death. There have been many martyrs since the death of Christ, and there will be many more before the end of time including those who refuse to worship the beast during the **end time**. The martyrs live and reign with Christ in heaven during the millennium, but the other dead must wait until the end of time to be resurrected. Christians only die once and will be resurrected at the end of time with a glorious body and will go to heaven. At the end of time the unrighteous will be resurrected and judged, then they will experience a second death in the lake of fire.

Verses 7-10 *"Now when the thousand years have expired, Satan will be released from his prison and will go out to deceive the nations which are in the four corners of the earth, Gog and Magog, to gather them together to battle, whose number is as the sand of the sea.' "They went up on the breadth of the earth and surrounded the camp of the saints and the beloved city. And fire came down from God out of heaven and devoured them. The Devil who deceived them was cast into the lake of fire and brimstone where the beast and the false prophet are. And they will be tormented day and night forever and ever."*

During the end time Satan and the demons will be released from the bottomless pit and go out over the earth to deceive the leaders of the nations turning them against God, Christ, and the Church. That is the time when the Lawless One (Antichrist) led by Satan will be in power and the time when the great battle takes place, the battle called of Armageddon in chapter 16.

All of the nations will be gathered together in a rebellion against God. The nations are symbolized as Gog and Magog, and their number will be too great to count. Gog and Magog were common rabbinical titles for the nations in rebellion against the Lord. (Notes from NKJV) The nations will surround the church, symbolized as the Great City of God. The battle will be brief, because fire will come down from heaven and destroy the great army led by Satan. Then Satan and the demons will be cast into a lake of fire where the beast and the false prophet will have been cast.

2nd Peter 3:10-13 "But the day of the Lord will come as a thief in the night, in which the heavens will pass away with a great noise, and the elements will melt with fervent heat; both earth and the works that are in it will be burned up. Therefore since all these things will be dissolved, what manner of persons ought you to be in holy conduct and godliness, looking for and hastening the coming day of God, because of which of which the heavens will be dissolved, being on fire, and the elements will melt with fervent heat? Nevertheless we according to His promise, look for new heavens and a new earth in which righteousness dwells."

Judgment of The Great White Throne

Verses 11-15 *"Then I saw a great white throne and Him who sat on it, from whose face the earth and the heaven fled away. And there was found no place for them. And I saw the dead, small and great, standing before God, and books were opened.' "And another book was opened, which is the Book of Life. And the dead were judged according to their works, by the things, which were written in the books. The sea gave up the dead who were in it, and Death and Hades delivered up the dead who were in them. And they were judged, each one according to his works. Then death and Hades were cast into the lake of fire. This is the second death. And anyone not found written in the Book of Life was cast into the lake of fire.”*

The great white throne symbolizes God's throne in heaven where He judges all creation and determines their fate based on their righteousness or unrighteousness. Everyone who has ever existed is subjected to the judgment of God. The books symbolize the knowledge of God concerning the life and works of every individual, including those who were in Hades and those who die before the great judgment. The dead will be resurrected and stand before God's judgment. Everyone will be judged except for the martyrs already in heaven. The unrighteous people of all times will be cast into the lake of fire, and the righteous will go to a new heaven and new earth that has been prepared for them by God.

Those who failed to become righteous through faith in Christ will be cast into the lake of fire and experience a second death.

During the early days of the church, some Christians did not believe there would be a resurrection. In the 15th chapter of 1st Corinthians, Paul taught about the resurrection of the dead at the end of time. One reason some failed to believe in the resurrection is because they did not understand how the resurrection would be possible.

1st Corinthians 15:33-34 “Awake to righteousness, and do not sin; for some do not have the knowledge of God. I speak this to your shame.”

1st Corinthians 15:40-44 “There are also celestial bodies and terrestrial bodies; but the glory of the celestial is one, and the glory of the terrestrial is another. There is one glory of the sun, another glory of the moon, and another glory of the stars; for one star differs from another star in glory. So also is the resurrection of the dead.’

“The body is sown in corruption, it is raised in incorruption. It is sown in dishonor, it is raised in glory. It is sown in weakness, it is raised in power. It is sown a natural body, it is raised a spiritual body. There is a natural body, and there is a spiritual body.”

1st Corinthians 15:50-57 “Now this I say brethren, that flesh and blood cannot inherit the kingdom of God; nor does corruption inherit incorruption. Behold I tell you a mystery: We shall not all sleep, but we shall all be changed—in a moment, in the twinkling of an eye, at the last trumpet.’ “For the trumpet will sound, and the dead will be raised incorruptible, and we shall be changed. For this corruptible has put on incorruption, and this mortal has put on immortality, then shall be brought to pass the saying that is written: “Death is swallowed up in victory.” “O Death where is your sting? O Hades, where is your victory?” The sting of death is sin, and the strength of sin is the law. But thanks be to God, who gives us the victory through our Lord Jesus Christ.”

The New Heaven and The New Earth

Chapter 21:1-21 *“Now I saw a new heaven and a new earth, for the first heaven and the first earth had passed away. Also there was no more sea. Then I, John, saw the holy city, New Jerusalem, coming down out of heaven from God, prepared as a bride adorned for her husband. And I heard a loud voice from heaven saying, “Behold, the tabernacle of God is with men, and He will dwell with them, and they shall be His people. God Himself will be with them and be their God. And God will wipe away every tear from their eyes; there shall be no more death, nor sorrow, nor crying. There shall be on more pain, for the former things have passed away.’*

"Then He who sat on the throne said, "Behold, I make all things new." And He said to me, "Write, for these words are true and faithful."

"And He said to me, "It is done! I am the Alpha and the Omega, the Beginning and the End. I will give of the fountain of the water of life freely to him who thirsts.' "He who overcomes shall inherit all things, and I will be his God and he shall be My son. But the cowardly, unbelieving, abominable, murderers, sexually immoral, sorcerers, idolaters, and all liars shall have their part in the lake which burns with fire and brimstone, which is the second death. Then one of the seven angels who had the seven bowls filled with the seven last plagues came to me and talked with me, saying, "Come, I will show you the bride, the Lamb's wife.'

"And he carried me away in the Spirit to a great and high mountain, and showed me the great city, the Holy Jerusalem, descending out of heaven from God, having the glory of God.'

"Her light was like a most precious stone, like a jasper stone, clear as crystal.' "Also she had a great and high wall with twelve gates, and twelve angels at the gates, and names written on them, which are the names of the twelve tribes of the children of Israel: three gates on the east, three gates on the north, three gates on the south, and three gates on the west.'

"Now the wall of the city had twelve foundations, and on them were the names of the twelve apostles of the Lamb. And he who talked with me had a gold reed to measure the city, its gates, and its wall. The city is laid out as a square; its length is as great as its breadth. And he measured the city with the reed; twelve thousand furlongs. Its length, breadth, and height are equal.'

"Then he measured its wall: one hundred and forth-four cubits, according to the measure of a man, that is, of an angel. The construction of its wall was of jasper; and the city was pure gold, like clear glass. The foundations of the wall of the city were adorned with all kinds of precious stones.' "The first foundation was jasper, the second sapphire, the third chalcedone, the fourth emerald, the fifth sardonyx, the sixth sardius, the seventh chrysolite, the eighth beryl, the ninth topaz, the tenth chrysoprase, the eleventh jacinth, and the twelfth amethyst. The twelve gates were twelve pearls: each individual gate was of one pearl. And the street of the city was pure gold, like transparent glass."

John was allowed to see the new heavens and a new earth. He saw the Holy City, the New Jerusalem, which is the church, and it was coming down out of God's heaven. The Spirit brought a symbolic view of the church to John's mind—the redeemed church came into his view. The church looked like a bride beautifully dressed for her husband who is Christ.

John saw the fulfillment of all of the prophet's writings and the gospel of Christ; the culmination of God's redeeming plan. John heard a voice saying, *"Behold the tabernacle of God is with men, and He will dwell with them, and they shall be His people. God Himself will be with them and be their God. And God will wipe away every tear from their eyes; there shall be no more death, nor sorrow, nor crying. There shall be no more pain, for the former things have passed away. Then He who sat on the throne said, Behold, I make all things new. And He said to me, "Write, for these words are true and faithful." And He said to me, "It is done."*

The church will live in a new heaven and new earth with God and Christ for all eternity. The people will be God's people, and they will be with God. Everyone who is saved will become a pillar in the temple of God in heaven. The church is the temple. Life in heaven will be glorious, blissful, and peaceful, because there will be no death, mourning, crying, or pain, and the saints will live eternally. Jesus sent this message to the churches, and he emphasized the fact that he is coming back soon, so that the church will be ready for his coming. Jesus doesn't know the exact time he will return. Only God knows the time, but Christ always stressed the imminence of his coming.

Jesus didn't say he is coming to set up a kingdom or to remain on earth, however he does stress the fact that he is coming to reward the faithful and bring them into heaven. Christ will shut out those who are ungodly and they will perish forever. Christ is the First and the Last in God's redeeming plan.

Colossians 1:15-20 "He is the image of the invisible God, the firstborn over all creation. For by him all things were created that are in heaven and that are on earth, visible and invisible, whether thrones or dominions or principalities or powers.' "All things were created through Him and for Him. And He is before all things, and in Him all things consist. And He is the head of the body, the church, who is the beginning, the firstborn from the dead, that in all things He may have the preeminence.' "For it pleased the Father that in Him all the fullness should dwell, and by Him to reconcile all things to Himself, by Him, whether things on earth or things in heaven, having made peace through the blood Of His cross."

Verses 22-27 "But I saw no temple in it, for the Lord God Almighty and the Lamb, are its temple. The city had no need of the sun or of the moon to shine in it, for the glory of God illuminated it. The Lamb is its light. And the nations of those who are saved shall walk in its light, and the kings of the earth bring their glory and honor into it.' "Its gates shall not be shut at all by day (there shall be not night there). And they shall bring the glory and the honor of the nations into it. But there shall by no means enter it anything that defiles, or causes an abomination or a lie, but only those who are written in the Lamb's Book of Life."

John saw the old heaven and earth disappear and there was a new heaven and earth, but there was no sea. John saw the Holy City, the New Jerusalem that came down from heaven to occupy the new heaven and the new earth. The new city of Jerusalem was a bride that was made ready for her husband.

John is still using comparisons between the Old and New covenants. Jerusalem was the literal city of God and his people during the Old Covenant. The church is God's people in the New Covenant and is the equivalent of the Holy City of Jerusalem.

John is not trying to establish a chronological order of events. He is revealing that it is the church that is the bride of Christ and the church will enter the new heaven and the new earth.

John heard a loud voice say that God would also be living in heaven with the church. All of the redeemed of every age will be there. The loud voice John heard from the throne was the voice of God announcing that his plan for mankind was complete. God is the first and last of everything in existence. The people who hunger and thirst for righteousness in this life will inherit all of God's blessings in the new heaven and new earth.

The New Jerusalem

One of the seven angels who had the bowls of God's wrath told John he would let him see the bride who is the wife of Christ, the Lamb. John was immersed in the Holy Spirit enabling him see the bride of Christ. The Spirit took John to a high mountain, and John could see the Holy City, which is the church coming down out of the heaven from God. The new heaven and the new earth John described is a city that shines with God's glory. It was like a precious jewel that is as clear as a crystal. The city had a high wall with twelve gates and an angel at each gate.

The names of the twelve tribes of Israel were written on the gates. The names of the twelve tribes of Israel indicates that the faithful people of the tribes of Israel will be in the city with the faithful church and all the redeemed. The names of the twelve apostles were written on the twelve foundations of the city. The twelve tribes of Israel and the twelve apostles were the foundations of the redeemed from both covenants.

The angel talking to John had a rod of gold to measure the city, the gates and the wall. Measuring represents discovering the total number of people who would be living in the square city. The image of the city John saw was a glorious city adorned with precious stone, the gates were made of pearls, and the street was made of gold. John was using terms that humans can relate to in order to show its glory and magnificence.

"I fell down to worship before the feet of the angel who showed me these things. Then he said to me, "See that you do not do that. For I am your fellow servant, and of your brethren the prophets, and of those who keep the words of this book. Worship God. And he said to me, "Do not seal the words of the prophecy of this book, for the time is at hand."

No sun or moon is needed, for the city gets light from the glory of God and Christ. There will be no unrighteous people in the city.

Chapter 22:1-21 *"And he showed me a pure river of water of life, clear as crystal, proceeding from the throne of God and of the Lamb. In the middle of its street, and on either side of the river, was the tree of life, which bore twelve fruits, each tree yielding its fruit every month. The leaves of the tree were for the healing of the nations. And there shall be no more curse, but the throne of God and of the Lamb shall be in it, and His servants shall serve Him. They shall see His face, and His name shall be on their foreheads. There shall be no night there: They need no lamp nor light of the sun, for the Lord God gives them light.*

And they shall reign forever and ever. Then He said to me, "These words are faithful and true." And the Lord God of the holy prophets sent His angel to show His servants the things, which must shortly take place. "Behold, I am coming quickly! Blessed is he who keeps the words of the prophecy of this book." Now I, John, saw and heard these things. And when I heard and saw, He who is unjust, let him be unjust still; he who is filthy, let him be filthy still; he who is righteous, let him be righteous still; he who is holy, let him be holy still."

And behold, I am coming quickly, and My reward is with Me, to give to every one according to his work. I am the Alpha and the Omega, the Beginning and the End, the First and the Last. Blessed are those who do His commandments, that they may have the right to the tree of life, and may enter through the gates into the city. But outside are dogs. "I, Jesus, have sent My angel to testify to you these things in the churches. I am the Root and the Offspring of David, the Bright and Morning Star." And the Spirit and the bride say, "Come!" And let him who hears say, "Come!" And let him who thirsts come. Whoever desires, let him take the water of life freely.'

"For I testify to everyone who hears the words of the prophecy of this book: If anyone adds to these things, God will add to him the plagues that are written in this book; and if anyone takes away from the words of the book of this prophecy, God shall take away his part from the Book of Life, from the holy city, and from the things which are written in this book. '"He who testifies to these things says, "Surely I am coming quickly." Amen. Even so, come Lord Jesus! The grace of our Lord Jesus Christ be with you all. Amen."

The angel showing the city to John showed him the river of life, and the water was as clear as crystal. The water of life symbolizes eternal life on the new earth. God gives eternal life to those who are righteous. The river will run down the middle of the street, and everyone will have access to it. There will be two trees of life, one on each side of the river.

The trees will grow a new crop every month. The leaves of the trees will be used for medicine to promote health and strength. God will no longer need to pronounce a curse of judgment, because the blood of Christ has covered the sins of everyone in the city, and there is no sin there. God and Christ will be in the city where everyone can worship them, and there will be no night, because the Lord God will be the light. The angel who was speaking to John assures him that everything he had seen and heard is true. John received a message from Jesus saying that he is coming soon, and those who have been faithful to obey the prophecies of Revelation will be blessed. When Jesus said He is coming soon, it is a symbol of an indefinite length of time that God alone will determine. Jesus will come as soon as God sends Him.

John fell down to worship the angel, but the angel forbad him to worship him, because angels are servants of God the same as people who serve God. John was instructed to make the message in the book of Revelation known to everyone—the righteous and the sinner. Christ emphasizes that his coming will be soon, and He will reward everyone according to his or her deeds. All of the righteous will be able to enter the gates of the city where they can eat the fruit from the tree of life, and everyone else will be shut out. There is no other choice, because Christ is the first and the last, the beginning and the end.

Revelation 3:20 "Behold, I stand at the door and knock. If anyone hears My voice and opens the door, I will come in to him and dine with him, and he with Me. To him who overcomes I will grant to sit with Me on My throne, as I also overcame and sat down with My Father on His throne."